MAGIC ON THE EARLY ENGLISH STAGE

Magic on the Early English Stage investigates the performance of magical tricks, illusions, effects and their staged appearance in the medieval and early English theatre. Performers who created such magic were not known as conjurors, as we might refer to them today, but as jugglers. Records concerning jugglers on the medieval stage have been hitherto misunderstood or misapplied. These references to jugglers are re-examined in the light of discussions of 'feats of activity' that also include tumbling, vaulting and 'dancing on the rope'; appearances and disappearances of the 'Now you see it, now you don't' variety; and stage versions of these concepts; magic through sound in terms of ventriloquy and sound through pipes; mechanical images and puppets; and stage tricks. Information that has remained dormant since original publication is discussed in relation to jugglers such as Thomas Brandon, the King's Juggler, and William Vincent, alias 'Hocus Pocus'.

PHILIP BUTTERWORTH is Reader in Medieval Theatre at the University of Leeds. He is the author of *Theatre of Fire: Special Effects in Early English and Scottish Theatre*, and has published widely in journals on the subject, including essays in *Medieval English Theatre*. He is currently working, with Joslin McKinney, on *The Cambridge Introduction to Scenography*, to be published in 2007.

MAGIC ON THE EARLY ENGLISH STAGE

PHILIP BUTTERWORTH

Reader in Medieval Theatre, University of Leeds

CAMBRIDGE
UNIVERSITY PRESS

CAMBRIDGE UNIVERSITY PRESS
Cambridge, New York, Melbourne, Madrid, Cape Town, Singapore, São Paulo

Cambridge University Press
The Edinburgh Building, Cambridge CB2 2RU, UK

Published in the United States of America by Cambridge University Press, New York

www.cambridge.org
Information on this title: www.cambridge.org/9780521825139

First published 2005

Printed in the United Kingdom at the University Press, Cambridge

A catalogue record for this publication is available from the British Library

Library of Congress Cataloguing in Publication data
Magic on the early English stage / Philip Butterworth
p.   cm.
Includes bibliographical references and index.

ISBN 0 521 82513 X
1. Magic tricks – England – History.   2. Theater – England – History.   I. Title
GV1543.3.E54B48 2005
793.8′0942–dc22   2005045725

ISBN-13 978-0-521-82513-9 hardback
ISBN-10 0-521-82513-X hardback

For
S. A. B., J. R. B.,
I. N. and J. E. N.

For the ende of this skil is not to doo simplely, but to stretche out imaginations euen vnto apperaunce, of whiche there shall afterwarde no sign appeare.

Heinrich Cornelius Agrippa, *Henry Cornelius Agrippa of the Vanitie and vncertaintie of Artes and Sciences, Englished by Ja. San. Gent., Imprinted at London, by Henry Wykes dwelling in Fleete streat, at the signe of the blacke Elephant. ANNO. 1569*

Contents

x   *Contents*

Illustrations

Foreword

Treatises on the history of what in Britain today is generally referred to as conjuring, and our American cousins prefer to term magic, usually begin with an account of Dedi's decapitation illusion performed in Egypt for King Cheops around 2600 BC, originally described in a papyrus discovered by Henry Westcar in the early nineteenth century. Sacerdotal temple mysteries of a similar era produced by the application of pneumatics, hydraulics and acoustics were subsequently explained by Hero of Alexandria in about AD 62, while the first authenticated reference to a sleight-of-hand trick, the Cups and Balls, dates from Seneca (3 BC–AD 65) at a time when it was already a very familiar feat.

Although it is evident that performances of magic for entertainment purposes existed long before the birth of Christ, there is a lacuna in the history of magic during the Dark Ages. Clearly, itinerant practitioners would be plying their craft during these largely unrecorded centuries, establishing a continuum with the earliest performers identified in the Middle Ages. Simultaneously the Christian Church was developing apace, and from this source the origin of much medieval drama may be attributed. The miraculous was an essential feature of the Church's teachings and thus the dramatisation of biblical lore required the presentation of magical effects, the nature of which has provided the stimulus for this present work by Philip Butterworth.

The first detailed explanation in the English language of how to perform conjuring tricks was Reginald Scot's *The Discouerie of witchcraft*, published in 1584. His aim was to demonstrate that the tricks of contemporary magicians were achieved by purely natural means and not by any diabolical influence, as part of his major crusade against the then prevalent belief in witchcraft. In divulging these methods his conscience was clearly pricked, 'being sorie that it falleth out to my lot, to laie open the secrets of this mysterie, to the hindrance of such poore men as live thereby'. Obviously the tricks he described, learned from Jean Cautares, a French conjurer then working in London, were not new at the time he described them and had been in the repertoire of performers for many years.

To Scot we are indebted for the names of some of the conjurors who were operating within the living memory of his sixteenth-century readers, but undoubtedly there were others. Yet who were they and where might their identities be ascertained? Philip Butterworth, in this pioneering research on magical effects portrayed in Early English drama, has simultaneously found some welcome answers to this question in his searches of county and city records, together with interesting information about their remuneration from treasurers' accounts, principally sourced from the *Records of Early English Drama* project of the University of Toronto. In doing so he has also been able to take us back in time closer to the seemingly impenetrable past of conjuring during the Dark Ages, and we are indebted to him for the invaluable references and annotations he provides.

For the student of magic history it is interesting to observe how the employment of magical effects in dramatic presentations characteristic of the medieval theatre, as related in this book, essentially disappeared after the seventeenth century. They were to be resurrected in the second half of the nineteenth century, not by dramatists, but by a scientist and also a magician. The scientist was John Henry Pepper, Director of the Royal Polytechnic Institution in Regent Street who, on Christmas Eve 1862, introduced the illusion that bears his name (though Henry Dircks was its inventor) in a representation of Charles Dickens' *The Haunted Man*. Its tremendous impact led to a number of plays being written during the following year purely as vehicles for this single illusion.

It may well have been the great success attendant on the Pepper's Ghost illusion dramas that influenced John Nevil Maskelyne at the outset of his magical career in 1865, leading him to pioneer a new genre of magical dramatic sketches to clothe the brilliant illusions he and his colleagues created at the Egyptian Hall in Piccadilly, London, from 1873 until 1905, and subsequently at St George's Hall. It was a lead that other famous illusionists of the early twentieth century were happy to follow, for Lafayette, Horace Goldin, Arnold de Biere and Servais le Roy all featured magical playlets in their shows.

So this present book, by extending our knowledge of the interaction of magic and early drama, will be warmly welcomed by historians of conjuring and of drama alike and, indeed, by anyone who shares an interest in the theatrical fare that both instructed and entertained our forebears.

EDWIN A. DAWES
Historian, The Magic Circle

Prefatory note

Although this work is rooted in the medieval theatre of England it contains a number of allusions to medieval theatre in Europe. Equally, there are many references made to sixteenth- and early-seventeenth-century theatre in England. The scope of this range exists because of shared practical issues and insights provided by the later evidence that illuminate or explain earlier practice.

Also, in this investigation there are a number of techniques and solutions to performers' tricks, illusions and stage devices that have been cited from appropriately published evidence as a means of demonstrating how these effects were or might have been produced. Such citation does not necessarily provide evidence that these declared methods work or have worked. Their use in this book is to indicate the possible means by which tricks and illusions might have worked, but more importantly, to demonstrate the kinds of ingenuity, insight, lateral thinking and guile of the perpetrators. Even if a proposed solution to the means by which given tricks were performed does not work, or has not worked, it is not excluded for that reason.

References to the 'stage' in this book are concerned with both the physical stage and that performance space created by the ambit that surrounds the performer, whether he be actor or juggler.

Acknowledgements

Funding to complete this work has been made possible through the Arts and Humanities Research Board Study Leave Scheme. Matched funding to that of the AHRB has been provided by the Faculty of Music, Visual and Performing Arts (now the Faculty of Performance, Visual Arts and Communications) at the University of Leeds. Chris Baugh, Peter Meredith and David Mills have supported efforts to obtain funding for the work. My colleagues have also been particularly supportive.

Meg Twycross was one of the readers of the initial proposal to Cambridge University Press, and has maintained her support throughout. Eddie Dawes has been consistently generous with his time and effort. Both Meg's and Eddie's contributions have been of enormous help.

It will be obvious that I have had considerable support from a number of translators who have worked diligently and with good humour on my behalf. I wish to express my sincere thanks to Philip A. Shaw (Latin); Peter Meredith (Latin); Meg Twycross (Latin); Elsa Strietman (Dutch); Cécile Brabban (French); Brian Richardson and Arthur Pritchard (Italian). Any mistakes in their transcriptions are mine.

The editors of the journals *Medieval English Theatre*, *Theatre Notebook* and *European Medieval Drama* have permitted me to use large sections of the articles 'Magic through sound: illusion, deception and agreed pretence', 'Brandon, Feats and Hocus Pocus: jugglers three' and 'Substitution: theatrical sleight of hand in medieval plays' in Chapters 1, 5, and 7.

Eila Williams and John McGavin, who are currently working on *REED: Scotland*, have generously helped in checking material in the Advocates Library, Edinburgh. Elizabeth Baldwin and David Mills, who await publication of their Cheshire records for *REED*, have helpfully supplied material from their forthcoming edition. I would also like to thank Jo Mattingly for the hospitality that enabled me to check and transcribe Cornish material in Truro.

Staff at the following libraries have offered their customary and valued support: the British Library; the Bodleian Library; the Brotherton Library; the John Rylands Library; University of London (Special Collections) and the Biblioteca Torino.

Finally, I would like to thank Vicki Cooper at Cambridge University Press for her continued confidence in and support of this work from the outset.

Note on the text

Throughout the text, abbreviations in original manuscripts and early printed books have been expanded. Expansions are indicated by the use of italics.

Introduction

This work is concerned with sleight of hand, illusion and magic both on and off the medieval and early English stage. Thus, its central preoccupation is with pretence – its nature and purpose in the creation of magic. The kinds of communicated magic under consideration are of different sorts and brought about by different intentions, processes, skill and understanding. There is an inherent concern for the appearance of something as opposed to its existence in reality. These interrelated notions are extended to convince the witness that the appearance of something is indeed the reality. The same fundamental relationship between appearance and reality conditions the core of activity conducted by both conjurors and the staged presentation of illusion in the theatre.

The conjuror does not need a stage upon which to perform his work, any more than does the actor, although many in modern times do perform on the stage and exploit the physical circumstances of staging conditions and conventions. The conjuror only needs the immediate space that surrounds him in order to manipulate its interaction with the space of the witness. Magic created through staged illusions, however, operates in space that extends beyond the conjuror's ambit to that where the increased scale is implicit to the nature and purpose of the illusion. Such discrepancies in scale serve to condition the similarities and differences between the work of the conjuror and the creation of staged illusion in the theatre.

The extent to which perceived pretence and its purpose is communicated by the conjuror is different from that which is brought about by staging conditions. The theatrical event and its purpose, whether in a building or outdoors, acts as a constant reminder to the audience as to the artificiality of the proceedings. Thus, the audience becomes involved in a conscious process of pretence by virtue of the occasion and its declared and communicated purpose. The conjuror does not need to depend on a prearranged agreement with his audience as to the nature of the event; he is able to create an agreement about pretence at the point of delivery through an implicit or explicit question: 'Would you like to see some magic?'

When it comes to the relationship between appearances and reality, there are no rigid lines of demarcation between conjuring and theatre. Some evidence exists of medieval characters who are seemingly required to perform magical tricks in plays. However, there is also evidence of scenes in medieval and early English plays concerned with conjuring as content that is realised by organisation of staging conditions involving, for example, trap doors, screens and curtains. This is particularly so in relation to appearances and disappearances.

Manipulation of pretence may be brought about openly in theatre where there is a tacit agreement about its nature and intention by those who create it and those who witness it. The audience knows what the pretence is. Pretence that occurs through the conjuror is not only the content but it is also the means; content and means are fused to determine the pretence. This convergence determines the nature of the agreement or collusion between conjuror and witness: the relationship is one of unequal collusion. A different, yet related, form of collusion occurs when the conjuror is supported by a confederate.

There is considerable evidence of the working of these concerns in medieval stage directions, civic records, ecclesiastical accounts, eye-witness descriptions, *books of secrets* and early books on magic from which to determine its significance – both to conjuring and the staging of theatre.

Today, the principal term that is used to encompass magical activity is *conjuring*. However, the action that relates to this word as it is understood in the twenty-first century, whether witnessed on television, on stage or in the open air, is not to be found in medieval or early English plays or documents that refer to itinerant performers. *Conjuring*, as a term employed to describe the act of performing magical tricks, was not used in its current sense in England until the nineteenth century. The words *conjuration, conjure, conjurer* and *conjury* first come into use with related meanings in the eighteenth and nineteenth centuries.[1] So, the term *conjuring* and its derivatives will not be used in this work unless it is to draw a modern comparison. Since the word *conjuring* is not to be found in relation to the sort of processes under discussion, what are appropriate terms to describe such activity? The chief designations in use from the twelfth to the seventeenth centuries are: *tregetry, legerdemaine, prestigiation, juggling* or *jugglery, feats, feats of activity* and *sleight of hand. Conveyance* and *confederacy* are two of the named means of bringing about magical acts. The principal, and some tangential, perpetrators of these processes are the *tregetour, praestigiator, joculator, circulator, mountebanke, emperick, quacksalver* and *juggler*. Each of these terms will be discussed further in Chapter 9.

The most consistently used words to describe the production of magic throughout this period are *juggler* (for the exponent) and *juggling* (for the activity). The term *juggling*, however, has been referred to as 'the lexicographer's nightmare', for this meaning and its creator, the *juggler*, are perhaps the least understood and most misunderstood words used to describe the creation of acts of magic.[2] In the twenty-first century the term *juggler* is applied to that kind of entertainer who throws up objects from one hand to another in a continuous rhythmical sequence without dropping them to the floor. This meaning of *juggler* is a nineteenth-century development in England and was only recently defined by the *Shorter OED* (1993).[3] This modern definition does not occur in the 1901, 1933 (and supplement), 1970 (and supplement) or the second 1989 editions of the *OED*. Nor does this recent definition appear in the latest online editions of the *OED* until the Additions Series of 1997. It is curious that the first inclusion of the modern definition appears in the *Shorter OED* before being recorded in the complete *OED*. Although there is pictorial evidence that this kind of action was performed in the Middle Ages it was not the principal activity of those identified as jugglers. All the definitions contained in the *OED* concerning medieval use of the terms *juggle, juggler, jugglery* and *juggling* refer to *conjuring* in its modern sense. However, evidence exists of medieval jugglers in other countries who operated as skilled conjurors and jugglers (in the more recent sense).[4] These jugglers both performed sleight of hand and juggled objects. Evidence concerning the activities of medieval jugglers in England that identifies the nature of juggling overwhelmingly, if not exclusively, refers to conjuring or illusion as it is understood today. Thus, throughout this work, the terms *juggling* and *jugglers* will be used in all medieval references to *conjurors* as understood by the modern term and its use. The term *conjuror* is not therefore an appropriate one to use in this context.

Roger Bacon (1214?–94) offers a clear description of the juggler's art. Even so, this is a description by a witness of juggling and not one that might have been provided by a juggler:

Nam sunt qui motu veloce membrorum apparentia singunt, aut vocum diversitate, aut instrumentorum subtilitate, aut tenebris, aut consensu multa mortalibus proponunt miranda, quae non habent existentiae veritatem. his mundus plenus est, sicut manifestum est inquirenti. Nam joculatores multa manuum velocitate mentiuntur.[5]

The earliest, and somewhat free, translation of Bacon's comments is offered by 'T. M.' in *Frier Bacon his Discovery of the Miracles of Art, Nature, and Magick. Faithfully translated out of D' Dees own Copy, by T. M. and never before in English* [1618]:

We have many men that by the nimblenesse and activity of body, diversification of sounds, exactness of instruments, darkness, or consent, make things seem to be present, which never were really existent in the course of Nature. The world, as any judicious eye may see, groans under such bastard burdens. A Jugler by an handsome sleight of hand, will put a compleat lie upon the very sight.[6]

The identity of many medieval jugglers as conjurors has not been known. Where identification of given jugglers has been made it may have been assumed previously that their skills were concerned with throwing up objects and not conjuring. Clear evidence of juggling activity in England exists from the thirteenth century and all such evidence where it identifies the nature of the activity does so in respect of the modern understanding of conjuring. No English evidence that identifies the nature of juggling from the thirteenth to the seventeenth centuries illustrates the activity as throwing up objects and catching them.

However, the act of throwing up objects and catching them may well have occurred as a skilled activity by those performers such as tumblers, vaulters and dancers on the rope whose skills and activity were collectively and individually known as *feats of activity*. Even so, there is no written evidence of this activity in England during the period under investigation. Since juggling is a qualitatively different kind of activity from the physically exacting activities of tumbling, vaulting and dancing on the rope, it is not possible to confirm that these skills were performed by the medieval juggler. It does seem clear, however, that this range of skills was performed by small groups consisting of distinctively skilled performers whose work developed from the core of family companies that included jugglers.

The purpose of this work has not been previously undertaken in monograph (or any other) form and thus the evidence upon which the examination is based permits the presentation of some material that has not been published since its original publication. Also, a considerable amount of hitherto unpublished material has now been published through the *Records of Early English Drama* (*REED*) project based at the University of Toronto. The present work makes extensive use of some of this information together with that collated in the *Malone Society Collections* series. Although it might be considered that some of the medieval and early English records presented here are repetitious in their collective volume, particularly in respect of jugglers, it is important to appreciate both the quantity and quality of such records in order to point to their hitherto unfocused significance.

Many accounts of the period under investigation refer to the related operation of two concepts and their associated practices as used by the medieval and early English juggler: conveyance and confederacy. Conveyance refers to sleight of hand and confederacy is concerned with collusion of different sorts. Individually, or in association, these two processes account for much of the recorded activity of medieval jugglers.

The modern phrase, 'Now you see it, now you don't' embodies the central concern of the juggler in respect of that which appears and that which disappears. Most of the juggler's repertoire is concerned with these two states and their relationship. The same point may be made in respect of the conduct of theatre. Whether the delivery of appearances and disappearances is real or illusory depends on the existence of theatrical conventions by which the perpetrators communicate or deliberately deny communication of their intentions.

Another popular and yet fallacious phrase concerning sleight of hand is summed up by the modern saying, 'The quickness of the hand deceives the eye'. However, jugglers' hands cannot move fast enough to deceive the eye. In order to be successful, sleight of hand must be slow, deliberate and undetectable, unless the intention is to create a ploy to mislead the spectator by attracting his attention. This may amount to misdirection of the eye although such misdirection is not the only sensory apparatus by which the juggler works. Auditory misdirection is required by stage directions in some medieval and early English plays, and this is also the basis of communicated ventriloquial sound of which there is further evidence.

Development of ventriloquial sound may be inferred from many medieval accounts concerning puppetry. Such accounts exist from the thirteenth century in a variety of staging and presentational modes. Additional evidence in this area has been made available through the *REED* project.

The inanimate figure as represented by the puppet or mechanical image is linked to the substitution, or partial substitution, of bodies and/or their limbs. In general, such replacements are intended to portray or, alternatively, convince an audience of the authenticity of the body or limb(s) to their ostensible owner. Some ingenuity in their use is apparent in a number of accounts.

Perhaps the greatest inventiveness in respect of both juggling and staging considerations may be seen in the range of stage tricks that are articulated and, in some instances, explained. Evidence concerning tricks that involve knives, daggers, wounds, blood, hanging, snakes and water effects may be found in stage directions as well as eye-witness accounts.

Many of the perpetrators of these tricks and effects are unknown, but a surprising number of medieval and early English jugglers and other presentational personnel are recorded, as may be seen from what follows.

CHAPTER I

Jugglers: the creators of magic

Who were the jugglers that created magic and what is the nature of the evidence that identifies them? The spread of available evidence is determined at one end of the spectrum by brief references to jugglers in financial accounts and at the other by detailed descriptions from eye-witnesses or those who write in the eye-witness mode.

There are many accounts of named jugglers and these are more plentiful than might be imagined. However, as might be anticipated, a number of these records simply refer to the juggler by his first or last name and exist as records by virtue of payment to him. These sorts of records generally offer limited information concerning the nature of the activities of jugglers although they are useful in recording the juggling activity as a distinct one that is different from and identifiable with other types of performance. Sometimes these records offer information of place, event, patronage, context and purpose, and it is these concerns that affect the value of such accounts. Records of some payments are of additional value in that they demonstrate something of the variety and synonymity of the terms outlined in the Introduction that are used to identify the juggler as the *tregetour* and the *ioculator*. Even so, the prospective understanding that might develop knowledge of these individuals and their activities is limited. A few examples will serve to reinforce these points: a tregetour by the name of 'Janin' is recorded in British Library, Cotton MSS, Nero C VIII, fol. 86v as the recipient of a payment of 20s for performing before Edward II between 1311 and 1312. The account reads: 'Janino le tregettor, facienti ministralsiam suam coram rege, &c.' [to Janin le Tregettur, for making his minstrelsy in the presence of the King].[1] Another payment to a named 'Ioculator' occurs in the *King's College Mundum Book* for 1503–4 and on this occasion the juggler's name is Matthew: 'Item xxvj° die Maij in regardis datis Matheo Ioculatori ij sx' [Likewise on the twenty-sixth day of May as rewards given Matthew, a juggler].[2] Frequent payments are recorded to jugglers in the *Account Book of Prior William More* of

Worcester: William More [Peers], 1471/2–1552, prior of Worcester, kept a
journal in which he recorded his day-to-day expenses. Records of payments to a wide variety of entertainers are contained in this work. In 1534
he records payment to 'William': '*A Ioguller* Item to William (blank) A
Ioguller at crowle xij d'.[3] 'Crowle' was one of More's three manors; the
other two being Battenhall and Grimley. The *Accounts of the Lord High
Treasurer of Scotland* for 1552–3 record payment to 'Jaques the Jouglar':
'Item, be commande of the said lordes, to Jaques the Jouglar . . . iij li.'[4]
In a letter to Sir Thomas Carden, 'knight master of the kinges maiesties
Revels' from George Fferrers, the Lord of Misrule to Edward VI, a
request is made in 1552 for 'an attyre for Clarinse my Iuggler, now of
late intertayned'.[5] Although detail in these records may be scant they
do collectively inform of payment for juggling activity at the court of
Edward II between 1311 and 1312; the Scottish court in 1552/3; the court
of Edward VI in 1552 and an ecclesiastical estate in 1534.

So, some understanding may emerge from this sort of evidence although it needs to be supported, developed and clarified from more
detailed information. In addition to the many itinerant jugglers who
operated both with and without appropriate licences, there are records
of a good number of jugglers who operated under the name of their
patrons. Evidence accumulated by the *REED* project indicates considerable movement of itinerant performers throughout the country during
the late Middle Ages and Tudor period. Performing troupes frequently
claimed patronage from members of the royal family, nobility or gentry.
The same is true of entertainers, such as jugglers, bearwards and minstrels,
who worked alone or in small groups. The general position appears to
have been one where respective entertainers received rewards from their
patrons at Christmas and Shrovetide and yet were free to travel and earn
money at other times of the year when not specifically obliged to the
patron. Those records that deal with payment to jugglers and other performers frequently distinguish the contributions of jugglers from other
entertainers as may be seen in the following examples of payments to
patronised jugglers. For instance, the *Chamberlains' Account Rolls* for
1520–1 at King's Lynn, Norfolk, record: 'Et in regardo dat' Ioculatori &
Berwarde ducis Suffolcie vj s viij d' [And given as a reward to the Duke of
Suffolk's juggler and bearward 6s 8d].[6] The MS 27449 of the *Hunstanton
Papers* in the Norfolk Record Office for 1533–4 records payment: 'To
Mr Hogons/Mynstrells & to the Iogeler my lord Fytzwater's servant
0.3.0.'[7] The *St George's Guild Accounts* at Chichester, Sussex for 1543–4
record payment to a juggler under the patronage of the Earl of Arundel:

'Et Mimis Comitis Arundel ac ad vnum Ioculatorem infra et extra le hape et pro pane & vino apud Mr Molens vij s.' [And to performers of the earle of Arundel and to one juggler inside and outside 'le hape' and for bread and wine at Mr Molens 7s.][8]

Extensive patronage, particularly in the sixteenth century, clearly operated within a context in which the office of the 'King's juggler' also existed. Throughout the sixteenth and early seventeenth centuries there was a growing number of records that refer to the 'Iogeler [Iugulatori; Iocular; Ioculatoribus] domini Regis', or the King's juggler. The bulk of these records are sixteenth-century ones. However, the earliest such record occurs in the *Anglo-Saxon Charters* for 1042–66, where land is granted to 'Nithard, formerly King Edmund's ioculator'.[9] Whether the meaning of *joculator* at this date refers to *juggler* in the sense that is being discussed here, or whether it refers to a wider meaning of *minstrel* is unclear, although given the date, the latter may be more likely. The *Chamberlains' Account Rolls* at King's Lynn for 1369–70 record: 'Item de. xx. Dat' Iugulatori domini Regis'[10] [Item, 20d given to the Lord King's juggler]. Here, too, it is not certain whether the role is one of a more generalised minstrel entertainer or one concerned with juggling in the terms under discussion. The earlier reference to 'Janino le tregettor' who played in front of Edward II between 1311 and 1312 may also have been the King's juggler. However, by the early sixteenth century the role of the 'King's juggler' as *conjuror* (modern meaning) is clearly established.

Records of payment to the King's juggler from 1517/18 to 1540/1 frequently refer to the occupant of the role as Thomas Brandon. Sometimes he is labelled as 'Brandon the King's juggler'. Whether he is named as the 'King's juggler' or 'Brandon', the two kinds of records support identification of Brandon as the King's juggler between these dates and lend support to identification of his business as that of conjuring (modern sense). Some slightly earlier records concerning the King's juggler from 1511/12 to 1517/18 also refer to the title/role but not to him. It seems likely, however, that these too might be records concerning him. Some of these records are as follows: at Lydd in Kent, the *Chamberlains' Accounts* for 1511–12 record payment as: 'Item paid in reward to a Iugeler of the kynges xijd'.[11] The *City Chamberlains' Accounts* at Canterbury for 1515–16 record payment to the 'kynges Iogler': 'Item paied to the kynges Iogler the xxth day of May gevyn to hym for reward ijs'.[12] The *Chamberlains' Accounts* at Dover, Kent for 1515–16 record: 'It[em] payed for reward*es* gevyn to the kyng*es* mynstrell my lord wardens mynstrell & to diu'se other mynstrell*es* & to the kyng*es* Iogeler xvij s.'[13] Records of further payments to the King's juggler in Kent exist at

Sandwich and New Romney.[14] Also, in 1515–16 the *Chamberlains' Accounts* at Rye, Sussex, record: 'Item payd to the kynges gogeler ij s iiij d'.[15] A similar payment is recorded in the same accounts in 1518.[16]

The preceding records of payments to the King's juggler simply refer to the office; they do not identify the role by the name of the holder. Three occupiers of the role are known to have held the position in the sixteenth century. In addition to Brandon, two jugglers by the names of Smyth and Stanweye are also recorded. Payment of 'iij^s iiij^{d}' is recorded to 'M Smyth ioculer domini rege' in the *Assembly Books* at Thetford, Norfolk for 1538/9.[17] The same payment is recorded in the same accounts for 1536/7 in payment to 'M Brandon the kyng*es* ioguler'.[18] Do these two records mark a possible changeover from Brandon to Smyth as the King's juggler? This seems likely since there are currently no further records of payments to Brandon as the King's juggler after 1536/7. Whether Smyth's engagement as the King's juggler continued up to Elizabeth's reign is unclear for the role was taken over by Stanweye as recorded in the *Corporation Chamberlains' Accounts* at Gloucester for 1563–4: 'Also geven Stanweye the Quenes Iugler for shewinge pastimes and other *of* his Iuglinge feates to Mr mayor and other of his bretherne'.[19] The Ludlow *Bailiffs' and Chamberlains' Accounts* for 1575–6 record: 'Item geven to Stanney the Queens man in waye of reward by assent of a nomber of the companie x s'.[20] Before he became the Queen's juggler payment is recorded to Stanweye in the *Bailiffs' Accounts* at Shrewsbury for 1553–4: 'Et Datum in regardo Thome staney Le Iugler ijs'.[21]

A growing amount of evidence has emerged concerning Brandon and this may be used to extend already cited evidence concerning the King's juggler. Although Brandon and Smyth are referred to as the 'King's juggler' and Stanweye is recorded as the 'Quenes Iugler' at different times in the sixteenth century, later individuals are not described in this way. For instance, William Vincent worked during the first half of the seventeenth century and did so 'with Commission from the Kings Majestie'.[22] Many of the records concerning Vincent refer to his activities as being licensed by the King.

Brandon is first recorded by name in the *St George's Guild Accounts* at Chichester for the years 1517–18. The record reads: 'Et solutum Magistro brandon Iogeler ijs'[23] [And paid to Master Brandon, juggler, 2s]. It is not until the accounting period of 1520–2 in the *Bailiffs' Accounts* at Shrewsbury that Brandon again appears by name and this time he is also recorded as the 'Joculatori domini Regis' [the lord king's juggler]. The role of the 'Joculatori domini Regis' is recorded as early as the eleventh century, although this is the earliest record to date that identifies Brandon as the King's juggler. It reads:

Regardo dato Magistro Brandon Joculatori domini Regis pro honestate ville xi.d. Et in vino expendito per ballivos & compares suos videntes lusum & joculacionem dicti Joculatoris ultra ii denarios collectos de qualibet persona ville extraneis exceptis, xvi.d.[24]

[On a reward given to Master Brandon, the lord king's juggler, for the honour of the town, 11d. And on wine dispensed by the bailiffs and their fellows while seeing the sport and entertainment of the said juggler above and beyond the 2d collected from every person of the town, outsiders excepted, 16d.]

Another record of 1521 contained in the *Account Book of Prior William More* of Worcester refers to payment to Brandon as: 'Item rewarded to the kynges joguler Thomas brandon iijs iiijd'.[25] The wording of this payment to the King's 'joguler' points to the synonymity of the terms *juggler* and *joculator* as recorded in 1520–2 and 1534–5 at Shrewsbury.[26] The 'kynges joguler' and the 'Joculatori domini Regis' at Worcester and Shrewsbury, respectively, not only refer to the same person but also the same role. It seems, therefore, that the *joculator* and its grammatical variants refer to the *juggler* as *conjuror* and not to some other more generalised form of entertainer. Further evidence confirms this identity and will be presented later in this chapter.

An increasingly consistent feature of payments recorded to Brandon and the 'King's juggler' (when they are recorded as separate designations), is that of the payment of 'iijs iiijd'. Most of the recorded payments to Brandon and/or the 'King's juggler' are set at this rate. Present evidence indicates that the 'King's juggler' is the only juggler to receive this rate of pay consistently, although other performing servants of the King such as bearwards and minstrels also receive this rate ($\frac{1}{2}$ noble). In 1521 Brandon is again recorded as the recipient of 3s 4d in the *Account Book of Prior William More* of Worcester: 'Item rewardes to the kynges joguler Thomas brandon iijs iiijd'.[27] The regular payment of 3s 4d is further recorded to Brandon every year from 1523 to 1534 in the *Account Book*.[28]

In 1527 Brandon was seemingly accompanied in performance by 'his chylde': 'Item to his [thomas brandan] chylde for tumblyng viijd'.[29] The role of children, both boys and girls, in this sort of capacity is not unusual in the sixteenth century. Small troupes, often based on given families, frequently combined the respective skills of juggling, tumbling, vaulting and dancing on the rope in their performances. These activities and their relationships are discussed in the following chapter.

In addition to Brandon's touring in Kent and Sussex and his visits to Shrewsbury and Worcester, he performed in Cornwall, Devon and Oxford.[30] Norfolk, Suffolk and Cambridge also feature in Brandon's itinerary; the *Register of Thetford Priory* for the accounting year 1526–7 records the payment: 'Item sol' to the kyng*es* Iogular iij[s] iiij[d]'.[31] The same source records payment to Brandon and/or the King's juggler, for the years 1521–2, 1529–30, 1530–1 and 1536–7.[32] The *Account (Paper Roll) of Receipts and Payments of Thomas Cutler and Jeffry Gilbert, Chamberlains of Ipswich* for 1530–1 records the following: 'To M[r] brandon the Kyng*es* Iugler Item payd to Mr brandond the Kyng*es* Iugler for hys Reward vj[s] viij[d]'.[33] Again, double the regular payment is also recorded in the Cambridge *Town Treasurer's Books* for the accounting year 1535–6: 'Item payed To Brandon The Kynges Gugeler by the commaundement of the Maier vjs viijd'. Further payment is recorded for this event 'for a Soper ffor Mr Brandon & other at Maister Mayers xxd'.[34] The immediate implication here is that Brandon simply doubled up the number of his performances. Brandon does not receive his regular payments on his visits to Cambridge. In payment recorded in the *Town Treasurer's Books* for 1532–3 it is clear why the payment is different from the apparent norm of 3s 4d: 'Item in rewarde govyn to Mr. Brandon the Kynges Iugguler at Mr Hassylles & in a banket ther made with all the charges &c xs. iiijd'.[35] A somewhat lower rate of payment is recorded in the *King's Hall Accounts*, Cambridge, for 1534–6: 'to braunden the Kynges Iogular ijs xjd'.[36] These irregular payments appear to be based on the norm of 3s 4d and presumably account for additional performances and/or different performance offerings with shorter or longer programmes.

Despite the limitations inherent in the kind of information offered by financial accounts, further identification and confirmation of details concerning Brandon and his work occur in differently presented evidence. For instance, Brandon's work seems to have been sufficiently well known and appreciated for him to be admitted as a freeman of the City of London in 1522: 'Itm this day was Redde the kyng*es* lre for oon Thomas brandon the kyng*es* player to be admytted into the libties of this Citie.'[37] However, the principal evidence that concerns the nature of Brandon's work is that contained in Reginald Scot's *Discouerie of witchcraft* of 1584. Scot (1538?–99) cites Brandon's 'Example of a ridiculous wonder':

What wondering and admiration was there at Brandon the iuggler, who painted on a wall the picture of a doue, and seeing a pigeon sitting on the top of a house, said to the king; Lo now your Grace shall see what a iuggler can doo, if he be his craftes maister; and then pricked the picture with a knife so hard and so often, and with so effectuall words, as the pigeon fell downe from the top of the house starke dead. I need not write anie further circumstance to shew how the matter was taken, what woondering was thereat, how he was prohibited to vse that feat anie further, least he should emploie it in anie other kind of murther; as though he, whose picture so euer he had pricked, must needs haue died, and so the life of all men in the hands of a iuggler: as is now supposed to be in the hands and willes of witches. This storie is, vntill the daie of the writing hereof, in fresh remembrance, & of the most part beleeued as canonicall, as are all the fables of witches: but when you are taught the feate or sleight (the secrecie and sorcerie of the matter being bewraied, and discouered) you will thinke it a mockerie, and a simple illusion. To interpret vnto you the reuelation of this mysterie; so it is, that the poore pigeon was before in the hands of the iuggler, into whome he had thrust a dramme of *Nux Vomica*, [strychnine] or some other such poison, which to the nature of the bird was so extreame a venome, as after the receipt thereof it could not liue aboue the space of halfe an houre, and being let lose after the medicine ministred, she alwaies resorted to the top of the next house: which she will the rather doo, if there be anie pigeons alreadie sitting there, and (as it is alreadie said) after a short space falleth downe, either starke dead, or greatlie astonnied. But in the meane time the iuggler vseth words of art, partlie to protract the time, and partlie to gaine credit and admiration of the beholders. If this or the like feate should be done by an old woman, eurie bodie would crie out, for fier and faggot to burne the witch.[38]

Scot's description and 'discovery', or revelation, of Brandon's work is the most detailed of any of the surviving records that indicate the nature of his work as a juggler and presents a qualitatively different kind of evidence to that located in financial accounts. In addition to the specific stunt described here the account confirms Brandon's identity as a juggler who performed before the king (presumably Henry VIII). Scot's *Discouerie of witchcraft* is an important work that not only denounces witchcraft as superstition (the only one at this time to do so) but declares the means by which such practices and beliefs were carried out through legerdemain. Scot's work was subsequently refuted by James I in his *Daemonologie* (1597).[39] In 'The Preface to the Reader' James says:

such assaultes of Sathan are most certainly practized, & that the instrumentes thereof, merits most severly to be punished: against the damnable opinions of two principally in our age, whereof the one called s c o t an Englishman, is not ashamed in publike print to deny, that ther can be such a thing as Witch-craft: and so mainteines the old error of the Sadducees, in denying of spirits.

Consequently, a whole chapter in the *Discouerie of witchcraft* is devoted to explaining how tricks, ruses and illusions were performed by jugglers. This book is also regarded as the earliest English one to deal with such juggling revelations.[40] As with a number of such apparent exposés, many questions remain concerning details that are omitted. For instance, how does the juggler determine the resting place of the pigeon when it flies on to the roof? How does the juggler know the appropriate dose of poison? The juggler's confederate behaviour might provide an answer to the first question through prior positioning of food on the roof. The answer to the second question seems to imply some experimentation with pigeons in respect of an appropriate dosage of strychnine. The relative imprecision with regard to the strength of the dose and the time taken for the pigeon to fall from its perch is accounted for in the flexibility offered through the juggler's ability to 'protract time' through patter.

Brandon is only one of the jugglers of whom Scot writes: Bomelio Feats; Steeuen Tailor and his confederate, Pope; Iohn Cautares; and Kingsfield are each identified by Scot, and their work will be discussed later.[41] Of these jugglers Scot provides most information on Bomelio Feats. Although Feats was not the King's juggler he was relatively well known in the mid sixteenth century: so much so, that other writers such as George Peele and Sir Richard Carew the younger also wrote about his exploits.

George Peele refers to Feats in his *Merrie Conceited Iests* (1627), where further information is provided as to one aspect of his skill:

George was not so merry at London with his Capons and Claret, as poore Anthony the Barber was sorrowfull at Brainford for the losse of his Lute, & therefore determined to come to London to seeke out George Peele, which by meanes of a kinsman that Anthony Nit had in London, his name was Cuts or Feats, a Fellow that had good skill in tricks on the Cards, and hee was well acquanted with the place where Georges common abode was: and for kindred sake he directed the Barber where he should haue him, which was at a blinde Alehouse in Sea-cole Lane.[42]

Although Peele's account describes Feats' ability in relation to 'good skill in tricks on the Cards', it is clear that his skill went beyond such close manipulation of cards. Peele also records that Feats sometimes went by another name of 'Cuts'. According to Scot, Feats was not only a juggler but a 'witch or conjurer, euerie waie a cousener: his qualities and feats were to me and manie other well knowne and detected'. As a 'witch or conjurer' he appears to have operated under the name of Hilles.[43] From Scot's accounts it seems that Feats worked some of his feats with a trained dog. Scot declares his understanding and admiration of the juggler's ability to train animals as part of a performance:

in so much as they be not by mans industrie or cunning to be made familiar, or trained to doo anie thing, whereby admiration maie be procured: as *Bomelio Feates* his dog could doo; or *Mahomets* pigeon, which would resort vnto him, being in the middest of his campe, and picke a pease out of his eare.[44]

The principal information concerning Feats comes from quite a different source; that is a manuscript written in the early seventeenth century by Sir Richard Carew, the younger, 1579/8–1643[?]. A copy of this manuscript exists in the Cornish Record Office, Truro, under the title *The ms works of Sir Richard Carew CZ/EE/32/C*. I shall quote in full the section that relates to Feats:

A little before his [i.e. Dr Burcott's, a physician] ende, his familier left him, then hee dealt with a Jugler, called Feates, (a man of the same trade, but one that vsed double iuglinge,) to procure him a new famylyer: Now Feates, that was a very cunninge knaue, so to mingle the helpe hee had from his Master, with the subtill tricks of his owne witt, as made his wickednes the lesse suspected, told him, that for on hundred pound in hand, and on condition, hee would remayne, one whole hower, in the same Roome, where hee would bringe him, and not once stepp out of doores, in that space; hee should haue what hee asked. Where vnto hauinge agreede, Feates left him, in a Chamber ouer a stable, whose planchinge was loose; and the Boards were neuer ioyned to gether; then vnder this roome Feates setts fire to wett hay, and straw, and so filles the Doctor with smoake, that either hee must bee choaked, or else get out, and so was well payd, for his hundred pounds; with which hee meant to haue bought a new deuill. And not longe after, died a begger. This story, each of the partyes, before named, told; by seuerall peices, as if they had mett on purpose, to relate his life, and death . . . And this Feates, had many fine tricks, to delude men by; which hee wold after discouer; how hee did them; that what hee did, in deede by the deuill, might bee taken, to be but a pleasant kinde of cozeninge,. Now three things, the same gentleman, my Cousen Fortescue, told mee, he saw him doe; two whereof, seeme strange, but the third, I can not conceiue, how any man can doe it, but by the helpe of a spirite; The first was, when this Feates, dininge at a table, amongst diuers knights, and Gentlemen, hee sittinge at the lower end, of the table, by one Mr. Powell; who duringe the meale, made himselfe very merry, with Feates, his pretious nose, and the rubyes of his face. For hee loued good liquor; and carried those tokens thereof. When the meale was ended, Feates to make sporte, called for a dish of nuts; bade one of the knights, thinke on some carde; and asked the other, whither hee would haue the name of the carde, so thought on, to bee written, in red letters, or black,? Hee sayd redd; then hee bade him, take out a nutte, and cracke it, which hauinge don, within the hud, which contaynes the kernell, was founde, a little rolle of parchm[t]: curiously folded, and therein, the seauen of spades written, in fine Roman letters. Which was in deede, the name of the carde, the other knight thought on, then hee turned him to mr. Powell, and sayd, you haue taken youre pleasure on mee, this meale, yet you shall see, I will doe some thinge for you; and bade another, thinke on a carde, and then spake to mr. Powell, to take a nutte, and crack him; which when hee had don, such filthy, black, stinkinge stuff, flew thence, in to his mouth, and a bout his face, as hee could hardly, in halfe an hower, get it away,. After which time, hee still held him, in as greate admiration as beefore hee had don in contempt; and would often bestow the wine on him.[45]

This entry in Carew's manuscript relates to the telling of these stories by Fortescue, his cousin. How much is factual and/or apocryphal is unclear, for the trick outlined here is contained in Scot's *Discouerie of witchcraft*. However, Scot writes of the 'tricke' in such a way as to suggest that it was a known contemporary trick with the possibility of some variations of treatment. He writes: 'This tricke they commonlie end with a nut full of inke, in which case some wag or vnhappie boie is to be required to thinke a card; and hauing so doone, let the nut be deliuered him to cracke, which he will not refuse to doo, if he haue seene the other feate plaied before.'[46] Scot outlines the 'tricke' as follows:

Take a nut, or a cheristone, & burne a hole through the side of the top of the shell, and also through the kernell (if you will) with a hot bodkin, or boare it with a nall; and with the eie of a needle pull out some of the kernell, so as the same may be as wide as the hole of the shell. Then write the number or name of a card in a peece of fine paper one inch or halfe an inch in length, and halfe so much in bredth, and roll it vp hard: then put it into a nut, or cheristone, and close the hole with a little red waxe, and rub the same with a little dust, and it will not be perceiued, if the nut or cheristone be browne or old. Then let your confederate thinke that card which you haue in your nut, etc: and either conueie the same nut or cheristone into some bodies pocket, or laie it in some strange place: then make one drawe the same out of the stocke held in your hand, which by vse you may well doo. But saie not; I will make you perforce draw such a card: but require some stander by to draw a card, saieng that it skils not what card he draw. And if your hand serue you to vse the cards well, you shall prefer vnto him, and he shall receiue (euen though he snatch at an other) the uerie card which you kept, and your confederate thought, and is written in the nut, and hidden in the pocket, etc. You must (while you hold the stocke in your hands, tossing the cards to and fro) remember alwaies to keepe your card in your eie, and not to loose the sight thereof. Which feate, till you be perfect in, you may haue the same priuilie marked; and when you perceiue his hand readie to draw, put it a little out towards his hand, nimblie turning ouer the cards, as though you numbered them, holding the same more loose and open than the rest, in no wise suffering him to draw anie other: which if he should doo, you must let three or foure fall, that you may beginne againe. This will seeme most strange, if your said paper be inclosed in a button, and by confederacie sowed vpon the doublet or cote of anie bodie.[47]

Carew goes on to describe a trick that is not contained in Scot's *Discouerie of witchcraft*. Nor is the trick printed in any of the early seventeenth-century works such as Samuel Rid's *The Art of Iugling* of 1612; Henry van Etten's *Mathematicall Recreations* of 1633 or *Hocvs Pocvs Ivnior* of 1634.[48] The description is as follows:

Now once, when my cousen Fortescue, and ffeates, were to-gether in Welles, (if I mistake not the name of the place) meetinge this mr. Powell, hee told him, You haue don mee many courtesyes, now if you will bestow a quarte of wine, on this gentleman, and mee, I will requite, all youre former kindnes, which hee presently agreed vnto, and so, into the Tauerne they goe; and Feates calles for the chamberlaine, and asked him, how many maydes there were in the house? Hee named him three, A: B: C; then bids him, bringe him three kniues; and a bason of water; When hee was gon, hee takes a roote, out of his pockett, which seemed to be a furse roote: names each seuerall knife, by one of the maydes names; and tells mr. Powell, hee would now teach him a trick, to know, whither anyone hee meant to marry, were a mayd, or noe. Then whetts the kniues vpon his roote, and putts them in to water, and sayes to the knife which hee called: A if A: bee a mayde, gett vp presently, vp flyes the knife, and sticks in a beame of the roofe, then sayes hee, to the knife, called: B, if B: bee a mayde, gett thou vp too,. Then vp mounts that knife, and sticks in the haft of the other, then calls hee vpon C,: if C: were a mayde, to follow her fellowes; But that knife was deafe, and would not stirr, wher-vpon, Ffeates calls againe to the Chamberlain, and seemes, to fall out with him, for sayinge, there were three maydes in the house; the Chamberlayn tells him againe, so there bee; Feates begins to chide him, for offeringe to mayntaine such a lye, before him, and sayes, hee knew: A; and B, were mayds, but: C: was none, the Chamberlyn answeares, the truth is S^r, shee had a younge sonne, some three monethes since, but beinge my fellow seruant it was reason, I should conceale it, and speake the best of her, and desired them, to doe so too, for the Creditt of the house; where vpon, Mr. Powell agrees, to buy this roote of him, which hee saw, to bee of such proofe; and payes him 40^{oe} [40 shillings] for it, And I thinke, hee might well haue tryed, all the maydes in Christendome, before hee should make his knife leape, as the two first did:[49]

To my understanding, this description has not hitherto been known to the magic fraternity. Although this trick is not contained in Scot, a similar one is recorded and Scot's description of the necessary conditions for the successful working of the trick may be used to illuminate the possible technique involved in the 'tricke' described by Carew. Scot's trick is recorded as follows:

With words to make a groat or a testor to leape out of a pot, or to run alongst vpon a table

You shall see a iuggler take a groat or a testor, and throwe it into a pot, or laie it in the midst of a table, & with inchanting words cause the same to leape out of the pot, or run towards him, or from him ward alongst the table. Which will seeme miraculous, vntill you knowe that it is doone with a long blacke haire of a womans head, fastened to the brim of a groat, by meanes of a little hole driuen through the same with a Spanish needle. In like sort you may vse a knife, or anie other small thing: but if you would haue it go from you, you must haue a confederate, by which meanes all iuggling is graced and ammended.[50]

So, this trick may also be performed with 'a knife, or anie other small thing: but if you would haue it go from you, you must haue a confederate, by which meanes all iuggling is graced and ammended'. It seems likely, therefore, that the 'chamberlaine' of Carew's account is a confederate as required by Scot in his description. The 'chamberlaine' not only brings in the knives and basin (presumably pre-prepared) but also provides the necessary information to the story of the maids. No doubt the 'chamberlaine', or possibly another un-named confederate, positions himself in the room above and draws up the knives on some kind of thread. In a marginal note to his trick Scot describes how the physical conditions of the trick need to be prepared: 'This feat is the stranger if it be doone by night; a candle placed betweene the lookers on & the iuggler: for by that means their eiesight is hindered from discerning the conceit.'[51]

Carew offers a further observation concerning Feats which completely baffles him. He writes:

An other time, when Feates my cozin Fortescue, and others, were in company, hee would needes, haue one of them, to thinke on a carde, and haue him to name the carde, when hee answeared, hee could not tell, what carde it should bee, He replied, any carde, which comes first in to youre mynde,. When suddenly as by the shortest puffe of breath, the name of the Ace, of hearts, was buzzed into his eare, And hee sayd, hee could not tell what carde it should bee, if not the Ace of hearts,. Which was indeede, the very carde, the other had thought; Now this kind of Instruction, passes my Capacity for one man, by any naturall meanes, to giue to an other, in this sorte.[52]

Carew's accounts of the activities of Feats are thought to have been written in the late 1620s. This appears to be sometime after the death of Feats, for Scot, writing in 1584, talks of Feats 'whilest he liued'. So, George Peele's reference to Feats and those of Carew appear to be written some forty or so years after his death.

As is evident from the kind of information outlined above, financial records offer only partial detail in their contribution to the picture of the juggler's activities and his methods. Some useful accounts of the juggler's work arise out of critical responses to his skill. Heinrich Cornelius Agrippa von Nettesheim (1486–1535) in his *De incertitudine & vanitate scientiarum & artium, atque excellentia verbi Dei, declamatio* (1531) attacked the astrologers and magicians of his time. The work denounces scholasticism, the veneration of relics and saints, and canon law and its hierarchy. Agrippa makes a marginal note that refers the reader to the Greek lexicon, *Suidae lexicon*, of the late tenth century for details of the work of a juggler called Pasetes. Of Pasetes, Agrippa states: 'Legimus quoque Paseten quendam praestigiatorem refertissimum conuiuium hospitibus monstrare solitum, idque cum libuit, rursum euanuisse, discumbentibus omnibus fame ac siti elusis.'[53] The earliest English translation of this work by James Sandford was published in 1569. He translates this passage as: 'we haue reade also that one *Pasetes* a Jugler was wonte to shewe to straungers a very sumptuouse banket, & when it pleased him to cause it vanishe awaie, all they whiche sate at the table beinge disapointed both of meate & drinke'.[54] The working of this trick is discussed later in Chapter 4. Pasetes' work, along with that of other ostensible jugglers, is also referred to by the writer Robert Burton (1577–1640) in his *The Anatomy of Melancholy* (first published in 1621). Here, stunts and illusions of similar scope and magnitude as that described by Agrippa are recorded:

> Now and then peradventure there may be some more famous Magiciens like *Simon Magus, Apollonius Tyaneus, Pasetes,* Jamblicus, udo de stellis, that for a time can build Castles in the aire, represent armies, &c. as they are said to have done, command wealth and treasure, feed thousands with all variety of meats upon a sudden, protect themselves and their followers from alll Princes of persecution, by removing from place to place in an instant, reveal secrets, future events, tell what is done in far Countries, make them appear that dyed long since, &c.[55]

The 1620s mark the development of another juggler by the name of William Vincent. Some of the material presented here was first published by Nigel Bawcutt in his article 'William Vincent, alias Hocus Pocus: a travelling entertainer of the seventeenth century'. Bawcutt states in his paper that 'These are all the performance records known to me, though more will undoubtedly surface when the *Records of Early English Drama* project is finally completed.'[56] Although the *Records of Early English Drama* project has not yet been completed, some additional records have now been made available and this makes it possible to develop the discussion. The earliest reference, to date, concerning Vincent is from 1619, when mention is made of: 'A Licence to William Vincent vnder the Signet, to exercise the art of Legerdemaine in any Townes within the Relme of England & Ireland during his Ma^ts pleasure'.[57] The Leicester

Chamberlains' Accounts for 1622 record further payment to Vincent: 'Item given to Vincent and his Company, by Mr Maiors Appointm^t, having authoritye from the King to shew feats of Activitye . . . x^{s}'.[58] These two records concerning payment for 'Legerdemaine' and 'feats of activity' refer to juggling. Although the terms 'legerdemain' and 'feats of activity' appear to be synonymous in this case, the term 'feats of activity' is also used to embrace other activities that involve tumbling, vaulting and dancing on the rope. The identity and distinctions concerning these activities are discussed in the following chapter.

Further confirmation of the relationship between 'legerdemain' and 'feats of activity', as it applies to Vincent, occurs in the *Chamberlains' and Wardens' Account Book* at Coventry in 1630: 'Paid given to William Vincent who came with Commission from the Kings Majestie to shew feats of Acivitie & legerdemaine in August last as appearethe by a bill vnder Maister Maiors hand v s'.[59]

In 1625, identification is recorded of William Vincent's alias, namely, that of 'Hocus Pocus'. The record exists because of Vincent's alleged involvement in a fraud upon Francis Lane of Campsey Ash, Suffolk. It is recorded that Lane 'saith that he was cosened and deceyved of ix*li.* in money, whiche he had in his purse, by Edward Butler [blank] Vincent, [blank] Archis, and others, by playeinge at tables the game ticke tacke, and betting with them or some of them'. Confirmation of Vincent's identity is revealed by the following statement in the same account:

William Vincent, alias Hocus Spocus, of London, the Kinge's Majestie's servant, to use his faculty of feales (?) [feates] &c, saith he was in company with the said Francis Lane and played at [ ] for vj*d.*, and soe till Hocus Spocus lost iij*s.* to Francis Lane, and said he would be halves with him, and would have had him fourth of the roome at Spencer's house into a private place.[60]

This record first appeared in 1895 in the *Reading Records* in the *Diary of the Corporation* and was re-discovered in 1993 by Richard Burt.[61] However, the correlation of these two identities makes it possible to build up a clearer picture of the work of Vincent through records of him and 'Hocus Pocus'. Effectively, 'Hocus Pocus' was Vincent's stage name and it is from this designation that all subsequent references to 'Hocus Pocus' derive.

References are to be found in the *Diary of Thomas Crosfield* for 1634 and 1635 to 'His maiesties Hokus Pokus' and 'Hokuspokus' played at 'ye Kings armes' below 'ye flower de luce'.[62] Sir Henry Herbert records in his Office Book for 1634: 'From Vincent – For dancing on the Ropes this Lent at y^e

Fortune by Blagrove 7 March 1634—2^{li}.[63] The *Mayors' Court Books* at Norwich for 1635 record that 'William Vincent is to shewe Feates' as determined by:

A warrant signed by his Maiestie vnder his highnes privie Signett bearinge date the xiijth day of December in the Third yeare of his Reigne & Confirmed by the master of the Revelles vnder his hand & deale was yesterday shewed to mr Maior & diuerse Iustices & Aldermen by william vincent one of the patentees, hee hath tyme to exercise his feates till wednesday night next.[64]

The above records demonstrate that Vincent not only performed 'Legerdemaine' but also 'feats of activity' which, in his case, involved 'dancing on the ropes'. Further, in the accounting year for 1636–7 the *Gloucester Corporation Chamberlains' Accounts* record: 'Item payd vnto Vincente that Caries Sightes and shewes with dauncing on the Ropp wch was by order of the Iustices 1-6-8'. Additional payment is recorded as: 'Item payd more vnto Vincent at his Retorning to towne in that the tyme of contagious sicknes might prove dangerous by the order of the Iustices – 0-13-4'.[65] Here is yet another payment in compensation during times of 'contagious sicknes'. Vincent was again given permission to perform in Norwich in 1639 where the *Mayors' Court Books* record that: 'william Vincent hath leaue for his servantes to exercise feates of activity according to his Maiesties lycence vpon Thursdaie ffryday and Satterday next and then he consenteth to depart this City and not to stay any longer'.[66] The *Chamberlains' and Wardens' Account Book* at Coventry for 1638 records: 'paid given to the Kinges players, and hocus pocus xxs'.[67] The last extant payment to Vincent occurs in the Chamberlains' and Wardens' Account Book at Coventry for 1642: 'given to William Vincent who had commission for him and his company to daunce vpon the ropes & shew other trickes of legerdemaine xs'.[68] There are no further records of Vincent's performances beyond this point although references to 'Hocus Pocus' continue up to the present day.

There are many contemporary references to 'Hocus Pocus' and the nature of his work. Not only are a number of his tricks and routines suggested but several references include details of his presentational patter. Versions of his patter have survived to the present day. The *Boy* in Jonson's *The Magnetic Lady* of 1632 asserts: 'Doe they thinke this Pen can juggle? I would we had *Hokos-pokos* for 'hem then, your *People*; or Travitanto Tudesko.' *Dam* says: 'Who's that *Boy*?' The *Boy* replies 'Another Juggler, with a long name.'[69] In John Kirke's *The Seven Champions of Christendome* of 1638 the Clown says:

Forgive me this, and if the obeying of your wil, wil bring me to you, let me alone; I'le not be long from home: But Father, what, no trick, no invention to make me famous e're I come to you? why, my Mother could juggle as well as any Hocus Pocus I'th world, and shall I doe nothing?[70]

In the anonymously authored *The Knave in Graine* of 1640 in a carefully crafted confederate 'scam', the Country Fellow naively declares:

They talke of Cheaters, here is a twenty shillings peece that I put into my mouth, let any Cheater in Christendome cousen me of this, and carry it away cleanly, and Ile not only forgive him, but hugge him and embrace him for it, and say he is a very *Hocus Pocus* indeed.[71]

Needless to say, the Country Fellow is tricked out of his 'twenty shillings peece' (see Appendix 4). In Jonson's *The Staple of Newes* of 1626 some indication is offered of the appearance of 'Hocus Pocus'. 'Mirth' states that 'Iniquity came in like Hokos Pokos, in a Iuglers ierkin, with false skirts, like the Knaue of Clubs!'[72] John Rushworth, in his *Historical Collections*, published in 1680 and 1682 refers, in a somewhat seditious letter, dated 9 January 1633, to the Archbishop of Canterbury as 'the little medling Hocus-Pocus' and the 'little Urchin, Vermin, little Hocus Pocus in the Velvet Jerkin'.[73]

A number of references to Vincent through his alias 'Hocus Pocus' indicate the style of his presentation through details of his patter. The earliest extant reference to 'Hocus Pocus' occurs in Ben Jonson's *The Masque of Augeres* in 1622, some three years after the earliest reference to William Vincent, and here Jonson writes phonetically of Dutch attempts to speak English: 'O Sir, all de better, vor an Antick-maske, de more absurd it be, and vrom de purpose, it be ever all de better. If it goe from de Nature of de ting, it is de more Art: for deare is Art, and deare is Nature; yow shall see. Hochos-pochos, Paucos Palabros.'[74] A further example of possible 'Hocus Pocus patter' occurs in Thomas Randolph's *The Jealous Lovers*, of 1632, when a page states: 'If I do not think women were got with ridling, whippe me: Hocas, pocas, here you shall have me, and there you shall have me.'[75] The implication here is that Vincent opens his hands one by one to reveal that he conceals nothing. Further patter occurs later in the play when Asot, the prodigal son to Sino, offers the opinion: 'I think Cupid be turn'd jugler. Here's nothing but Hocas pocas. Praesto be gon, Come again Jack; and such feats of activitie.'[76] These references are interesting in that they appear to state or parody the patter of 'Hocus Pocus' in making objects disappear and reappear. The latter quotation also confirms the process of juggling as that which is synonymous with 'feats of activity'. In turn, 'feats of activity' are again confirmed as conjuring. In *Observations upon Anthroposophia Theomagica, and Anima Magica Abscondita* a further statement refers to the patter that accompanies opening of the hands to reveal that nothing is hidden: 'Here Philalethes like the Angell of the bottmlesse Pit, comes jingling with the Keyes of Magick in his hands. But hee opens as Hokus Pokus do's his fists, where we see that here is nothing and there is nothing.'[77]

Two examples of William Vincent's repertoire refer to his apparent ability to swallow and expel daggers from his mouth. *The Character Of A London-Diurnall*, a satire ridiculing the London newsbooks of the day, was published in 1647 by the poet John Cleveland and here it is recorded that:

> Before a *Scot* can properly be curst,
> I must (like Hocus) swallow daggers first.[78]

In the *Harleian Miscellany* further reference to Vincent's ability with daggers is described: 'Now the game begins: room for the Roman actors. Here the Bishops rack themselves in a pulpit, vomiting up daggers, like Hocus, to amaze the people.'[79]

An epitaph to Hocus Pocus appeared in 1650 and since the last recorded payment to him was at Coventry in 1642, it may be inferred that he died sometime within these dates. The epitaph reads:

> Here *Hocas* lies with his tricks and his knocks,
> Whom death hath made sure as his Juglers box:
> Who many hath cozen'd by his leiger-demain,
> Is presto convey'd and here underlain:
> Thus *Hocas* he's here, and here he is not,
> While death plaid the *Hocas*, and brought him toth pot.[80]

The name 'Hocus Pocus' not only occurs as the pseudonym of William Vincent but is also involved in the title of one of the important early works on magic that is titled *Hocvs Pocvs Ivnior*; the earliest surviving edition of this work is dated 1634.[81] For many years it has been questioned as to whether 1634 represents the date of the first edition of the work. Sydney W. Clarke declares that the work 'ran in various editions and forms from 1622 to 1850 or thereabouts' and adds 'It is doubtful whether any copy of the first edition now exists, but numerous copies of the second edition [of 1635] are to be found in public and private collections.'[82] Clarke recognises that the date of 1622 is a perpetuated mistake that should be recorded as 1722.[83] Clearly Clarke was not aware of the four extant copies of the 1634 edition.[84] Others who have speculated on the date of the first edition of *Hocvs Pocvs Ivnior* are Henry Ridgely Evans, Harry Houdini and John Ferguson.[85] Trevor H. Hall conducts a careful discussion about the early editions of *Hocvs Pocvs Ivnior* in his *Old Conjuring Books*.[86] He summarises known information about the earliest edition of *Hocvs Pocvs Ivnior* and separates this from poorly informed speculation that has been handed down or plagiarised. In the absence of firm evidence, he too, makes a number of assumptions through his declared opinions. The 1635 edition of *Hocvs Pocvs Ivnior* refers to the edition on its title page as 'The second Edition'. It may be inferred, therefore, that the first edition is that of 1634. Considerable speculation has been expended on attempts to identify the author of *Hocvs Pocvs Ivnior*. In the absence of firm evidence some erroneous assertions, arguments and faulty interpretation of available evidence have taken place. However, I do not wish to discuss these statements at this time for it is now clear from my investigation that the 1634 edition is the first one and that its author is William Vincent, alias Hocus Pocus.

Evidence for these two assertions occurs in Randle Holme's *The Academy of Armory; Or, A Storehouse Of Armory and Blazon* of 1688. The following statement occurs in the Third Book, Chapter XII, during a discussion on 'Leger De Main Implements'. Holme says: 'Of which I shall give you an example of some, for the rest I referr you to *Hocus Pocus Iunior*, Printed by him in the yeare 1634.[87]

To whom does the 'him' of the quotation refer? The only answer to this question is to the juggler 'Hocus Pocus'. The larger context in which this quotation occurs does not refer to the identity of any other person so the 'him' can only refer to the content of the sentence. The other point that the quotation confirms is that the publication date was '1634'. Does the description that the book was 'Printed by him' mean that he wrote, compiled, edited or published the work? Given that the title page of the 1634 edition records that the work was 'Printed by T.H. for R.M.' [Thomas Harper for Ralph Mabb] it is more probable that Vincent was the author and/or compiler. Although Holme's statement is clear there is still a need for further evidence to reinforce Vincent's authorship of *Hocvs Pocvs Ivnior*.

Identification of William Vincent as the author of *Hocvs Pocvs Ivnior* enables another issue to be resolved. In the 1634 edition there is a trick labelled, 'Bonus Genius or Nuntius invisibilis' which involves the appearance and disappearance of a small doll 'the bignesse of your little finger'. A subsequent edition of *Hocvs Pocvs Iunior* of 1654 titles the trick as: 'Bonus Genius, or Nuntius, invisibilis, or Hiccius Doccius, as my Senior calls it'.[88] Much discussion has centred upon the phrase 'as my Senior calls it'.[89] To what or whom does this refer? If the book is referred to as the *Junior* then 'my Senior' suggests its author and not an earlier edition. Given that Randle identifies the author as Hocus Pocus then 'my Senior' appears to be William Vincent.

Although it is clear that William Vincent, alias 'Hocus Pocus', performed 'feats of activity' through legerdemain and wrote about it in *Hocvs Pocvs Ivnior*, it is also clear that he and/or his company performed 'feats of activity' through dancing on the rope. These dextrous skills are quite different in their nature and the relationship between them and tumbling and vaulting as other 'feats of activity' is discussed in the next chapter.

CHAPTER 2

Feats of activity: juggling, tumbling and dancing on the rope

Feats of activity is a phrase that has gone unnoticed as both a distinctive and generic term that specifically refers to juggling, tumbling, vaulting and *dancing on the rope*. These activities and their requisite skills were combined sometimes through individuals and on other occasions through groups, companies or families of jugglers. Because of this multi-skilled ability it is sometimes difficult to separate the skills in order to determine their nature in relation to *feats of activity*.

The term *feats* is regularly used to describe acts of physical skill, tricks and other forms of theatrically devised activity. For example, the *Mayors' Court Books* at Norwich for 1634 record that 'This Day Iohn Tandy one of the assistantes vnto Robert Tyce Iames Gentleman & Thomas Galloway did bring into this Court a lycence vnder the hand & seale of the maister of the Revilles to shew feates . . . they are forbidden to shewe their feates . . . yet afterward there was leave granted to him to shewe his feates till satterday night next.'[1] Again, the *Mayors' Court Books* at Norwich record payment to an itinerant juggler, Danyell Abbot, in 1638. He too operated under licence 'vnder the seale of the maisters of the Revells'. Even so, 'Mr Maior' asked Abbot not to play and 'offered him xxij s for a gratuity to forbeare his shewes which hee refused'. In the end 'Mr Maior' relented and allowed him 'to shewe his feates here till this Day at noone'.[2]

More precise use of the term *feats* occurs where it is coupled with particular skills. For instance, records exist of 'Iuglinge feates'; 'feates of legerdemaine'; 'feats of agilitee'; 'feates of vaulting' and 'feats of tumblinge'. As seen in the last chapter, the *Corporation Chamberlains' Accounts* for 1563–4 at Gloucester record payment to 'Stanweye the Quenes Iugler for shewinge pastimes and other of his Iuglinge feates to Mr mayor . . . xs'.[3] The *Quarter Sessions Roll* for 1623 at Somerton, Somerset, records that Iohn Gerrard was given money by 'some gentlemen & others . . . for shewinge them feates of Leigerdemaine & slightes of the hand'.[4] Robert Laneham [Langham] in his *Letter* describes performance of 'feats of agilittee' by 'an Italian'.[5] For the accounting year 1579–80 the *Dramatic Records in the Declared Accounts of the Treasurer of the Chamber* record payment of 'x^{li}' to 'the Lorde Straunge his Tumblers vpon a Warr*ant* signed by her Maiesties pryvie Counsell dated at Whitehall xxv^{to} Ianuarij 1579 in considerac*i*on of certen feates of Tumblinge by them done before her Matie'.[6]

Clear references to feats of activity as juggling occur in the play *Beggars' Bush* by Beaumont and Fletcher (1622) where Prig, the juggler, asks: 'Will ye see any feates of activity, / Some sleight of hand, leigerdemaine? hey passe, / Presto, be gone there?' [Appendix 3].[7] A similar reference is contained in *The Jealous Lovers* by Thomas Randolph (1632) where Asotus, the prodigal son to Simo, declares: 'I think Cupid be turn'd jugler. Here's nothing but Hocas pocas. Praesto be gon, Come again Jack; and such feats of activitie.'[8] Reginald Scot in his *Discouerie of witchcraft* further confirms the meaning of *feats of activity* as *juggling* when he declares that: 'There are certeine feats of actiuitie, which beautifie this art [juggling] exceedinglie: howbeit euen in these, some are true, and some are counterfet; to wit, some done by practise, and some by confederacie.'[9] Although the above examples make it clear that the phrase *feats of activity* refers to juggling, some further records indicate a wider use. However, the meaning of this evidence needs to be clarified. For instance, in *The Declared Accounts of the Treasurer of the Chamber* for 1582, payment is recorded to Iohn Simons: 'To Iohn Simons vppon a warr*ant* signed by ^{mr} Secr' walsingham and the ll*es* of the Counsell xvij^{mo} Febr' 1582 for showinge ce*r*ten Feates of Actiuitye and Tomblinge before her ma^{tie} on Newyeres day last at Windsor xiij^{li} vj^{s} viij^{d}.[10] Does this record mean that 'Tomblinge' was an additional activity to 'Feates of Actiuitye'? Initial consideration of this question may suggest that this is what is meant. However, payment is also recorded in the same accounts for 1584–5 where activity in relation to 'feates of Actiuitye' is on this occasion recorded as 'vawtinge' [vaulting]: 'To Iohn Symons and other his fellowes Servant*es* to Therle of Oxforde vppon the Counsell*es* warr*ant* dated at Grenew^{ch} xiiij^{to} m'cij 1584 presentinge before her ma^{tie} vppon Newyeares day at nighte last feates of Actiuitye and vawtinge by way of her ma^{tes} rewarde x^{li}.[11] Is 'vawtinge' a separate pursuit to 'feates of Actiuitye'? At Coventry, the *Chamberlains' and Wardens' Account Book II* for 1630 records payment to William Vincent in a similarly itemised payment: 'Paid given to William Vincent who came with Commission from the Kings Majestie to shew feats of Activitie & legerdemaine in August last as appearethe by a bill vnder Maister Maiors hand v s'.[12]

In this instance, are 'feats of Activitie' different ones to 'legerdemaine'? The *Mayors' Court Books XVI* at Norwich for 1632 record that 'Henry Miller and ffower Assistantes are lycenced to shewe feates and sleight of hand &c'.[13] Again, are 'feates' different from 'sleight of hand'? Part of the answer to these questions lies in the knowledge that Renaissance style frequently used doublets for synonyms where the second explicated the first. Another part of the answer may be seen in the consistency of use of these phrases. Even though these records seemingly point to the activities of 'Tomblinge', 'vawtinge', 'sleight of hand' and 'legerdemaine' as additional and different ones from 'Feates of Actiuitye' and 'Feats', it seems that the processes of 'Tomblinge', 'vawtinge', 'sleight of hand' and 'legerdemaine' are expressed in this stylistic way so as to qualify the term 'Feates of Actiuitye' or 'Feats'. Use of the word 'and' to join the term 'Feates of Actiuitye' or 'Feats' and 'Tomblinge', 'vawtinge', 'sleight of hand' and 'legerdemaine' does not appear to refer to these activities as additional ones but to determine that of which the activities consist. In other words, references to 'Tomblinge', 'vawtinge', 'sleight of hand' and 'legerdemaine' exist to qualify and constitute 'Feates of Actiuitye'. This consideration may be further supported with reference to the work of John and Caleb Hassett in payment for their performance at Hampton Court: 'To Iohn Hassett & Caleb Hassett vpon the Councell warraunt dat xxiij^{tio} die Septembr 1608 for feates of Activity by them per*formed* vpon a Vaughting horse before his Matie at Hampton Courte by way of his Maties reward xiij^{li} vj^s viij^{d}'.[14] Here is further confirmation that 'vaulting' qualifies as one of the 'feates of Activity'. The same sort of relationship is apparent in records concerning *dancing on the rope*. William Pedle and members of his family appear as recipients of payment in *The Declared Accounts of the Treasurer of the Chamber*: 'To William Pedle the Father and Willm Pedle the sonne vpon the Councell*es* warraunte dated xx° Aprilis 1609 for themselves and their Company in presentinge of feat*es* of activitie vpon a rope at Whitehall before his ma^{tie} the xviijth of Aprill 1609 xiij^{li} vj^s viij^{d}'.[15]

Although the manouvres employed in *dancing on the rope* may be considered as 'feat*es* of activitie' in their own right there remains the question as to whether 'feat*es* of activitie' refer to juggling tricks carried out whilst 'dancing on the rope'. This concern may be made clearer in the light of another account recording payment to William Pedle that states: 'To William Pedell vpon like warr^t dated at whitehall viij^{uo} Die Aprilis 1616 for dauncing on the Ropes and showing other feates of Activitie on Tewseday in Easter weeke laste xx^{li}'.[16] The important difference recorded in this account is to 'other' feats of activity than those 'for dauncing on the

Ropes'. Further clarity concerning the relationship between dancing on the rope and juggling is contained in recorded payment to William Vincent [Hocus Pocus] in the *Chamberlains' and Wardens' Account Book III* at Coventry. In this case, 'other' tricks of legerdemain are recorded in relation to 'daunce vpon the ropes'. The account states: 'paid given to William Vincent who had commission for him and his company to daunce vpon the ropes & shew other trickes of legerdemeane x s'.[17] *The Declared Accounts of the Treasurer of the Chamber* for 1585–6 also record 'other' feats of activity in relation to 'Tumblinge': 'To Iohn Symondes and m^r Standleyes Boyes vppon the Counsells warr*ant* dated vltio Ianuarij 1585 for Tumblinge and shewinge other feates of activitie before her ma^{tie} one the Sondaie nighte next after Twelve daie laste paste, vj^{li} xiij^s iiij^d and for her ma^{tes} speciall rewarde lxvj^s viij^d in all x^{li}.[18]

The same sort of distinction for 'other' feats of activity is made in relation to 'dauncing & vaulting' in a record concerning William and Thomas Peadle at Coventry. The *Chamberlains' and Wardens' Account Book* records: 'paid given to William Peadle & Thomas Peadle his sonn & fower children & Charles Sale & the rest of his assistants that had authority by Commission for dauncing & vaulting & other feats of activity the 24th of december 1639 as appeareth by a bill vnder Maister Maiors hand'.[19]

Since 'dauncing' and 'vaulting' are specified in this account then 'other' feats of activity may be presumed to consist of juggling or legerdemaine. The *Dramatic Records of Sir Henry Herbert* record that: 'A license was granted to Henry Momford, and others, "for tumbling, and vaulting, with *other tricks of slight of hand*"'.[20] The importance of these records, that specify 'other' feats of activity, is that they both imply one or other of the four activities involved here and at the same time confirm the named activity as one of the *feats of activity*. Two further references suggest with more certainty the way in which the phrase *feates of activitie* is intended to embrace juggling, tumbling and *dancing on the rope*. The first of these concerns William Vincent and his company:

1627, Dec. 13 – 'A license vnder the Signett vnto Wm Vincent wth the rest of his Company to exercise and practize the Arte of legerdemaine wth all his other feates of activitie, As vaulting, danceing on the ropes for his best Comodotie in any Convenient place wthin any his Ma^{ts} Dominions, Any provinciall lawe or any other lawe or Restraint whatsoeuer to the contrary notwthstanding'.[21]

The second record is incorporated in an indictment of the juggler, John Jones, at Upton on Severn, Worcestershire, in 1629. This account corroborates the relationship established by the previous record:

and putteing downe of all & euery Playes Players & Playmakers As of all other shewes whatsoever in all places within his maiesties Realme of England as well w[ithin] as without I have by these presentes lycenced and authorised Iohn Iones Anne his wief Richard Payne Richard Iones and their assistance To sett forth and shew a [. . .] Motion with dyvers storyes in ytt As alsoe tumbleing vaulteing sleight of hand and other such like feates of Activety Requyreing you and euery of you in [. . .] suffer and permytt the said Iohn Iones Anne his wief Richard Payne Richard Iones and their assistances quietly to passe.[22]

Even though these separate activities may be grouped under the generic term *feats of activity*, the activities and skills required to produce them were clearly quite different. Juggling skills that require sleight of hand, misdirection or confederate preparation and execution are clearly different from the necessary agility, balance, poise, nerve and fitness that are essential to successful tumbling, vaulting and dancing on the rope. Yet all or most of these skills operated across a number of small companies. But what were the skills and how did they translate into performance? What was the nature of these separate, yet related, activities and by whom were they performed? It transpires from the above records that William Vincent was not simply a lone performer. He ran a company as did William Peadle, Henry Miller, John Simonds, John Jones and Henry Momford. These small companies, often based on family members, seem to have drawn upon the full range of *feats of activity*.

The earliest records that concern the Peadle family are earlier than was previously thought and are contained in the *Dramatic Records in the Declared Accounts of the Treasurer of the Chamber* for April, 1609 (cited earlier) where payment is recorded to 'William Pedle the Father and Willm Pedle the sonne in presentinge feat*es* of activitie vpon a rope'.[23] The extent of the Peadle family company may be appreciated from the following records that build up a cumulative picture of their company. William Peadle – the father, rather than the son – is implied in the minutes of the *Council of Leyden,* Netherlands, in November 1608, where 'Willem Pedel, versochte aen die van de Gerechte der stadt Leyden omme te mogen speelen verscheyde fraeye ende eerlicke spelen mettet lichaem, sonder eenige woorden te gebruycken, stont geappostileert'.[24] [W[illiam] Pedel petitioned the authorities of the city of Leyden to allow him to exhibit various beautiful and chaste performances with his body, without using any words, was determined.] Father and son William are again accounted for in the *Public Record Office* in 1615 where payment is recorded for 'feates of Activitie vpon Ropes'.[25] It is not clear whether father or son is intended to receive payment as recorded in the *Treasurer of* *the Chamber* accounts for 1615–16 where 'William Pedell' is paid for 'dauncing on the Ropes and showinge other feates of Activitie'.[26] An extension to the family company is recorded at Norwich in the *Mayors' Court Books* for 1616 where: 'William Peadle senior william Peadle Iunior & Abraham Peadle' are 'lycensed to vse dancinge on the Roape and other feates of activity'.[27] Payment is further recorded to Peadle and possibly other members of his family at Coventry in 1621: 'Paid which was given to William Peadle & other players Dauncers vpon Ropes the 29th of November last as appeareth by a Bill vnder Maister Maiors hand x s.'.[28] Another Peadle, so far not referred to, is Thomas Peadle, who was arrested for theft in Wells, Somerset, in 1633. Peadle's skills as a juggler were insufficient to extricate him from the charge of 'the felonious takeinge away of ffower Ruffes' from the wife of Thomas Pecke of Wells. Pecke's wife was a 'laundress' who 'havinge washed ffower Ruffes and hanginge them vppon her hedge in Tucker streete they were stolne away and after vppon search Made they were found in the house of Thomas Wills an [. . .] Inkeeper'.[29] Thomas Peadle is again recorded in 1631 when a *Licence from the Master of the Revels* was granted to: 'Sisley Peadle; Thomas Peadle her sonne Elias Grundling and three more in theire Company to vse and exercise daunceing on the Roapes, Tumbling, Maulling [boxing or wrestling?] and other such like ffeates which they or any of them are practized in or can performe . . . with such musiccke drumme or Trumpettes as they shall thinke fitting'.[30] If Thomas was the son of Sisley as determined by the above record and William was the father of Thomas as recorded in an earlier account in this chapter then William the father and Sisley were married and their sons were William, Thomas, Abraham and Jacob. In 1614 a decree of appointment that supports this assertion concerning the sons was 'made out for the brothers William, Abraham and Jacob Pedel' along with others by the Elector John Sigismund in Germany. Although *dancing on the ropes* and other *feats of activity* appear to be the principal activities of the performances, the 1631 account that includes 'Maulling' is a later development.

John Simons and his company performed before Elizabeth throughout the 1580s.[31] The particular orientation of this company appears to have been concerned with tumbling and vaulting as feats of activity. There is no evidence of sleight of hand in their performances.

The company led by John Jones in the 1620s appears to have consisted of his wife, Anne Jones, and another family member, Richard Jones (possibly their son), together with Richard Payne and 'their assistance' [assistants].[32] The *Mayors' Accounts* at Lyme Regis, Dorset, for 1623–4 record payment to Jones as: 'Item given to one Iohn Iones whoe had a licence to shew feates of actiuity to depart the Towne by consent of the Company ij s.'.[33] In 1625 the *Chamberlains' Accounts XI* at Norwich record payment to John Jones as a tumbler: 'Item paid to Iohn Iones and Boxer Tumblers as a gratuity the vij[th] of may 1625 As by warrant appeareth xs.'.[34] The feats of activity performed by the company are recorded as 'tumbleing vaulteing sleight of hand and other such like feates of Activety'.[35]

Another company that involved stories in the performance was that of Francis Strolly at Norwich: 'This Day ffrancis Strolly brought into this Court alycence for him his wiffe and assistance to shewe sundry storyes with slight of hand Dated xx° Septembris 1637 to hold for a yeare, they haue leaue to shewe till Satterday night next, and noe longer.'[36]

The Somerset *Quarter Sessions Roll* for 1623–4 records evidence of the examination of Henry Wian, late of London, groom in the service of Richard George 'who travells vnder authority graunted from the master of the Revells to shew feates of activity, and ever synce he hath continued in the said Georg's service, travellinge the cuntry, the said George gyvinge him weekly for his hire ij s.'.[37]

A company, cited earlier, that visited Norwich in 1634, consisted of Robert Tyce, James Gentleman, Thomas Galloway and their assistant, John Tandy. The company was given limited access to 'shew feates' as recorded in the *Mayors' Court Books XX*, 1634: 'for reason of the said Contagion they are forbidden to shewe their feates for the cause before mencioned, yet afterward there was leave granted to him to shewe his feates till satterday night next'.[38] Although the plague was frequently cited as the reason for prohibiting players from playing there was often some form of compensation awarded to the companies. However, inaccurate or out-of-date licences also provided another reason for the Mayor or other authorities to veto performance. Again, at Norwich the *Mayors' Court Books XV* for 1622 record:

Iohn Dowman brought a Testimoniall vnder the handes of my Lord of Suffolk & others authorisinge them to shew feates of actiuity which Testimoniall ys dated the xxxj[th] of March 1618 And because yt appeareth that he was here with the same Certificate the xxiiij[th] day of May 1620 & had then xxij s giuen him & forbidden to vse his feates then in this Citty And because he nowe confesseth that he accepted the said xxij s & yet shewed his said feates contrary to the then maiors Comandement, he ys therefore nowe comanded to surcease.[39]

The *Chamberlains' and Wardens' Account Book* at Coventry for 1629 records payment to a juggler called 'Lacy': 'Paid which was given to one

Lacy who had a warrant to show feates of Activity the 5th of Iune last xj s.'.[40] Companies such as the Queen's Men, the Lord Admiral's Players and Lord Strange's Players, which are primarily known as acting companies, are also recorded as having performed *feats of activity*. In these cases the preponderant skill appears to be tumbling. In 1588 the 'Lorde Admyrall his Players' presented 'twoe Enterludes or playes wch were playde before her ma^{tie} thone one the sondaye after xpmas daye and thother vppon Shroueteusdaye and for showinge other feates of activitye and tumblinge by waye of her maisties liberalitye xx^{li}'.[41] Again on Childermas Day, 1589, 'the Servaunt*es* of the Lorde Admirall' were paid 'vj^{li} xiij^s iiij^d' for 'shewinge certen feat*es* of activitie before the Queenes ma^{tie}'.[42] Occasionally, this work is performed in the presence of dancers on the rope but these performers are not recorded as members of the company.[43] In the *Declared Accounts of the Treasurer of the Chamber* for 1590–1 payment is recorded:

To George Ottewell and his Companye the Lorde Straunge his players vppon the Councell*es* warra*u*nte dated at the Courte vij^{mo} Marcij 1590 for showinge or presentinge one Enterlude or Playe before her ma^{tie}, the one on St Iohns daye & thother on Shrovetwesdaye laste paste & for other feates of Activtye then also done by them xiij^{li} vj^s viij^d & more by waye of her ma^{tes} further rewarde vj ^{li} xiij ^{s} iiij ^{d} in all xx^{li}.[44]

Ottewell is thought to be 'Attewell' who was possibly one of the Queen's Men in 1595 and further associated with 'Attewell's Jig' of 1595.[45] It is not clear from this account whether Ottewell was a juggler, for the payment is to him 'and his Companye'. Additional payments for feats of activity are recorded by players under the patronage of the Queen and the Earls of Essex, Suffolk, Stafford and Warwick.[46] Again, these accounts are mainly for tumblers. There are also sporadic records to the King's tumbler.[47]

Although there are many records of tumbling, dancing on the rope and vaulting activity across the whole of the country, they are often of the kind that simply record payment for the activities.[48] There are some accounts, however, that record idiosyncratic detail of a kind that enables a clearer understanding of relevant processes to emerge. For instance, the *Household Accounts* of Edward Stafford, Duke of Buckingham, for 1520–1 record payment to 'a yong maide a Tumbeller': 'Item in Rewarde geven by the said Dukes coimmaundement vnto certain frenshe men and ij frenshe women playing afore the said Duc the passion of oure lorde by a vise and also to a yong maide a Tumbeller by Reaport of Iohn kyrk being present maister poley xl s'.[49] In addition to payment to the 'yonge maide a Tumbeller' the account also implies payment to the 'ij frenshe women' as puppeteers. Could the 'vise' be a clockwork arrangement? Could it be that the figures involved in the 'passion of oure lorde' are operated by thread or wires? This record is also of interest because it is one of the early references to the tumbling activities of women. Later accounts allude to the talent and skill that women bring to tumbling and dancing on the rope. For instance, at Norwich the *Mayors' Court Books XV* for 1616 record that:

The same Day in the afternoone Iohn De Rue and Ieronimo Galt ffrenchmen brought before mr Maior in the Counsell Chamber A Lycence Dated the 23th of ffebruary in the xiij[th] yeare of the Reigne of Quene Elizabeth & in the yeare of our Lord 1616 thereby authorisinge the said Iohn De Rue & Ieronimo Galt ffrenchmen to sett forth & shewe rare feates of Actiuity with Dancinge on the Ropes performed by a woman.[50]

Two further accounts suggest that tumblers were accompanied by musicians. The *Household Accounts of Thomas Walmesley* for 1631–2 record payment 'giuen the tomlinge fidlers when Sir Gilbart Houghtonn was heare v s'.[51] Similarly, the *Chamberlains' Accounts* at Carlisle for 1616–17 record: 'Item geuen to A tumbler & his musicions iiij s'.[52] Was music played in the background as an accompaniment or did it provide tempo or rhythm to help the tumblers keep time?

A graphic moment in the tumbler's sequence of action is described by Richard Brome in his *The Antipodes* (1640):

> And when you have spoke, at end of every speech,
> Not minding the reply, you turne you round
> As Tumblers doe; when betwixt every feat
> They gather wind [gather breath],
> by firking [hitching] up their breeches.[53]

An additional feature of the tumbler's repertoire is alluded to in Beaumont and Fletcher's *The Noble Gentleman* of 1626, where Jaques, when asked if all his goods are packed up, replies: 'All, all Sir, there is no tumbler, / Runs throw his hoop with more dexteritie / Then I aboute this businesse.'[54] The same skill is referred to in the *Wardens' Accounts* at Dover for 1477–8 where payment is recorded as: 'Item paid to A playrre thurow hopys xijd' (see Figures 2.1a and b).[55] It is possible, although not always certain, that references to 'tumbling' and 'vawting' may sometimes refer to the same skills and activity as appears to be the case at Bristol where the *Mayor's Audits* for 1575–6 record payment for 'certeign feates of vaulting' to Edmond Iones: 'Item paid to one Edmond Iones a Tumbler for shewyng

Figure 2.1a. Tumbler with hoop from a drawing, *The Overthrow of the Magician* by Pieter Bruegel the Elder (1564). Engraving by Jan van der Heyden (1565).

Figure 2.1b. Tumbler with hoop from John Amos Comenius, *Orbis sensualium pictus: hoc est omnium principalium in mundo rerum, & in vita actionum, pictura & nomenclatura*, p. 170.

(a)

Figure 2.2a.   'The Hercules Leape', from William Stokes, *The Vaulting Master; or, the Art of Vaulting*, Figure 7.

(b)

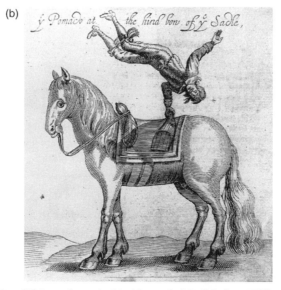

Figure 2.2b.   'Y^e Pomado at the hind bon of y^e Sadle', from William Stokes, *The Vaulting-Master; or, the Art of Vaulting*, Figure 8.

before master Mayer and the Aldermen certeign feates of vawting vpon a horse and tumbling agilitie of his bodie vjs. viijd'.[56]

Modern practice of 'vawting vpon a horse' takes place over a piece of gymnasium equipment that is referred to as a 'vaulting horse'. However, in the Bristol record it is likely that the horse was a real one. The same may be said with reference to the item in *The Diary of Thomas Crosfield* where Crosfield outlines: 'Things to be seene for money in ye City . . . vaulting upon ye sadle'.[57] That 'vawting vpon a horse' or upon 'ye sadle' refers to this kind of activity is corroborated by William Stokes in his *The Vaulting Master* of 1652, where he describes various routines that he recommends to would-be vaulter (see Figures 2.2a and b).[58] In each of these cases the horse is a real one.

Further tumbling skills are evident in the vivid description by Robert Langham of a display of tumbling as 'part of the entertainment vntoo the Queenz Maiesty, at Killingwoorth [Kenilworth] Castl, in Warwik Sheer, in this Soomerz Progress 1575'. It reads:

Noow within allso in the mean time waz thear sheawed before her highnes, by an Italian, such feats of agilittee, in goinges, turninges, tumblinges, castinges, hops, iumps, leaps, skips, springs, gambaud [gambado], soomersauts, caprettiez [caprettie], and flights: forward, backward, syde wize, doownward, vpward, and with sundry windings gyrings and circumflexions: allso lightly and with such easines, az by mee in feaw words it iz not expressibl by pen or speech I tell yoo plain. I bleast me by my faith to behold him, and began to doout whither a waz a man or a spirite, and I ween had doouted mee till this day: had it not been that anon I bethought me of men that can reazon & talk with too toongs, and with too parsons at onez, sing like burds, curteiz of behauiour, of body strong and in ioynts so nymbl withall, that their bonez seem az lythie and plyaunt az syneuz.[59]

This description reflects the novelty of the action to the witness. Robert Langham is simply dazzled by what he sees and is virtually rendered speechless by the seeming audacity and level of skill of the Italian tumbler. A similar first-time witness, 'Dr. Taylor', describes another tumbling performance by 'an hongarian' and others at Shrewsbury in 1589. This account is again full of wonder at the breath-taking skill of the tumblers:

This yeare and the xxiiij^th [of] ⌐day of July¬ there was a scaffolld put vp in the cornemarket in salop vpon the which an hongarian and other of the queenes Maiesties players and tvmblars vsid and excersised them selves in sutche maner of tvmblinge and tvrninge as the the [sic] lick was never seene in shrewsburie before, that is to saye in this maner, they wold tvrne them selves twise bothe backward and forward without towchinge any grownde in lightinge or fallinge vpon theire feete som of them also wold apeare in a bagge vpright in the same beinge tieed fast at the mowthe above his head and wold beinge in the sayde bagge turne bothe foreward and backward without towchinge any grownde in falling vpright vppon his feete in the sayde bagge marvelous to the beholders.[60]

Perhaps an unusual and unexpected part of this description is that of the tumbler whose operations from inside a bag are 'marvelous to the beholders'. Presumably, the bag is a relatively close-fitting one in order that it and the tumbler are able to turn together and not independently of each other. Additionally, a close-fitting bag is likely to permit the audience to appreciate the skill of the tumbler. Although the bag recorded in this eye-witness account is effectively a necessary property to the tumbler's impressive action, it may also be regarded as an item of costume if its nature is such that it both permits and promotes appearance of the action. Do records of payment towards costume for jugglers, tumblers or dancers on the rope point to differences in the nature of these activities and their requisite skills?

A concern for close-fitting apparel is expressed in letters from and about the Lord of Misrule contained in the *Loseley Manuscripts* for 1551. Here, account is made for 'a Iyrkyn for the Tumbler strayte to his bodye'.[61] Such a close-fitting jerkin may be what is again accounted for in 1552–3 where payment is recorded for the 'Tumbler' as 'j Gerkyn & a pair of sloppes of yellow & blew satten paned conteyning vj yardes at viij^s ye yard all out of ye store xlviij^s'.[62] Again, in 1552–3 the same accounts record payment to 'Rycharde homes for makinge of one Ierkynne and one paire of Sloppes of silke garded for my lordes Tumbler iiij^s'.[63] Also in 1552 the same accounts record payment for what appear to be close-fitting suits for 'a masque of tumblers' at Court:

The seyd Iohn Carowe viij^t pere of legges and half bodies with leggpeces lyke armes and handes Ioyned to gether by him made and prouided of past and cement mowlded woorke for a maske of tumblers to goe vpon theyr handes at xxv^s the pece – x^{li}. and for viij hedpeces for the same of the lyke mowlded woork – xv^s. in the hole } x^{li} xv^s.[64]

The details contained in this account point to the illusion of tumblers walking on their hands when in fact they are effectively dancing. Whether the 'tumblers' are tumblers or court dancers who imitate tumblers is unclear, although the latter suggestion seems more probable. Another record of payment to John Simons and his company in 1584 refers to their costumes, some of which were 'spoyled'. Presumably, the ripping or tearing of tumbling garments, whether they be close fitting or otherwise, was an occupational hazard and it may be conjectured that these costumes were 'spoyled' in this manner:

Dyuers feates of Actyuytie were shewed and presented before her maiestie on newe yeares daye at night at Grenewich by Symons and his fellowes wheron was ymployed the pages sute of Oringe tawney tissued vellet which they spoyled . . . yardes of white Cotten/ a batlement and ij Ianes [jeans] sutes of canvas and iiij ells of sarcenett.[65]

Accounts from the *Office of the Revels* during the reign of Elizabeth record that 'Sundrey feates of Tumbling and Activitie were shewed before her maiestie on Newe yeares daie at night by the Lord Straunge his servauntes. ffor which was bought and Imploied xxj[tie]. yardes of cotten for the Matachins. [sword dancers in fantastic costumes] iij. ells of sarcenet and viij. paire of gloves'.[66] Further payments for gloves to tumblers are recorded in the same accounts for 1588–9:

ffor gloves geven to the players the children of Powles & tumblers in the xxx[th] yeare of her maiesties raign xxxix[s].

ffor gloves geven to the players the children of Poules & tumblers in y[e] xxxj[th] yeare of her maiesties raign xlv[s]. [Total] iiij[li] iiij[s].[67]

Payments for the provision of gloves frequently exist in records and accounts for players. Often such payments are for gloves that accompany other costume. Sometimes payments are made for gloves that fulfil a ceremonial role. It is often stated that performers playing before Elizabeth were required to wear gloves.[68] Here, in addition to possible Court procedure, payment for gloves may relate to the function of protecting hands from friction burns and/or splinters from wooden floors and perhaps most importantly to enable sufficient 'grip' to take place. The modern-day use of powdered rosin that is rubbed on hands and feet performs part of this function. Such gloves would presumably need to be close-fitting (see Figure 2.3).[69]

Functional clothing paid for in relation to tumblers gives way to some colourful costume when it comes to the provision for jugglers. The *Accounts of the Lord High Treasurer of Scotland* for 1538–9 record payment on behalf of James Atkinsoun: 'Item, deliverit to ane tailzeour iij elnis 1/2 elne of reid [red] and zallow [yellow] to be ane cote to James Atkinsoun, jugleor, price of the elne of the dymmegrane [name of textile fabric] xxiiijs and of the zallow xxs.; summa . . iijli. xvijs.'[70] Payment for similarly colourful costume is recorded in 1551–2 on behalf of 'George fferys apoynted lorde of Mysrule in the Courte': '[his Iuggeler] A Cote of grene

Figure 2.3.   Tumbler wearing gloves, from *Stories in Stone: The Medieval Roof
Carvings of Norwich Cathedral*, ed. Martial Rose and Julia Hedgecoe
(London: Herbert Press, 1997; repr. 2000), p. 17.

and yellowe satten with sloppes j payre large made of clothe of gowlde
cheverned with a blacke strype, and a payre of sleves trunked to the cote,
of the same, ye makynge besydes stuff owt of the store iij^s. iiij^{d}.[71] Further
payment is recorded in the same accounts for 1552 where similarly vivid
materials are designated: '[Iuggeler] A longe coate and cap of blew satten
with wide sleves conteyning vij yardes at viij^s ye yard lvj^s garded with
yellowe satten ij yardes at viij^s ye yard. xvj^s in all besides ye workemanshipp
and other charges of prouisions bought lxxij^{s}'.[72]

   The last three items all refer to payment for materials required to make
coats for jugglers. One of the payments is for 'A longe coate'. Although
these garments are intended for jugglers they do not appear to be ones
designed to permit tumbling. Indeed, the last of these three payments is
distinguished as a separate one from an adjacent payment to a 'Tumbler'
(cited earlier).[73] In these accounts the 'Iuggeler' and the 'Tumbler' are
quite differently costumed. Such colourful materials accounted for in

relation to jugglers in the preceding records may have been designed and constructed to resemble what may be described as a late-sixteenth-century juggler's costume or uniform as described by Henry Chettle in his *Kind-Harts Dreame*:

The third (as the first) was an olde fellowe, his beard milkewhite, his head couered with a round lowe crownd rent silke hat, on which was a band knit in many knotes, wherein stucke two round stickes after the Iuglers manner. His ierkin was of leather cut, his cloake of three coulers, his hose paind with yellow drawn out with blew, his instrument was a bagpipe, & him I knew to be William Cuckoe, beter knowne than lou'd, and yet some thinke as well lou'd as he was worthy.[74]

The vivid description of William Cuckoe, the juggler, refers to some colourful clothing and to what appears to be a custom with regard to his head gear. Chettle's description of the sticks held by the band around the hat may simply refer to a costume effect. However, such costumed appearance may seem to be particularly quirky unless the sticks relate to the juggler's craft. Just as more recent conjuror's 'wands' may look the same from the outside it is known that these objects can be made in a variety of different ways for various magical purposes. Irrespective of specific functions of the 'wand', Professor Hoffmann declares:

To the uninitiated its use may appear a mere affectation, but such is by no means the case. Apart from the prestige derived from the traditional properties of the wand, and its use by the wizards of all ages, it affords a plausible pretext for many necessary movements, which would otherwise appear awkward and unnatural, and would thereby arouse the vigilance of the audience at possibly the most critical period of the trick.[75]

Although *feats of activity* may be seen to refer to juggling, tumbling and dancing on the rope, the foregoing payments for costume indicate that those worn by respective practitioners of these activities were of different kinds. The implication here is that individuals within the same group or company of players produced different skills in order to exhibit different feats. Jugglers dressed in coats with wide-fitting sleeves or baggy trousers as 'sloppes' are less likely to have performed feats of tumbling. Close-fitting clothes, at least to the upper part of the body, along with gloves appear to constitute the provision for tumblers. The supply of costume to enable tumbling to take place seems to have been primarily determined by functional value and purpose. However, loose-fitting clothes were, no doubt, of considerable benefit to the juggler in enabling objects to be secreted about his person in order to perform some of his tricks.

Little evidence exists concerning the dress or appearance of dancers on the rope. However, Girolamo Cardano in his *De subtilitate* records: 'Itaque quidam puer sphæris ligneis pedibus suppositis, aliquando etiamsacco inclusus totus præter brachia, super funem inter cacumina turrium extensum maximo nostro pro illius uita metu ambulabat.'[76] [And so a certain boy, with wooden balls placed beneath his feet, and sometimes even wholly enclosed in a bag except for his arms, used to walk on a rope stretched out between the tops of towers whilst we were in the greatest fear for his life.] Cardano was born in 1501. He studied at the University of Pavia and afterwards at the University of Padua where he gained a doctorate in medicine. He was later awarded chairs at the Universities of Pavia and Bologna and became well known as a physician. His reputation was such that he travelled to Scotland to treat the Archbishop of Edinburgh. He died in 1576. A similar account of dancing on the rope is offered by Johann Weyer in his *De praestigiis daemonvm* (1583). Weyer is thought to have been born in 1515 in Graves on the Meuse river near the border of Brabant between the Netherlands and Belgium. During his late teens he studied under Heinrich Cornelius Agrippa von Nettesheim and later read medicine at the University of Paris. After university he became a physician and first published *De praestigiis daemonvm* in 1563.

Funambulorum preterea siue schoe nobaton gressus equilibres uel equati ad libram, aut ponderibus utrinque; librati, naturae miracula augere solent. Fuit talis superiorib. annis per omné Italiá satis notus, Venetianello cogno minatus, eo quòd & Venetus natus, & paruae staturae esset, non solum in eo negocio tantae dexteritatis & peritiae, ut modò sacco insutus, liberis tamen manibus, quibus aequilibrium dirigebat, modò unicuique; pedi pelue rotundissima supposita, modò pilis magnitudinis oui durissimis ac rotundissimis plantae pedum subligatis.[77]

The feats of rope-walkers, whether performed under their own equilibrium or with the help of balancing weights on either side, can also be ranked among the wonders of nature. In years past, one such fellow was well known through all of Italy; he was called Venetianello, because he was born in Venice and was of small stature. He possessed such great skill and experience in this type of work that he could walk with perfect ease on a rope running from the palace-tower at Bologna, through the middle of the public square, to the roof of a private house – sometimes while sewn in a sack (with his arms free so as to maintain his equilibrium), sometimes with an absolutely round basin placed under each foot, and sometimes with hard, round, egg-sized balls tied under the soles of his feet.

These accounts point to the importance of free arm-movement in maintaining balance irrespective of the nature of costume, and they also present examples of the way in which dancers on the rope placed objects between their feet and the rope so as to develop feats of increased difficulty. It is quite possible that Cardano and Weyer refer to the same rope dancer since Weyer, writing in 1583, speaks of the rope dancer as working in 'years past'. Cardano published his account in 1550. The development of such performances was apparently built up from relatively simple tasks to ones that were intended to amaze audiences. Edward VI on his entry into London in 1547 witnessed one such amazing feat. Holinshed records:

Now as he rode through London toward Westminster, and passed on the south part of Pauls churchyard, an Argosine came from the battlements of the steeple of Paules church vpon a cable, being made fast to an anchor by the deanes gate, lieng on his breast, aiding himselfe neither with hand nor foot, and after ascended to the middest of the cable where he tumbled and plaied manie pretie toies, whereat the king and the nobles had good pastime.[78]

The same event is described by another witness recorded in Leland's *Collectanea* where some more detail is added:

When the King came almost to St. Georges Church in Powles Churchyard, there was a Rope as great as a Cable of a Ship, stretched in length from the Battlements of Powles Steple, and with a great Anker at one End, fastened a little before Mr. Dean of Powles House Gate. And when his Majesty approached neere the same, there came a Man, a Sranger [stranger] being a Native of Arragon, lying on the same Rope, his Head forward, casting his Armes and his Leggs abroad, running on his Breast on the said Rope from the said Battlements to the Ground. Then he came to the Kings Majesty, and kyst his Foot, and so after certaine Words to his Highnes, departed from him again, and went upwards upon the said Rope till he was come over the Midst of the said Churchyard, where he having a Rope about him, played certain Misteryes on the said Rope, as tumbling and casting one Legg from another. Then tooke he the said Rope, and tyed it to the Cabell, and tyed himselfe by the Right Legg a little beneath the Wrist of the Foot, and hung by the one Legg a certaine Space, and after recovered himselfe up again with the said Rope, and unknet the Knot, and came downe again, which staid the Kings Majesty with all the Trayne a good Space of Time.[79]

Here, the feats played on the rope are referred to as 'Misteryes' and these perhaps involved balancing, turning, twisting, swinging, hopping and skipping. The description of 'casting one Legg from another' presumably refers to a stylised form of hopping on the rope. The most daring and spectacular part of this funambulist's performance appears to have been his splayed descent of the rope. Cardano refers to the same feat: 'Idem se è turri absq*ue* ponderibus pronus per funem usq*ue* ad solum extensis manibus demittebat, nam robur adeò manibus & brachijs constans erat ac firmum, ut illis ponderum uice uteretur.'[80] ['Likewise he used to lower himself down from the tower to the base without weights, laid flat on the rope with his hands stretched out, for so much constant and firm strength was in his hands and arms, that he used them in place of weights'.] Although such descent of the rope is one involving strong nerve, concentration and remarkable balance, his descent may have been aided by some form of protection to his chest. This could have been achieved through leather clothing and/or by securing to his chest a piece of wood with a grooved section to fit over the rope in order to enable greater stability and guidance to the descent and, additionally, prevent friction burns. This technique is recorded in a graphic account of an eighteenth-century performance at All Saints' Church, Hertford:

A rope was stretched from the top of the tower of All Saints church, and brought obliquely to the ground about fourscore yards from the bottom of the tower, where, being drawn over two strong pieces of wood nailed across each other [in the form of an X], it was made fast to a stake driven into the earth; two or three feather-beds were then placed upon the cross timbers, to receive the performer when he descended, and to break his fall. He was also provided with a flat board having a groove in the midst of it, which he attached to his breast; and when he intended to exhibit, he laid himself upon the top of the rope, with his head downwards, and adjusted the groove to the rope, his legs being held by a person appointed for that purpose, until such time as he had properly balanced himself. He was then liberated, and descended with incredible swiftness from the top of the tower to the feather-beds, which prevented his reaching the ground. This man had lost one of his legs, and its place was supplied by a wooden leg, which was furnished on this occasion with a quantity of lead sufficient to counterpoise the weight of the other.[81]

Strutt records the above description as having been provided by a friend who assisted in the feat. In a note, Strutt additionally records that: 'He performed this three times in the same day; the first time, he descended without holding any thing in his hands; the second time, he blew a trumpet; and the third, he held a pistol in each hand, which he discharged as he came down.'[82] Need of the same or similar technique to descend the rope is indicated in the *Diarey of Robert Birrel* (1598), where he describes how the rope walker 'raid doune the tow'. Robert Birrel was a burgess of Edinburgh and appears to have kept his diary from 1532 to 1605. He records:

The 10 of Julii, ane man, sume callit him a juglar, playit *sic* sowple tricks upone ane tow, qlk wes festinit betwix the tope of S[t] Geills Kirk steiple and ane stair beneathe the crosse, callit Josias close heid, the lyk wes nevir sene in yis countrie, as he raid doune the tow and playit sa maney pavies [tricks] on it.[83]

It is uncertain whether or not such aids and precautions were adopted by another rope walker in 1554 at the entry of Prince Philip of Spain into London. On this occasion the same kind of descent of the rope was attempted with tragic results:

Not that I reprehend the art of the Latine verses, which was fine and cunning; but that I passe ouer the matter, hauing other grauer things in hand, and therefore passe ouer also the sight at Paules church side, of him that came downe vpon a rope tied to the battlements with his head before, neither staieng himselfe with hand or foot: which shortlie after cost him his life.[84]

This account records that the rope dancer did not guide himself by 'staieng himselfe with hand or foot'. Cardano describes what might have been a more conventional form of descent:

Fingebant ambo se cadere praecipites, summa ueró pedis herebant funi capite prono, quantum pedis summitati illius roboris inesse necessarium fuerit intelligis, nam sola curuatura digitorum atque ea in syluestrem partem sustinebantur.[85]

They used to make it look as though they were both falling headlong, but with the end of their foot they were clinging to the rope with their head down, you will understand how much strength they had to have in the end of their foot, for they were held up by just the curving of their toes ['and that backward' – Wecker, trans. Read].

Danger does not seem to be much in evidence as portrayed in the account contained in the *Mayors List* at Chester in 1606–7. Here the novelty of the event is indicated: 'A strange man Came to this Cittye and his wife & the did daunce vpon A Rope. Tyed overCrosse the streete: with other pleasante trickes: which was rare to the behoulders.'[86]

An account titled 'A pretty pastime', based on the Diary of Sir Simonds D'Ewes (1619–20) and described in Marsden's *College Life*, records unexpected delight at witnessing dancing on the ropes. D'Ewes' original journal is now lost and it is unclear to what extent the version contained in Marsden's *College Life* is a faithful copy of the original. However, the account follows:

In the lack of other means to divert his thoughts during this period of comparative solitude, Symonds went into the town to see 'a pretty pastime called dancing upon the ropes'. He had some misgivings as to the propriety of visiting such a place of amusement; and both in London and at Bury, where the same performance had lately been exhibiting, he had denied himself the indulgence. He came away, however, 'highly contented for the money' he had paid, finding that 'there was little hurt in it, save some few idle words'.[87]

Such unfamiliar activity as dancing on the rope is again evident from *Dr Taylor's History* at Shrewsbury in 1589–90. In addition to his earlier description of tumbling he also creates a vivid impression of the work of the 'hongarian' on the rope. Here, there are details of the rope-dancer's act not recorded elsewhere in eye-witness descriptions:

also a litill from the sayde stadge there was a gable roape tighted and drawen strayte vppon poales erectid against master pursers place in the sayde corne market vpon the whiche roape the sayde hongarian did assende and goe vppon withe his bare feete having a longe poale in his hanndes over his headd and wold fall stridlenges vppon the sayde roap and mowntinge vp againe vpon the same withe hys feete verey myraculous to the beholders at soondrie tymes and in soondrie maners, aso vppon the topp of the same roape goinge streight from bothe the sloapes he went to & fro the same in daunsinge and turninge hym sellff withe holdinge still his saide poale which wayed above xxxviij li. weight and also he put on two broadshues of copper vpon hys feete not towching them with hys handes and went vpright vpon the saide roape never suarvinge on no syde in woonderfull maner and after he had put downe the poale he shewyd woonderfull feates and knackes in fallinge his head and handes downewardes and hangid at the roape by his feete and assendid vp agayne and after that hangid by his handes and all his feete & body downewardes and turnid hys body backward & forward betwyxt his handes & the rope as nymbell as yf it had been an eele in sutche woonderfull maner that the licke was neuer seene of the inhabitantes there before that tyme.[88]

This account seems to be the earliest one in England to refer to use of the 'longe poale' to assist in the maintenance of balance although its use 'over his headd' is unusual in terms of later practice. Taylor even states the weight of the pole as being above 'xxxviij li' (38 lb). He also records that the 'hongarian' danced 'withe his bare feete'. No doubt contact of bare feet with the rope would enable greater sensitivity and responsiveness to shifting balance. The account also points to the distinction between what later became known as the 'slack' wire and the 'tight' wire. Here, the rope seems to be of the slack kind in that the dancer is recorded as 'goinge streight from bothe the sloapes'. The implication is that the rope dips in the middle to create the 'sloapes'.

As with a number of artistic innovations in England in the sixteenth century, foreign exponents are labelled as the instigators of such activity. Not only is 'an hongarian' recorded at Shrewsbury but French, Italian and Turkish dancers on the rope are cited at Edinburgh, Newcastle, Norwich and Bristol while Turkish, French and Dutch tumblers and vaulters are recorded at Ipswich, Dover and London. However, such foreign labels are not always verifiable and it is not inconceivable that such designations might have been adopted by some of the performers themselves in order to strengthen the perceived mysteriousness or publicity value of their performed feats. The *Chamberlains' Accounts* at Ipswich for the accounting year 1579–80 record payment 'to the Frenche tumbler at Mr Bayliffes commandement x^s'.[89] James Melville (1556–1614), Church of Scotland minister and diarist, went to school in Montrose and later matriculated at St Leonard's College, St Andrews in 1570. In his *Autobiography and Diary of Mr James Melvill* for 1600 he records: 'At that tyme, being in Falkland, I saw a funambulus, a Frenchman, play strang and incredible prattiks [tricks of legerdemain] upon stented [stretched] takell [rope tackle] in the Palace-clos befor the King, Quein, and haill court.'[90]

Although reference to such political motivation may well appear in a diary it is unlikely to be found among records. However, it seems that the same Frenchman may have performed at Newcastle in 1600. This 'fune ambule' was, according to the *Chamberlains' Account Books*, paid 1 s for his work: 'Paide wche was given to a ffrenchman a fune ambule or rope walker playing before mr maior the aldermen with others in the Manners commanded to paie l s'.[91]

Similarly, 'Iaques Babell A ffrenchman' is recorded in the *Mayors' Court Books* at Norwich in 1608 for possessing 'A lycense from Lords of the Counsell to play vppon A Roape and other actyvities dated in Aprill 1607'.[92] It is also recorded in the Norwich *Chamberlains' Accounts* for 1589–90 that payment of 40 s is made to the Queen's men: 'when the Turke wente vponn Roppes at newhall xl s'.[93] In the accounting year for 1589–90 payment is recorded in the *Chamberlains' Accounts* at Ipswich for Turkish tumblers: 'Item, geuyn vnto the Torkey Tumblers 1£'.[94] It seems likely that the 'Turke' who 'wente vponn Roppes at newhall' in the Norwich accounts is the same Turk, or possibly from the same company, as the tumbler recorded at Ipswich. A 'Turcke' is again recorded in the same accounting year of 1589–90 in the *Mayor's Audits* at Bristol:

Item paid by master Mayor and Thaldermans appoyntementt vnto the Queens Players which tumbled before them at the ffree schole where was tumblinge shewen also by a Turcke vpon a Rope. with runninge on the same - xxx s. et for wyne drancke there by master Mayor ij s.[95]

Award of a licence to a Dutch vaulter is recorded in the *Dramatic Records of Sir Henry Herbert* to permit performance at the Globe and the Blackfriars in 1630: 'a licence to Mr. Lowins, on the 18th of February 1630, for allowing of a *Dutch vaulter*, at their Houses'.[96] Payment is also recorded to Italian tumblers in the *Chamberlains' Accounts* at Dover for 1574–5 as: 'Item payd to the Italian tumblers or players x. s.'.[97] It is possible that one of the tumblers from this company played before Elizabeth at Kenilworth in 1575.[98] Italian performers are also recorded in the *Dramatic Records of Sir Henry Herbert* where an award of a warrant is made to 'Francis Nicolini, an Italian, and his Company, "to dance on the ropes, to use Interludes, and masques", and to sell his powders, and balsams'.[99]

CHAPTER 3

Conveyance and confederacy

Conveyance and confederacy are different contributory concepts and processes that are used by the juggler to bring about acts of magic. Conveyance functions implicitly in the work of the juggler and confederacy operates explicitly. Although the term 'conveyance' is often used synonymously and interchangeably with the words 'juggling', 'legerdemain' and 'sleight of hand', such use may be misleading for its meaning is rather more particular. Conveyance is concerned with the real or apparent transference of objects from one location to another that takes place in front of an audience and yet is not perceived by it. This notion and the requisite ability to perform it is essentially a practical one that is successfully completed through another related concept and practice of 'misdirection'.[1] The processes of conveyance and misdirection support each other towards the successful completion of sleight of hand.

Reginald Scot describes the embodiment of conveyance and misdirection when he states: 'Such are the miracles wrought by jugglers, consisting in fine and nimble conueiance, called legierdemaine: as when they seeme to cast awaie, or to deliuer to another that which they reteine still in their owne hands; or conueie otherwise.'[2] The ability to 'retaine still in their owne hands' is critical to the repertoire of the juggler's skills. The secrecy of what may be retained in the hand is alluded to in John Lydgate's early-fifteenth-century translation of Giovanni Boccaccio's mid-fourteenth-century work, *A Treatise excellent and compendious, shewing and declaring, in maner of Tragedye, the falles of sondry most notable Princes and Princesses* of 1554. This volume contains also *The daunce of Machabree* where 'Death speaketh to master John Rikil Tregetour':

> Master John Rikil whilom Tregetour
> Of Noble Henry King of England
> & of Fraunce ye mightie conquerour,
> For al the sleightes and turning of thine hond
> thou must come nere my daunce to vnderstond

nought may auayle al thy conclusions,
For death shortly nother on sea ne lond,
is not deceiued by none illusions.[3]

The key phrase in this verse that demonstrates understanding of the
juggler's skill is that of 'turning of thine ho*nd*' [hand]. The ability secretly
to convey objects from one place to another or feign this action relies on
the juggler's ability to secrete objects in the hand and to hide them by
turning it to mask its contents from the audience. Scot iterates the value
of the skill to hide objects in the hand when he writes of John Cautares as
'A matchles fellowe for legierdemaine' who 'hath the best hand and
conueiance (I thinke) of anie man that liueth this daie'.[4]

An explicit stage direction in Robert Tailor's *The Hogge Hath Lost His
Pearl* (1613) encapsulates the key components of conveyance: 'Enter
Hogge in his chamber with Rebecka laying downe his bed, and seeming
to put the keyes vnder his boulster conuayeth them into her pocket'.[5] This
simple illustration both defines and opens up the possibilities of more
involved conveyance such as that recorded in *The Loyal Observator; Or,
Historical Memoirs of the Life and Actions of Roger the Fidler* (1683) where
in the dialogue between Nobbs and Ralph, Nobbs asks: 'Did you never
see a little *Hocus* by slight of hand popping a piece several times, first out
of one Pocket, and then another, perswade Folks he was damnable full of
money, when one poor *Sice* [sixpence] was all his Stock[?]'.[6] Another clear
example of the essential qualities of conveyance is offered by Scot in
relation to the following basic manoeuvre: 'This plaie is to be varied a
hundreth waies: for as you find them [balls] all vnder one candlesticke, so
may you go to a stander by, and take off his hat or cap, and shew the
balles to be there, by conueieng them thereinto, as you turne the bottome
vpward.'[7]

The nature of conveyance is again referred to by Scot when he warns
that: 'You must take heed that you be close and slie: or else you discredit
the art.'[8] John Baret, lexicographer, first published his dictionary, *An
Alvearie, or Triple Dictionarie, in Englishe, Latin, and French* in 1574. In
this work Baret refers to the same understanding when he articulates the
verb 'to Conueigh' as 'Slie and deceitfull conueyance'.[9] John Stephens,
satirist and playwright, published his *Satyrical Essayes Characters and
Others* in 1615, and here he spurns the ability of the 'Lawyers Clarke' by
saying: 'You can make no question that he is not ignorant to dispatch
readily; for he hath his businesse at his fingers end. Hee may pretend
Schollership, but all *that* is nothing to a Iugglers, who exceedes in the slight
of hand; which is the Art of both.'[10]

The words *crafty*, *closely*, *finely*, *cleanly*, *smoothly* and *nimbly* are frequently used to describe the finesse of conveyance. These qualifications refer to the quality of the unobserved skill and its successful completion. Many perceptive references exist to the respective qualities involved in successful conveyance. What, then, is 'crafty conveyance'?

Sir Thomas Elyot (*c.* 1490–1546) in his *The boke named the Gouernour* (1531) refers to the illusory function of 'crafty conueiaunce' in relation to the pretence of stabbing someone: 'they will be called faire plaiars or in some company auoide the stabbe of a dagger if they be taken with any crafty conueiaunce.'[11] Suitable methods of creating such 'crafty conveyance' are revealed by Scot and discussed later in Chapter 8. In *Hall's Chronicle* (1548), Edward Hall also identifies the nature of crafty conveyance: 'The which matter for the subtyl iuggelyng & craftie coⁿueighaunce of the same, no lesse deceytfull then ligier de meyne in the hand of a iuggeler, was to be estemed emoⁿgest all wyse men.'[12] In the British Library, Harl. MS, 2252 it is recorded that: '"Singulare Commoda" . . . seythe, By sotell pretens all thyngᵉs conveyethe, & Craftely hathe contryvyd to banysshe hyr fromⁿ every degre'.[13] As Hall and Elyot indicate the nature and use of 'crafty conveyance' so does John Skelton in *Magnyfycence* (*c.* 1515), in which his personification, 'Craftie conueyaunce', is seen as one of the negative influences upon the main character, 'Magnyfycence': 'Who so to me gyueth good aduertence / Shall se many thyngys donne craftely: / By me conueyed is wanton insolence.'[14] 'Craftie conueyaunce', by virtue of his identity, is able to perform some of the conventional tricks of the juggler. He can 'knyt togyther many a broken threde. / It is great almesse the hunger to fede.'[15] The allusion here is to the juggler's capacity seemingly to put several threads into his mouth and retrieve the separate threads as one joined-up thread. 'Craftie conueyaunce' describes the basic skills of conveyance as possessed by him when he says he can 'Conuey it be crafte, lyft and lay asyde'. Here, also, 'Craftie conueyaunce' boasts that he can perform a trick of substitution in which 'I wyll, and I can, / Save a strong thefe and hange a trew man'.[16] The bodies of the two men are switched through conveyance in order for the trick to be completed.

'Closeness', as it refers to conveyance, is concerned with secrecy. William Pemble (1591/2–1623) in his posthumous description of Arminius (1625) reflects: 'as in other his opinions: so in the publishing of this [he] vsed much closenesse and cunning conveyance'.[17] R. Willis, in a rare type of description of the play, *The Cradle of Security*, which he saw at Gloucester in the 1570s, refers to the secret nature of conveyance: 'these

three Ladies joyning in a sweet song rocked him asleepe, that he snorted
againe, and in the meane time closely conveyed under the cloaths where
withall he was covered, a vizard like a swines snout upon his face, with
three wire chaines fastened thereunto, the other end whereof being holden
severally by those three Ladies'.[18] Such secret conveyance of the 'vizard
like a swines snout' is pivotal to the developing narrative. Count Lurdo, in
John Day's *Law-trickes; or, Who Wovld have Thovght it* (1608), outlines
the growth in his ability to deceive potential clients by punning on the
word 'conveyances' as used in the lawyer's transference of property and
sleight of hand:

> Then did I learne to countefeit mens hands,
> Noble-mens armes, interline Euidences,
> Make false conueyances, yet with a trick,
> Close and cock-sure, I cony-catch'd the world.[19]

Earlier in the play Lurdo again refers to the quality of conveyance for
deceitful purposes: 'The deepest wit could not haue bettered, / Our
smooth conueyance, but vpright and streight, / Vnknowne, vnseene, ile
worke vpon conceit.'[20]

'Fine' conveyance refers to the quality of successfully unobserved
conveyance. Stage directions in Thomas Lupton's play, *All For Money*
(1577) require the different personifications of 'Pleasure', 'Sinne' and
'Damnation' to be in turn 'finely conueyed' from under a chair in which
'there must be some hollowe place for one to come by in'. The entry of
'Damnation' is required as: 'Here shal damnation be finely conueyed as
the other was before, who shal haue a terrible vysard on his face, & his
garment shalbe painted with flames of fire.'[21]

'Cleanly' conveyance not only refers to the quality of the conveyance
but also the necessary adroitness, dexterity or deftness to implement it.
John Palsgrave in his *L'éclaircissement de la Langue Française* (1530) explains the word 'Jogyll' by refering to 'Mathewe' who 'jogyled the cleanest
of any man in our dayes'.[22] John Stephens in 1615 refers to the klepto-
maniac 'Begging Scholler' who: 'Being admitted (for Hospitality sake) to
receiue lodging; he hath a slight of hand, or cleanely conueiance, which
threaten siluer spoones; and leaues a desperate sorrow among all the
houshold seruants, because he departed so soone.'[23] The anonymous
author of *Wily Beguild* (1606) creates an entrance for a juggler who asks:
'Why how now humorous *George*? what as me-choly [melancholy] as a
mantletree? Will you see any trickes of Leigerdemaine, slight of hand,
clenly conueyance, or *deceptio visus* [deception of vision]? what will you

see Gentleman to driue you out of these dumps?'[24] The 'Clown' in *The Birth of Merlin* (1608) reassures the 'Spirit': 'Yes, my little juggler, I dare show it, ha, cleanly conveyance agen, ye have no invisible fingers have ye? 'Tis gone certainly'.[25]

Scot's description (1584) of how 'To cut halfe your nose asunder, and to heale it againe presentlie without anie salue' requires that the technique should be applied with 'nimble conueiance'. In a marginal note he adds: 'This is easilie doone, howbeit being clenlie handled it will deceiue the sight of the beholders.'[26] This and other tricks involving knives are more fully discussed in Chapter 8. 'Nimble conueiances' are again referred to by Scot when he urges the reader/juggler to declare to an audience, after concluding his tricks, that 'no supernaturall actions' have been conducted:

And so long as the power of almightie God is not transposed to the iuggler, nor offense ministered by his vncomlie speach and behauiour, but the action performed in pastime, to the delight of the beholders, so as alwaies the iuggler confesse in the end that these are no supernaturall actions, but deuises of men, and nimble conueiances.[27]

When Scot outlines the means by which balls may be secreted or palmed in the hand he states that: 'These feats are nimbly, cleanly, & swiftly to be conueied; so as the eies of the beholders may not discerne or percueiue the drift.'[28] Scot continues to insist on the necessary high standards involved in conveyance when he states that 'This conueiance must be closelie doone: *Ergo* it must be no bunglers worke.'[29] 'Crafty Conueyaunce' in *Magnyfycence* is also critical of people who do not possess sufficient skill to create successful conveyance: 'But some man wolde conuey, and can not skyll, / As malypert tauernars that checke [cheek] with theyr betters'.[30] Additionally, Sir John Harington, in his *A New Discovrse of a Stale Svbiect, called the Metamorphosis of Ajax* (1596) points to the potential penalties of poor-quality conveyance: 'A certaine Gentleman that had his fingers made of lime twigges, stole a peece of plate from Claudius one day at a banket; the conueyance was not so cleanly [done], but one had spyed it, and tolde the Emperour, and offered to accuse him of it, whereby hys goods might haue been al confiscate.'[31] Thomas Nash, in his attributed work *The Returne of the renowned Caualiero Pasquill of England, from the other side of the Seas* (1589), also alludes to poor-quality conveyance: 'A chip of ill chance, you haue lost your iugling stick, your conueighance is such, that you shatter, and carrie not halfe so cleane as your freends would haue you.'[32]

The skill of conveyance is well illustrated in the ability to pick pockets either for criminal or entertainment purposes. The reverse action of this same skill, for entertainment purposes, is today referred to as 'body loading, that is, the transference of objects to individuals without them knowing that it has taken place'.[33] Robert Greene, in his *A notable discouery of coosnage* (1591), explains the necessary qualities required of the pickpocket for criminal purposes and relates them to acts of legerdemain:

Therefore let all men take this caueat, that when they walke abroad amid any of the forenamed places, or like assemblies, that they take great care for their purse, how they place it, and not leaue it carelesse in their pockets or hose, for the Foist is so nimble-handed, that he exceeds the jugler for agilitie, and hath his *legiar de maine* as perfectly. Therefore an exquisite Foist must haue three properties that a good Surgeon should haue, and that is, an Eagles eie, a Ladies hand, and a Lions heart. An Eagles eie to spy out a purchese, to haue a quick insight where the boung [bung, purse] lies, and then a Lions heart, not to feare what the end will bee, and then a Ladies hande to be little and nimble, the better and the more easie to diue into any mans pocket.[34]

According to Greene, the 'Foist' lifts purses from pockets and the 'Nip' cuts purses with a knife. The qualities and ability required of the foist, as described by Greene, are evident in Skelton's *Magnyfycence* (c. 1515) where a bet is made by Folly that he can get 'Crafty conueyaunce' to remove his cloak. Here, both 'body loading' and 'pickpocketing' appear to take place in this short sequence:

FOL. I holde [bet] the a grote That I shall laughe the out of thy cote.
CRA. CON. Than wyll I say that thou haste no pere.
FAN. Nowe, by the rode [rood], and he wyll go nere.
FOL. Hem, Fansy! *regardes, voyes vous.*
  Here FOLY *maketh semblaunt* [pretends] *to take a lowse from*
    CRAFTY CONUEYAUNCE *showlder.*
FAN. What hast thou found there?
FOL. By God, a lowse.
CRA. CON. By Cockes harte, I trowe thou lyste.
FOL. By the masse, a Spaynysshe moght [moth] with a gray lyste [stripe]!
FAN. Ha, ha, ha, ha, ha, ha!
CRA. CON. Cockes armes! it is not so, I trowe.
  Here CRAFTY CONUEYAUNCE *putteth of his gowne*
FOL. Put on thy gowne agayne, for thou has lost nowe.
FAN. Lo, John*n* a Bonam, where is thy brayne?
    Now put on, fole, thy cote agayne.
FOL. Gyue me my grote, for thou hast lost.

Here FOLY *maketh semblaunt to take money of* CRAFTY CONUEYANCE,
   saynge to hym,
Shyt [shut] thy purse, dawe, and do no cost.[35]

Body loading may not actually take place here, for the louse, being so small, is quite likely to be implied rather than presented or represented, whereas the humour of the situation may permit extraction of the 'grote' by 'Craftie conueyaunce', which may be exhibited to characters and audience in a similar manner to that described earlier by Nobbs in *The Loyal Observator.*

Like conveyance, confederacy also brings about sleight of hand but by external conditions that may also reinforce misdirection. 'Confederacy', as a term that is specifically concerned with juggling, is not contained in the *OED* or the *MED* although collusion and conspiracy are cited as relevant processes.[36] Scot makes full use of the term and creates a distinction between 'priuate' and 'publike confederacie' as follows:

Priuate confederacie I meane, when one (by speciall plot laid by himselfe, without anie compact made with others) persuadeth the beholders, that he will suddenlie and in their presence doo some miraculous feat, which he hath alredie accomplished priuilie. As for eaxample, he will shew you a card, or anie other like thing: and will saie further vnto you; Behold and see what a marke it hath, and then burneth it; and neuertheles fetcheth another like card so marked out of some bodies pocket, or out of some corner where he himselfe before had placed it; to the wonder and astonishment of simple beholders, which conceiue not that kind of illusion, but expect miracles and strange works . . . Publike confederacie is, when there is before hand a compact made betwixt diuerse persons; the one to be principall, the rest to be assistants in working of miracles, or rather in cousening and abusing the beholders.[37]

Scot's definitions and their differences are clear enough and they do encapsulate the meanings of the process as they are used in juggling. An earlier critical use of the notion of confederacy is recorded by John Northbrooke in 1577 in a dialogue between 'Youth' and 'Age' as to the nature of the 'craft and deceit at Cardplaying':

YOVTH. Is there as much craft and deceit at Cardplaying, as there is in Diceplaying?
AGE. Almost one. I will not giue a strawe to choose: they haue such sleightes in sorting and shuffling of the Cardes, playe at what game ye will, all is lost aforehande, especially if two be confederate to cousin the thirde.
YOVTH. As howe I pray you?
AGE. Eyther by pricking of a Carde, or pinching of it, cutting at the nicke, eyther by a Bumbe carde finely vnder ouer, or in the middes. &c. And what not to deceyue?[38]

Something of the range of deceitful ploys and tactics concerning confederacy are alluded to by Scot through examples that require some caution from the would-be juggler. There is often a fine line between entertainment and nefarious activity through use of confederacy. Scot is well aware of the distinction when he writes of 'dice plaie': 'I dare not (as I could) shew the lewd iuggling that chetors practise, least it minister some offense to the well disposed, to the simple hurt and losses, and to the wicked occasion of euill dooing.'[39] He continues to warn anyone who indulges in dice play by saying: 'but if he haue a confederate present, either of the plaiers or standers by, the mischiefe cannot be auoided. If you plaie among strangers, beware of him that seemes simple or drunken; for vnder their habit the most speciall couseners are presented.'[40] Dice players are further warned to: 'Beware also of bettors by, and lookers on, and namelie of them that bet on your side: for whilest they looke in your game without suspicion, they discouer [reveal] it by signes to your aduersaries, with whome they bet, and yet are their confederates.'[41] John Fletcher, in his *The Fair Maid of the Inn* (1626), develops a simple but seemingly effective confederate relationship between Forbusco (a cheating mountebank) and Clown (the mountebank's man, a setter) where they deny their confederate relationship in front of others who witness the Clown dancing in a state of undress. The Clown dances wildly as if compelled by Forbusco. The onlookers are afraid that the Clown may take off all his clothes.[42] This simple confederate arrangement is also referred to by Scot when he says: 'Make a poore boie confederate with you, so as after charmes, &c: spoken by you, he vncloth himselfe, and stand naked, seeming (whilest he vndresseth him) to shake, stampe, and crie, still hastening to be vnclothed, till he be starke naked.'[43]

The relationships involved in these two examples from Fletcher and Scot imply that the 'Clown' and 'a poore boie' are under the influence of Forbusco and Scot's juggler as hypnotists. However, hypnotism does not take place but the pretence of it does. In *The Wonderful Discoverie of the Witchcrafts of Margaret and Phillip Flower* (1619) cheating, deceiving and cozening are plainly regarded as being achieved through confederacy: 'As for the conceit of wisemen or wise woemen, they are all meerly coseners and deceiuers; so that if they make you beleeue that by their meanes you shall heare of things lost or stolne, it is either done by Confederacy, or put off by protraction to deceiue you of your money.'[44]

A clear example of the use of this kind of confederacy is offered by Scot. He names two confederates, namely 'Steeuen Tailor and one Pope', who commit a trick by confederacy. Effectively, the trick is a swindle or a fraud. Today, the action may be referred to as a 'con-trick' or a 'scam'. However, the confederate relationship is clear:

By meanes of confederacie, Steeuen Tailor and one Pope abused diuers countrie people. For Steeuen Tailor would hide awaie his neighbours horsses, &c: and send them to Pope, (whom he before had told where they were) promising to send the parties vnto him, whome he described and made knowne by diuers signes: so as this Pope would tell them at their first entrance vnto the doore. Wherefore they came, and would saie that their horsses were stollen, but the [that] theese should be forced to bring backe the horsses,&c: and leaue them within one mile south and by west, &c.[45]

Scot offers a number of tricks created by means of both private and public confederacy. The trick concerning Brandon's pigeon, referred to earlier, is a clear example of both private and public confederacy, particularly if the public confederacy ascribed to this trick arises from Scot's suggestion that: 'This might be done by a confederate, who standing at some window in a church steeple, or other fit place, and holding the pigeon by the leg in a string, after a signe giuen by his fellowe, pulleth downe the pigeon, and so the woonder is wroght.'[46] Scot describes an example of private confederacy when he reveals how to: 'throwe a peece of monie into a deepe pond, and to fetch it againe from whence you list'. Here, a duplicate coin, with identical markings to the one thrown into the pond, is hidden and retrieved by the 'beholders [who] will maruell much at it'.[47] A clear example of public confederacy demonstrates something of the carefully organised stance towards deception and the attitude to it:

Laie a wager with your confederate (who must seeme simple, or obstinatlie opposed against you) that standing behind a doore, you will (by the sound or ringing of the monie) tell him whether he cast crosse or pile: so as when you are gone, and he hath fillipped the monie before the witnesses who are to be cousened, he must saie; What is it, if it be crosse; or What ist, if it be pile: or some other such signe, as you are agreed vpon, and so you need not faile to gesse rightlie. By this meanes (if you haue anie inuention) you may seeme to doo a hundreth miracles, and to discouer the secrets of a mans thoughts, or words spoken a far off.[48]

The mechanism involved in this subterfuge may be seen to have many variant applications that are completed by prior arrangement with the confederate. This illustration also demonstrates something of the necessary care, effort and attention to detail that jugglers need to put into preparation of their work.

A different kind of confederacy takes place when the confederate is an animal, which, of necessity, needs to be a trained one. Sir Thomas Roe records a story that he heard during his Embassy to the Court of the Great Mogul between 1615 and 1619.[49] A similar description is also recorded by Edward Terry, who was Roe's chaplain (1655).[50] A third account occurs in an anonymous pamphlet titled *A Trve Relation Withovt All Exception, of Strange and Admirable Accidents, which lately happened in the Kingdome of the great Magor, or Magvll* (1622).[51] These accounts do not appear to be eye-witness ones although the last of these three sources claims that the description is 'Written and certified by persons of good import, who were eye-witnesses of what is here reported'. Roe introduces his version by saying: 'The other story is this', and Terry, who travelled with Roe, declares that the event happened 'but a few years before our abode there'.[52] Terry goes to some lengths to reinforce the supposed authenticity of the account by saying: 'it hath been often confirmed there in its report unto me by divers *persons*, who knew not one another, and were differing in Religion; yet all agreed in the *story*, and all the *circumstances* thereof.'[53] However, Terry makes it clear that the author of the anonymous pamphlet, *A Trve Relation . . .*, 'told his Reader that I had often seen that Ape while I lived in those parts, which particular he should have left out; but for the Relation it self, I believe it was so.'[54] Terry's correction therefore makes it clear that he did not witness the event but believed in its existence. Similarly, Roe claims that the story may be trusted by saying 'no doubt is to be made of the truth of the matter of fact'. Roe's account is as follows:

A juggler of *Bengala*, of which craft there are many, and very notable at it, brought before the king a great ape, which as he said could devine and prophesy; and to this beast some of the *Indian* sects attribute a sort of divinity. The king took a ring off his finger, and caused it to be hid under a boy's girdle, there being a dozen present; then bid the ape divine who went to the right child, and took it out. His majesty being somewhat more curious, caused the names of twelve law-givers, as *Christ, Moses, Mahomet, Haly*, and others to be writ on twelve papers in the *Persian* tongue; and shuffling them in a bag, bid the beast divine which was the true law, who putting in his paw, took out that inscribed with the name of *Christ*. This amazed the king, who suspecting the ape's master could read *Persian*, and might assist him, wrote them anew in court characters, and presented them the second time. The ape found the right [paper], and kissed it. At this a great officer grew angry, telling the king it was some imposture, and desiring he might have leave to make the scrolls anew, offering to undergo any punishment if the ape could deceive him. He writ the names, putting only eleven in a bag, and kept the other in his hand. The monkey search'd, but refused all; the king commanding it to bring one, it tore them in a fury, and made signs the true lawgiver's name was not among them. The king asked where it was, and the ape ran to the nobleman and caught him by the hand, in which was the paper inscribed with the name of *Christ Jesus*. The king was concerned, and keeps the ape. This was done in publick before thousands, and no doubt is to be made of the truth of the matter of fact.[55]

Despite concerted efforts by Roe and Terry to authenticate these apocryphal events there remains doubt as to the credibility of them. However, there is some possibility that such an ape could have been trained to perform the physical acts required by the story and operate in a confederate mode. If the narrative embellishment is stripped away from Roe's and Terry's stories and the actions performed by the ape are examined then the following may be seen to happen: the ring is placed 'under a boy's girdle', the ape takes the ring from the boy, twelve pieces of paper are placed in a bag; the ape picks out one piece of paper, this happens a second time, the ape goes to the bag and apparently looks at each piece of paper and tears them up, the ape takes one person by the hand and reveals a piece of paper in it. This is the action of the story. Clearly, the actions of the ape do not need to have anything to do with the development of the story; he merely performs some simple physical actions around which details of the story are woven. The juggler creates the context for these physical tasks, and human attributes that help to create the story are applied to the behaviour of the ape who presumably responds to pre-determined visual and/or aural signals from the juggler. This sort of explanation may enable the story to retain elements of truth in a way that does not automatically relegate its authenticity to the status of legend. Support for this kind of explanation may be seen by the example of the French jugglers at Norwich in 1616, when 'Iohn De Rue & Ieronimo Galt ffrenchmen' performed with 'A Baboone that can doe strange feates'.[56] Further support is offered by the example of Bomelio Feats and his dog who could be 'traind to doo anie thing, whereby admiration maie be procured'.[57]

Perhaps the clearest and most detailed of confederate relationships between jugglers and animals may be seen in the work of William [Richard] Banks, and his horse, Morocco or Marocco. Relative to other sixteenth-century jugglers there is a considerable amount of evidence concerning Banks and his horse in relation to the content of their respective performances and confederate relationship.[58] The horse was effectively a trained confederate. A French translation of Lucius Apuleius' *Les metamorphoses, ov l'asne d'or* with a commentary by J. de Montlyard was published in Paris in 1601, and Montlyard inserted a section on Morocco into the text. Here Morocco is regarded as being 'âgé d'enuiron douze ans' [approximately twelve years of age] which thus suggests a birth date around 1589.[59] The *Dictionary of National Biography* states that the horse 'was certainly some three or four years older'.[60] Morocco is described in *Les metamorphoses* as a 'bay'. He is likewise described as a 'Bay Horse' on the title page of *Maroccus extaticus. Or, Bankes Bay Horse in a Trance*, by John Dando and Harrie Runt, of 1595.[61] Another account in the manuscript of Patrick Anderson (1574/5–1624) in the Advocates Library in the National Library of Scotland, Edinburgh, describes the horse as 'a Chestane [chestnut] colloured naig' in 1596.[62] Although these two descriptions are similar, another account in *Dr Taylor's History* at Shrewsbury for 1591 describes Banks' horse as a 'white horsse'.[63] This account records the earliest reference to both Banks and his working horse although it does not name the horse as Morocco, as do the previous accounts, and it is therefore possible that Banks worked with more than one horse, one being the bay, Morocco, and the other identified as the unnamed white horse. This seems entirely possible if Banks' reported claim in Lucius Apuleius' *Les metamorphoses* is true. Here it is recorded that: 'L'Escossois asseure n'y auoir cheual auquel il n'en apprenne autant en vn an' [The Scotsman swears there is not one horse that he cannot train within the space of one year]. Banks and Morocco appear to have worked through the 1590s and it is recorded in John Marston's attributed work, *Iack Drvms Entertainment* (1601) that: 'It shall bee Cronicled next after the death of Bankes his horse'.[64] This might suggest that Morocco died before 1601, yet he was still working in Paris in 1601 and Banks did not return to England until 1608.[65] Banks is recorded in Patrick Anderson's manuscript as 'an Englishman'; he is 'a staffordshire gentilman' in *Dr Taylor's History*, and a Scotsman in *Les metamorphoses* and the *Dictionary of National Biography*.[66]

Banks clearly trained his horse to fulfil certain physical tasks that were given contextual significance by him in performance. Sir Walter Raleigh in his *The History of the World* (1614) refers to Banks, the instructor: 'And certainly if *Bankes* had liued in elder times hee would haue shamed all the Inchanters of the World: for whosoeuer was most famous among them, they could neuer master or instruct any Beast as he did his Horse.'[67] Similarly, Ben Jonson refers to Banks' role as an instructor: 'Old Bankes the iuggler . . . Graue tutor to the learned horse'.[68] In *Hogs Character of a Projector*, attributed to Thomas Heywood (1642), a central feature of the training is referred to as 'His eye observes Master Attourney, as Banks' Horse did his Master', and the inducement to perform specific tasks 'is rewarded as they feed Apes with a bitt and a knock' – or, in modern parlance, 'the carrot and stick'.[69] The insistence and importance of eye-contact between Banks and his horse is further reinforced in Thomas Killigrew's *The Parsons Wedding* in a scene between Lady Wild (A rich (and somewhat youthful) Widow) and Mrs Pleasant (A handsome young Gentlewoman, of a good Fortune) where Mrs Pleasant asks:

PLEAS. How do's she do it? is there not a trick in't?
WID. Onely patience, but she has a heavy hand with 'em
(they say) at first, and many of them miscarry; she
governes them with signes, and by the Eye, as Bank's breedes his Horse.[70]

Eye-contact and the transmission of instructions through signs and signals is critical to the development of confederate performance. The title page of *Maroccus extaticus* shows a woodcut of 'Bankes and his beast' (Figure 3.1). Banks holds a pointer in his hand; the 'beast' stands on his hind legs and holds a stick in his mouth; two large dice lie on the floor between Banks and the horse. There is some evidence of processes that create the impression that the horse could count. There is also evidence that indicates the importance of the pointer.

Considerable insight into the training of the horse that alludes to the specific feats performed by Morocco is offered in Gervase Markham's *Cavalarice; Or, The English Horseman* of 1607. Markham wrote a number of books on horsemanship, husbandry and veterinary medicine. In *Cavalarice* he describes how horses need to be trained in order to perform the kind of feats achieved by Morocco. The trainer's stick is of central importance, both to administer corrective strikes and to point to the object of the task. Markham writes:

looke to what place you point your rodde, to that place also you must most constantly place your eye, not remouing it to any object, till your will bee perform'd, for it is your eye and countenance, aswell as your wordes, by which the Horse is guided, and whosoeuer did note *Bankes* Curtall, might see that his eye did neuer part from the eye of his Maister.[71]

The requirement outlined here by Markham may be seen to be fundamental to most of the tasks completed by Morocco. Many of the available accounts that describe the abilities of the horse focus on his capacity seemingly to select and subsequently extract a given person from the audience. Generally, the means by which this was done was by the horse grabbing the clothing of the selected person with his teeth and pulling him towards Banks. *Dr Taylor's History* at Shrewsbury demonstrates how local circumstances and knowledge of them condition the narrative and its justification of the horse's behaviour:

Figure 3.1. 'Bankes and his beast', from John Dando and Harrie Runt,
Maroccus extaticus, title page.

yf the partie his master [his master] wolld name any man beinge hyd neuer so
secret in the company wold fatche hym owt with his mowthe either naminge
hym the veriest knave in the company or what cullerid coate he hadd he
pronowncid further to his horse and said sir ha there be two baylyves in this
towne the one of them bids mee welcom vnto the towne and vsid me in frindly
maner I wold haue the goe to hym and gyve hym thanckes for mee And he wold
goe truly to the right baylyff that did so vse hys sayd Master as he did in the sight
of a nvmber of people vnto master baylyffe sherar and bowyd vnto hym in
makinge curchey [curtsy] withe hys foote in sutche maner as he coullde withe
sutche strange feates for sutche a a [*sic*] beast to doe that many people iudgid that
it were vnpossible to be don except he had a famylar or don by the arte of
magicke &c.[72]

Although the horse did not have a 'famylar', nor were his feats 'don by the art of magicke &c/', i.e. witchcraft, he did have a confederate relationship through his training with Banks. In an epigram in Thomas Bastard's *Chrestoleros. Seuen bookes of Epigrames* (1598) the same ability to pick out an individual is identified by the question: 'But Bankes, who taught your horse to smel a knaue?'[73] The apparent capacity to distinguish between individuals and choose as instructed is referred to in another epigram in *A Strappado for the Diuell* by Richard Brathwait in 1615. Here the horse is regarded as having been able to distinguish an honest woman from 'a whoore':

> If I had liu'd but in our Banks his time,
> I doe not doubt, so wittie is my Iade,
> So full of Imitation, but in fine,
> He would haue prou'd a mirrour in his trade,
> And told Duke *Humphreis* Knights the houre to dine
> Yea by a secret instinct would had power,
> To know an honest woman from a whoore.[74]

Identification of distinctive individuals in the audience who are labelled as 'knaues', 'whores', 'fools' or dressed in a 'cullerid coate' etc. provides comic engagement with the task of the horse but such narrative elaboration does not affect performance of the task itself. So much so, that on one occasion the task of drawing someone from the audience was conducted for a more serious purpose. According to Thomas Morton (*c.* 1564–1659, Bishop of Chester and later of Coventry, Lichfield and Durham), in his *A Direct Answer vnto The Scandalovs Exceptions, which Theophilus Higgons hath lately obiected against* (1609), when Banks was 'in *France* among the Capuchins . . . he was brought into suspition of Magicke, because of the strange feats which his horse *Morocco* plaied (as I take it) at *Orleance*'.[75] Under such suspicion Banks contrived to demonstrate to the authorities that Morocco was not an agent of the devil:

To this end he commanded his horse to seeke out one in the preasse of the people, who had a crucifixe on his hat; which done, he bad him kneele downe vnto it; & not this onely, but also to rise vp againe, and to kisse it. And now (Gentlemen quoth he) I thinke my horse hath acquitted both me, and himselfe; and so his Aduersaries rested satisfied: conceauing (as it might seeme) that the Diuell had no power to come neare the Crosse.[76]

The same situation is described in *The Booke of Bulls* (1636):

Bankes being at Orleance in France and making his famous horse do tricks, which to the French seemed so strange and wonderfull that they thought they could not be done without the helpe of the divell. the monkes and friars caused him to be apprehended and brought him before the magistrate, and accused him to be a witch or a conjurer; whereupon Banks desired them he might send for his horse and then he would give them a plaine demonstration that hee was no divell. They granted his request, and when the horse was come, hee entreated one of them to hold up his crucifixe before the horse, which he no sooner did but the horse kneeled downe before it, whereat they greatly marvelled, and saying the beast was inspired, dismissed Banks not without money and great commendations.[77]

The range of actions performed here by Morocco is the normal one as accumulated by this and other accounts. The purpose of the performance in placating the authorities is given significance by the narative patter developed by Banks. All that the horse does is to go to a person in the audience, kneel down and nuzzle up to the hat. Banks weaves the rest of the narrative. Further confederacy is implied when Richard Tarlton, a well-known clown and possibly the most popular entertainer of his generation, is dragged, seemingly against his will, by Morocco from the audience at the 'Cross-Keyes in Gracious-street' where:

Banks perceiuing (to make the people laugh) saizs Signior (to his horse) Go fetch me the veryest foole in the company. The Jade comes immediatel[y], and with his mouth drawes Tarlton forthe: Tarlton (with merry words) said nothing, but God a mercy Horse. In the end Tarlton seeing the people laugh so, was angry inwardly, and said, Sir, had I power of your horse, as you haue I would doe more then that. What e're it be, said Bankes (to please him) I wil charge him to do it. Then (saies Tarlton) charge him to bring me the veryest whore-master in this company. He shall (saies Banks) Signior (saies he) bring Master Tarlton here the vertest whore-master in the company. The Horse leades his Master to him. Then God a mercy horse indeed, sayes Tarlton. The people had much ado to keepe peace: but Bankes and Tarlton had like to haue squar'd, and the horse by to giue aime, But euer after, it was a by-word thorowe London, God a mercy Horse, and is to this day.[78]

The ability to draw someone out of the audience either from a direct instruction from Banks or from a seemingly reasoned choice made by the horse was clearly a feat that impressed contemporary audiences. However, such reasoned responses are unlikely although the patter provided by Banks that supports the physical actions of the horse may make it appear that this is what happens. George Sandys (1578–1644), writer and traveller, refers in *Sandys Travailes* (1658) to the same distinction in relation to trained asses in Cairo: 'Asses they will teach to doe such tricks, as if possessed with reason: to whom *Banks* his horse would have proved but a *Zany*.'[79] Such was the amazed response of audiences that it provokes the question: How was Morocco able to select these individuals? Markham's training techniques offer some insight into the potential practices adopted by Banks. Continuous eye-contact between Banks and Morocco was essential and Banks needed to point his stick at the object or individual concerned in order to guide the horse. The distinctive identity, as recorded in these accounts, of the individual drawn from the audience does not seem to have been important in respect of Morocco's ability to select them, for Banks could direct the horse to anyone in the audience. No doubt there was some showmanship about this kind of action that served as misdirection for the audience but not for the horse. Should the pre-determined range of signals not produce the correct response from the horse then Markham suggests the following:

If your Horse out of ignorance bee about to doe contrary to your will, then to vse this worde: *Bewise*, at which if hee do not stay and take better deliberation, but wilfully pursue his error, thē to correct him & vse this word *Villayn* or *Traytor*, or such like, so you vse this but one word; and when he doth as you would haue him, to cherish him, & vse this word *So boy*, in a short space you shall bring him to that knowledge that hee will wholy bee directed by those wordes and your commaundment.[80]

Markham puts considerable stress on the necessary discipline to train the horse. The trainer should only use the prescribed words to instruct the horse in his actions and must not feed or reward him when he does not perform the correct action. When successful completion of the task is achieved then the horse may be 'cherished'.

A related and developed task performed by Morocco was that of returning or retrieving a glove from someone in the audience. Lucius Apuleius in *Les metamorphoses* describes this physical ability by saying:

Il donne vn gand à quelqu'vn de la trouppe, & commande à son Moraco de luy amener par le manteau l'homme auquel il l'a donné. Le Cherual le va prendre par le manteau, & l'estreint si fort auec les dents, que l'homme est contraint de le suyure: & se fait amener de mesme tous ceux qu'il veut, les luy designant par quelque marque, comme de pennache noir, blanc, rouge, &c. voire quelqu'vn qui porte sous son aiselle vn sac de papiers, encore, qu'il le cache: ce que nous auons veu faire.[81]

He gives a glove to someone in the audience and commands his Morocco to fetch the man who received it, by his coat. The horse takes hold of the coat with his teeth, pulling it so tightly that the man is forced to follow him. He can make him fetch anyone he wants in the same way, describing them by some distinctive feature such as a black, white or red feather or even someone carrying a parcel hidden under his arm; this we saw being done.

Although Banks may have referred to 'black, white or red feather[s]' as part of his patter, such designations are likely to have been irrelevant to the horse and his task. Similarly, an account claiming Banks seemingly whispered instructions in the ear of Morocco is contained in Sir Kenelm Digby's *Two Treatises* (1644). Digby (1603–65), a natural philosopher and courtier, wrote that Banks' horse 'would restore a gloue to the due owner, after his master had whispered that mans name in his eare'.[82] The narrative of this event may seem to require a whispered instruction into Morocco's ear but it is likely that the supposed action is one of misdirection. Apuleius, in *Les metamorphoses*, also refers to the glove task: 'Son maistre iette vn gand emmy la place, luy commande de l'aller querir, & le porter à celuy de la compagnie qui porte (pour exemple) des lunettes.'[83] [His master throws a glove on the ground and orders him to fetch it and take it to a member of the audience wearing (for example), spectacles.] Again, identification of someone in the audience with '(for example), spectacles' is part of the narrative account but not does not condition Morocco's task.

Banks' horse performed other physical tasks that were contextualised, justified and explained in such a way as to make it appear that Morocco could count coins, identify a specific card picked out by a member of the audience, pretend to be dead by lying on his back with his legs in the air, curtsy, dance, fight, piss and operate whilst blindfolded. In *Doctor Taylor's History* it is recorded that the horse could 'Tell how many peeces of money by his foote were in a mans purse'.[84] Banks' patter would presumably have set up the task and all that the horse was required to do was to tap out the answer with his foot. The same routine is referred to in an imagined address in Edmund Gayton's *Pleasant Notes upon Don Quixot* (1654) from 'Bancks his Horse to Rosinant' (the horse belonging to Don Quixote) where the skill of Banks' horse was to 'Tell mony with his feet'.[85] In Bastard's *Chrestoleros* the epigram 'Of Bankes horse' states that the horse can 'finde your purse, and tell what coyne ye haue'.[86] The limitations upon Morocco's apparent ability to count are referred to as 'Moroccoes dumbe Arithmeticke' in Hall's *Virgidemiarvm* (1598).[87] A variation of the 'counting of coins' tricks is referred to in Patrick Anderson's manuscript, where Banks 'wold borrow from xx. or xxx. of the spectators a piece of gold or silver, put all in a purse and shuffle them togither, thereafter he wold bid the horse give everie gentleman his own piece of money againe'. This was followed up by Banks requiring Morocco 'to tell by so many thapps or patos with his foote how many shillings the piece of money was worth'.[88] According to Digby in his *Two*

Treatises Banks' horse 'would tell the iust number of pence in any piece of siluer coyne barely shewed him by his master'.[89] Digby's surprise that the horse could perform the trick with the 'coyne barely shewed him by his master' indicates that the horse's response was not determined by what kind of coin it was. An elaboration on this kind of routine is vividly described in *Les metamorphoses*:

Son maistre luy couure les yeux d'vn manteau; puis demande à trois de la compagnie trois pieces differentes d'argent ou d'or. Nous auons veu luy donner vn sol, vn quart d'escu, vn escu; puis les mettre dans vn gand, desboucher son Moraco, luy demander combien de pieces il y auoit dans le gand: le Cheual frapper trois coups de pied contre le carreau pour diretrois. Plus son maistre demander combien il y en auoit d'or: & Moraco ne batre qu'vn coup, pour dire vne. Item l'interroger combien de francs vaut l'escu: & luy, donner trois fois du pied en terre. Mais chose plus estrange, parce que l'escu d'or sol & de poidsvaut encor maintenant au mois de Mars 1601. plus que trois francs: l'Escossois luy demanda combien de sols valoit cest escu outre les trois francs: & Moraco frappa quatre coups, pour denoter les quatre sols que vaut l'escu de surcroist.[90]

His master covers the horse's eyes with a coat, and then asks three people in the audience to give him three different coins of gold or silver. He is given a Sol, a quarter Ecu and one Ecu, and he puts them in a glove; he then uncovers Morocco's eyes and asks him how many coins are in the glove. The horse knocks three times on the ground with his hoof to indicate three. His master then asks how many gold coins there are and Morocco knocks once only, to indicate one. He asks how many Francs there are in one Ecu and the horse knocks three times. But even more amazing, because a gold Ecu is now worth more than three Francs, since it is March 1601, the Scotsman asks him how many Sols extra there are in that Ecu. Moraco knocks four times, meaning the four extra Sols the Ecu is worth.

Confederate signals from Banks to Morocco, whether visual or auditory, enable another developed variation on the routine of tapping out answers. In this instance, Morocco is required to identify a specific card as chosen from a pack of cards by a member of the audience:

L'Escossois fait apporter vn ieu de cartes, les mesle fort & ferme, en fait tirer vne par quelqu'vn de l'assemblée: puis commande à son Cheual de heurter autant de coups que la carte vaut de points: s'elle est rouge, qu'il frappe du pied droit: si noire, du gauche. Ce que nous luy auons veu faire d'vn cinq de picque.[91]

The Scotsman fetches a deck of cards, shuffles them firmly and thoroughly and then asks someone in the audience to pick one: he then orders his horse to knock the number which corresponds to the points on the card; if it is a red card, to knock with his right hoof, if it is a black one, to knock with his left hoof. The one we saw was the five of spades.

Presumably, the audience knew of this arrangement with regard to use of left and right feet through patter from Banks. Patrick Anderson also indicates something of the imaginative context that Banks created through patter in order to direct Morocco in particular kinds of movement:

He wold cause him ly down as dead. He wold say to him, I will sell you to a Carter, then he wold seeme to die. then he wold say Marroco, a gentleman hath borrowed you, and you must ryde with a Lady of Court. then he wold most daintilie Hackney, amble, and ryde a pase, and trots and play the Jade at his command when his Maister pleased . . . By a signe given him, beck [curtsy] for the King of Scots, and for Queene Elizabeth and when he spake of the King of Spaine, wold both byte and strike at you and many other wonderfull things.[92]

Other sources also make reference to the same content as described by Anderson. Apuleius, in *Les metamorphoses*, provides evidence of the imaginative context in which the horse performed:

Il luy commande qu'il ait à marcher comme il feroit s'il auoit à porter. vne damoiselle. Moraco fait deux ou trois tours par la sale, & va tresdoucement l'amble. Qu'il marche comme s'il portoit vn valet: il chemine vn trot rude & fascheux. Puis luy demande comme il feroit si quelque Escuyer estoit monté sur luy. Cet animal se prend à faire des courbetes aussie iustes que aucun cheual en puisse faire, bonds & passades, & tous autres saults qu'on fait faire aux chenaux de manege. Si son maistre le tance comme faisant du lasche, & le menace de le donner à quelque Chartier qui le fera trauailler tout son saoul, & luy baillera plus de foüet que de foin: Moraco, comme s'il entendoit son langage, baisse la teste, & par d'autres gestes faict cognoistre qu'il n'en est pas content: il se laisse tomber en terre comme s'il estoit malade; roidit les iambes, demeure longuement en ceste posture, & se contrefait si bien qu'on le croiroit de faict estre mort.[93]

He orders him to walk as if he were carrying a lady. Moraco goes round the ring two or three times very slowly. He is ordered now to walk as if he were carrying a servant: he trots away angrily and harshly. He is then asked to walk as if carrying a ringmaster. The animal starts to curvet like no other horse could, to jump, to parade and do all sorts of other leaps a ring horse could be made to do. If his master berates him for being lax and threatens to give him away to some rag-and-bone man who will make him work all his strength and give him more whip than hay, Morocco, then, understanding his words, bows his head and shows his discontent by other gestures. He lets himself fall to the ground as if he were ill, stiffens his legs and stays in this posture for a long while to such an effect that one might think him dead.

The repertoire of Morocco's abilities may be seen to be extended as demonstrated in Bastard's *Chrestoleros*, where it is declared that the horse 'can fight, and pisse, and daunce, and lie'.[94] Digby, in his *Two Treatises*, comments on the same activity in more delicate terms when he refers to the horse 'discharging himselfe of his excrements'.[95] Ability to respond in this way may be developed through Patrick Anderson's observation when he says: 'He wold mak him take a great draught of water as oft as he lyked to command him.'[96] The different qualities of movement performed by Morocco are further extended in *Les metamorphoses* where it states that: 'Apres vne infinité de tours de passe-passe, il luy fait danser les Canaries auec beaucoup d'art & de dexterite.'[97] [After an infinite number of tricks, he makes him dance the 'Canaries' with great skill and dexterity.] So-called dancing skill is alluded to by Dudley Carlton in a letter to John Chamberlain concerning a 'maske brought in by a magicien of China' at Court in 1603. Carlton was, at this time, the ambassador's secretary in Paris, and he frequently corresponded with Chamberlain who is described by the *DNB* as a 'letterwriter'. At one end of the hall there was devised and constructed 'a faire horse colt of Busephalus race and had this virtu of his fire that none could mount him but one as great at lest as Alexander'. James seems to have been in good humour for he reportedly 'made himself merry wth threatening to send this colt to the stable and he could not breake loose till he promised to dance as well as Bankes horse'.[98]

Perhaps the most revealing account of the combined abilities of Bankes and his horse may be seen in the explanation of their routines from a juggling perspective in Samuel Rid's *The Art of Iugling or Legerdemaine*. Here, Rid reinforces the importance of eye-contact between Bankes and his horse and specifies the kind of signals used by the juggler to instruct the horse in 'pawing' out answers:

Such a one is at this day to be seene in London, his master will say, sirra, heere be diuers Gentlemen, that haue lost diuers things, and they heare say that thou canst tell them tydings of them where they are: if thou canst, prethee shew thy cunning and tell them: then hurles he downe a handkercher or a gloue that he had taken from the parties before, and bids him giue it the right owner, which the horse presently dothe and many other pretty feates this horse doth, and some of those trickes as the Asse before mencioned did, which not one among a thousand perceaues how they are done, nor how he is brought to learne the same: and note that all the feates that this horse doth, is altogether in numbering: as for example, His master will aske him how many people there are in the roome? the horse will pawe with his foote so many times as there are people: and marke the eye of the horse is alwaies vpon his master, and as his master moues, so goes he or stands still, as he is brought to it at the first: as for example, his master will throw you three dice (see Figure 3.1), and will bid his horse tell how many you or he haue throwne, then the horse pawes with his foote whiles the master stands stone still: then when his master rises hee hath pawed so many as the first dice shewes itselfe, then he lifts vp his shoulders and stirres a little: then he bids him tell what is on the second die, and then of the third die. which the horse will doe accordingly, still pawing with his foote vntill his master sees he hath pawed ynough, and then stirres: which the horse marking, wil stay and leaue pawing And note, that the horse will paw an hundred times together, vntill he sees his master stirrs: and note also that nothing can be done, but his master must first know, and then his master knowing, the horse is ruled by him by signes. This if you marke at any time you shall plainely perceaue.[99]

This account is recorded from the perspective of a juggler and not an audience member. In each of the examples offered by Rid, the horse is simply required 'to paw' the answer. The number of 'paws' are potentially endless and brought to an end by slight movement from Bankes when he 'lifts vp his shoulders and stirres a little'. Presumably, the relative subtlety of the movement remained undetected by the audience. All the so-called counting routines appear to have been fulfilled through these procedures.

A remarkable feat performed by Banks' horse involved him climbing to the top of St Paul's Cathedral. It may be presumed that Banks accompanied him. Thomas Dekker makes a number of references to Banks and his horse and their climb to the top of the cathedral. In *Satiro-Mastix* (1601–2) he says: 'I, I, I, excellent sumpter horses carry good cloathes; but honest roague, come, what news, what newes abroad? I haue heard a the horses walking a'th top of *Paules*.'[100] In Dekker's *The Gvls Horne-booke*, the perilous nature of the achievement is not merely related to the difficulty of the task for the horse but the deteriorating condition of the cathedral roof:

before you haue paid to buke [book] to the top of Powles steeple with a single penny: And when you are mounted there, take heede how you looke downe into the yard for the railes are as rotten as your great Grand father: and thereupon it will not be amisse if you enquire how Kit Woodroffe durst vault ouer, and what reason he had for, to put his necke in hazard of reparatione. From hence you may descend to talke about the horse that went vp, and striue if you can to know his keeper, take the day of the Moneth, and the number of the steppes, and suffer your selfe to belieue verily that it was not a horse, but something else in the likenesse of one.[101]

In 1609 when Dekker published this account the spire of St Paul's was also in poor condition. The steeple caught fire in 1561 through what was at the time thought to be lightning. Some years later it was divulged that the fire had been caused by a negligent plumber.[102] Within one month of the fire the steeple was patched up and clad with boards covered with lead. It was not until 1621 that a new spire was commenced. The late-sixteenth-century wooden spire effectively sat on top of the stone tower of the Cathedral, which permitted a walkable circuit around the base of the spire (Figure 3.2). This space provided a viewing platform for those wishing to pay 'a single penny' for the opportunity to see across London. This is presumably where the horse was paraded. Although the spire could be climbed on the inside and possessed windows at different levels of its 260 feet it is unlikely that the horse could have been seen behind the windows from the ground. It is also possible that the space in the spire would not have been sufficient to accommodate the horse.[103] These concerns are illuminated by Dekker and Wilkins in their *Jests to make you Merie*:

When the Horse stood on the top of Poules, a Seruingman came sweating to his Maister, that was walking in the middle Ile, and told him the wonder he had seene, and what multitudes of people were in the streetes staring to behold it, the fellow most vehemently intreating his Maister to goe and make one. Away thou foole (sayd hee) what neede I goe so farre to see a Horse on the top, when I can looke vpon so many Asses at the bottome: O yes, Sir, replyed the Seruingman, you may see Asses heere every day, but peraduenture you shall never see a Horse there againe, though there were a thousand beasts in the cittie.[104]

Interestingly, none of the above references concerning the horse seen at the top of St Paul's Cathedral refer to the horse by the name Morocco. Dr Taylor's description at Shrewsbury refers to a 'white horse' and not a 'bay' as recorded elsewhere. Does this mean that the horse that performed this feat was not Morocco? It seems possible that the horse that performed this stunt was another 'white horse'. Even William Rowley in his *A Search for Money* (1609) does not refer to Morocco when he refers to 'the transforming of the top of Paules into a stable'.[105] Similarly, the address from 'Bancks his Horse to Rosinant' in Gayton's *Pleasant Notes upon Don Quixot*, where the qualities of the two horses are compared, does not refer to Morocco: 'Let us compare our feats; thou top of Nowles / Of hils hast oft been seen, I top of *Paules*'.[106] When Dekker again refers to this incident in his *Northward Hoe* the Cap[tain] asks: 'Could the little horse that ambled on the top of Paules, / cary all the people; els how could they ride on the roofes!'[107] Could such a 'little horse' be a different one from Morocco? This seems quite likely, for the feat might only be possible with a 'little horse'. In William Cavendish's *The Country Captain* the horse is referred to as 'the dainty docile horse, that snorts at Spaine, by an instinct

Figure 3.2.   St Paul's Cathedral, from Sir William Dugdale, *The History of S.t Paul's Cathedral in London*, after p. 133.

of Nature'.[108] It appears also that the horse did not climb up the steeple as recorded in the *DNB*, where it states: 'About 1600 the horse is reported to have performed his most famous but hardly credible exploit – that of climbing the steeple of St Paul's.'[109] None of the accounts that refer to Banks' horse climbing to the top of St Paul's allude to the horse climbing the steeple; the *DNB* might well refer to the 'hardly credible exploit' if it assumes that the horse did this. The ambulatory circuit provided by the intersection of the base of the steeple and the roof of the stone tower seems to have been the horse's destination.

CHAPTER 4

Appearances and disappearances

The well-known twentieth-century magician's patter of 'Now you see it, now you don't' exemplifies the related notions of 'appearances' and 'disappearances' as they are effected by the juggler using sleight of hand. In addition, actual appearances and disappearances – that is, 'being in view' and 'not being in view' of the audience – have been made possible in early English theatre through use of Tudor halls and private/public theatres in the sixteenth century. Under these conditions, physical appearances and disappearances were made possible through use of architectural features such as traps, doors and screens. These kinds of conditions and their related theatrical conventions have survived in some theatre to the present day. Development of proscenium-arch theatre enabled progression and reinforcement of such conventions. The twin concepts of 'entrances' and 'exits' under proscenium-arch conditions have become synonymous with appearances and disappearances.

Before the existence of purpose-built theatres in England the predominant, although not exclusive, custom was that of performing outdoors. This practice does not provide evidence of a synonymous relationship between entrances and appearances with exits and disappearances. A character who was required to 'exit' did so without necessarily disappearing from view of the audience. The exit was one from the focus of the scene or its action. On exiting, the character did not normally need to hide from the audience after completion of the withdrawal. Similarly, the appearance was signalled, not from a hidden position to a sighted one, but from a sighted one in which the character communicated his intention to 'come forth'.[1] Examples of the use of this sort of convention may be seen in many plays. For instance, the *Conspiracy and Capture* in *The Towneley Plays* begins the play with Pilate ordering: 'Peas, carles, I commaunde!'[2] The conscious ambiguity of the order is directed at both audience and characters. Similar opening lines are delivered by Pilate in the *Scourging*: 'Peasse at my bydyng, ye wyghtys in wold!' and in the *Crucifixion*: 'Peasse

I byd euereich wight!'[3] These are not only lines to command attention within the narrative but they also perform the function of creating focus through a staging convention that does not depend on an appearance in order to effect an entrance. The convention is also clearly identified in and through the texts and performances of extant Mummers' plays where the standard entry line is 'In comes I . . .' where the character announces his/her intention to create staging focus from a sighted position.[4]

The appearances and disappearances under consideration here consist of those that are: firstly, actual, in that they create the circumstances of being in view and not being in view of the audience; secondly, those in which the appearance or disappearance is brought about by an illusion created by a juggler and/or staging conditions; thirdly, one in which the appearance or disappearance is imaginary and communicated through a convention; and fourthly, those created primarily to fulfil the requirements of the dramatic and/or biblical narratives.

By their very nature appearances and disappearances happen suddenly. Although the physical act of appearing or disappearing, as in 'coming forth' or 'vanishing', may take place over a short period of time, the perception or realisation of it needs to happen instantaneously.[5] But to whom is the suddenness communicated? Is it to the characters, audience or both? Many explicit stage directions are ambiguous in this respect. Because they fulfil requirements of the biblical narrative in the first instance, the purpose and relevance of the content of stage directions is often indistinct in respect of staging requirements. A case in point is the incident concerning the disappearance of Christ from his disciples on the road to Emmaus. In the *Chester Cycle* play of *Christ on the Road to Emmaus: Doubting Thomas* a stage direction records: 'Tunc Jesus evanescit' [Then Jesus vanishes].[6] Christ's disappearance in the equivalent play of *Cleophas and Luke: The Appearance to Thomas* in the *N-Town Plays* is also recorded by an explicit stage direction: 'Hic subito discedat Christus ab oculis eorum' [Here let Christ suddenly disappear from their eyes].[7] In this instance the stage direction reinforces the biblical narrative requirement that the disappearance should be 'from their eyes', that is, Cleophas and Luke, and not necessarily the eyes of the audience. A similar requirement dealing with the same incident in the biblical narrative is made by a stage direction in the *The Pilgrims* from the *Towneley Plays* where it is recorded of Christ and the disciples: 'Tunc recumbent, et sedebit Iesus in medio eorum; tunc benedicet Iesus panem et franget in tribus partibus, et postea euanebit ab oculis eorum; et dicet Lucas' [Then they sit down and Jesus shall sit between them, then Jesus shall bless bread and breaks [it] into three pieces & afterwards shall disappear out of their sight & Luke shall say].[8] This stage direction also records that the disappearance shall be 'out of their sight'. These stage directions primarily fulfil the requirements of the biblical narrative without demanding that the respective disappearances should be those perceived by the audience.

Some stage directions that conform to the biblical narrative do make additional requirements concerning appearances and disappearances that are not included in the original. For instance, in the *Chester Cycle* play of *Lazarus* a stage direction declares: 'Tunc colligunt lapides et statim evanescit Jesus' [Then they gather stones, and Jesus suddenly vanishes].[9] This aspect of the biblical narrative is recorded in John 10.39 but does not offer detail of the disappearance. It says: 'Et extivit de manibus eorum' [But he escaped out of their hands]. Similarly, the disappearance recorded in another stage direction in the *Chester Cycle* in the play of *Christ on the Road to Emmaus: Doubting Thomas* is not recorded in the Bible. The stage direction reads: 'Tunc evanescit Jesus, et ibunt discipuli Bethaniae; et obviantes Thomas dicat Petrus' [Then Jesus vanishes, and the disciples shall go to Bethany; and, meeting Thomas, let Peter speak].[10] In another stage direction in the same *Chester Cycle* play a stage direction states: 'Tunc ibunt omnes iterum ad mansionem et recumbent. Et subito apparebit Jesus dicens' [Then they shall all go again to the house and they lie down. And suddenly Jesus shall appear, saying].[11] Although the source is contained in John 20.26, there is no record of Christ 'appearing' or that his presence should happen 'suddenly'. These explicit stage directions may therefore be seen to interpret the biblical narrative in order to produce dramatic effect through appearances and disappearances.

A stage direction in the later inserted Belyall episode in *The Conversion of St Paul* requires of Belyall and Mercury: 'Here þei shal vanyshe away wyth a fyrye flame, and a tempest.'[12] The imperative that the two devils 'shal vanyshe away' does not specify from whom the vanishing occurs, nor indeed does it identify their resting place. To 'vanyshe away' carries the same meaning as 'vanish' and since this scene involves only Belyall and Mercury it seems that the disappearance from sight is that witnessed by the audience.[13] There are no other characters from whom to 'vanyshe away'. Thus, it might appear that the destination of the devils needs to be out of sight of the audience. Although different cases have been put forward as to the method of staging this play, the requirement to 'vanyshe away' suggests a resting position among or behind the audience that is achieved by simply removing themselves from the playing focus.[14] This, of itself, may be seen to satisfy the requirement of the stage direction. In which case, the audience may still be able to see the devils although they are not witnessed as participants in the developing action. They may be seen to have removed themselves from the action and thus comply with the requirements of the stage direction through an understood performance convention where the audience acknowledges sight of the characters but consciously relegates them from its concentration.

Appearances and disappearances present different opportunities and conventions when they operate on constructed stages. During the *Bourges Effects* for the *Mystery of the Acts of the Apostles* instructions are given that:

There must be a court (*parquet*) where the king, queen, Denis, Pelagia, and all the household are baptized. This being done, St. Thomas must vanish under the stage (*par soubz terre*) and return to where Abanes is.

Having done this [freed St. Peter], Gabriel must vanish and go under the stage (*par soubz terre*) to give the news to the Virgin Mary.[15]

Here, outdoor platform staging enables a character to disappear and re-emerge in another part of the staging. No doubt traps are involved in these disappearances since they are recorded in other Bourges accounts.[16] In *The Two Noble Kinsmen* a stage direction declares that one of Emilia's attendants carries 'a silver Hynde, in which is conveyd Incense and sweet odours'.[17] This figure is set upon an altar and another stage direction records: 'Here the Hynde vanishes under the altar: and in the place ascends a Rose Tree, having one Rose upon it.'[18] This disappearance also seems to have been completed through a trap device where 'a Rose Tree' that 'ascends' is swiftly exchanged for the 'Hynde'. In *Histrio-Mastix; Or, The Player whipt* a stage direction states: 'Enter Pride, Vaine-glory, Hypocrisie, and Contempt: Pride casts a mist, wherein Mauortius and his company vanish off the Stage, and Pride and her attendants re-maine.'[19] The requirement for 'Mauortius and his company [to] vanish off the Stage' is presumably effected through a door. However, the stipulation that Pride 'cast[s] a mist' is not a literal requirement but a metaphoric one that is concerned with producing mystification.[20]

Use of false bottoms or partition walls to boxes or cabinets that enable a disappearance to take place forms an important part of modern-day conjuring. However, Scot was clearly aware of such devices for he says: 'There be diuers iuggling boxes with false bottoms, wherein manie false feats are wrought' and also 'There is another boxe vsuall among iugglers, with a bottome in the middle thereof, made for the like purposes.'[21] No doubt such an arrangement, on a large enough scale, would be suitable in performing the appearance of Christ out of the tomb in the Resurrection. Staging requirements of the *Resurrection* were seemingly satisfied by another technique as described in the *Volume of Secrets of a Provençal Stage Director's Book* (late fifteenth or early sixteenth century). This work is derived from the manuscript, MS X 29 in the National Library, Turin, and contains a sequence of notes drawn up to illuminate or explain the use of 'fintas' or special effects in the staging of a Passion play:

> E faut que la fin[ta de-]
> la post, quant se [leva-]
> ra, ago una care[la de-]
> part dejost e q[ue]
> la post sia trauq[uada]
> un pan del cap, [e]
> lo que tenra lo rolle
> tire la cordela [de-]
> sus quant la volr[a]
> fa baisa; e que q[uant]
> la volra leva [que]
> la layse ana.[22]
> (Figure 4.1)

It is necessary that the mechanism of the cover, when it will be lifted, should be equipped with a pulley on its lower part and that the cover be rigged [bored?] at a *spanna* [unit of measurement – relating to the span of a hand?] from its end, and the actor should pull the rope when he will want to lower it, and when he will want to raise it he will let go.

The purpose of a single pulley is to enable a change of direction from which to pull the rope. If the rope is pulled by the actor in order to lower the cover then there must be some form of resistance provided by the cover in order to need pulling. Otherwise, the weight of the cover would enable it to drop of its own accord. Such resistance might be provided by a spring. This would also allow the cover to be raised by letting go of the rope. The middle section of the sketch seems to be a plan elevation in which two hinges are shown together with what appears to be two bored holes through which the rope is looped. This loop is fed through the pulley. If the loop is not continuous, and this seems to be the case, then the single rope is fastened at the right-hand bored hole and the lid is lowered by pulling upwards on the right-hand end of the rope. Even so, there must be some form of resistance offered to the action of pulling on the rope if it is to be raised when the actor releases the rope. What is clear

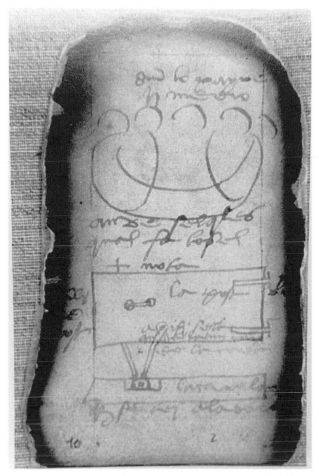

Figure 4.1. Christ's tomb from the *Volume of Secrets of a Provençal Stage Director's Book*
MS X 29, fol. 23v.

is that the device was intended to enable the actor playing Christ to appear out of the tomb at a slow rate that could appear miraculous.

Appearances and disappearances are vividly portrayed through use of light and darkness in different versions of Sir John Mandeville's *Mandeville's Travels* (*c.* 1400), where descriptions of the activities at the Court of the Great Khan are offered. The techniques offered here are ones that may be found in Europe between the end of the fifteenth century through to the early seventeenth century. Essentially, the Egerton and Cotton MSS that contain these descriptions, are the ones, in English, that offer most detail concerning entertainments at Court. The relevant section from the Egerton MS is as follows:

An þan commez iugillours and enchantours and dose many meruailes; for þai make to comme in þe aere as it semez þe sonne and þe mone to do him reuerence, whilk schynes so bright þat men may noȝt behald þam. And seyne þai make so grete myrknes þat it semez nyght; and efterwardes þai make þe light to appere agayne. And þan þai make damysels to comme in carolland, as men thinkes þat seez. Seyne þai make oþer damysels to comme in, bringand cowpez of gold full of meere mylk, and proffers lordes and ladys to drink off. And after þis þai make knyghtes to iust in þe aere wele armed; and þai smyte so sammen [together] with þaire speres þat þe trunschouns of þam flyes aboute all þe tablez in hall.[23]

The same section in the Cotton MS similarly reads:

And þan comen JOGULOURS and ENCHAUNTOURES, þat don many meruaylles, For þei maken to come in the ayr the sonne + the mone be semynge to euery mannes sight. And after þei maken the nyght so derk þat noman may see no thing, And after þei maken the day to come aȝen fair + plesant with bright sonne to euery mannes sight. And þan þei bryngen in daunces of the faireste damyselles of the world + richest arrayed. And after þei maken to comen in oþer damyselles, bryngynge coupes of gold full of mylk of dyuerse bestes, + ȝeuen drynke to lordes + to ladyes And þan þei make knyghtes to iousten in armes full lustyly + þei rennen togidre a gret raundoun, + þei frusschen togidere fulle fiercely + þei breken here speres so rudely þat the tronchouns flen in sprotes + peces all aboute the halle. And þan þei make to come in huntyng for the hert + for the boor, with houndes rennynge with open mouth. And many oþer thinges þei don be craft of hire enchauntementes, þat it is merueyle for to see. And such pleyes of desport þei make til the takynge vp of the boordes.[24]

Both accounts refer to the sun and moon as appearing 'in þe aere' and the Egerton text states that the sun shines so brightly 'þat men may noȝt behold them'. Thus, it may be inferred that the sun and the moon actually exude brightness and do not merely represent it. One possibility of this effect might be caused by circular mirrors that are held aloft. If this were the case, light sources would need to reflect upon the mirrors in such a way as to be able to reflect the light to an audience with different viewing perspectives. This, therefore, seems unlikely within this context. However, this sort of arrangement may be seen in an observation of the *Transfiguration* at Revello in 1483:

And when Jesus is on the mountain let there be a polished bowl (*bacillo*) which makes the brightness of the sun striking the bowl reflect on Jesus and towards his disciples. Then Jesus shall let fall his crimson garment and appear in white garments. And if the sun is not shining, let there be torches and some other lights.[25]

Effectively, the polished bowl works as a mirror: the depth of the bowl in relation to its diameter affects its ability to converge or spread light. Similarly, the rim of the bowl enables the rough limits of direction to be determined. Presumably, in the Revello example, the bowl needed to be hand-held in order to follow any movement of Jesus and his disciples.

A further possibility might be that the sun and moon consist of glass globes that contain candles or torches. The problem with this suggestion is that such an arrangement is unable to produce the necessary magnification to create the required brightness unless the glass 'skin' of the globe be made of two 'skins' with a space in-between. If a double-skinned globe, which is open at the top, contains a candle or a torch and is filled with water between the two 'skins', the globe will shimmer and radiate light in all directions. Sir Hugh Platte, in his *The Jewell House of Art and Nature*, describes this arrangement:

Cause a round & double Glasse to bee made of a large size, & in fashion like a globe, but with a great rounde hole in the toppe, and in the concaue part of the vppermost Glasse place a Candle in a loose socket, and at some hole or pipe which must bee made in the side thereof, fill the same with spirite of Wine or some other cleare distilled water that will not putrifie, and this one Candle will give a great and wonderfull light, somewhat resembling the Sun beames.[26]

Another way of producing intensified and magnified light is to fill a glass globe with water and hold a torch, or two, in a near and fixed relationship to the globe. The resultant light will be magnified and the globe will look like the sun. The same arrangement needs to be made for the effect of the moon but the water in the globe should contain something to colour it. A milky-white light is capable of being produced through use of burning camphor, which will float on the water.[27]

The descriptions in both MSS concerning the 'knyghtes to iust' are essentially the same, with one major and significant difference. The Egerton MS states that the knights joust 'in þe aere'. How can the knights joust in the air? When the knights joust the Egerton text declares that 'þai smyte so sammen [together] with þaire speres þat þe trunschouns of þam flyes aboute all þe tablez in hall'. The Cotton MS states that the knights 'þei frusschen togidere full fiercely + þei breken here speres so rudely þat the tronchouns flen in sprotes + peces alle aboute the halle'. These descriptions make little sense until it is realised that the jousting knights and the hunting of the hart and boar sequences are depicted in fire. The

Cotton MS records that 'at o syde of the Emperours table sitten many PHILOSOFRES þat ben preued for wise men in many dyuerse sciences, as of ASTRONOMYE, NIGROMANCYE, GEOMANCYE, PIROMANCYE, YDROMANCYE, of Augurye + many oþer sciences'. Given that 'wise men' in 'PIROMANCYE' were present at the Court of the Great Khan it seems appropriate that pyrotechnic skill was employed during the celebrations.[28] One method of creating the jousting knights and hunt is by portraying them in quickmatch (cotton wick, coated with gunpowder slurry and allowed to dry) that is shaped into the desired image of the jousting knights and hunt. A simple alternative version of this treatment may be achieved by impregnating old rope with almost any flammable substance. When this is ignited, the image, hanging on a lightweight frame, will burn to complete the respective fights. As the burning sequence comes to an end the spent sections fly off and away from the image and thus fulfil the description that they 'flyes aboute all þe tablez in hall' or in 'sprotes + peces alle aboute the halle'. An anonymous yet similar description to this one is of the firework events 'upon the Thursday before the Wedding' of Frederick and Elizabeth (*Heaven's Blessing and Earth's Joy*) in London, 1613:

> After this, in a most curious manner, an artificiall Fire-worke with great wonder was seene flying in the ayre, like unto a Dragon, against which another fierie vision appeared, flaming like to St. George on horsebacke, brought in by a burning Inchanter, betweene which was there fought a most strange battell continuing a quarter of an hower or more; the Dragon being vanquished, seemed to rore like thunder, and withall burst in peeces and so vanished.[29]

Here, the description of 'an artificiall Fire-worke' represents the battle between St George and the Dragon as a 'fierie vision [that] appeared flaming'. Observation of the 'flaming' representation suggests that the figures were realised and defined in flame and this points towards use of impregnated rope or quickmatch. The account states that the dragon 'burst in peeces and so vanished' and this indicates what happens at the end of a fired sequence. The same conclusion may be offered in respect of Mandeville's jousting knights and hunt.

James Sandford in his translation of Heinrich Cornelius Agrippa's *De incertitudine & vanitate scientarum & artium* (1531), which was published as *Of the Vanitie and vncertaintie of Artes and Sciences* (1569), describes the work of a juggler by the name of Pasetes (see Chapter 1): 'we haue reade also that one *Pasetes* a Jugler was wonte to shewe to straungers a very sumptuouse banket, & when it pleased him to cause it vanishe awaie, all they whiche sate at the table beinge disapointed both of meate & drinke'.[30] It seems that the same illusion is referred to by an explicit stage direction in Shakespeare's *The Tempest* (1611): 'Enter Ariel, like a harpy; claps his wings upon the table; and, with a quaint device, the banquet vanishes'.[31] Some insight into the means by which Agrippa's description and the stage direction in *The Tempest* might have been realised is offered by two stage directions in the anonymous play, *The Wasp* (1630).[32] The first direction is in response to the request for the provision of 'A Banquet, Musick, & royall attendaunts for yo[r] new king there'; the direction simply requires 'A Table ffurnisht'. Later, the second stage direction states that 'the table turns & such things apeare'. The 'such things' that suddenly appear are 'snakes toads & newtes'. It seems, therefore, that the table-top, or part of it, that contains the items for the banquet, is turned over to reveal the reptiles. Items on either side of the top must be fastened in position. The idea suggests that a smaller table-top lies flush within the larger table-top and is allowed to revolve on a bar or rod that is possibly disguised and fixed lengthways down the middle of the underside of the smaller top. Thus, it is possible to rotate the top within the larger top to achieve two positions that may be locked off by a transverse bar or rod to prevent further turning. This may be operated from the side of the table. Further confirmation of this kind of device may be seen in the *Bourges Effects* for the *Mystery of the Acts of the Apostles*, where it is recorded that: 'St. Bartholomew shall be placed on a revolving table (*une table tornisse*) with a nude (*ung nud*) underneath, and when he is covered with a cloth the table must be turned secretly.'[33] Some modern illusions make use of similar devices.[34] Timing of the appearance and disappearance is clearly important as is the necessary misdirection. The stage direction in *The Tempest* offers some indication of misdirection when Ariel is required to 'clap his wings upon the table'. This action may be regarded as a physical form of patter, as if casting a spell, and at the same time is intended to mask the manoeuvre. Chaucer alludes to this kind appearance as demonstrated at banquets in *The Squire's Tale*: 'He lyeth, for it is rather lyk / An apparence ymad by som magyk, / As jogelours pleyen at thise feestes grete.'[35]

Since so much of the juggler's repertoire is concerned with the creation of appearances and disappearances it is hardly surprising that any such intention is supported by whatever means may be laid at the juggler's disposal. Perhaps the most important means to support sleight of hand concerns use of appropriate language by which to communicate that which the juggler wishes or does not wish to communicate to his audience. Such language may be conventional in order to describe, contextualise or misdirect the audience. The latter possibility is also frequently assisted by means of 'patter'. Samuel Rid, in his largely plagiarised work *The Art Of Iugling or Legerdemaine*, uses some of Scot's words and some of his own to describe the purpose and value of patter to the juggler:

You must also haue your words of Arte, certaine strange words, that it may not onely breed the more admiration to the people, but to leade away the eie from espying the manner of your conuayance, while you may induce the minde, to conceiue, and suppose that you deale with Spirits: and such kinde of sentenses, and od speeches, are vsed in diuers mannuers, fitting and correspondent to the action and feate that you goe about. As *Hey Fortuna, furia, nunquam, Credo*, passe passe, when come you Sirrah: or this way: hey Jack come aloft for thy masters aduantage, passe and be gone, or otherwise: as *Ailif Cafil, zaze*, Hit, metmeltat, Saturnus, Iupiter, Mars, Sol, Venus, Mercurie, Luna? or thus: *Drocti, Micocti, et Senarocti, Velu barocti, Asmarocti, Ronnsee, Faronnsee*, hey passe passe: many such obseruations to this arte, are necessary, without which all the rest, are little to the purpose.[36]

Most of the above recorded patter is copied directly from Scot's *Discouerie of witchcraft*; Scot's emphasis on the need to 'use words' prefigures that of Rid.[37] Many of Scot's revelations require the juggler to 'then use words' or to 'use words of course'.[38] Such words, or patter, nearly always occur at the pivotal point of a trick. A changed state occurs in relation to use of the patter. Usually, something appears or disappears and the audience is led into the belief that the patter provides the finesse and power to bring about the revelation. In his trick 'To consume (or rather to conueie) one or manie balles into nothing', Scot advises that 'If you take one ball, or more, & seeme to put it into your other hand, and whilest you vse charming words, you conueie them out of your right hand into your lap; it will seeme strange'.[39] In another trick, labelled 'With words to make a groat or a testor to leape out of a pot, or to run alongst vpon a table', Scot describes how 'You shall see a iuggler take a groat or a testor, and throwe it into a pot, or laie it in the midst of a table, & with inchanting words cause the same to leape out of the pot, or run towards him, or from him ward alongst the table.'[40] In a trick 'To make a groat or a testor to sinke through a table, and to vanish out of a handkercher verie strangelie', Scot requires of the juggler: 'Then will he send for a bason, and holding the same under the boord right against the candlesticke, will vse certeine words of inchantments; and in short space you shall heare the groat fall into the bason.'[41] Not only does patter operate as a pivotal point in a trick but it may also enable additional functions to be fulfilled as Scot describes: 'But in the meane time the iuggler vseth words of art, partlie to protract the time, and partlie to gaine credit and admiration of the beholders.'[42] The ability to 'protract the time' is effectively the means by which the juggler maintains control and timing of the trick.

Examples of 'charming words' or 'inchanting words' may be found in other works. Henry Chettle, in his *Kind-Harts Dreame*, suggests some specific patter when he reports 'they vse not our olde tearms of hey-passe, re-passe, and come aloft'.[43] Yet the 'olde tearms' are precisely those used in the prologue of *Wily Beguild* (1606). Here, the Iuggler says: 'Marry sir I wil shew you a trick of cleanly conueiance. *Hei fortuna furim nunquam credo*, With a cast of cleane conueyance, come aloft *Iack* for thy masters aduantage (hees gone I warrant ye.)'[44] The phrase *Hei fortuna furim nunquam credo* is virtually identical to that advanced by Scot (Appendix 2).[45] Some of these words are also used in Beaumont and Fletcher's *The Beggars' Bush* (Appendix 3) where Prig asks if the two Boores would like to see some sleight of hand. He declares: 'hey passe, Presto, be gone there?' When Prig throws up three balls that he designates as bullets he claims 'Presto, be gone: they are vanish'd.'[46] The word 'presto' appears to make use of two meanings simultaneously. One meaning is concerned with that which is 'at hand, in readiness' and the other refers to the quickness or instantaneousness of the action.[47] In attempts to pluck the three bullets from the Boores' noses Prig uses some corrupted Latin patter: 'Titere, tu patule—', 'Recubans sub tegmine fagi' and 'Silvestram-trim-tram' in order to aid the apparent extraction of the bullets. To aid the withdrawal further he demands: 'Come aloft bullets three, with a whim-wham.' A second trick in which the Boores are relieved of money from their pockets leaves Prig to demand: 'Hey, come aloft: sa, sa, flim, flam, taradumbis? East, west, north, south, now flye like Jacke with a *bumbis*.' After this patter the Boores again find money in their pockets.[48]

William Vincent, in *Hocvs Pocvs Ivnior*, reinforces Scot's insistence on the need for patter from the juggler when he declares: 'he must have strange termes, and emphaticall words, to grace, and adorne his actions, and the more to astonish the beholders'.[49] Clearly, Vincent employed this thinking in his own performances. A number of references to Vincent through his alias, Hocus Pocus, indicate the style of his presentation through indications of his patter. Not only does Vincent require the juggler to use such patter but he also stresses the need for a more or less continuous monologue in some of his descriptions to support and license his actions. An example of this, in communication with his audience, may be seen in his account of how to perform the trick of the Cups and Balls. The introductory section of this description serves to focus this concern:

Then let him draw his foure balls, and lay three of them upon the table, (and retain the fourth in his right hand) and say, Gentlemen, here are three bals you see, 1. *Meredin*, 2. *Benedic*, and 3. *Presto Iohn*, then let him draw his cups, and hold them all three in his right hand also, saying, Here are also three Cups, saying, See theres nothing in them, neither have they any false bottoms: Then say, See I will set them all on a row, and clap them all on a row, and in clapping them downe, convey the ball that you reteined under the middlemost cup, saying as you set them downe, Nothing there, there, nor there. Then shew your hands, and say, Gentlemen, you see here is nothing in my hands, and say, Now to begin, and take up with your right hand one of the three bals that you layed downe, and say this is the first, and with that seeme to put it into your left hand, and presently shut your left hand, and being shut clap it unto your eare, saying, This is for the purging of the braine, *Presto* be gone, then move both the utmost cups (noted with A, and B[)], with both your hands, saying, And there is nothing there nor there, and in the clapping them downe conveigh the ball in your right hand under the Cup noted B.[50]

The rest of the description continues in this vein and completes what appears to be skilful patter of a kind that might even be witnessed in a modern-day version of the trick. In another trick outlined by Vincent concerning 'How to make a great Ball seeme to come through a Table into a Cup' similar patter to that encouraged by Scot is suggested as: 'Hei Fortuna nunquam credo, vade couragious'.[51] The juggler is then required to say to the audience 'Now see if it be there or not.' Vincent concludes by saying to the reader: 'which when they see, they will imagine was conjured into it by vertue of your words'. Further patter is outlined by Vincent in a trick that involves sleight of hand with balls. At the climax of the trick Vincent's advice to the juggler is: 'reteining the ball firmely pronovnce these words: *Iubeo celeriter*, come all into my hand when I bid you'.[52] Another trick concerned with 'How to make a stone seeme to vanish out of your hand' is outlined by Vincent and assumes that the juggler sits at a table and says:

You see, Gentlemen, here is a stone, a miraculous stone: Will you have it vanish, vade, or go away invisible; which being said, withdraw your hand to the side of the table letting the stone slip down into your lap, in which time stare about you, saying, chuse you whether. Then reach out your hand and say: *Fortuna variabilis, lapis inestimabilis Iubeo, vade, vade, couragius*. Open your hand then tossing it up, and blow a blast, and look up, saying, Do you see it is gone. Your looking up will make them to looke up, in which time you may take the stone againe in the other hand, and slip it into your pocket.[53]

If the juggler does not sit down during the delivery of the trick then a different kind of support may be necessary to the creation of appearances and disappearances. Jugglers frequently carried a bag that was fastened around the waist. Such bags could be left open or closed by a flap. These bags contained the accoutrements of the juggler and were also a means of enabling items to disappear. Terms used to describe such bags were the *purse*, the *budget* and the *gibecière* or *gipser*. Use of the terms was not restricted to the work of the juggler but also extended to other functions and occupations.[54] William Vincent, in his *Hocvs Pocvs Ivnior*, alludes to the purpose of the budget: 'Some I have seen sit with their Codpiece open, others play standing with a budget hanging before them, but all comes to one end.'[55] In Charles Hoole's translation of *Orbis sensualium pictus* by John Amos Comenius he presents a composite illustration of entertainers who perform 'sleights' and 'Praestigiae' (Figures 4.2a and b). In respect of the juggler, the picture is captioned 'The Juggler, sheweth sleights, out of a Purse'. The juggler wears the purse in front of him and it is fastened round the waist. The juggler's left hand can clearly be seen delving into the purse.[56] In his description of the necessary preparation to the old and now well-known trick of the Cups and Balls, Vincent declares that 'Some feats may with more grace be performed sta*n*ding then sitting.'[57] In this regard another means of fulfilling the function of the budget is suggested when he says:

He that is to play must sit on the farther side of a Table, which must be covered with a carpet: partly to keepe the balls from rolling away, and partly to keepe them from ratling: likewise he must set his hat in his lap, or sit in such manner as that he may receive any thing into his lap, and let him cause all his spectators to sit downe.[58]

Another account of the preparatory arrangements to performance of the long-established Cups and Balls routine further indicates the importance of the *gibecière*:

Ce Boccal, comme nous avons dit cy-devant, estoit Bergamasque. Iceluy accourant incontinant tire de sa sarcote quelques pieces recousuës, & plus sales que le devantail d'un cuisinier. D'entre ces drappeaux il prend une gibeciere, laquelle soudain il met à sa ceinture pendante au cofté droict: puis ayant rangé deux treteaux met une table dessus; & se tenant au devant d'elle, comme si un bancquier vouloit compter argent, il retrousse habilement la manche deson pourpoint & de la chemise, & les rebrasse jusques au coude, comme fait une lavandiere quand elle veut laver la buée fur le bord de l'eau & montrer ses grosses jambes aux barqueroliers . . . lequel avoit jà tiré de la besace trois ou cinq gobelets de cuivre, & je ne scay combien de petites pelottes plus grandes que pilules . . .

(a)

Figure 4.2a. Entertainers showing 'Sleights' or 'Praestigiæ' from John Amos Comenius, *Orbis sensualium pictus*, p. 170.

(b)

Figure 4.2b.   'The Juggler, sheweth sleights, out of a Purse' from John Amos Comenius, *Orbis sensualium pictus*, p. 170.

Il commence à jouer de son art de passepasse, & si habilement que Saramelle ne joüa jamais mieux devant le Duc Borse C'estoit merveille comme il avoit la main subtile, remuant si bien dessus dessous ces petites bales que de trois en paroissoit cinquante. Il met tantost un gobelet sur l'autre, tantost les tenversant les divise & separe le cul contre-mont, & sur iceluy il met tantost trois, tantost cinq de ces petites pelotes, & une seule tantost paroist.[59]

This Boccal, as we have mentioned before, was a Bergamask [a native of Bergamo, Italy]. The man, running quickly, takes some patched rags from inside his coat and they look dirtier than a cook's apron. From amongst these cloths he produces a *gibecière*, which he hurriedly hangs at the right side of his belt: then, having arranged 2 trestles he makes a table and, standing in front of it like a banker wanting to count his money, he skilfully rolls up the sleeves of his doublet and his shirt, up to his elbows, just like a washer woman does, at the edge of the water, when she wants to wash the steam away and therefore showing her fat legs to the boaters . . . [Boccal] has already taken 3 or possibly 5 copper goblets and also a number of little balls, how many I know not, which were bigger than pills, . . . He begins to play his magic trick, so skilfully that Saramelle himself never did it better while in front of the Duke of Borse. It was wonderful how his subtle hand moved the balls about so well that having only 3 it looked like there were

50. Now he places a goblet on top of another, now he turns them upside down, separating them as he does and placing them over 3, sometimes 5 of the little balls, now only one appears.

In tricks like the Cups and Balls where appearances and disappearances are in a constant state of flux the *gibecière* is an essential item to the juggler who stands in front of his audience. In Skelton's *Magnyfycence* some bragging takes place between 'Clokyd colusyon' and 'Crafty conuyaunce' as to who is the more skilful lock picker. 'Counterfet counte*naunce*' acknowledges their respective skills but regards their bickering as inconsequential. It appears from this dialogue that the 'bowget' [budget] is capable of being locked:

CRA.CON. Thou sawe neuer yet but I dyd my parte,
The locke of a caskyt to make to starte.
COU.COU. Nay, I know well inough ye are bothe well handyd
To grope a gardeuyaunce [travelling trunk],
though it be well bandyd.
CLO.COL. I am the better yet in a bowget.
CRA.CON. And I the better in a male [travelling bag].
COU.COU. Tushe! these maters that ye moue are but soppys in ale;
Your trymynge and tramynge by me must be tangyd,
For had I not bene, ye bothe had bene hangyd,
When we with Magnyfycence goodys made cheuysaunce.[60]

The same might be said of any small-scale trick involving close manipulation. At the other extreme of a potential range of tricks and illusions that are concerned with appearances and disappearances is the renowned illusion of the so-called Indian Rope trick. An account that is roughly contemporaneous with *Mandeville's Travels* contains descriptions offered by Ibn Batuta of entertainment at the palace of the Amír Kurtai in China (*c.* 1348). This description refers to the apocryphal event that has been transmogrified into the Indian Rope trick. It is perhaps the ultimate disappearing act – or at least it appears to be. Sir Henry Yule's translation, together with variant readings from H. A. R. Gibb (given in square brackets), of Batuta's description is as follows:

That same night a juggler, who was one of the Kán's slaves, made his appearance, and the Amír said to him, 'Come and show us some of your marvels.' Upon this he took a wooden ball, with several holes in it through which long thongs [cords] were passed, and (laying hold of one of these) slung it into the air. It went so high that we lost sight of it altogether. (It was the hottest season of the year, and we were outside in the middle of the palace court.) There now remained only a little of the end of a thong in the conjuror's hand, and he desired one of the boys who assisted him to lay hold of it and mount. He did so, climbing by the thong, and we lost sight of him also! The conjuror then called to him three times, but getting no answer he snatched up a knife, as if in a great rage, laid hold of the thong, and disappeared also! Bye and bye he threw down one of the boy's hands, then a foot, then the other hand and the other foot, then the trunk, and last of all the head! Then he came down himself, all puffing and panting, and with his clothes all bloody, kissed the ground before the Amír, and said something to him in Chinese. The Amír gave some order in reply, and our friend then took the lad's limbs, laid them together [attached them to each other] in their places, and gave a kick, when, presto! there was the boy, who got up and stood before us [he stood up intact]! All this astonished me beyond measure, and I had an attack of palpitation like that which overcame me once before in the presence of the Sultan of India, when he showed me something of the same kind. They gave me a cordial [medicine], however, which cured the attack. The Kazi Afkharuddin was next to me, and quoth he, 'Walláh! tis my opinion there has been neither going up nor coming down [or cutting off of limbs], neither marring nor mending; 'tis all hocus pocus [conjuring]!'[61]

This account has been unwittingly, or otherwise, attributed to Marco Polo, since it was included as part of a long note by Sir Henry Yule in his *Book of Ser Marco Polo* (1875).[62] The misappropriation of this account was not due to Yule, who carefully acknowledged Ibn Batuta as the source. Indeed, Yule had printed the account in an earlier work in which he duly and accurately recorded Ibn Batuta as the author.[63] However, this description remains the touchstone for other subsequent and similar accounts in different cultures. For example, an Irish account known as the *Ceithearnach Ui Dhomhnaill* (the 'Kern of O'Donnell': *c.* 1537–50) stresses the basic elements of Ibn Batuta's account but takes on different detail and possesses a stronger narrative identity where the qualities of the story seem to take precedence over any possible eye-witness credibility:

Tug an clesaidhe ceirtle síoda amach as a mhála cleasaighecht 7 tug urchar a nairde dho go ndeachaidh a neal an æoir, 7 tug gearfhiadh amach as an mhala cheadna 7 dimthigh an gearfhiadh na rith suas air an tsnaithe 7 tug cu bheag 7 do leig a ndiaigh an ghearfhiadh i 7 do bhí si taffann go binn ar a lorg, tug giolla beag amach as an mhala ciadhna 7 dubhairt leis dul suas air ⌈a⌉ tsnaithe andiaigh na con 7 an ghearfhiadh, tug oigbhean alainn inniolta amach as mhala eile bhi aige ogus dubairt leithe an giolla 7 chu do leanmhainn 7 an gearfhiadh do chaomhnadh gan masladh on ccoin, do rith an rigbhean na ndiaigh go luath 7 dob aoibhinn le taodhg o ceallaidh beith ag amharc na ndiaigh & ag eisteacht le seastain na sealga go ndeachadar suas san neal as aithne go lear, Do bhadar seal fada na ttost iar sin, go ndubhairt an cleasaidhe, is eagal liom, ar se go bhfuil droch char ga dheanamh an sud shuas, 7 ma ta ni rachaidh gan dioghal, cred sin air taodhg o ceallaidh: ata air an cleasaidhe go mbiodh an chu ag ithe an ghearfiadh 7 an giolla dol chum na mna,,, bu dual sin fein air taodhg,,, tairngios an tsnaithe iar sin agus fuair an giolla idir dhá chois na mná, 7 an chú ag crinn chnama an ghearfhiadh,,[64]

The juggler/trickster/acrobat took a ball of silk out of his conjuring bag [budget?] and threw it upwards so that it went into a cloud in the air. He took a hare out of the same bag, and the hare went running up the thread; and he took out a little dog, and let it go after the hare, and it was barking sweetly in pursuit. Then he took a small youth out of the same bag and told him to go up the thread after the hound and the hare. From another bag that he had he took a beautiful, neat young woman, and told her to follow after the youth and the dog and to protect the hare from harm by the hound. The young woman quickly ran up after it. And Tadhg Ó Ceallaigh enjoyed looking at them and listening to the noise of the hunt, until they finally were up into the cloud completely out of sight. They were silent for a long time, until the juggler said: 'I'm afraid there's mischief going on up there, and if there is it won't go unpunished.' 'What's that?' asked Tadhg Ó Ceallaigh. 'The dog will be eating the hare', said the juggler, 'and the youth making love to the woman'. 'That would be natural', said Tadhg. He pulled down the thread and found the youth between the woman's legs and the hound gnawing at the hare's bones.

Johann Weyer, in his *De praestigiis daemonvm* of 1566 includes a structurally similar account to the Irish example, although with different creatures that ostensibly climb the silk/rope:

Praestigiator quidam magicus Magdiburgi equulum in theatro frequenti per circulum transilientem ostentabat certa stipe: in fabulae exitu paucam se apud mortales colegisse pecuniam questus, se in coelum conscendere uelle ait. Hinc in sublimes eiecto fune, consequitur in altum equulus: praestigiator quasi eum cauda retenturus, quoque, ascendit: cuius uxor maritum apprehendens affectatur, ibidem ancilla, ut uiderentur ascensu contiguo uelut concatenati, simul aera petere. Haec dum populus ad stuporem spectaret, cuidam ciui eò forte declinanti, quaerentique, quid nam rerum ibi agere tur. responsum est, circulatorem cum equulo in aera conscendere: hic se statim uidisse eum eum [sic] in uico ad diuersorium abeuntem asseuerauit. Illusos itaque se ubi animaduerterent, discesserunt.[65]

For a fixed fee, a magician [juggler] of Magdeburg displayed in a crowded theater a little horse leaping through a hoop. At the end of the act, after complaining that he had collected little money among mortals, the magician said that he wished to mount up to heaven. Thereupon, he threw a rope into the air, and the little horse followed it upward, and the illusionist (as though intending to hold him back by the tail) also ascended, and his wife followed, holding on to her husband, and likewise their maid, so that it seemed they were all flying up into the air, linked together, as it were, in a continuous line of ascent. While the crowds were gazing at these things in amazement, one of their fellow citizens happened to come in and ask what was going on there. They replied that the charlatan was mounting into the air along with his little horse; but the newcomer stoutly maintained that he had just seen him in the street heading towards the inn. And so, when the spectators realized that they had been deceived, they went away.

A further statement is recorded in the *Memoirs of The Emperor Jahangueir, Written by Himself.* The Emperor ruled in Delhi between 1605 and 1627 although it is thought that this account is taken from one of a number of extant MSS at a later date:

They produced a chain of fifty cubits in length, and in my presence threw one end of it towards the sky, where it remained as if fastened to something in the air. A dog was then brought forward, and being placed at the lower end of the chain, immediately ran up, and reaching the other end, immediately disappeared in the air. In the same manner a hog, a panther, a lion, and a tiger were alternately sent up the chain, and all equally disappeared at the upper end of the chain. At last they took down the chain and put it into a bag, no one even discovering in what way the different animals were made to vanish into the air in the mysterious manner above described. This, I may venture to affirm, was beyond measure strange and surprising.[66]

These accounts each refer to one or more persons or animals who climb up the thong, cord, silk, rope or chain and disappear from view of the audience. These disappearances are what supply the mystery and power to the descriptions. The record of each disappearance is vague and lacks explanation. Similarly, the limbs that seemingly drop from the uppermost parts of the rope are not explained. We, the audience, think that we know what the limbs are and how they have come to be in existence. These two conditions concerning the disappearances and the dropped limbs hold immense power for the respective imaginations that constitute an audience. The audience brings its imagination to bear and completes, accurately or inaccurately, the narrative that develops these two conditions.

Yule, in *The Book of Ser Marco Polo*, produces an illustration of the rope being cast upwards, the boy ascending the rope and the limbs falling to the ground. He acknowledges that the illustration or 'The cut on the preceding page is taken from Melton's plate.' This reference is to Edward Melton's *Zee-en Land-Reizen* of 1681 (Figures 4.3 and 4.4).[67] Comparison of the two illustrations makes it clear how Yule has abstracted his version to focus on the throwing and climbing of the rope and the putative dismembered limbs. He does this in order to illustrate Ibn Batuta's description. However, Melton's illustration contains other features that are not drawn upon by Yule. The importance of Melton's full picture relates to his text. The relevant section and its translation is recorded in Appendix 1.

Figure 4.3. 'Chinese conjuring extraordinary', from Colonel Henry Yule, *The Book of Ser Marco Polo*, 1, p. 309. This image is extracted by Yule from Eduward Melton, *Zee-en Land-Reizen*, after p. 468.

What is remarkable about this account is the declared self-consciousness concerning the intended honesty with which Melton describes the event. Melton can hardly believe that which he claims to have seen and yet it seems important to him that the reader believe his extraordinary observation. The apparent fact that the event was experienced by a thousand eye-witnesses is used to bolster the seeming truth of the account. However,

Figure 4.4. Chinese feats of activity, from Eduward Melton, *Zee-en Land-Reizen*, after p. 468.

the principal questions to be faced by the reader of Melton's description are: Where is the end of the rope?; How is the rope supported?; and How does the rope achieve its rigidity? Melton's illustration does not answer these questions and only serves to add further mystery to the reported activity. These questions are common to all the related examples so far considered and they are the ones that baffle the witness/reader. The questions also baffle modern-day conjurors who generally consider that this stunt cannot be performed in the open air as described by witnesses such as Melton.[68] This trick has been performed in more recent times in the theatre by making use of the theatre building and its apparatus, i.e. the rope being secured in the flies of a proscenium-arch theatre, but realisations of the accounts outlined here are not considered to be performable. Recent work in this area has strongly identified these accounts as legends.[69]

John Nevil Maskelyne, the well-known twentieth-century conjuror, set out to expose a fraudulent medium known as Madame Blavatsky. She claimed to have seen the Indian Rope trick performed in India and repeated the story with many of the features so far encountered. Maskelyne and his colleagues set out to discover the secrets of the trick: 'We spent a considerable sum in advertising for information from any persons who had witnessed the trick. We also offered to pay £5000 a year to any juggler who could perform the trick as it has been described.'[70] One person came forward to offer a potential explanation:

He explained the secret. He had been stationed for some years at one of the frontier military posts and he had noticed that the troop of Indian jugglers always arrived at the same time of day when the sun was in one position and its rays were so strong that Europeans could not be exposed to them. The audience, said our informant, occupied the balcony of the bungalow, and were sheltered from the sun by an awning. The jugglers brought a coil of what appeared to be a large rope. As they uncoiled it and held it up it became stiff; it was evidently jointed bamboo with the joints made to lock. It was covered to look like a rope, and it formed a pole about thirty feet long. A diminutive boy, not much larger than an Indian monkey, climbed up to the top of the pole and was out of sight of the audience unless they bent forward and looked beneath the awning, when the sun shone in their eyes and blinded them. As soon as the boy was at the top of the pole the jugglers made a great shouting, declaring he had vanished. He quickly slid down the pole and fell on the ground behind the juggler who held the rope. Another juggler threw a cloth over the boy and pretended that he was dead. After considerable tom-tomming and incantation the boy began to move, and was eventually restored to life. This account was subsequently confirmed by another gentleman who had evidently witnessed the same jugglers perform the feat.[71]

Even though this explanation proposed by Maskelyne may seem plausible in its attempt to account for the flexible rope becoming a rigid one, the description offered by Maskelyne is not verifiable. It is sometimes the case that explanations offered by jugglers or modern-day conjurors of their tricks are in themselves further obfuscations designed to misdirect; the plausible is meant to represent reality. However, Maskelyne's description concerning sections of jointed bamboo may be seen in Melton's illustration.

The apparent inability to perform this trick in the open air only serves to create the need for further caution in the treatment of so-called eye-witness accounts.

CHAPTER 5

Magic through sound: illusion, deception and agreed pretence

The conscious working of the reality–illusion relationship is not only central to the conventions by which theatre exists, but also to the creation of magic through conjuring, legerdemain or sleight of hand, ventriloquy and other forms of overt deception or pretence. The perpetrators of magic feats or tricks frequently rely on diversion and deception as a means of confusing the visual sense of the audience. It is the ability to visualise that is most frequently diverted or disorientated when acts of magic are created. However, the reality–illusion relationship may also be affected by the use of sound.

In the *Origo mundi* of the *Cornish ordinalia* a stage direction requires the following action: 'Et fodiet et terra clamat et iterum fodiet et clamat terra.' [And he shall dig, and the earth cries: and again he shall dig, and the earth cries.][1] The significance of the action within the biblical narrative is that God has expelled Adam and Eve from Paradise and Adam now attempts to dig the earth so that he 'may raise corn'. However, he declares that 'The earth will not let me break it.' The inherent ambiguity in the stage direction is intriguing. Clearly, it may not be possible to say how the requirement expressed in the stage direction was originally achieved, but it is possible to consider some implications and their potential influence upon the nature of the inherent theatrical statement.

Firstly, how does the earth cry? Presumably, the sound of the crying earth is intended to communicate just that to the audience. The audience needs to know that it is the earth that cries. What does this sound like? Who knows what the crying earth would sound like? Clearly, whatever sound was produced to indicate that the 'earth cries' would have needed to appeal to the imagination of the audience in order to contextualise and give significance to the sound. The possibilities surrounding the nature of this sound and its production invite interesting questions about the character of and implicit conventions in its communication to the audience. It might be presumed that the sound is a 'live' one and produced by someone and/or something. If it is made to occur through the latter, what kind of object or instrument might be used? Is the creator of the sound, whether person and/or instrument, seen by the audience? Is it important that the audience be able to recognise that the 'cries' actually come from the earth at the point where the digging is carried out by Adam? Answers to this question inevitably lead towards concerns about the nature of reality, illusion, deception and agreed pretence in the communicated statement.

If it is that the sound is intended to come from, or seem to come from, the point at which the earth is dug, the pretence may lead to use of illusion, although this is not inevitable. What are the means of its creation? A person may be positioned out of sight beneath the 'earth' in some sort of cavity in order to produce the sound *in situ*. Alternatively, a person who is in view of the audience may make, or cause to make, the sound 'as if' it comes from the ground. A further possibility exists in the sound being regarded as that which 'represents' the sound of the earth crying, in which case, the terms of reference by which the significance of the sound is communicated would need to be established. In such an instance the audience does not primarily appreciate the sound for its supposed verisimilitude but for its meaning.

Of itself, the stage direction in the *Origo mundi* does not divulge sufficient information to determine how the 'earth cries', but two other stage directions in the *Resurrexio Domini* of the *Cornish ordinalia* offer the following information in respect of the attempted burial of Pilate:

> et tunc proicietur extra terram
> And then he shall be thrown out of the earth

> et tunc ponent eum in terra et proicietur iterato sursum[2]
> And then they shall put him in the ground,
>   and he shall be thrown up again

The implication here is that the 'earth' possesses sufficient depth to enable the ejection of Pilate. This might be achieved by a depression of some kind in the natural earth or within some built-up staging. If the information contained in the text may be trusted to indicate accurate action, then the instruction given by the Carcerator or Gaoler to Garcon, the Servant, to 'take the head, By the feet I will let him down, Within the earth' suggests that Pilate ends up on his back. In this position Pilate is unlikely to throw himself out of the earth. It is more likely that others cause his ejection. Perhaps the most obvious method might consist of Pilate being tossed in a strong earth-coloured cloth.[3] This kind of action would seem to meet the intention behind the requirement expressed in the stage direction, although it presupposes sufficient space and depth in which to stage manage the action. Given the need for such space it is possible that the creation of sound to signify that the 'earth cries' in the stage direction in the *Origo mundi* may take place in and from the same space. The 'earth' may well be a designated *locus* within the performance space. Further support for this possibility may be found in the stage direction in the *Passio Domini* of the *Cornish ordinalia* that requires an earthquake to occur.[4] Where better could such an earthquake take place than in a *locus* designated as 'the earth'? Indeed, the same means suggested for the ejection of Pilate may be adopted for the visual effect of the earthquake. Accompanying sound would presumably also take place at this point. Such treatment is recorded in the late-fifteenth- or early-sixteenth-century Passion play in Provençal:

> E a fa la
> finta de fa terra–
> tremol qual que,
> ce hon fa
> an tellas, lo que hon
> faça core las tela[s]
> a cobri lo trovat.[5]

And to perform the trick of the earthquake one covers the stage with pieces of cloth and shake[s] them.

In this instance, the sound of the earthquake is provided by rolling stone balls on a wooden framework below the stage platform that is supplemented by firing cannons ten or twelve times 'promptly'.[6]

Since no one knows what the crying earth in the *Origo mundi* would have sounded like, nor indeed knows what the actual sound would be, it seems that the help needed by the audience to contextualise the sound would have been strongly influenced by its location. If the sound comes from the 'earth' where Adam digs, then identification of the source of the sound, in relation to the delivered text and its timing, may carry meaning over and above that of its nature. The theatrical option as to whether creation of the sound be hidden or seen by the audience is not immediately clear. However, communication of sound may be imprecise or indistinct if its creation is not witnessed by the audience. Additionally, recognition of the source of a given sound is likely to be affected by the nature of the acoustic environment in which it occurs.

The nature and source of the sound to implement requirements of the *Cornish ordinalia* stage directions is clearly important. However, such a source, as communicated to an audience, may be a real one or one that creates the impression of it. This distinction becomes significant when considering the deliberately communicated appearance of someone or something from which sound is supposed to issue. During Queen Mary's Progress before her Coronation in London in 1553, a pageant contributed by the Florentines consisted of the following:

> verie high, on the top whereof there stood foure pictures, and in the middest of them and most highest, there stood an angell all in greene, with a trumpet in his hand: and when the trumpetter (who stood secretlie in the pageant) did sound his trumpet, the angell did put his trumpet to his mouth, as though it had beene the same that had sounded, to the great maruelling of manie ignorant persons.[7]

Whether the 'angell all in greene' who stood 'most highest' was an artificial figure or simply a person who could not produce the required sound is uncertain, although the former seems more likely given the apparent 'great maruelling' response by the audience. Also, there seems little point in making use of a real, unseen trumpeter if he himself could have been placed in the position 'most highest'. This account, contained in Holinshed, refers to the imprecise behaviour of sound and its communication as means of creating deliberate deception to produce required illusion.

A similar effect was sought during Elizabeth's entry to Kenilworth Castle in 1575. Both Robert Langham and George Gascoigne refer to the action, its creation and effect. Langham records:

> he ['a porter'] cauzd hiz Trumpetoourz that stood vppon the wall of the gate thear, too soound vp a tune of welcum: which, besyde the nobl noyz, was so mooch the more pleazaunt too behold, becauz theez Trumpetoourz beeing six in number, wear euery one an eight foot hye, in due proportion of parson besyde, all in long garments of sylk sutable, each with hiz syluery Trumpet of a fiue foot long, foormed Taperwyse, and straight from the vpper part vntoo the neather eend: whear the Diameter waz a 16. ynchez ouer and yet so tempered by art, that being very eazy too the blast, they cast foorth no greater noyz nor a more unpleazaunt soound for time and tune, then any oother common Trumpet bee it neuer so artificially foormed. Theese armonious blasterz, from the foreside of the gate at her highnes entrauns whear they began: walking vpon the wallz, vntoo the inner: had this musik mainteined from them very delectably while her highness all along this tiltyard rode vnto the inner gate next the base coourt of the Castl.[8]

Gascoigne's account makes clearer the relationship between the artificial figures and the trumpeters:

> Her Maiesty passing on to the first gate, there stode in the Leades and Battlementes therof, six Trumpetters hugelie aduaunced, much exceeding the common stature of men of this age, who had likewise huge and monstrous Trumpettes counterfetted, wherein they seemed to sound: and behind them were

placed certaine Trumpetters who sounded in deede at her maiesties entrie. And by this dum shew it was ment, that in the daies and Reigne of K. *Arthure,* men were of that stature. So that ye Castle of *Kenelworth* should seeme still to be kept by *Arthurs* heires and their seruants.[9]

In responding to Langham's letter, John Nicholl misinterprets the account by suggesting that: 'It would appear that these were but figures constructed like all those used in ancient triumphs and pageants, of hoops, deal boards, pasteboard, paper, cloth, buckram, &c. which were gilded and coloured on the outside; and within this case the real trumpeter was placed.'[10] However, deception of the kind interpreted by Nicholl may be found in the play of St George of 1429, which was probably performed in Turin, where the property list contains the following: 'Item: another idol in which is hidden a person who speaks.'[11] As in the previous example, sound is required to emerge from an inanimate object in the form of an idol. In this instance the sound does not simply appear to issue from the idol, it actually does so. Both or either of the techniques outlined above may be applicable to two further instances in the records of the Bourges *Mystery of the Acts of the Apostles* of 1536 where 'There must be a dog which will sing at the command of the aforesaid [*Simon Magus*]. There must be in the temple an idol which will laugh at the command of the said Simon.'[12] Similar requirements are made by stage directions in some late-sixteenth-century plays that require disembodied heads to speak.

In George Peele's *The Old Wives Tale* (c. 1590) two stage directions embrace the following:

> Heere she offers to dip her Pitcher in, and a head speakes in the Well.
> *Head.* Gently dip, but not too deepe,
> For feare you make the golden birde to weepe,
> Faire maiden white and red,
> Stroke me smoothe, and combe my head,
> And thou shalt haue some cockell bread.
> *Zant.* What is this, faire maiden white & red,
> Combe me smooth, and stroke my head:
> And thou shalt haue some cockell bread.
> Cockell callest thou it boy, faith ile giue you
> cockell bread.
> Shee breakes hir Pitcher vppon his heade, then it thunders and lightens, and Huanebango rises vp: Huanebango is deafe and cannot heare.[13]

The 'heade' appears to be a physical entity rather than just a disembodied voice, for the breaking of 'hir Pitcher vppon his heade' is a requirement stipulated by the stage direction on behalf of the communicated statement to the audience. The stage direction tells us that the 'head speakes', but how does it do this?

In Greene and Middleton's *Friar Bacon and Friar Bungay* (1591) both text and stage directions require the use of a 'brasen head' created by Friar Bacon in order to 'tell out strange and vncoth Aphorismes'.[14] The relevant stage directions are as follows:

Enter Frier Bacon drawing the courtaines with a white sticke, a booke in his hand, and a lampe lighted by him, and the brasen head and miles, whith weapons by him.

the Head speakes.

Heere the Head speakes and a lightning flasheth forth, and a hand appeares that breaketh down the Head with a hammer.[15]

The stage directions signify that the 'brasen head' is a portable property and Miles' words in the text may indicate the eventual resting place of it when he says, 'now sir I will set me downe by a post, and make it as good as a watch-man to wake me if I chaunce to slumber'. If the 'post' is a real one, then it is possible that the head is placed on top of it. If, on the other hand, the post is one of the pillars that supports part of the upper structure of the theatre, then the head may be simply hooked on to it and the curtain from behind which the hand appears may be positioned immediately behind the pillar.[16]

Stage directions in *Alphonsus King of Aragon* (1599) by Robert Greene make the following requirements:

Let there be a brazen Head set in the middle of the place behind the iv.i Stage, out of the which, cast flames of fire, drums rumble within, Enter two Priests.

Cast flames of fire forth of the brazen Head.

Speake out of the brazen Head.[17]

In this case the text informs us that the 'brazen Head' is a representation of 'Mahomet', before which the two Priests and King Belinus kneel in order to focus their dialogue with 'Mahomet'. The positioning of the 'brazen Head', as determined by the stage direction, is precisely located as 'the place behind the iv.i Stage' (forestage). Thomas Dekker, in his *If this be not a good play, the Devil is in it*, includes a 'golden Head' called Glitterbacke, which both 'ascends' and 'descends'. Glitterbacke is involved in considerable dialogue with Shackle-soule and Scumbroath. At the end of the scene a stage direction instructs that the golden head

'Goes downe'. 'Ascending' and 'descending' are therefore presumed to be carried out through or on a trap.[18]

Positioning of the respective heads in each of the above examples appears to be important. The 'well of life', 'a post', 'iv.i Stage' and a presumed trap are all locations at which heads are sited. Such fixed sites for the heads might lend themselves to the technique of constructing brazen heads of the kind offered by William Bourne in his *Inuentions or Deuises* (1578):

> And as the brasen head, that seeme for to speake, might bee made by such wheele work, to go either by plummets or by springs, and might haue time giuen vnto it, that at so many houres end, then the wheeles and other engines should bee set to worke: and the voyce that they did heare may goe with bellowes in some truncke or trunckes of brasse or other mettall, with stoppes to alter the sound, may bee made to seeme to speake some words, according vnto the fancie of the inuenter, so that the simple people will maruell at it.[19]

The mechanical intricacies suggested in Bourne's account may appear too complex or inflexible for the kind of theatrical use cited above, in that timing of the sequence is determined by 'plummets or by springs'. However, the fact that the conveyance of sound 'in some truncke or trunckes of brasse or other mettall, with stoppes to alter the sound, may bee made to seeme to speake some words, according vnto the fancie of the inuenter', seems to be most appropriate in respect of manipulation of the 'head' to produce spoken words. Whether the heads stipulated in the above stage directions possess moveable jaws is unclear, for within their respective contexts such articulation is not necessary: the heads simply speak as icons.[20] Bourne develops his repertoire of established and potential techniques with regard to sound production through artificial birds:

> and also to make birds of mettall to sing very sweetly, and good musicke, it may bee done with wheeles, to goe at any houre or time appoynted by plummets, and then to haue pipes of tinne or other fine mettall to go with bellowes, & the pipes to haue stops, and to go with a barrell or other such like deuise, and may bee made to play or sing what note that the inuenter shall thinke good when he dooth make it: and also there may bee diuers helpes to make it seeme pleasant vnto the eares of the hearers, by letting the sound or wind of the pipes to passe through or into water, for that will make a quauering as birds do. &c.[21]

The technique of passing sound through pipes in water to 'make a quauering as birds do' is one of the ones employed today among the range of 'bird calls and decoys' produced by the 'Acme Whistle Company'. The instrument to produce the nightingale call consists of a metal container about the size of a cotton reel out of which projects a short pipe (mouthpiece). Instructions to the user are stated as follows: 'Remove filler cap and mouthpiece cover. Fill quarter full with water. Blow gently and firmly. Obtain 'trills' by vibrating tongue (as in pronouncing 'r-r-r-r'). Only replace cap screw and cover AFTER use, thus keeping the instrument watertight.'[22]

Giambattista della Porta also writes of the transmission of sound through pipes in 1589. Although the principle of sound conveyance here is the same as in previous examples, the scale is considerably developed:

si quis ductus plumbeos longissimos confecerit, longitudine bis, vel tercentum passuum (vt expertus sum) & in eis aliqua verba, immo multa intra illos locutus fuerit, incedunt vera per ductus illos, & ex alia parte audiuntur, vt ex ore loquentis.[23]

if any man shall make leaden Pipes exceeding long, two or three hundred paces long (as I have tried) and shall speak in them some or many words, they will be carried true through those Pipes, and be heard at the other end, as they came from the speakers mouth.

The conveyance of sound through pipes is also referred to by Henry van Etten in 1633 when he describes a means 'to helpe the hearing':

trunkes are used to helpe the hearing, being made of silver, copper, or other resounding materiall; in funnell-wise putting the widest end to him which speaketh, to the end to contract the voyce, that so by the pipe applyed to the eare it may be more uniforme and lesse in danger to dissipate the voyce, and so consequently more fortified.[24]

Further corroboration of the technique of speaking through tubes or pipes is offered by Nicolo Sabbatini in his *Pratica di fabricar scene e machine ne teatri* (1638):

Si potrebbe ancora far rappresentare quasi del naturale, che la fantasima dicesse qualche parola, col mezo d'una ciarabottana lunga altretanto quanto è l'ombra, una cima di cui deve essere accomodata alla bocca della maschera, e l'altra alla bocca dell'operanti, il quale al debito tempo pronunciando ciò che deve su per la ciarabottana farebbe risonare le parole nel volto della maschera.[25]

Greater verisimilitude can be attained by making a ghost say a few words. A speaking tube is run from the face of the mask down to the mouth of the operator who will speak into it the required words at the proper time, making them seem to come from the face of the mask.

Given the apparent artificiality of the speaking heads in the plays of Greene, Middleton, Peele, Dekker and the ghost in Sabbatini's account, how do the nature and use of sound affect communication of the respective theatrical statements? Presumably, words spoken through tubes that emanate from the open mouth of a speaking head would be equally artificial. So, it may be that successfully communicated verisimilitude, if it is known what this might be, is not the theatrical aim. However, the perceived location of sound needs to be attributed to the head. Bourne describes the phenomenon as 'the brasen head, that seeme for so to speake'. Similarly, Sabbatini, in translation, refers to words that 'seem to come from the face of the mask'. Such illusion is bolstered in its intention by dialogue and staging focus in each of the above plays. We, the audience, expect the heads to speak and our imagination enables us to confirm that this is what we hear. It may not be essential that we be able precisely to locate the words as those coming from the head, since our respective imaginations are capable of compensating for any lack of precision. We know that the sound is intended to come from the head and thus imaginatively we will it to do just that. In this sense, as indicated earlier, sound is a less precise tool in conditioning imaginative responses than is light in determining visual perception. This point is well illustrated by Robert Harrison in his translation of Ludwig Lavater's *Of ghostes and spirites walking by nyght* (1572), when he relates the 'famous historie of foure monkes of the order of preachers (who were brent at Berna in Heluetia in the yeare of our Lord 1509, the last daye of May) by what subtilties they deceyued a poore simple Frier who they had lately reteined into their monastrie'. He writes:

After long instruction and teaching, they placed him on the altar of our Lady, kneeling on his knees within a chappell before the image of the holy virgine: Where one of the Monkes standing behinde a cloath, spake thorough a cane reede, as if it were Christ talking with his mother, in this wise: Mother why dost thou weep; haue I not promised thee, ye whatsoeuer thou willest, shal be done; Wherto the image made answere. Therfore I weepe, bicause this businesse findeth no end. Then sayd the image of Christ: Beleeue me mother, this matter shall be made manyfest. This doone, the Monke priuely departing, the chappell dores were shut. As soone as these things were scattered about the citie, by & by ther was a great thronging of people.[26]

Thomas Nash, in his *The Vnfortvnate Traveller*, records a less deceitful use of sound through pipes in his description of the production of melodious bird song:

On the well clothed boughes of this conspiracie of pine trees against the resembled Sunne beames, were pearcht as many sortes of shrill breasted birdes, as the Summer hath allowed for singing men in her siluane chapels. Who though there were bodies without soules, and sweete resembled substances without sense, yet by the mathematicall experimentes of long siluer pipes secretly inrinded in the intrailes of the boughs whereon they sate, and vndiscernablie conuaid under their bellies into their small throats sloaping, they whistled and freely carold theyr naturall field note. Neyther went those siluer pipes straight, but by many edged vnsundred writhings, & cranked wandrings aside strayed from bough to bough into an hundred throates. But into this siluer pipe so writhed and wandering aside, if anie demand how the wind was breathed. Forsoth ye tail of the siluer pipe stretcht it selfe into the mouth of a great paire of belowes, where it was close soldered, and bailde about with yron, it coulde not stirre or haue anie vent betwixt. Those bellowes with the rising and falling of leaden plummets wounde vp on a wheele, dyd beate vp and downe vncessantly, and so gathered in wind, seruing with one blast all the snarled pipes to and fro of one tree at once. But so closely were all those organizing implements obscured in the corpulent trunks of the trees, that euerie man there present renounst coniectures of art, and sayd it was done by inchantment. One tree for his fruit bare nothing but inchained chirping birdes, whose throates beeing conduit pipt with squared narrow shels, & charged siring-wise with searching sweet water driuen in by a little wheele for the nonce, that fed it a farre of, made a spirting sound, such as chirping is, in bubling vpwards through the rough crannies of their closed bils.²⁷

Another form of illusion occurs in a trick described by Hanss Jacob Wecker in 1582. Here, both the hearing and speaking functions of the pipe are used in the same trick:

Demortui caput mensae apposuit, quod patefacturum esse nobis auditoribus promisit, quisnam ex nobis filiam ciuis cuiuspiam miserè deperiret, quis etiam futurus esset amoris exitus caput id hoc esse praedicturum. Ludicrum id non intelligentibus horrorem induxit, perinde atque si caco daemonis ope vaticinium id processisset. Verum ijs qui iocum animaduerterent, risum mouit. Hac autem arte res haec instituta erat. Mensa quatuor columnis pedum instat suffu ciebatur, quarum vna excauata erat, mensae perforatae subdita: Foramen id, totaque mensa subtili quodam tapeto tegebatur, ne mensae foramen conspiceretur: Eo loco demortui caput positum consistebat. Pauimentum autem in ea parte perforatum etiam erat, in qua columna excauata mensam sustinebat, vt ex inferiori aedificio, in superius, & vicissim ex superiori in inferius voces transmitti possent. Quamobrem is qui in inferiori erat, tubo quodam in excauatam mensae columnam immisso, & altera eiusdem tubi parti auri admota, facilè quid alter in superiori conclaui consistens rogaret, exaudiebat, responsaque dabat quaesitis apprimè conuenientia. Successit hoc eò facilius, quòd vterque amatoris eludendi secreta nouissent: Sic enim fabulam hanc communicatis ante consilijs dexterè peregerunt. Ad maiorem etiam vaticinij fidem, candelas cereas accensas circa demortui caluariam posuit, verbaque peregrina recitauit.²⁸

He set a dead Mans head upon a Table, and he promised unto us that the head should reveal which of us was deeply in love with a certain Citizens Daughter.

We that understood not that Pastime were troubled at it, as if that Oracle should be pronounced by help of the Devil, but they that observed the Jest, laughed at it. The business was thus: The Table stood upon four Pillars, like to feet, and one foot was hollow set under the Table that was perforated quite through that hole, and all the Table was covered with fine Tapistry, that the hole of the Table should not be seen: upon that place stood the dead Mans head: the Pavement also in that part had a hole made through, where the hollow Pillar held up the Table, that from the lower Room to the upper, and from the upper Room to the lower a voice might proceed. Whereupon he that was in the lower Room putting a Pipe into the hollow Pillar of the Table, and setting the other part of the Pipe to his ear, heard with ease what the other in the upper Room asked, and he answered according to his questions. This succeeded the better, because they knew the secrets of both these Lovers, and so knew how to delude them: for so they handsomely acted their parts, having conferred together before. And to make this Oracle the more to be believed, he set lighted Wax Candles about the skull of the dead Man, and he repeated some strange words.

Later examples of the method of speaking through tubes exist, although the efficacy, for magical purposes, of the technique has more recently been questioned.[29] If the sound from 'the brasen head, that seeme for so to speake' is not produced through tubes or pipes, how else might the illusion or effect be created? The sound described in the accounts of Bourne and Sabbatini should appear to come from the 'brasen head' and the 'face of the mask'. If this is the case then the actual sources must be located elsewhere as demonstrated in the examples offered by Lavater, Wecker and Nash. A further method that makes use of sound from another source, and one that might equally apply to the production of sound in the *Origo mundi* of the *Cornish Ordinalia* where the 'earth cries', is that produced by ventriloquy.[30]

The practice of ventriloquy depends upon the successful manipulation of conscious deception and production of resultant illusion. Such ability to deceive the audience would lead to an abuse of trust were it not for the fact that the audience normally knows of the process and tacitly agrees that it should take place. The audience is willing to be deceived and enjoy both the content and skill of its creator.[31]

Although ventriloquy frequently exists in its own right, as diverting entertainment, it may also be used in furthering the purpose and communication of theatrical statement. Conventionally, ventriloquy takes place when someone, whose face is visible to the audience, creates live, vocal sound or speech that purports to come from someone or something and from some other place than that occupied by its instigator. Early writers who refer to ventriloquy do not indicate a clear understanding of the processes involved in its successful completion. Roger Bacon, in his *De Secretis Operibus Artis et Naturae, et de Nullitate Magiae*, repeats a frequently held belief that ventriloquists spoke from their bellies:

> & Pythonissae vocum varietaté in ventre, & gutture fringentes, & ore, formant voces humanas à longè vel propè prout volunt, ac si spiritus cum homine loqueretur; etiam sonus brutorum confingunt. Cannae verò gramini subditae, aut latebris terrae conditae, ostendunt quod vox humana est, & non spiritus, quae magno fingunt mendacio.[32]

> The Pythonesses [the oracles of Delphi and Cumae, and here described as ventriloquists], twittering (?) with a variety of voices in their stomach, throat, and mouth, make human voices from a long way off or close by, as they will, as if a spirit were conversing with a man: they even imitate the sound of beasts. Canes placed under the grass, or hidden in the secret places of the earth, show that it is a human voice, and not a spirit: which things they pretend with a great lie.

During the nineteenth century, three distinct kinds of ventriloquial 'voices' were identified in relation to performed statements. These effects varied according to both the physical and imagined distance between the creator and the apparent source of sound. Common terminology referred to 'near', 'near-distant' and 'distant' ventriloquial sound, and these distinctions continue to be made today by ventriloquists.[33] Some frequently used examples have been employed to illustrate these different kinds of sound. For instance, 'near' ventriloquy was that used in relation to a dummy or doll held by or positioned near the ventriloquist: 'near-distant' ventriloquy produced the sort of sound that would seemingly emerge from a dummy being shut up in a nearby box or trunk: 'distant' sound was often cited as that belonging to 'a man in the cellar' or 'on the roof'.[34] Writers on ventriloquy frequently refer to the ventriloquised sound itself as being insufficient to create the required illusion.[35] So, reinforcement of illusion is necessary from supporting dialogue, description or 'patter':

> if he [the ventriloquist] is doing the 'man on the roof', he either tells you first of all that he is about to call to his friend on the roof, or he points to the spot. The audience therefore expect to hear a voice from the roof, and the Ventriloquist, correctly imitating the sound as it would appear if a man had in reality called from the spot indicated, and assisted by the imagination of those present, completes the illusion, and everyone is astonished.[36]

In Peele's *The Old Wives Tale*, Zantippa may be seen to reinforce this possible technique by conducting an exchange of dialogue with the 'heade' that 'speakes in the Well'. In *Friar Bacon and Friar Bungay*, the audience has already been told by Bacon that the 'brasen head' will speak 'strange and vncoth Aphorismes' before it actually speaks. Each time the 'brasen head' speaks, subsequent dialogue from Miles refers back to the 'brasen head'. In *Alphonsus King of Aragon*, reinforcement of the illusion is provided by the three-way discussion between the two priests and the 'brazen Head' as Mahomet. The same condition may be observed of Glitterbacke, the golden head, Shackle-soule and Scumbroath in *If this be not a good play then the Devil is in it.*

The power of ventriloquial sound does not necessarily rely upon the quality or volume of sound itself or in its correspondence to an original, but in the relationship between the ventriloquist and the created effect. The likeness of the sound as an imitation of its original may be produced by means other than ventriloquy if such fidelity is necessary to the theatrical statement.

A related technique to ventriloquy is that which has been referred to as *polophony*.[37] This term describes straightforward mimicry of sound. The Smiths' Accounts at Coventry for the years 1573, 1574 and 1578 record payment 'to Fawston for Coc-croyng iiijd'.[38] Presumably Fawston possessed the necessary vocal skill to be able to produce the required effect in the Smiths' pageant of the *Trial, Condemnation and Crucifixion of Christ*. Similar skill was no doubt needed for effects to support the early-sixteenth-century liturgical Easter ceremony at Granada, where it was necessary 'to find some people who can do bird song (*música de aves*)'.[39] Like the Coventry account concerning Fawston, the implication here is that the required people would possess the vocal skill to perform their duties. Should vocal skill not be that which was sought or paid for, then the instruments 'Of Voices, Calles, Cryes, and Sounds' described by John Bate in his 1635 edition of *The Mysteries Of Nature and Art* might be useful aids to producing the required effects. Bate describes the making and use of devices to reproduce the sounds of the following: 'Of the Cooko Pipe; A Cock; The Drake, Bitern, Hare, Leurat, Peacock and Hedgehog; A Stag and Foxe; The Hogge, Cow, and Lyon; A Plover and a Puppie; A Call for Small Birds; A Quaile Call; A Larke, Linnet, and Kite'.[40] According to Bate, these instruments 'are known among some Shopkeepers, by the names of Calles, and there are long white boxes of them, which are transported hither from France, each box containing eleven in number'. He further declares that 'They are very seldomsold [sic] alone, and altogether at a very deare rate. There is no difficulty in their making.'

Other artificial aids to the production of vocal mimicry make use of thin membranes placed in the mouth that are allowed to vibrate in relation to varying positions of teeth, tongue and lips. Bate relates the following: 'An Irishman I have seen (which I much wonder at) imitate with his mouth the whistling of a Blackbird, a Nightingall and Lark, yea almost of any small Bird, as exquisitely almost as the very Birds themselves; and all is by the cunning holding the artificiall blade of an Onyon in his mouth.'[41]

The same principle and technique are at work in the description offered by Frank Bellew in his *The Art of Amusing*, where he requires a piece of green leaf to be cut from a leek, some 1 to $1\frac{1}{2}$ inches in length. Then part of the surface of the leaf should be scraped away with a thumb nail, leaving the fine membrane or outer skin of the leaf intact. Bellew describes the technique:

The way of using this instrument is to place it in the roof of the mouth with the side on which is the membrane downwards; then press it gently in its place with the tongue, and blow between the tongue and the upper teeth. After the first two or three attempts, you will be able to produce a slight sound somewhat, so that in the course of a couple of days you can imitate the barking of a dog and the neighing of a horse. With two or three weeks' practice, you will be able to imitate some of the song-birds.[42]

Mimicry, by its nature, demands accuracy in likeness to an original in order to accomplish illusion. Whether creation of the sound is seen or unseen by the audience, its imagination is required to complete the illusion through acceptance of verisimilitude. This is particularly so in respect of sound as sound. Words as sound, however, inevitably carry integral meaning that may compensate for any lack of precision as to the source of their creation. This notion is reinforced by a requirement in the list of effects for the Bourges *Mystery of the Acts of the Apostles* in 1536, where a simple account describes precisely the nature of intended deception and resultant pretence when an item records: 'There must be a small child, aged eight, the son of the satrap, who will be put on a trapdoor (*une trappe coulouere*) through which someone else will speak.'[43]

The foregoing stage directions either require sound to come from an object/location or to seem to come from one. If the means of producing sound through the brasen head is conducted via pipes, then the sound actually comes from the head. If ventriloquy is used then the sound merely seems to come from the head. Do either of these techniques lead to a more or less realistically perceived effect? If so, does this matter? Just as the speaking voice should 'seeme for to speake' from the 'brasen head', so, by implication, should the sound come from or seem to come from the earth at the point at which the 'earth cries' in the *Origo mundi* of the *Cornish Ordinalia*. The communicated location of sound to an audience may be supportive of an intention to create illusion or it may exist as a signal from which to create meaning. The two possible intentions are not mutually exclusive. Each of the methods is concerned with verisimilitude, but to varying extents that arise through seemingly different theatrical intentions.

CHAPTER 6

Mechanical images, automata, puppets and motions

The kinetic properties of static images determine the starting point at which automata and puppets may be considered. If the static image represents a person or an animal then the action of giving it a voice or sound may begin the process of developing the appearance of motion. Once an image appears to move it is not a large visual or theatrical step to the creation of its actual movement. The quality and expression of such movement is determined by means of its articulation. Mechanical means may be said to fall into two categories: one, in which the movement is started and left to run its course, i.e. some form of clockwork arrangement, and secondly, mechanical means through continued attention of an operator. These two modes are capable of variation of function and purpose. Similarly, the function of the operator may also be conditioned by purpose. Is the operator seen or unseen in such manipulation? Do the witnesses of such movement recognise the terms of reference by which movement occurs? If the answer to this question is 'Yes' then the skill of the operator and the created action may be enjoyed and appreciated in relation to the movement. If the answer is 'No' then some form of deception, illusion or pretence is likely. This distinction lies at the centre of notions of theatre and its acceptance is one with which the performance of magic is in constant negotiation.

Movement may be suggested by the static image where the image itself represents motion. Natural development of this condition depends on actual movement created by articulated joints. For instance, a critical description of the giants that featured in the *Midsummer Shows* in London in the 1540s indicates that they were constructed in order 'to make the people wonder [and there] are set forth great and vglie Gyants marching as if they were aliue, and armed at all points, but within they are stuffed full of browne paper and tow, which the shrewd boyes vnderpeering, do guilefully discouer and turne to a great derision'.[1] Giants appearing to move 'as if they were aliue' is presumably intentional and suggests articulated movement.

Giants of a 'huge stature' formed part of the celebrations to mark the return of Henry V and his wife Katherine to London in 1421, and here among the 'triumphal arches and castles, bands of singing boys and maidens, fountains running with wine' there were 'giants of a huge stature ingeniously constructed to bow at the right moment, lions which could roll their eyes and make other appropriate gestures.'[2]

It is not clear from this account whether the giants were two-or three-dimensional in their construction. Articulation of the giants through pivotal joints presumably occurred at the waist and/or the neck to create the 'bow'. Timing of the 'bow' at the 'right moment' implies at least one operator. The ability of the lions to 'roll their eyes' and make 'other appropriate gestures' suggests use of operators who might time the movement of the lion's heads and tails. It may be presumed that rolling of the lion's eyes concerned vertical movement achieved by lifting the pupils up or down; a similar requirement was made of the construction of a giant during the visit of Philip II of Spain to Antwerp in 1549:

Aspectum habet planè gigantæum, crudelem, formidabilem, tyrannicum, barbam prolixam, ruffam, oculos ardentes, toruos, introrsum cauos, supercilia hirsuta, oculis minaciter incumbentia: Brachia ei nuda, fæmora, tibiæ, suræ nudæ: Pedes cothurnis, pectum antique ritus thorace tectum est: nutat nonnumquam capite, grandes*que* oculos mouet, aliquot scilicet ad intrinsecus agente. Adueniente PRINCIPE, visus est solitò blandior ac festiuior: habebat caput pulchrè ornatum candidis, puniceísque rosis, quod huic Urbe est Insigne. Ab altero humero dependentem, cocco tinctam, festiuè rubentem, gestabat togam: manu dextera ligneum, suæ magnitudine par, tenebat sceptrum, albo rubròque colore distinctum. Ex latere sinistro, ingens, incuruus, pendebat ensis.[3]

His look was conspicuously that of a giant: cruel, terrifying, tyrannical, with a long tawny beard; burning eyes, [which were] grim, hollow within [possibly meaning 'deep-sunken' or, alternatively, hollowed out inside the head]; bristling eyebrows, bending down menacingly over the eyes; his arms naked, his thighs, shins, and calves naked; his feet in buskins, his chest was covered in the ancient manner with a breastplate: he frequently nodded his head, and moved his huge eyes, evidently worked by several people on the inside. When the prince approached, he seemed to be milder and more cheerful than normal: his head was beautifully decorated with white and crimson roses, which is the emblem of this city. He wore a toga hanging from one shoulder, dyed with scarlet, glowing festively; in his right hand he held a sceptre, in proportion to his size, painted variously in red and white. From his left side hung a huge, curved, fearful sword.

The same giant, known as *Antigonus*, was again paraded in Antwerp in 1581 during the *Duke of Anjou's Entertainment*, where he 'was made cunning to turne his face towards the Duke as he passed by, and to let fall the armes of Spaine which he held in his hand, and to put up the armes of Anjou'.[4] *Antigonus* was a seated figure of some 27 feet in height. He was again paraded on 14 June 1594 for the *Ceremonial Entry of Ernst, Archduke of Austria* into Antwerp.[5]

Articulation of joints and limbs is frequently referred to as being created by 'vices'.[6] The term is used to refer to a range of techniques that are essentially mechanical. The scope of the methods and processes includes pivotal arrangements controlled by materials such as packthread, rope, wire, springs, pulleys, counterweights and clockwork mechanisms. William Bourne, in his *Inuentions and Deuises* of 1578, exposes some of these techniques:

As touchyng the makyng of any strange workes that the world hath maruayled at, as the brasen head that did seeme for to speake: and the Serpent of brasse for to hisse: or a Doue of woodde for to flie: or an Eagle made by arte of woode and other mettall to flie: and byrdes made of brasse, tinne or other mettall to sing sweetely, and such other lyke Deuises, some haue thought that it hath bene done by inchantment, which is no such thing, but that it hath bene done by wheeles, as you may see by clockes, that doo keepe tyme, some goyng with plummets, and some with springs, as those small clockes that be vsed in tablets to hang about mens neckes.[7]

Charles Wriothesley's *Chronicle* contains an account of 'An idoll made of vices and shewed at Poules crosse' where in 1547 'Doctor Barlowe, Bishopp of Sainct Davides':

shewed a picture of the resurrection of our Lord made with vices, which putt out his legges of sepulchree and blessed with his hand, and turned his heade; and their stoode afore the pilpitt the imag of our Ladie which they of Poules had lapped in seerecloth, which was hid in a corner of Poules Church, and found by the visitors in their visitation. And in his sermon he declared the great abhomination of idolatrie in images, with other fayned ceremonies contrarie to scripture, to the extolling of Godes glorie, and to the great compfort of the awdience. After the sermon the boyes brooke the idolls in peaces.[8]

'Vices' in this account are referred to in the notes as 'Moveable joints', but the term is more concerned with the means by which the 'Moveable joints' operated – albeit in a generalised way. The account informs specifically that the head moves and it may be presumed that the 'legges' and 'hand' also move since the nature of the 'picture' is one 'made with vices'. Given the ostensible purpose of the device it is likely that the operator was out of sight.

At the reception to mark the visit of the emperor Charles V to London in 1522, at the little conduit in Cheap there was a pageant that 'dyd stand . . . representyng hevyn . . . w^t the assumpcion off owr lady mervelous goodly conveyde by a vyce and a clowde openyng'.[9] A more complicated sequence of manoeuvres occurred earlier on the route where:

> ther dyd stand a pageaunte off an ylonde betokenyng the Ile off englonde . . . where were dyuers bestes goyng abowte the mountayns by vyces and dyuers maner off trees herbys and flowres as roses, dayses, gylofloweres, daffadeles and other[s] so craftely made thatt hitt was harde to knowe them from very naturall flowres, and in the mountayns pondys off fressh water w^t fisshe. And att the comyng off the emprowr the bestys dyd move and goo, the fisshes dyd sprynge, the byrdes dyd synge reioysyng [at] the comyng off the ij princes the emprowr and the kynges grace. Also ther were ij goodly ymages one in a castell lyke to the emprowr in visage, and the other in an herbar wyth rosys lyke to the kynges grace with ij swerdys nakyd in ther handys. Which castell, garden, and the ymages dyd Ryse by a Vyce. The ymages dyd beholde eche other, and then cast away ther swerdys by a vyce, and w^t another vyce ioyned eche to other and embrasede eche other in tokennyng off love and pease, whiche don an ymage off the father off hevyn all in burnyd golde dyd disclose and appere and move in the topp off the pageant.[10]

A complicated process conditioned by use of 'vyces' is not one that is necessarily determined by complexity of the 'vyces' themselves but one that is affected by timing and sequence of action. '[D]yuers bestes goyng abowte the mountayns' suggests figures held on a circular base that is capable of continuous horizontal rotation and wound by an operator. The 'ymages [that] dyd Ryse by a Vyce' were presumably raised by rope/line and pulley and required to turn into each other, in the first instance in order to 'beholde eche other' and secondly, at a later stage, to move towards each other in order to have 'embrasede eche other in tokennyng off love and pease'. So, three actions seem to have been required: one, to lift the images; two, to turn the images into or away from each other; and three, to move the images closer together. The capacity to reverse these actions is also implied. During the procession of Edward VI to his coronation at Westminster in 1547, also at the little conduit in Cheap, a tower was constructed upon which played waits and an old man representing Edward the Confessor sat on a throne. In front of this figure lay a lion of gold, 'which moved his Head by Vices'.[11]

Interpretation of such so-called 'eye-witness' accounts presents interesting considerations. For instance, does that which is described determine that which happened or that which was intended to happen? Does the implied narrative of the event condition the received meaning or is it the action that creates the communicated sense? When the description informs that the images 'embrasede eche other', is this merely the language of the narrative or is it a description of the action? Clearly, there was a sequence of movement of images that moved towards each other that was intended to symbolise that the figures 'embrasede eche other in tokennyng off love and pease'. The significance and meaning of the narrative may not be apparent to the viewer from what is seen but supplied as pre- or post-rationale or explanation. It is important therefore that such accounts be treated with caution.

The notion of figures held on a base plate or board that rotates is also implied in Act v, Scene i of Thomas Middleton's *A Game at Chess* by an explicit stage direction in one of the extant manuscripts: 'Musique an Altar discouered and Statues, wth a Song'.[12] In another manuscript version the editor interprets the song and provides the following stage direction: 'Music. An altar is discovered with tapers unlit, and divers images about it.'[13] This editor also develops the action with another stage direction: 'Flames rise from the altar, the tapers take fire, and the images move in a dance.' The song is as follows:

> Wonder work some strange delight,
> (This place was never yet without),
> To welcome the fair White-House Knight,
>   And to bring our hopes about!
> May from the altar flames aspire,
> Those tapers set themselves on fire!
> May senseless things our joys approve,
>   And those brazen statues move,
>   Quicken'd by some power above,
> Or what more strange, to show our love![14]

After the song is over the B[lack] Knight says: 'A happy omen waits upon this hour; All move portentously the right-hand way.' The last comment indicates that the 'brazen statues' move in a circular fashion and in a clockwise direction. Thus, it is suggested that a base upon which the figures are fastened is allowed to rotate. That which drives the figures in their circular path is not stated. However, a remarkably well-fitting device that would meet the requirements of the above stage directions and song is suggested by John Babington in his *Pyrotechnia; Or, A Discovrse of Artifical Fire-works* of 1635 (Figure 6.1). His device is described as follows:

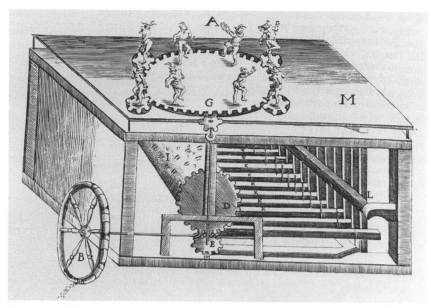

Figure 6.1.   'How to present musick playing, (by the help of fire) with anticks dancing',
from Babington, *Pyrotechnia*, p. 38.

How to present musick playing, (by the help of fire) with anticks dancing.

Cause an instrument to bee made, representing the Virginals, and to it fit a
Barrell set with severall tunes, (as I shall shew you in another Treatise hereafter)
then let there be a wheele with teeth fastened on this barrell, and a fire wheele,
with a screw on the axeltree, as I have shewed before, which screw may be so
fitted, that as it moves round the barrell one way, so it may move another wheele,
being placed on the side, which wheele shall move certain anticks, as the musick
playeth. This and many more may bee performed by the motion of wheele
work.[15]

The 'fire wheele' outlined by Babington consists of a number of
stickless rockets that are connected end to end by impregnated packthread
(usually from a slurry of gunpowder and allowed to dry) and fastened
round the rim of the wheel. The rockets, when lit, power the fire wheel
in order to drive the rest of the mechanism. The power to drive the
'brazen images' in *A Game at Chess* could be powered in this way, or by
an operator turning such a driving wheel. Although Babington's device
presents an almost complete means of achieving the requirements of
the stage directions (and their interpolations) in respect of the 'brazen

statues', the observation in the song that 'Those tapers set themselves on fire' is not explained by this method. However, Thomas Hill, in his *A briefe and pleasaunt treatise, entituled, Naturall and Artificiall conclusions* of 1581, offers a straightforward and reliable technique to enable the tapers to ignite. He writes:

How to drawe many Candles the one after the other, beyng laied a foote distaunce or more asunder.

For to dooe this, take Brimstone, Orpiment, and Oile, these labour together, and make thereof an oyntment, after take so many Candles as may well serue your Table, whiche laie on the Table a large foote asunder and all a roe, the one behinde the other as long as you list to laie them, yea, a hundred maie you laie downe on this wise a length if you laye them streight, then take a long threed, and anoynt the same in this oyntment, whiche after laye a lang on the Candles, and after drawyng the formost, all will followe by order.[16]

In the margin of the Huntington Library copy of this text is a handwritten comment: '[. . .]ie them all in a packthread and you may draw them without a yoke of oxen'. The intention here is that the 'long threed' [packthread] be smeared by the ointment (and probably allowed to dry) and then laid across the tops of the candles/tapers so that it touches all the wicks and is able to convey fire once the first candle/taper has been lit. This sort of technique is common in firework *Books of Secrets*, although the specific ingredients may vary.[17] Hill does not exaggerate the number of candles that may be used in this way when he says that 'a hundred maie you laie downe'. These may be placed in any number of configurations.

Although powered by a 'fire wheel', Babington's device makes use of mechanical components in the form of geared wheels, screw threads and connecting rods. The arrangement of these components in this device is not unlike others that possess the capacity to change direction of the motion. This ability is one of the valued features of geared wheels and screw threads in such combinations, and is integral to clockwork mechanisms.

During the First Provincial Progress of Henry VII to Bristol in 1486 there was a pageant constructed that showed 'The Resurrection of oure Lorde in the highest Tower of the same, with certeyne Imagerye smytyng Bellis, and al went by Veights merveolously wele done'.[18] This account refers to similar mechanical workings to those at the cathedrals of Wells and Salisbury. A modern account describes the arrangements concerning the clock at Wells:

Placed close to the main dial, Wells's interior hour-bell is struck by a quaint and colourful quarter-jack (so called because it also strikes the quarter-hours) known as Jack Blandifer. This is the figure of a seated man, carved in oak and painted, with jointed elbows and knees. He holds an iron hammer in each hand, and a short iron bar projects backwards from each of his heels. With his right hand he strikes the hours on the bell hanging in front of him. He strikes the quarters by kicking his iron-tipped heels backwards against two bells under the seat of his chair. The clock's exterior dial is sited on a buttress of the north face of the north transept. Its hands are driven by the main works through a simple linkage. It is adorned by two very handsome quarter-jacks representing knights in full armour, each holding a halberd with which he strikes a bell. Carved in oak, the knights stand upright. Each pivoted on a vertical spindle, they turn backwards and then forwards to swing and strike.[19]

Two accounts that describe mechanical images at Salisbury in 1466 occur from members of the retinue of Baron Leo von Rozmital who travelled Europe seeking support for the King of Bohemia. Gabriel Tetzel, who was in the party, described the mechanical images:

We saw also some fine carved figures which were so worked with weights that they moved as if to show how the Three Holy Kings brought gifts to our Lady and her Babe, how our Lord reached out to take the gifts, and how our Lady and Joseph bowed and did obeisance to the Three Kings, and how they took their leave. All this was presented with rare and masterly skill as if they were alive. There was also a similar carving showing our Lord rising from the tomb and the angels ministering to him. This was a splendid and praiseworthy thing to see.[20]

Rozmital's squire, Schaseck, also referred to the images:

I have nowhere seen more elegant figures. One represents the Mother of God, holding the infant Christ in her arms while the Three Kings offer gifts. The other shows the angels opening the Sepulchre with Christ rising from the dead, holding a banner in his hand. Both scenes are so represented that they do not appear to be fashioned but alive and actually moving before our eyes.[21]

Of these two accounts it is that of Tetzel that establishes that the 'carved figures' moved and did so 'with weights'. Inclusion of weights in this arrangement indicates a sequence of movement governed in its timing and duration by the length of 'drop' of the weights. At the end of the drop the apparatus must be reset. The artifice is also determined by the declaration that the carved figures moved 'as if to show' the coming of the Three Kings. Tetzel's description states that 'our Lord reached out to take gifts' and that 'our Lady and Joseph bowed' to the Three Kings. The account also informs us that there was 'a similar carving showing our Lord rising from the tomb and the angels ministering to him'. It is possible that the figures were sculpted in particular poses in such a way that 'our

Lord' may well have been created with an outstretched arm. The Three Kings may well have been similarly positioned in proffering their gifts. The comment that 'our Lady and Joseph bowed' implies but does not state movement. Their positions might simply be ones carved and posed in obeisance. In order to realise the biblical narrative the respective carved tableaux of the 'Three Holy Kings', 'her Babe' and 'our Lady and Joseph' simply need to move as independent tableaux and be brought into close proximity to complete the narrative.

Lincoln Minster also had an 'old clock being in sad condition' that was replaced around 1380 and lasted until the eighteenth century. A sketch of the clock is said to be in the Gough collection in the Bodleian Library 'showing three quarter jacks or figures of men, one at the top striking the hour, and two at the sides for the quarters'.[22]

A record from Barcelona of 1453 concerning a mechanical bird deals with an agreement between members of Barcelona City Council and a priest, Johan Çalom, which concerns the renovation of floats. This account is specifically concerned with the float of the Annunciation:

In addition it is agreed and understood that the said Johan Çalom is to make or have made a dove with its mechanism (*una coloma ab son exercici*) which is to issue from the mouth of God the Father in the float of the Annunciation and descend with its wings extended (*ab les ales steses*) until it reaches Mary. And it is to emit certain rays of light or fire which are to do no damage when it is before Mary. And afterwards it shall return to God, "flapping" its wings (*fahent exercici de les dites ales*).[23]

This sort of dove and its mechanism might well be what Bourne had in mind when he referred to 'a Doue of woodde for to flie: or an Eagle made by arte of woode and other mettall to flie'.[24] Bourne further describes the mechanism of such birds:

And for to make bird or foule made of wood & mettall, with other things made by arte, to flye, it is to bee done to goe with springs, and so to beate the ayre with the wings as other birds or fowles doe, being of a reasonable lightnes, it may flie: . . . and also the birds made to flie by Arte, to flie circularly, as it shall please the inuenter, by the placing of the wheeles and springs, and such other like inuentions.[25]

Indeed, this kind of arrangement may well account for the description offered by William Lambarde in his *Dictionarium Angliæ topographicum & historicum*, concerning observations collated between 1567 and 1577. Lambarde was born in 1536 and became an antiquary and lawyer. He recalls a childhood memory that presumably dates from the 1540s:

The like Toye I my selfe (beinge then a Chyld) once saw in *Poules* Churche at *London*, at a Feast of *Whitsontyde*, wheare the comynge downe of the *Holy Gost* was set forthe by a white Pigion, that was let fly out of a Hole, that yet is to be sene in the mydst of the Roofe of the great Ile.[26]

Given the symbolism attached to the 'comynge downe' of the 'white Pigion' it is clearly important that the bird reach the ground. The description that the dove 'was let fly' may indicate a sloping and controlled descent, although it is equally possible that the effect might have been achieved by simply lowering the bird with wings open in a vertical drop. The account from Barcelona is more informative in that the dove is to 'descend with its wings extended' and return to God 'flapping' its wings. The account also declares that the bird was to 'emit certain rays of light or fire'. This latter effect may be achieved simply by attaching squibs or fisgigs to the wings of the bird and igniting them on its release.[27] Assuming that the dove descends on a cord or wire its drop may be governed by gravity in a free fall or it may be controlled in its descent by another attached line. A free-fall descent may happen too quickly for its dramatic value to be registered. If the bird is connected to a guiding cord or wire then it would have to be removed in order to face the direction of its subsequent rise. Alternatively, a second dove might be used for the ascent but the account only indicates use of one dove. Presumably, the 'mechanism' of the dove is that which enables it to keep its wings open on descent and to flap them on its return. Such a mechanism is recorded in a nineteenth-century description of 'A toy bird that effectively simulates a bird flying' (Figure 6.2):

The cord leading from the aperture below the mouth of the bird is attached at its outer end to a hook in the wall or other support, while its inner portion passes over an idler and around a pulley, to which it is attached. The pulley is a little smaller than another at its side, both pulleys being fast on the same shaft, and a cord from the larger pulley passes over an idler and out rearwardly, having at its end a finger-piece, on which the operator pulls in manipulating the toy. The cords are wound in opposite directions on their pulleys, so that the unwinding of the cord from the larger pulley, and the rotation of the same, winds up the cord on the smaller pulley, and causes the bird to move forward on what seems to be only a single length of cord, the backward movement taking place by gravity when the pull on the string is released. The movement of the wings is effected by a crank on each outer end of the pulley shaft, the crank being pivotally connected with an extension of a member of the inner one of two pairs of lazy tongs, and this member having also a pivotal bearing on a crossbar which turns in bearings on the outer side of the toy, just under where the wings are hinged to the body. The larger pair of lazy tongs is pivotally connected to the outer portion of the

Figure 6.2.   'A toy bird that effectively simulates a bird flying', from
Hopkins, *Magic: Stage Illusions and Scientific Diversions*, p. 413.

wing, giving a longer sweep thereto than to the inner portion, with which the
smaller lazy tongs are connected; and the pivotal connection to the lazy tongs
with the bearing in the crossbar gives an oscillatory movement to the wings,
which constitutes a very good simulation of the natural movement of the wings
of a bird in flight.[28]

The description of the construction of this bird corresponds with the
need expressed in the Barcelona agreement. What it does not do is to
provide precise answers to the staging of the device. However, the materials from which the mechanism is made – namely wire, metal strips
[possibly tin] and cord – constitute the components of other known
devices such as the notorious *Rood of Boxley*.

The *Rood of Grace* at the Abbey of Boxley in Kent was, according to
William Warham, Archbishop of Canterbury in 1524, 'much sought from
all parts of the realm' primarily because the Abbey was 'so holy a place
where so many miracles be shewed'.[29] The *Rood of Grace* was the apparent
source of these 'miracles' and consisted of a cross bearing an image of the
crucified Christ that was capable of moving. The notoriety of the image

arose from the apparent deception through mechanical means by the monks upon the viewers. Fortunately, there are a number of letters written in 1538 that indicate the nature of the *Rood of Grace*. However, these letters do not always confirm features considered in other letters. Later references to the moving image extend the apparent capacity of the device to fulfil certain tasks.[30] Some care needs to be taken therefore before ascribing exaggerated attributes to the image. Jeffray [Geoffrey] Chamber[s], employed 'on defacing the late monastery of Boxley and plucking down the images', wrote to Cromwell on 7 February 1538:

On defacing the late monastery of Boxley and plucking down the images, found, in the Roode of Grace, which has been had in great veneration, certain engines and old wire, with old rotten sticks in the back of the same, which caused the eyes to move and stir in the head thereof, like unto a lively thing, and also the nether lip in likewise to move as though it should speak, which was not a little strange to him and others present. Examined the abbot and old monks, who declared themselves ignorant of it. Remits the matter to Cromwell when the monks repair to London. The abbot is sore sick and not able to come now. Considering that the people of Kent had in time past a great devotion to the image and used continued pilgrimages there, conveyed it to Maidstone this present Thursday, being market day, and showed it to the people, who had the matter in wondrous detestation and hatred, so that if the monastry had to be defaced again they would pluck it down or burn it. Will bring up the image. Maidstone. 7 Feb.[31]

The image was clearly brought up to London as referred to by Chambers, for on the 23 February 1538 John Hugee wrote to Lord Lisle informing him that: 'The Rode of Grace shall stand tomorrow at Paul's Cross during the sermon time "and there shall the abusion be divulged".'[32] The following account written by John Hoker of Maidstone in a letter to Bullinger dated '24 Feb 1538' indicates something of the development of responses to the image:

Dagon is everywhere falling. Bel of Babylon has been lately broken to pieces, a wooden god of the Kentish men, a Christ hanging who might have vied with Proteus, for he nodded his head, winked his eyes, turned his beard, bent his body to receive the prayers of worshippers. This, while the monks were falling on his behalf, was found in their temple surrounded with a multitude of offerings. A brave fellow, a brother of Nic. Partridge, smelt the deceit, loosened it from the wall, and exposed the trick. The juggler was caught. The thing was worked by wires through little pipes. For ages they have deluded the people of Kent and of all England with much gain. It was shown to the people at Maidstone from the top of the house, and then brought to London and visited the Court, where it was made to act amid the jeers of the courtiers. The King hardly knew whether more to rejoice at the exposure or to grieve at the long deception. A few days after, the bishop of Rochester preached at London, with the image opposite him, when it performed again, and was afterwards cut to pieces and put in the fire.[33]

On 12 April 1538, Nicholas Partridge wrote to Bullinger:

Concerning the bearded crucifix called 'the Rood of Grace', near Maidstone, he says that while the bp. of Rochester was preaching at St. Paul's Cross it turned its head, rolled its eyes, foamed at the mouth, and shed tears, – in the presence, too, of many other famous saints of wood and stone. The bp. had before thundered forth against these images. The satelite saints of the Kentish image acted much the same way. It is expected that the Virgin of Walsingham, St. Thomas of Canterbury, and other images will soon perform miracles also in the same place; for the trickery was so thoroughly exposed that every one was indignant at the monks and imposters.[34]

The account in Wriothesley's *Chronicle* for 1538 declares that the image was 'made to move the eyes and lipps by stringes of haire, when they would shewe a miracle, and never perceyved till now'.[35] Construction of the image is further alluded to 'at the sermon made by the Bishopp of Rochester, the abuses of the graces [vices?] and engines, used in old tyme in the said image, was declared, which image was made of paper and cloutes from the legges upward; ech legges and armes were of timber'.[36] When Robert Southwell was first shown the image in 1538 he regarded 'the idolle that stode there, in myne opynyon a very monstruows sight'.[37]

Given that John Hoker writes that the 'brother of Nic. Partridge, smelt the deceit' and 'loosened it from the wall, and exposed the trick', it may be assumed that some form of casing or covering surrounded the image that was capable of hiding the mechanism when the whole arrangement was placed up against the wall. Chambers refers to this space as the 'back of the same' and it is in this space that he found 'certain engines and old wire'. What therefore constitutes 'an engine'? One possibility might refer to the use of springs to create and release tension. Another one might consist of pulleys to enable lifting operations. This might have been necessary if Wriothesley's description that 'ech legges and armes were of timber'. Further development might include geared wheels. However, this kind of relative sophistication seems unlikely given that Hoker claims that 'The thing was worked by wires through little pipes.' This information is important in that it suggests that the wires were capable of being both pushed and pulled. The technique of using wires in this way is made more reliable through use of pipes or tubes. The wires are less likely to snag or jam when guided and restricted through pipes, particularly when being pushed. This further indicates an arrangement dependent on an operator.

Where was the operator positioned if the apparatus was up against the wall? In a letter thought to have been written in 1538, William Peterson wrote to Conrad Pulbert and stated that 'These things were managed by the ingenuity of the priests standing out of sight.'[38] If this is so, where did they stand? Were the wires controlled through a hole or holes in the wall? Did the operator stand at the side of the image? Did the operator climb inside the device as experienced in the 'hollow image erected near St. Alban's shrine, wherein one being placed to govern the wires, the eyes would move and head nod, according as he liked or disliked the offering, and being young he had many times crept into the hollow part thereof'?[39] Individual wires through tubes could fulfil single tasks such as: causing the 'eyes to move and stir in the head' by lifting or dropping the pupils, or operating the 'nether lip' up or down (rather like the articulation of the jaw of the ventriloquist's doll). The ability to 'shed tears' may have been achieved by little tin cups containing liquid lifted to tilt into the eye sockets in order to release the contents. It is of course possible that the account in Wriothesley's *Chronicle* is correct when it states that 'stringes of haire' were the means of moving the 'eyes and lipps', providing that there was little or no weight to be lifted. Otherwise, the wire through tube method would have been more secure and reliable. Partridge's notion that the image 'foamed at the mouth', if correct, suggests that an operator created and blew foam or, alternatively, developed it in the mouth of the image through chemical interaction of substances. The implication here is that a tube or pipe led up to the edge of the mouth of the image for this purpose.

Although the *Rood of Grace* at Boxley can not be considered as puppetry, the techniques by which parts of the figure of Christ were manipulated are not dissimilar from some of those used in puppetry. Identification and revelation of the deception in purpose and communication by the *Rood of Grace* prevents it from being considered as puppetry. Even though puppeteers may be seen or unseen in performance, the tacit acknowledgement of their existence is critical to understanding of the agreement between puppeteer and audience. The anger reported in the above letters, when deception was discovered, is similar to that experienced by an audience when an actor, puppeteer or conjuror (modern sense) breaks the unspoken understanding concerning the nature of pretence. Under these conditions an audience feels betrayed and cheated. It is perhaps not too surprising therefore to encounter derogatory references inspired by the Reformation to the interplay of the *Pope* and *puppetry*. In a note of explanation to a definition of *puppetry*, the *OED* states: 'spec. applied to idolatrous or superstitious observances (in 16th c. often in form *popetry*, with play on *popery*)'.[40] An example of such play on words is offered through William Tyndale's use of the word *popetry* in 1528: 'no let not oure most holy father make them no moare so dronken with vayne names / with cappes of mayntenaunce and lyke bables, / as it were popetry for children'.[41] A similar play on words occurs with John Bale's use of the phrase 'popetly playes' in his *King Johan* of 1538: 'I wyll be sumewhat playne / yt is yow clargy, that hathe her In dysdayne / w^t yow^r latyne how^rs, sermonyes & popetly playes.'[42]

In recent years there has been made available a growing number of English records concerning puppetry. When George Speaight wrote his acclaimed and influential *The History of the English Puppet Theatre* the extant medieval records were such that he was able to write: 'The references to puppets in medieval England are scarce and doubtful.'[43] In consideration of existing records he was also of the view that 'Apart from this intriguing glimpse, no further references to puppets in medieval England seem to have survived.'[44] By 'this intriguing glimpse' Speaight refers to evidence provided by Chaucer, through a discussion of the word *popet*, *The Romance of Alexander*, the *Rood of Grace* and a puppet version of the *Resurrection* at Witney in Oxfordshire.[45] This compelled Speaight to conclude that 'unfortunately there is no clear documentary proof of the existence of puppet shows in England at any time during the Middle Ages'.[46] If, by this statement, Speaight refers to use of the specific term 'puppet show', then he is correct. However, there are references to the 'puppet play' and the 'puppet stage' in the sixteenth century and many earlier references to the workings of puppets, puppetry and puppeteers. Some of these references had been published when Speaight wrote his work but many more have now been identified and published under the auspices of the Malone Society and the *Records of Early English Drama* project.

Ian Lancashire makes a case for 'Ioly Walte and Malkyng' as the earliest record of puppetry in England.[47] References to these figures are made in the *City Chamberlains' Books* at York for 1447 and 1448.[48] The 1447 record reads: 'Et j ludenti cum Ioly Wat & Malkyn' [And to two playing Joly Wat and Malkyn], and the 1448 one records 'Et ij ludentibus Ioly Wat & Malkyn ijd' [And two playing Joly Walte and Malkyn]. The significance of these records is indistinct but a third reference makes their existence clearer. These figures, Jolly Walte (Walter) and Malkin (Molly) are noted in a complaint recorded in the *Court Rolls* for the 3 September 10 Henry VI (1431) at Grimsby, Lincolnshire. John de Rasyn brought an action against Hans Speryng 'to deliver him certain instruments of play called Joly Walte and Malkyng'. The entry is as follows:

Curia tenta ibidem die [sabbati primo] lune tercio die Septembris anno [ut supra] regni Regis Henrici sexti x^{mo}

Iohannes de Rasyn queritur de Hans Speryng de placito transgressionis plegium de prosecutore Walterus Whayte quesiuit et utraque parte parato de eo quod ubi concordatum fuit inter eosdem quod ei deliveraret certa instrumenta joci vocata Ioly Walte and Malkyng ultimo elapsi, et dictus defendens se elongauit dicto die et die sequenti ad diminutum viij d. et defendens dedicit quod nihil ei fecit transgressionis prout etc. et hoc petitt quod inquiratur.[49]

Court was held in the same place on Monday, the third day of September, in the tenth year of the reign of King Henry the Sixth.

John de Rasyn brings an action against Hans Speryng in a plea of trespass – the pledge for the plaintiff, Walter Whayte, has made inquiry and each party being prepared – about this: that whereas it was agreed between them that he would deliver to him certain instruments of play called Joly Walte and Malkyng on the last day of the past (month), and the said defendant was absent on the said day and on the following day, to the loss of 8d. And the defendant replied that he did no wrong against him, just as etc. And he asked that there be an inquiry.

It seems that Rasyn and Speryng were puppet players and it has been suggested by Lancashire that their work related to the *Interludium de clerico et puella*. This fragment of text is often referred to as the earliest English play text (fourteenth century). Lancashire suggests that the original Latin text of the action should be translated as 'a certain instrument of a play called Joly Walte and Malkyng'.[50] Certainly this might make sense, but care needs to be taken here in order that the formality of a structured 'play' not be imposed as assumed evidence.

However, evidence of a structured play does exist through references to the 'puppet play' and the 'puppet stage'. The 'puppet play' implies formality of a presented event over and above that of playing with puppets as a process. The 'puppet stage' suggests the formality of a focused and purposeful location irrespective of its specific nature. In his preface to Sir Philip Sidney's *Astrophel and Stella* of 1591 he writes: 'let not your surfeted sight, new come from such puppetplay [*sic*], think scorne to turn aside into this Theater of pleasure, for here you shal find a paper stage streud with pearle, an artificial heav'n to overshadow the faire frame'.[51] Here, the allusions to the 'paper stage' and the 'artificial heav'n' that 'overshadow the faire frame' are all ones to the structure of the contemporary London theatre of the day. The earliest use of the term 'puppet show' so far encountered is 1623, although notions of the 'puppet play' and the 'puppet stage' are recorded in the sixteenth century. The first stanza 'To the Reader' of Thomas Brewer's satirical work *A Knot of Fools* (1623) addresses the:

> Kind Reader (cause I'de finde thee so,
> I so enstile thee) I haue here
> (I will not call't a Puppit-show:
> Though those and these, come something neare,
> Compar'd with iudgment) Such a sight,
> As for thy Cost returnes Delight.[52]

Little is known about Brewer, although his name appears in the title pages of several early-seventeenth-century publications. *A Knot of Fools* is not a play but a satire in dialogue form where a number of fools meet and deliver numbered speeches. A play called *A Knott of ffooles; or, Come laughe and spare not* was performed at Court in 1613 but it is not clear whether this is Thomas Brewer's work.

John Hall, a 'Surgeon of Maidstone' (1529/30–1568/9), writes a section titled 'A maruaylous dreame of the Author: Anno 1561' in his work *The Courte of Vertu* (1565), in which the activities of a number of performers are detailed:

> Of these many were Juglers lewde,
> And some had apes and beares,
> And some had foolyshe puppet playes.
> And therby great gayne reares.[53]

Hall identifies jugglers, tumblers and minstrels in his 'dreame' as performers who play in order 'money to attayne', and his focus on 'foolyshe puppet playes' suggests formal presentation and yet activity that is banal or intended for children.[54] Accounts of puppetry exist that disparage such activity by regarding it as childish. For instance, Thomas Nashe, in his *Lenten Stuffe* of 1599, states that: 'my inuectiue hath relation, to such as count al Artes puppet-playes, and pretty rattles to please children'.[55] Nashe's attitude is further implied in his *The Terrors of the night* of 1594, where the 'puppet stage' is considered to be an 'idle childish invention'. He says: 'in the daye, comes some superfluous humour of ours, lyke a Iacke-anapes in the night, and erects a puppet stage, or some such ridiculous idle childish inuention'.[56] The account provided by Jonson in *The Alchemist* suggests that puppet plays were sometimes accompanied by fireworks when he alludes to: 'gamster, after gamster, / As they doe crackers, in a puppit-play'.[57] The Chatsworth, Bolton Abbey

MS 94 records payment in 1611 as: 'giuen this day in Rewarde by my Lo: and La: *Comanment* to twoe men & a woman that went about with puppitt Playes xijd'.[58] In Worcestershire in 1617, a Master (schoolmaster?), Griffin Glinn, was charged for arranging a puppet play in church although the record does not relate if it had a religious theme. The record contained in the *Visitation Act Book* for Martin Hussingtree reads:

contra magistrum Griffinum Glinn
detectus for [sufferinge] causinge a puppett playe to be in the Chauncell[59]

Against Master Griffin Glinn
Detected for causing a puppett play to be in the chancel.

Edmund Spenser, in his *Prosopoia; Or, Mother Hubberds Tale* of 1591, records that: '. . . all men him vncased gan deride, / Like as a Puppit placed in a play, / Whose part once past all men bid take away'.[60]

Most of the available records concerning puppets do not identify their nature, and usually such records permit only slender conjectural possibilities as to the types of puppets under consideration. Essentially, the two forms of puppets under discussion and to which the evidence alludes, are the glove puppet and the marionette. William Lambarde's eighteenth-century description of puppetry at Witney in Oxfordshire, 'in maner of a Shew, or Enterlude' comes near to to use of the term 'puppet show':

In the Dayes of ceremonial Religion they used at *Witney* to set foorthe yearly in maner of a Shew, or Enterlude, the Resurrection of our Lord and Saviour *Chryste*, partly of Purpose to draw thyther some Concourse of People that might spend their Money in the Towne, but chieflie to allure by pleasant Spectacle the comon Sort to the Likinge of Popishe Maumetrie; for the which Purpose, and the more lyvely thearby to exhibite to the Eye the hole Action of the Resurrection, the Priestes garnished out certein smalle Puppets, representinge the Parsons of *Christe*, the Watchmen, *Marie*, and others, amongest the which one bare the Parte of a wakinge Watcheman, who (espiinge *Christ* to arise) made a continual Noyce, like to the Sound that is caused by the Metinge of two Styckes, and was therof comonly called, *Jack Snacker of Wytney*.[61]

Lambarde does not state the kind of puppets involved in his description. The sound that is likened to the 'Sound that is caused by the Metinge of two Styckes' concerning *Jack Snacker of Wytney* does not appear to be the kind of clacking noise frequently produced by the limbs and feet of marionettes, since he is the only figure that is singled out in producing this 'continual Noyce'. This noise appears to be a characteristic one of this figure and is thus more likely to have been produced by a glove puppet. A clearer account of the nature of glove puppet activity

is contained in the description offered by William Horman in his
Vulgaria of 1519. Horman was a schoolmaster and grammarian, and
his *Vulgaria* consists of a collection of English sentences and model Latin
translations. He writes:

The trogettars behynd a clothe shew forth popettis that chatre/ chyde/ iuste/ and
fyghte to gether.

Praestigiatores/ interiecto velo/ minutas ostentant imagunculas/ quasi puppas
loquaces/ rixantes/ et inter se concursantes perque ludicrum plurifariam
gesticulatrices.[62]

   The activities of the puppets indicated here suggest physical interaction
of a kind that is likely to have been more controllable with glove puppets
than marionettes. The possibility of jousting and fighting marionettes
does not appear to be a strong one. Nor, indeed, is it likely that the
reference to the 'trogettars behind a clothe' indicates shadow puppets. To
countenance the likelihood of this possibility would require a light source,
inevitably involving flame, behind the cloth and performed in a darkened
context. In this instance, the notion that the 'trogettars' worked from
'behynd a clothe' suggests use of glove puppets (Figure 6.3).
   Gervase Babington, Bishop of Worcester, in his *An Exposition of the
Catholike Faith* of 1615, refers to 'The Papists' who 'shamefully . . . abuse
our Sauiour; when on Easter day in the morning they rayse vp a Poppet,
and make him walke by wyers and strings, saying, That is Christ.'[63]
   Babington's comments raise a number of issues. Does the account
point to the marionette? If so, this is possibly the earliest English reference
to the puppet form. However, use of 'wyers and strings' does not automatically imply use of marionettes. The description, cited earlier, in the
chapter from Wriothesley's *Chronicle* concerning the same subject matter
of the Resurrection points to control of the articulation of limbs but
without the implication that such mobility is that provided by the
marionette. The same point may be made with reference to the *Rood of
Boxley*. Another issue that arises from Babington's statement concerns that
of scale. Was the size of the puppet large enough to embody a supposed
likeness to Christ? Or does the account simply refer to the 'Poppet' as a
representation of Christ without the implication of verisimilitude? Babington's indictment is typical of the way in which theatrical illusion or
pretence was labelled as deceit in the hands of the Catholics. Such
denigration of the Catholics in the sixteenth and seventeenth centuries
provides many references to the use of illusion and pretence in the service
of theatre, juggling and puppetry. Marionettes involving idiosyncratic

Figure 6.3. Puppeteer and glove puppet. This may be one of the earliest, if not the
earliest, explicit illustrations of the puppeteer and his glove puppet. From *The
Overthrow of the Magician* by Pieter Bruegel the Elder (1564). Engraving by Jan
van der Heyden (1565).

operational techniques are referred to by Girolamo Cardano in his *De
subtilitate* of 1550 and Hanss Jacob Wecker in his *De secretis libri* of 1582:

Iam si enumerem quot quanta*que* statuis ligneis paruis, Magatellos uocat uulgus,
dies me deficiet. Nam ludunt, pugnant, uenantur, saltant, tuba canunt,
coquinariam exercent artem, atq*ue* hæc omnia ut mirabilia sunt, ita nullius ut
dixi utilitatis.[64]

Now if I were to relate how many and what sorts of small wooden statues they
have – the people call them *Magatelli* – the day would fail me. For they play, they
fight, they hunt, they dance, they play the trumpet, they practise the culinary art,
and as all these things are marvels, so, as I have said, they are of no use whatsoever.

Cardano's description is further developed in 1582 by Wecker and later translated into English by Dr R. Read in 1660:

Mira sunt, quae de duabus statuis ligneis paruis, & colludentibus, à duobus Siculis fieri vidi: erant autem vnico filo transfixae hinc inde, quae annexae altera quidem parte lignae statuaeque fixa manebat, reliqua tibiae, quam ille pulsabat, extenso vtrinque filo: nullum saltationis genus non aemulabantur, gesticulantes miris modis, capite, cruribus, pedibus, brachijs totque in varias formas, vt ingenue fatear me tanti artificij rationem non assequi: neque enim plura fila, neque modò extensa, modò remissa, sed vnicum filum in singulis statuis, & semper intentum: nam multas alias vidi, quae pluribus filis, atque his modò intentis, modô remissis agebantur, sed id nihil mirum. Id verò pulchrum erat, quod saltationes gesticulationesque modis cantilenæ congruebant.[65]

The things which I have seen done by two Sicilians with two small wooden statues, which were playing together, are marvellous: but they were pierced through here and there by a single thread, which, indeed, joined in one part to the wooden statue and remained fixed, and in the other part to his arm, which he was moving, with the thread stretched at both ends: no type of dance was not imitated by them, gesturing in marvellous ways with their head, legs, feet, arms, and in such various manners that frankly I confess that I do not understand the method of such artifice: for there were neither several threads, nor were they sometimes extended and sometimes slackened, but there was one thread on the individual statues, and it was always stretched: for I have seen many others, which were being operated by several threads, and those sometimes stretched and sometimes slackened, but that is no marvel. That, indeed, was beautiful, because the dances and gestures used to fit with the measures of a song.

Giralamo Cardano came from Milan and was a professor of medicine. John Ferguson, in his *Biographical Notes on Histories of Inventions and Books of Secrets*, refers to Cardano's *De subtilitate* as 'a summary of philosophy, science and the arts . . . Yet, as it does contain a description of secrets both of nature and art, it cannot reasonably be excluded (from John Ferguson's list), even though its name does not specify the secrets which it aims at elucidating.'[66] According to Ferguson the book was a 'standard one' and passed through many editions.

Hanss Jacob Wecker, a German doctor of medicine, first published his *De secretis libri* in 1582; it was not until 1660 that the work was translated into English by R[obert?] Read, a physician. The single thread described in the Wecker account is designed to pass through the pivotal points of the statues to permit articulation. Thus restrictions on the variety of movement are implied. Presumably, opposite limbs may have been linked with one string. For example, the right knee would have been linked through to the left wrist and passed out through the head. A more complicated

series of linkages may bind or create unreliable movement. No doubt the
weight of the statue permitted the stretched thread.

The word *mametts* is sometimes used to refer to puppets although
the various examples of its use do not refer to particular types of puppets.
It appears that glove puppets and/or marionettes may be included in
the scope of possible meaning. In the *Chamber Accounts* that contain
payments for revels spectacles, plays and other entertainments at Court,
payment of £4 is recorded in 1499 to 'The players with mamettes'.[67]
In connection with the *Midsummer Shows* in London in 1534, the *Skinners'
Renter Wardens' Accounts* record payment for 'the "refreshing" of the giant
and his "mametts", and for "refreshing" the same pageants after Midsummer'.[68] An additional payment of 10s was made to the bearers of 'the
"geant" and the puppet bearers'.[69] William Turner, the Dean of Wells,
physician and botanist, writes in his *Herbal*: 'ye herbe that we call
comenly Mandrag' refers to the roots of the plant as 'conterfited & made
like litle puppetts & maummettes which come to be sold in England in
boxes with heir'.[70] One further kind of puppet is alluded to by William
Bourne, who suggests yet another form of puppet operation through the
use of 'wheeles and springs'. He says: 'And also you may make a small
puppet, either like a man or woman, to seeme to goe by wheeles and
springs, and shall turne and goe circular according vnto the setting of the
wheeles and springs.'[71]

In recent years there has been some drawing together of disparate
information concerning the puppeteer William Sands. In 1623, Sir Henry
Herbert gave a license 'to William Sands and others to show "the *Chaos
of the World*"'.[72] Other evidence identifies William Sands as a puppeteer
and the *Chaos of the World* as a puppet show. Although there has been
appropriate speculation as to the content of the show, the most persuasive
evidence so far available is that entered into the *Diary of Thomas Crosfield*
for 1628.[73] Here, Crosfield, a fellow of Queen's College, Oxford, records
visits of a number of entertainers to the city of Oxford between 1626 and
1654. Among these recorded entertainments is one concerning 'ye sight
call'd Chaos doth present express'd by puppets wch one did invent In 17
yeares. & this as 'tis well knowne In Oxford City hath bene often
showne'.[74] The content of this show as outlined by Crosfield includes
reference to the 'Creation', 'Abell & Cain', 'Abraham & Isaac' and
'Nebuchadnezzar, Shadrach, Mesheck and Abednego' as Old Testament
material. New Testament content starts with the 'birth of Christ' and
continues with the fear that King Herod would have 'martyr'd the Child'.
This is concluded by reference to 'Lazarus and Dives'. Crosfield further

alludes to this, or a modified version of the show, when he records what might be seen in Oxford in 1631: 'Things to be seene for money in ye City . . . The history of some parts of ye bible, as of ye creation of ye world, Abrahams sacrificing his sonne, Nineveh beseiged & taken, Dives & Lazarus'.[75] This account introduces content involving that of 'Ninevah beseiged & taken'. It is not clear whether Jonson's reference to 'a new Motion of the citie of Niniueh, with *Ionas,* and the Whale' in his *Everyman Out of his Humour* refers to this version.[76]

The scope of William Sands' operation in production terms is offered by another record of the provision of his license: 'A license to William Sands Ric.^{d} Luke, & John [Sands with nine] assistants for a yeare Tis calld the *Caos* [Caos of the world, they have given 1. & have given bond for *mor* more 1. 10. o]'.[77] Thus, twelve people that include 'nine assistants' were involved in the presentation of the show. Further evidence as to the scope of the work is contained in Sands' will of 1638:

In the name of God Amen I William Sandes of Preston in Amoundernes in the County of Lancaster Ioyner being sicke in body but of good memory doe make my last will & testament in forme following . . . Item I giue & bequeath my Shewe called the Chaos, the Wagon, the Stage, & all the Ioyners tooles & other ymplementes & [p]appurtenances to the said Shewe belonging to my sonne Iohn Sandes.[78]

The wagon mentioned here appears to be the means of transporting the equipment of the production rather than the means of staging the show. The 'Stage' is recorded as a separate item presumably needing to be 'fitted up' using 'the Ioyners tooles & other ymplementes'. So, John Sands was William Sands' son. Another son is recorded as 'William Sands the yonger' in the *Quarter Sessions Orders* at Beaminster, Dorset in 1630, where:

complaint was made vnto this Court that William Sands the elder Iohn Sands and William Sands the yonger doe wander vp and downe the Countrey and about nine others of their Company with certaine blasphemous shewes and sights which they exercise by way of poppett playinge contrary to the Statute. made against such vnlawfull wanderers.[79]

One of the reasons behind the growth in popularity of the puppet show in the early seventeenth century was conditioned by the prohibition placed on the performance of plays that dealt with aspects of the Catholic faith. An example of such prohibited content may be seen in instructions contained in the document sent by the ecclesiastical commissioners at York to the bailiff, burgesses and others at Wakefield in May 1576. Here, the commissioners effectively sought to censor:

a plaie commonlie called Corpus Christi plaie which hath bene heretofore used there, wherein they are done t'understand that there be many thinges used which tende to the derogation of the Majestie and glorie of God, the prophanation of the sacramentes and the maunteynaunce of superstition and idolatrie, the said Commissioners decreed a lettere to be written and sent to the baylyffe, burgesses and other the inhabitantes of the said towne of Wakefeld that in the said playe no pageant be used or set furthe wherein the Ma^rye of God the Father, God the Sonne, or God the Holie Ghoste or the administration of either the Sacramentes of baptisme or of the Lordes Supper be counterfyted or represented, or anythinge plaied which tende to the maintenaunce of superstition and idolatrie or which be contrarie to the lawes of God ~~and~~ or of the realme.[80]

Since puppet shows were clearly not stage plays it was argued by the performers with puppets that their shows should not be prohibited as stage plays. The authorities at Beaminster, Dorset clearly responded differently to the 'poppett playinge' of Sands.

A further relative of Sands might have been Henry Sands, who was granted 'A license to Henry Sands, Alexander Baker & Robert Smedlyy to shew a motion called the *Creation of the World* for a y^r. 18 Sept. 3.^li'.[81] The *Corporation Clerks' Memoranda Book* for 25 October 1624 at Gloucester records that Henry Sands sought permission from the mayor to perform 'vnder Sir Henry Harberts hand & seale'.[82] *The Dramatic Records of Sir Henry Herbert* record the granting of this licence in 1623 as 'to show a motion called *the Creation of the World*'.[83] Two other puppeteers, Robert Tayler and Ann Mossock, players 'who came by warrant' to Coventry 'to shew the worldes Creation', are also recorded in receipt of payment in 1638: 'paid given to Robert Tayler and Ann Mossock, players who came by warrant to shew the worldes Creation the 12th. of Iuly 1638. iij s iiij d.'[84] In 1639 the *Creation of the World* was also performed by another puppeteer named Christopher Tomson who was 'Paid given to Christopher Tomson the 20th of february who came with Commission to shew the Creation of the world xiij s. iiij d.'[85] References to 'motions' in the accounts of Jonson and the licence granted to Henry Sands form part of the growth in use of this term in respect of puppetry from the late sixteenth century. The word alluded to a broad range of examples from mechanical ones to those involving glove puppets. The earliest use of the term appears to be in 1573 when recorded in the *Privy Council Minutes* for 14 July: 'A letter to the Lord Mayour of London to permitte libertie to certein Italian plaiers to make shewe of an instrument of strainge motiones within the Citie'.[86] An account some five days later in the same *Privy Council Minutes* indicates some regret that the first letter had not received a favourable response: 'A letter to the Lord Mayour to graunt libertie to certein Italians to make shewe of an instrument there, mervel-ing that he did it not at their first request'.[87] Does 'an instrument of strainge motiones' refer to puppetry or is this a mechanical device? Use of the word 'instrument' does not necessarily refer to mechanical motion, for the reference to the puppets 'Ioly Walte and Malkyng', cited earlier, refers to 'instruments of play'. However, use of the word 'strainge' does not indicate puppets but some sort of relatively unusual mechanical device. The same point may be made with reference to 'an artificiall motion to be shewed' as recorded in the *Licence of Court of Aldermen* in 1588:

This daye at the request of ye right honorable Sr Thom^{a}s Henage knight Vicechambleyn of her ma^{ties} howsehould yt is orderyd that Henricke Iohnson of Vtright [Utrecht] szstraunger shall durynge the pleasure of ye Co^{r}te & in the daye time only make shewe of an artificiall motion of his own devise to such of thinhabitant*es* of this Cyttye & others shalbe willynge to see the same.[88]

Use of the word 'artificiall' to describe the term 'motion' again indi-cates something other than puppets. Synonymity and difference is alluded to in the following prohibition from Cambridge in 1610–12, where the *Acta curiae* records:

Cancellario magistris et Scholaribus not to sett vpp or shewe any publique interlude motion or puppett playe or any other shewe by his maiesties letters prohibited, within Cambridge or the compasse of v myle/. he is admonished to departe presently without any more.[89]

Such an alternative 'motion' to puppets occurs in the *Chamberlains' and Wardens' Account Book* 11 at Coventry for 1624. Here the concern is for a 'Musicall Organ' with what appears to be moving figures: 'Paid which was given to Bartholomew Cloys being allowed by the Maister of the Revells for shewing a Musicall Organ with divers strang and rare Motions in September last as appeareth by a Bill vnder Maister Maiores hand vs.'[90] Bartholomew Cloys' device and its use was registered by the Master of the Revels the year before in 1623: 'On the 27th of August 1623, a license was granted to Barth. Cloys with three Assistants to make show of a *Musical Organ*, with divers motions in it'.[91] Among many letters in the correspondence between John Chamberlain and Dudley Carlton is one that refers to a performance at the masque to celebrate the wedding of John Ramsay, Viscount Hadlington, and Elizabeth, daughter of Robert, Earl of Sussex. Here, Chamberlain says of the event: 'I can send you no perfect relation of the marriage nor masque on Tuesday, only they say all, but especially the motions, were well performed.'[92] Such concern for the quality of performance suggests that it might have been potentially variable. Of itself, this also indicates use of puppets rather than mechanical devices.

The *Chamberlains' and Wardens' Account Book* III at Coventry for 1638 and 1639 respectively records visits of several puppeteers and their shows. Payment to the puppeteers of a motion titled the *worldes abuses* is recorded in 1638: 'paid given to Robert Browne, Georg Hall & Richard Iones players by warrant, who had a motion to shew expressing the worldes abuses the. 12th: of Ianuary last by bill vnder maister Maiors hand xij s.'[93] Although the term 'motion' appears to have been well established by 1619, a variation in the form of an 'Italian motion' is recorded at this time in the *Leicester Chamberlains' Accounts*: 'Item, given to the Playors that shewed Etalion Motion x[s].'[94] What was an Italian motion? Was it different from existing notions of motions? Was it that such motions were performed by Italians? Or was the content or style Italian? There are no clear answers to these questions, although it does appear that it might have been possible to create an Italian motion even if the puppeteers were not Italian. At Norwich the *Mayors' Court Books* XX *for 1639 record that permission to play an Italian motion was refused on the grounds that the work was created in London:*

Robert Browne and George Hall Did this Day exhibit a lycence from Sir Henry Herbert master of the Revelles to shewe an Italian motion but because he sayth his motion is noe Italian motion but made in London this Court thinkes fitt not to suffer them to shewe.[95]

Does it follow, therefore, that an Italian motion is one that comes from Italy? Or is the response at Norwich a parochial one concerned with local reasons for turning down Browne and Hall? Thomas Maskell does not appear to have suffered the same fate at Norwich in 1635 when the *Mayors' Court Books* XX record that 'Thomas Maskell did this day bringe a lycence from the Master of the Revelles Dated the xx[th] of Iune last past to sett forth an Italian motion, hee hath leaue so to doe till Tuseday night next & no longer'.[96] Is the content of an Italian motion concerned with Italian stories and characters? Does the content consist of *commedia dell'arte* material? Little evidence exists to answer these questions but the *Chamberlains' and Wardens' Account Book* II at Coventry for 1632 records payment for an Italian motion that consists of 'divers & sundry storyes': 'Paid to William Costine Thomas Hunter Henry ffussell with theire assistantes Licenced to set forth and shew an Italiann motion with divers & sundry storyes in it the 25th of September 1632 as appeareth by a Bill x s'.[97]

The following year, the same performers are recorded at Coventry in setting 'forth an Italian motion'.[98] Also at Coventry in 1640, Anthony Barker was paid when he 'brought Commission to shew an Italian motion & vaulting'.[99] Apart from the one refusal to permit playing of an Italian motion at Norwich there do not appear to be restrictions placed on performers from England in playing Italian motions. However, the normal restrictions placed upon travelling players did affect puppet players and players of motions. Newly emergent records collected and collated by the *REED* project demonstrate just how widely practised puppetry had become by the sixteenth and seventeenth centuries. Many records of payments to puppeteers exist that have not been enumerated here for there are simply too many of them. Additional impetus to the practice of puppetry clearly developed in relation to post-Reformation conditions that inhibited or suppressed Catholicism.

CHAPTER 7

Substitution

Evidence of medieval theatrical artifice exists to demonstrate use of artificial substitutions in replacing mutilated or amputated parts of the body. Such evidence also includes reference to the substitution of real bodies with dummies. Given the nature of the evidence in this area a key question is: To what extent is verisimilitude important in substitution? Is the mutilation or amputation intended to convince the audience of its realism? Is there any theatrical sleight of hand involved in such substitution? Does the audience know that it is witnessing substitution? If so, what does this mean?

Some accounts, particularly those in the form of explicit stage directions, are unequivocal in respect of substitution by dummies or dummy parts. Other stage directions are explicit in terms of dummy substitution through the action of the play. For instance, in *The Croxton Play of the Sacrament* (*c.* 1461) a dummy hand is used to develop a situation that is not derived from the biblical narrative but from a legend concerning the desecration of the Host by a group of Jews who eventually repent their actions and are converted to Christianity. Such stories were common throughout Europe from the fourteenth century. In *The Croxton Play of the Sacrament* when Jonathas' hand cannot be removed from 'þe Ost in hys hond' his fellows, Jason, Jasdon, Mashat and Malchas attempt to nail 'þe Ost' to a post it order to remove it.[1] At this point an explicit stage direction declares: 'Heres hall [here shall] thay pluke þe arme, and þe hond shall hang styll with þe Sacrament.'[2] The arm is ripped away from what is a dummy hand, which remains stuck to the nailed Host. The dummy hand and 'þe Ost' are still attached. Further attempts to separate 'þe Ost' from Jonathas' hand involve the attempted separation and destruction of the Host by boiling the two in a cauldron of oil. This attempted solution does not work and so resort is made to casting the hand and Host into an oven. An explicit stage direction requires the oven to 'ryve asunder' and out of the riven oven appears an image of Christ.

Jesus persuades Jonathas that he should 'wasshest thyn hart with grete contrycion' by putting 'hys hand into þe cawdron, and yt shalbe hole agayn'.³ This is indeed what happens. Jonathas presumably pushes his real hand through his sleeve to reveal the miracle.

A similar story that deals with Jewish outrages is contained in the thirteenth-century *Legenda aurea* (*The Golden Legend*) during the episode of the *Assumption of the Virgin*. In this retelling of the narrative of the *Assumption* Jocobus de Voragine tells how the Jews attempted to stop the burial ceremony of the Virgin and of their ultimate forgiveness and conversion. Here it is recorded that:

Tunc ad arma *om*nes concurrerunt et se mutuo hortabantur dicentes. Ven[i]te omnes discipulos occidamus. ac corpus illud quod seductorem illum portrauit ignibus co*m*buramus. Princeps aut*em* sacerdotu*m* hoc videns obstupuit. et ira repletus ait. Ecce tabernaculum illius qui nos et genus nostru*m* co*n*turbauit qualem glam nu*n*c accipit. Et hoc dice*n*s manus ad feretru*m* misit vol*e*ns illud euertere et ac ad terra*m* deducere. Tu*n*c manus eius subito ambe arruerunt. et lectulo adhaeseru*n*t. ita vt ad lectulu*m* manibus penderet. et nimio cruciatu vexatus lamentabiliter eiularet. Reliquus aut*em* poplius ab angelis qui erant in nubibus caecitate percussus est.⁴

At once they hurried to take arms and exhorted each other, saying: 'Come on, let us kill all those disciples and burn the body that bore the seducer.' The chief priest, seeing what was happening, was astounded and filled with rage, and said: 'Look at the tabernacle of that man who disturbed us and our people so much! Look at the glory that is now paid to that woman!' After saying this he put his hands on the litter, intending to overturn it and throw the corpse to the ground. But suddenly his hands withered and stuck to the bier, so that he was hanging by his hands; and he moaned and cried in great pain, while the rest of the people were stricken with blindness by angels who were in the cloud.

This incident is contained in the *Assumption of Mary* in *The N-Town Play* (late fifteenth century) where the Jews attempt to seize Mary's body from the Apostles. When the 'Primus Princeps' attempts to take hold of the bier, upon which Mary rests, his hands stick to it. An explicit stage direction states: 'Hic saltat insanus a[d] feretrum Marie et pendet per manus'⁵ [Here he dances madly towards Mary on her bier and hangs by the hand]. There is no precise moment indicated by the text when the hand of the 'Primus Princeps' is released or made whole again but in order to do this Petrus requires that he should 'beleue in Jesu Criste, oure Saveyour', wherepon, the 'Primus Princeps' states: 'I beleue in Jesu, mannys saluacyon.' Presumably, the hand is released at this point. In this version of the story there is no apparent need for the use of a false hand, for the actor concerned merely releases his hand at the appropriate moment. Similarly, in the ceremony of the *Assumption of the Virgin* at Elche, Spain, which continues to this day, the point at which the chief Jew's hands stick to the bier is simulated by the actor who mimes the action, and his hands remain about a foot away from the bier in a stylised manner as if held back by a 'force field'. However, the same incident is given theatrical form in the *Bourges Effects* for the *Mystery of the Acts of the Apostles* in 1536. Here, the description is translated as follows:

The Jews try to get hold of the Virgin Mary's body to take it from the apostles, and immediately their hands wither and they are blinded by the fire the angels throw (*gectent*) at them. Belzeray [*a Jewish prince*] puts his hands on the litter on which the Virgin Mary is being carried, and his hands remain attached to the said litter and much fire in the form of lightning (*fouldre*) is thrown at them, and the Jews must fall to the ground, blinded. Belzeray's hands must be detached and joined back onto his arms. Then he is given the palm which he carries to the others, by which those who wanted to believe were enlightened (*illuminez*), then he brought back the said palm.[6]

In this instance the Jew is named Belzeray and it is stated that his hands 'must be detached and joined back onto his arms'. This episode as contained in the *Legenda aurea* is also the presumed content of the *Play of Fergus* in the *York Cycle*. 'Fergus' is the name given to the character who is 'Belzeray' in the Bourges account and the 'Primus Princeps' in the *N-Town* version. The play itself has not survived but a document contained in the *A/Y Memorandum Book* at York for 1432 records attempts by the Goldsmiths to relieve themselves of the responsibility of their play of *Herod*. They pass on the play to the Masons, who appear to have been ready to accept it since they found their other play of the *Death and Burial of the Virgin* to have been unsatisfactory:

Ex altera parte vero quia Cementarij huius ciuitatis murmurabant inter se de pagina sua in ludo corporis christi vbi ffergus fflagellatus erat pro eo quod materia pagine illius in sacra non continetur scriptura & magis risum & clamorem causabat quam deuocionem Et quandoque lites contenciones & pugne inde proueniebant in populo ipsamque paginam suam raro vel nunquam potuerunt producere & ludere clara die sicut faciunt pagine precedentes ipsi igitur Cementarij affectabant desiderio magno ab huius modi pagina sua exonerari & alteri assignari que conueniens est scripture sacre. & quam producere & ludere poterunt clara die.[7]

On the other hand, indeed, the Masons of this city have been accustomed to murmur among themselves about their pageant in the Corpus Cristi Play in which Fergus was beaten because the subject of this pageant is not contained in the sacred scripture and used to produce more noise and laughter than devotion. And whenever quarrels, disagreements, and fights used to arise among the people from this, they have rarely or never been able to produce their pageant and to play in daylight.

The *Pageant of Fergus* is recorded in the *Ordo paginarum* in 1415 at York by Roger Burton, the common clerk. The list is a register of plays and their guilds to be performed in the annual play of *Corpus Christi*. At this time, the *Play of Fergus* is assigned to the Linenweavers: 'Quatuor Apostoli . . . Marie et fergus pendens super feretrum . . . is Iudeis cum vno Angelo'[8] [Four apostles carrying the bier of Mary, and Fergus hanging upon the bier with two oth*er* Jews and one angel]. Subsequently the play was taken over by the Masons who, in turn, relinquished it in 1432. It is not until 1476, some forty-four years later, that the pageant is again recorded, and by this time it had again become the responsibility of the Linenweavers.[9] Although this may be gleaned from the *Ordo paginarum*, the word *Lynweuers* is written over an erasure in a much later hand. The Linenweavers again drop the play in 1485 when the play is to be 'laid apart'. Even so, they are fined in 1486 for not playing it. Why might it have been claimed that the *Pageant of Fergus* was one that produced more noise and laughter than devotion? Was this due to the content of the play? Was the response dictated by the nature of the performance? What created the quarrels, disagreements and fights? Given that the Masons inherited the play of *Herod* from the Goldsmiths in 1432 it may be presumed that the Masons possessed the capacity to perform the play. It is possible from the context of the Goldsmiths' document that the resultant response arose because the subject of this pageant did not originate from sacred scripture. Such a response may have been founded in a theological sensitivity of the day. Did this prevent the subject of the play being credible? Did the quarrels, disagreements and fights occur out of arguments concerning the legitimacy of the content? Was the noise and laughter created at the expense of the performance or did it arise out of comic portrayal? Were these responses sought? Did the performance create such responses because it happened in darkness? Noise and laughter might have occurred because of a discrepancy between perceived realities dictated by performance conditions. In other words, the audience may not have been able to see that which they were intended to see, or directed to see. Another possibility for such audience responses concerns the content of the play in respect of the hand becoming stuck to the bier. This incident, without the authority of sacred scriptures, may have taxed the belief of the audience, and this physically simple act may have

produced slapstick overtones. Whether such potential disparity is consciously or unconsciously intended, the audience response may be the
same. Certainly, this incident is regarded as a consciously comic one
serving to divide performances of a two-day presentation of the *Auto de
la Asunción de Nuestra Señora* (sixteenth century: the incident itself
possibly fifteenth century).[10] A version of the incident, which appears to
be contemporaneous with that of the *Play of Fergus*, is the Catalonian
Assumpció de madona Sta. Maria, which was performed in Prades (in
either Tarragona or across the Pyrenees in France in the early fifteenth
century).[11] Here, the action of the play is thought to have been performed
on a stage consisting of at least five mansions representing the cabin of the
Jews, Hell, Paradise, the Virgin's house and the tomb. In this version the
Jews first pretend to be asleep and then they attack Mary's bed, whereupon the Rabí becomes stuck to it and is unable to release himself. The
other Jews are blinded. As with other examples, the Rabí must acknow-
ledge God, Jesus and Mary and kiss Mary's bed before he and the others
can be absolved of their afflictions.

A revealing account of the staging of this incident is contained in the
Volume of Secrets of a Provençal Stage Director's Book. Here, many of the
techniques are referred to as tricks thus creating the theatrical stance of
illusion and deception. The account reads:

> Ha fa la fin[ta]
> d'aquel que donet [lo]
> soflet a Nostra Da[ma]
> no qual mas que p[renga]
> un bras contrafach ala
> margo e que quant [li]
> aura donat lo soflet,
> que retire son bras e [que]
> faça sali lo contrafa[ch]
> e faça sa[nc]
> pel trovat.[12]

To do the trick of the man who strikes Our Lady, all that is necessary is to hold a
fake arm in the sleeve, and after the blow he pulls his arm back [inside the
sleeve], drops the fake one, and bleeds on the stage.

Later references to the implied use of false limbs are contained in
Edmond Ironside; or, War Hath Made All Friends (*c.* 1595). Explicit stage
directions require amputations to be conducted by Stich on behalf of
Canutus.[13] This action is carried out on the two 'Pledges' because their

'fathers did abuse theire tongues in periurye'. Stich has entered according to a stage direction 'wth an Axe'. In quick succession further stage directions determine that: 'Hee cutts offe one hand' and then 'Hee Cutts offe the other hande.' Four lines later another stage direction determines that 'Hee Cutts off his Nose.' Within the next eight lines '2 Pledge' is given the same treatment. A stage direction states: 'Hee Cutts his hand*es* and Nose.' The amputated '1 Pledge' refers to 'theis my stumpes' which are presumably held up in front of his face after chopping off his nose. Canutus permits this possibility by saying: 'Cutt off his nose then lett him praye againe.' Presumably, false hands extend beyond the length of partially sewn-up sleeve endings in order to produce 'stumpes'. It is less certain whether false noses were involved.

A stage direction in *The Tragedy of Claudius Tiberius Nero* of 1607 requires the two imprisoned and hungry characters, Nero and Drusus, to perform the following actions: 'They eate each others armes.' Presumably, false arms are used to fulfil the requirement and presented in such a way as to disguise the substitution.[14] Further macabre treatment is dispensed when Shacklesoule burns off the hand of Rauillac with a 'burning torch' in Thomas Dekker's *If This Be Not a Good Play* (1611).[15] An explicit stage direction determines: 'Enter Shacklesoule with a burning torch, and a long knife.' A few lines later, another stage direction states: 'Hand burn't off'.

In both the above examples, hands are severed. Do the audiences witness the severances? The respective texts are not clear in this respect. In *Edmond Ironside* the amputation at the wrist enables '1 Pledge' to refer to 'theis my stumpes'. Presumably, the audience was allowed to see these. If this is the case then the audience was similarly able to witness the 'before' and 'after' conditions, i.e. '1 Pledge' both with and without his hands. Even if the audience did not witness the feigned chopping off of hands some stage business concerned with hiding the real hands and the retrieval of false hands would have been necessary to manipulate the conditions in producing the 'stumpes'.

Not all Assumption plays include the incident in which the hand of the Jew sticks to Mary's bier but the *Valencia Assumption Play* of the early fifteenth century does include that which might be regarded as the simplest of theatrical sleight-of-hand techniques through substitution. This is not sleight of hand in the conventional sense of 'close manipulation' but it is that theatrical condition that enables an audience to 'see it' and 'not see it'. This is achieved through a simple staging device in which an 'image', or dummy figure, replaces the body of Mary in its ascent to heaven. The apparatus by which the ascent takes place is known as the 'araceli'. The staging routine that promotes the substitution is outlined as follows:

When Christ has spoken, Mary shall fall into the arms of the handmaidens as if dead (*faent com es morta*). Meantime there is to be loud thunder, and they are to place Mary beneath the stage (*devall lo cadafal*). And they are to carry up the image (*la ymage*) and say all the rest of the office.

On the second day of the play (*en la segona iornada*), after St Michael has returned the soul to the body, those who are beneath the stage (*devall lo cadafal*) are to receive the image quickly and make thunder and smoke, and the living person (*la viva*) is to emerge suddenly.

. . .

Then the angels, apostles, and everybody else are to crowd round Christ and Mary, and thunder and smoke are to be made, and Christ and Mary are to exit. And at once the lifting machinery (*la ara celi*) is to rise.[16]

The translation above does not quite convey the intention behind the act of 'everybody else' crowding round Christ and Mary. Here, the intention is that the crowd mask Christ and Mary so that they may depart without being seen. The thunder and smoke are not only intended as a contribution to the illusion but also as a distraction from the staged deception. Presumably, their destination is 'beneath the stage (*devall lo cadafal*)'.

A similar substitution of the Virgin Mary, in this instance played by an eleven-year-old boy, takes place today in the ceremony of the *Assumption of the Virgin* at Elche. The boy, as Mary, is placed on the bier with the apostles surrounding and masking him from the audience. Whereupon, the bier containing the boy is tipped up in such a way that he slides off it into a space beneath the platform. The 'araceli' descends from the roof of the Basilica and is permitted to drop into the space that was occupied by the bier below the platform. In turn, the 'araceli' rises to Heaven (through a square hole in the ceiling of the Basilica) with the substituted image of Mary.[17]

Although theatrical sleight of hand is frequently sought through manipulation of that which is seen and that which is not seen, the means by which it is achieved is often conducted 'secretly'. In the *Rouergue Judgement Play* (fifteenth century) dummies are substituted in the torture of the damned:

Then shall be prepared the throne (*cadieyra*) of Pride, and the devils come out of Hell leading Pride all dressed in fine clothes and a collar round the neck. And they set her on the throne and secretly they must put there a dummy figure made to look like her. And let him who plays Pride position himself behind the throne, and the devils shall torture the said person in silence.[18]

A similar stance to such artifice through secrecy occurs in the *Bourges Effects* of the *Mystery of the Acts of the Apostles* (1536):

There must be a nude (*ung nud*) or a body (*une carnacion*) for the flaying of St Bartholomew.

St Bartholomew shall be placed on a revolving table (*une table tornisse*) with a nude (*ung nud*) underneath, and when he is covered with a cloth the table must be turned secretly.[19]

In addition to this effect 'Several other dead bodies should appear in the water (*venir sur l'eaue*) moved by the waves, which can then disappear under the stage (*retirer soubz terre*) when it is time.' Also, dummies are substituted for Cidrat, Titon and Aristarcus when they are burned: 'There must be a pillar near Paradise to which Cidrat, Titon, and Aristarcus will be fastened to be burnt, and the said pillar shall be sited over a trapdoor (*sur une trappe*) and three dummy bodies fastened to the pillar in their place, surrounded by faggots.'[20]

During the battle sequence in the Mercade *Vengeance* (late fifteenth century) dummies are recorded to represent dead bodies:

And they raise the siege ladders, and it shall last as long as seems appropriate; and they throw [down] dummy bodies dressed like some of those inside the town. In addition, at the foot of the walls, the besieged must pull inside the walls one or two of the attackers and make a show of killing them: and then they must throw down dummy bodies dressed like those who were dragged to their death.[21]

A particularly gruesome sequence is recorded in the French *St Lawrence Play* in 1499. Even if audience members were conscious of the use of a dummy in the production of this effect the dramatic intent is sufficiently vicious for the power of the action to take over from any awareness of artifice:

Then they attach two horses to the hands in addition to the two which are at Ypolite's feet. And after he has been dragged on a hurdle across the playing area (*champ*) by the first two horses, he speaks what follows. And then when he has spoken, the torturers put a dummy, similar to him, in his place, to which they attach the four horses, one to each limb.

[Speech by Ypolite]

Then the torturers exchange and put a dummy in the place of Ypolite under the protection (?*custodes*) of the scaffold (*eschaffault*), and do not move . . .

[Dialogue in Paradise. The torturers each mount a horse.]

Then each one individually spurs his horse and drags away his limb of the dummy.

[Dialogue.][22]

Dummy 'souls' appear as doll-size representations in a number of accounts. A stage direction in the the text of *La Passion de Semur* of 1488 records: 'Here the soul descends and comes on a wire (*fillium*) onto the body in the tomb.'[23] The *Volume of Secrets of a Provençal Stage Director's Book* records a particularly vivid description concerning the hanging of Judas where a dummy soul and attendant entrails are allowed to fall from under his shirt:

> e que agues una
> arma que la lay-
> ses ana aitabe,
> e los diables
> venria que
> sarion jost el
> que amasarion
> las tripas e l'a-
> rma e ho po-
> rtaria en Ifern,
> e pueis venria
> serqua lo cors.[24]

there would be a soul that should also be allowed to go, and the devils would come, who would be below, and that they collect the intestines and the soul and bring them to Hell, and then will come to pick up the body.

The same effect is recorded in *Michel's Passion* for 1486: 'Here Judas bursts at the belly and the guts fall out and the soul comes out.'[25] The *Bourges Effects* for the *Mystery of the Acts of the Apostles* record similar treatment to St Barnabas: 'There must be wood to burn St Barnabas who will be bound to a cartwheel (*une roe de chareste*), and there must be a dummy corpse full of bones and entrails.'[26]

Yet another account of the same effect occurs in the *Modane Antichrist Play* where it is required that there shall be: 'two dummy bodies to rip or saw through the middle, from which shall come out entrails and blood and which will look as much as possible like the two Jesuits. And the officials (*syndics*) will supply the flesh of the said bodies and the pig skins and shall take back the said flesh afterwards.'[27]

Concern to produce realistic effects is not only found in the severance of limbs and simulated human entrails but also in decapitation or, as it is often termed, decollation. Different levels of reality may be inferred from available evidence. In some instances, decapitation is part of the dramatic narrative and finds its resolution through manipulated staging conditions, and in other cases it exists as part of the juggler's repertoire in the form of a trick involving sleight of hand.

In the *Majorca SS Crispin and Crispinian* (sixteenth century; possibly earlier) the two saints are beheaded: 'Llevar-los an los caps. Y a on steran y aurà dos cosos morts, que feran de bulto, plens de palla, y los caps de duas màscaras molt gentils.'[28] [They are to be beheaded. Where they are standing, there are to be two dead bodies which are to be dummies filled with straw, and the heads are to be made with masks with calm expressions.] The *Majorca Judith* (sixteenth century; possibly earlier) records:

Holofernes is to be sleeping in his bed; and there is to be made a head like his, so that it can be held and cut from a dummy body (*una stàtua*). And kneeling, she says: [prays to God]. Now she shall get up, take his knife, which is to be on the bolster, and taking the head by its hair, she says: [prays to God]. After these words, she is to cut off Holofernes' head and take it to the servant.[29]

Severed heads for St James and Josias are required properties in the *Bourges Effects*.[30] Further severed heads appear in the property list of the St George Play, Turin, in 1429.[31] The dummy heads are those of St Marcellin, St Cladien, St Cirin and St Anthony 'whom Dacien first beheaded'. Payment is recorded for the white paint required to paint 'the faces of the [false] heads'. In total the play required eleven severed heads complete with wigs and beards.[32]

In Thomas Dekker's *The Virgin Martyr* (1620) a stage direction requires that Dorothea's head be removed: 'Her head strucke off'.[33] The editor of John Marston's *The Insatiate Countess* of 1610 records the fate of Isabella: 'The executioner strikes off her head.'[34] In *Apius and Virginia* (1564) by R. B. [Richard Bower?], a stage direction requires of Virginius: 'Here let him profer a blowe' to his kneeling daughter, Virginia.[35] Another stage direction, some four lines later, instructs: 'Here tye a handcarcher aboute hir eyes, and then strike of hir heade.' Seemingly a dummy head is used, for Comfort says: 'Nomore Sir knight, but take the head, and wende a while with me.' If the 'handcarcher' is still in place at this point then imitation of the real head is made easier because the 'handcarcher' helps to define the head for the audience. One of two watermen in the *Two Lamentable Tragedies* by Robert Yarington (1601) trips over a bag lying on the floor. A stage direction states: 'Taking the Sack by the end, one of the legs and head drops out.'[36] The sack is likened to a 'hangman's budget' by waterman number one. The head is described by him as having 'many wounds' and that 'hoase and shooes' are still 'remaining on the legs'. This kind of specific detail implies false body parts to satisfy these descriptions.

Although not informed by an explicit stage direction, the intention of the narrative is clear in Fletcher and Massinger's *Sir John van Olden Barnavelt* (1619) in relation to Barnavelt's execution.[37] A kneeling Barnavelt invites the executioner to perform his task by saying: 'now: now: now I present –'. After the execution the executioner asks: 'is it well done mine Heeres?' The reply states: 'somewhat too much: yo^u haue strooke his fingers too'. The implication is that Barnavelt lays his hands at the side of his head on the block in a kneeling position. Whether the head and fingers are seen as false body parts by the audience is unclear.

In *Mankind* (*c.* 1465–70), Myscheff declares that 'I xall smytt of þi hede and sett yt on agayn.'[38] A few lines later he claims that 'I kan choppe yt of and make yt agayn.' Although this intention may be no more than a comic threat to remove the head of one of the three Ns and restore it within the narrative, the capacity to fulfil this action may have some basis in known juggling practice. Girolamo Cardano in his *De svbtilitate* of 1550 refers to the jugglers' repertoire as being extensive. With regard to decapitation he writes: 'Puerum sine capite, caput sine puero ostendunt, uiuunt tamen omnia, & nihil detrimenti puer patitur interim.'[39] [They show a boy without a head and a head without a boy, yet both of them are alive, and the boy suffers no harm in the meantime.]

In 1570, Ludwig Lavater (1527–86) published his *De spectris, lemuribus et magnis atque insolitis fragoribus etc.* in Geneva. The work was translated into English in 1572 by Robert Harrison and published in London as *Of ghostes and spirites walking by nyght, and of strange noyses, crackes etc.* A range of jugglers' skills is detailed here in this work and its translation. Lavater was born in Zurich and became a theologian who was ordained in 1549. He became the vicar of Horgen and later the Archdeacon of Zurich cathedral. In Harrison's translation, he says:

It is well knowne, a mans sight maye be so deceiued, that he verily thinkes that one deuoureth a sword, spitteth out money, coales, and suche like: that one eateth breade, and spitteth foorth meale: one drinketh wine, which after runneth out of his forehead: that one cutteth of his felowes head, which afterwardes he setteth on agayne: and that a cocke seemeth to drawe after hym a huge beame of tymber. &c. Moreouer it may be brought to passe by naturall things, as by perfumes and suche like, that a man woulde sweare in earnest, that all men sitting at the table wyth him, haue no heds at al, or else that they are like the heads of asses: & that som times a vine spreadeth it self as it were ouer al the house, when in deed it is a mere deceit, or a plain iuggling cast. Of whiche matter there be bookes commonly set abrode.[40]

These accounts of Cardano and Lavater pre-date that of Reginald Scot in his *Discouerie of witchcraft* of 1584, in which he explains the trick 'which the iugglers call the decollation of Iohn Baptist' (Figure 7.1). This description and the trick that it outlines have become the standard account of early forms of this trick from which later ones have been derived and developed. Cardano's account indicates knowledge of the trick in Italy in 1550. Lavater's description suggests that it was known in Switzerland in 1570. Lavater was able to claim that the trick of taking off someone's head and restoring it to its normal state was one: 'Of whiche matter there be bookes comonly set abrode'. If this was so, the books were ones available to him in his native Switzerland. No English works appear to have survived from 1572 or earlier.

Scot's *Discouerie of witchcraft* is generally regarded as the earliest extant work on the approaches and methods of early jugglers. He wrote the work, in part, to expose the growing mythology surrounding that which was being passed off as caused by supernatural forces. Scot wanted to assert that jugglers created these effects by conscious, deliberate and purposeful skill. Hence, the tricks were 'discovered', that is, 'revealed'. Scot outlines the trick as follows:

To cut off ones head, and to laie it in a platter, &c: which the iugglers call the decollation of Iohn Baptist.

To shew a most notable execution by this art, you must cause a boord, a cloth, and a platter to be purposelie made, and in each of them holes fit for a boies necke. The boord must be made of two planks, the longer and broader the better: there must be left within halfe a yard of the end of each planke halfe a hole; so as both planks being thrust togither, there may remaine two holes, like to the holes in a paire of stocks: there must be made likewise a hole in the tablecloth or carpet. A platter also must be set directlie ouer or vpon one of them, hauing a hole in the middle thereof, of the like quantitie, and also a peece cut out of the same, so big as his necke, through which his head may be conueied into the middest of the platter: and then sitting or kneeling vnder the boord, let the head onlie remaine vpon the boord in the same. Then (to make the sight more dredfull) put a little brimstone into a chafing dish of coles, setting it before the head of the boie, who must gaspe two or three times, so as the smoke enter a little into his nostrils and mouth (which is not vnholsome) and the head presentlie will appeare starke dead; if the boie set his countenance accordinglie: and if a little bloud be sprinkled on his face, the sight will be the stranger.

This is commonlie practised with a boie instructed for that purpose, who being familiar and conuersant with the companie, may be knowne as well by his face, as by his apparell. In the other end of the table, where the like hole is made, an other boie of the bignesse of the knowne boie must be placed, hauing vpon him his vsuall apparell: he must leane or lie vpon the boord, and his head vnder the boord through the said hole, so as his bodie shall seeme to lie on the one end of the boord, and his head shall lie in a platter on the other end. There are other things which might be performed in this action, the more to astonish the beholders, which because they offer long descriptions, I omit: as to put about his necke a little dough kneded with bullocks bloud, which being cold will appeare like dead flesh; & being pricked with a sharpe round hollow quill, will bleed, and seeme verie strange, &c. Manie rules are to be obserued herein, as to haue the table cloth so long and wide as it may almost touch the ground. Not to suffer the companie to staie too long in the place, &c.[41]

Although Scot's description gives the gist of the deception involved and method employed there is insufficient information divulged to enable the trick to be performed. Such is the case with many so-called explanations of tricks that are apparently designed to let the reader in on the secret(s) of the trick. However, some additional information is provided by William Vincent in his 1634 edition of *Hocvs Pocvs Ivnior* when he adds that the platter 'must, as also the table, be made to take in two peeces'.[42] If this were not the case there would be a sizeable gap between the boy's neck and the rim of the hole in the platter. Having the platter made in this way ought to ensure that the platter fits snugly around the boy's neck. Vincent also stresses the need for secrecy in setting up the basic situation by saying: 'Let no body be present while you doe this, neither when you have given entrance, permit any to be medling, nor let them tarry long'.[43]

David Calderwood, in his *The History of the Kirk of Scotland* for 1540, records that James Wedderburne

had a good gift of poesie, and made diverse comedies and tragedies in the Scotish tongue, wherein he nipped the abuses and superstitioun of the time. He composed in forme of tragedie the beheading of Johne the Baptist, which was acted at the West Port of Dundie, wherin he carped roughlie the abusses and corruptiouns of the Papists.[44]

What form of surmised 'decollation' took place in this account is unclear but other approaches involving different techniques to that advocated by Scot are recorded such as the one to produce a decollation as described by Richard Johnson in 1556 and published in 1599 in *Hakluyt's*

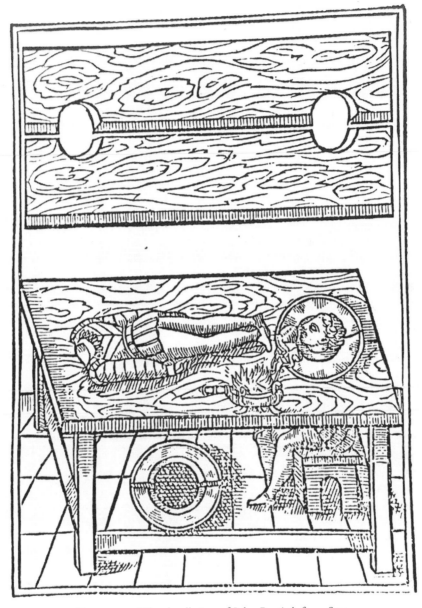

Figure 7.1. 'The decollation of Iohn Baptist', from Scot,
Discouerie of witchcraft, p. 352.

Collection of the Early Voyages. Johnson travelled with '*Steuen Burrowe* in the Serchthrift 1556. and afterwarde among the Samoedes, whose deulish rites he describeth':

Then they made a thing being foure square, and in height and squarenesse of a chaire, and couered with a gown very close the forepart thereof, for the hinder part stood to the tent side. Their tents are rounde and are called Chome in their language. The water still seething on the fire, and this square seate being ready, the Priest put off his shirt, and the thing like a garland which was on his head, with those things which couered his face, & he had on yet all this while a paire of hosen of deeres skins with ye haire on, which came vp to his buttocks. So he went into the square seate, and sate down like a tailour and sang with a strong voyce or halowing. Then they tooke a small line made of deeres skinnes of foure fathoms long, and with a smal knotte the Priest made it fast about his necke, and vnder his left arme, and gaue it vnto two men standing on both sides of him, which held the ends together. Then the kettle of hote water was set before him in the square seat, al this time the square seat was not couered, and then it was couered w^t a gown of broad cloth without lining, such as the Russes do weare. Then the 2. men which did hold ye ends of the line stil standing there, began to draw, & drew til they had drawn the ends of the line stiffe and together, and then I hearde a thing fall into the kettle of water which was before him in the tent. Thereupon I asked them that sate by me what it was that fell into the water that stoode before him. And they answered me, that it was his head, his shoulder and left arme, which the line had cut off, I meane the knot which I sawe afterwarde drawen hard together. Then I rose vp and would haue looked whether it were so or not, but they laid hold on me, and said, that if they should see him with their bodily eyes, they shoulde liue no longer. And the most part of them can speake the Russe tongue to bee vnderstood: and they tooke me to be a Russian. Then they beganne to hallow with these wordes, Oghaoo, Oghaoo, Oghaoo, many times together. And as they were thus singing & out calling, I sawe a thing like a finger of a man two times together thrust through the gowne from the Priest. I asked them that sate next to me what it was that I sawe, and they saide, not his finger; for he was yet dead: and that which I saw appeare through the gowne was a beast, but what beast they knew not nor would not tell. And I looked vpon the gowne, and there was no hole to bee seene: and then at the last the Priest lifted vp his head with his shoulders and arme, and all his bodie, and came forth to the fire . . . And I went to him that serued the Priest, and asked him what their God saide to him when he was dead. Hee answered, that his owne people doeth not know: neither is it for them to know, for they must doe as he commanded.[45]

It appears from this account that Richard Johnson attempts to report faithfully that which he saw and experienced. His observation, however, does not question the action that he reports as juggling activity. He has no inkling of the trick that is being performed. When he does question that which he sees he is placated by religious or quasi-religious reasons as to why he should not investigate the matter. All the individuals of whom he enquires appear to have a confederate relationship with the activity. In other words, they know of the deception that is taking place and provide him with responses to maintain its secrecy. At one level this may be considered to have been a naive response on the part of Johnson. But given the juggling intention of his hosts it is hardly likely that they would allow him to have the deception revealed. It is relatively easy to label responses as naive when the witness or audience does not share in or is not party to the juggling intention. A number of accounts refer to the juggling audience as 'simple people' and they do so with an apparent sense of superiority that arises out of knowledge of the deception. This is not necessarily knowledge of the means of deception; it is simply knowledge of the fact that the deception takes place. Take for instance the comments made by William Lambard in his *A Perambulation of Kent* (1576) where he refers to those people who were deceived by the *Rood of Boxley* as 'the sillie lambes of Gods flocke'.[46] John Gee, in his *The Foot out of the Snare* (1624), compares acts of the Catholic Church with those of 'puppets, apes-faces and gawds' through 'allures, masks, and disguises' and recipients of them as 'the poor silly people'.[47] William Bourne, in his *Inuentions or Deuises* (1578), refers to the communication of sound through 'trunckes of brasse or other mettall' to produce an effect that 'the simple people will maruell at it'.[48] Bourne, later in the same work, refers to responses to mechanical devices as ones 'which the common people would maruell at, thinking that it is done by Inchantment'.[49] Interestingly, those jugglers who write about juggling and those who know about it tend not to refer to their potential audiences as common, silly or simple.

Labels of naivety may be attached inappropriately to individuals or audiences because they do not appreciate or are not made aware of different realities. A number of early writers focus on this condition as a means of explaining the nature of juggling. James Sandford, in his 1569 translation of Heinrich Cornelius Agrippa's 'Of Iuglinge', attempts to explain the nature of it:

But let vs retourne to Magicke, wherof the Juglers skil is a parte also, that is, illusions, which are onely done according to the outwarde apparance: with these Magitiens doo shewe vaine visions, and with Juglinge castes [tricks] doo plaie many miracles, & cause dreams, which thinge is not so much done by *Geoticall* inchauntmentes, and praiers, and deceites of the Deuill, as also with certaine vapours of perfumes, lightes, medicines, colleries, bindinges, & hangings, moreouer with ringes, images, glasses, & other like receites and instruments of Magicke, and with a natural and celestial vertue. There are many thinges done also, with a readie subteltie and nimblenesse of the handes, as wee dayly see stage players and Juglers doo, whiche for that cause we terme *Chirosophi*, that is to saie, hande wise.[50]

The notion that illusions 'are onely done accordinge to the outwarde apparance' presents the beginning of an understanding concerning sleight of hand. Another way of articulating this condition is to consider that one reality stands for another. That which represents the 'outwarde apparance' stands for one reality and that which concerns the illusion represents the other. The likeness of the two realities may be such that they are promoted to become indistinguishable to the audience. The creation of this state is inextricably bound up with the juggler's purpose in the conduct of sleight of hand and misdirection. One of the results of this process is a form of juggled verisimilitude that conditions the nature of illusion. This process also possesses an equivalent in terms of theatrically staged verisimilitude. For instance, such convergence of realities is described in an account of the *Bourges Effects* of the *Mystery of the Acts of the Apostles* in 1536: 'It lasted forty days, and it was so admirably acted (as a contemporary historian assures us) that the greater part of the spectators judged it to be real and not feigned.'[51] The juggler's intention to develop sleight of hand through misdirection may be seen to present a further theatrical equivalent during the *Lucerne Passion Play* in the sixteenth century, in which a crude, but no doubt effective, manoeuvre is graphically described:

Meanwhile Esau sets off hunting, that is, in the Garden of Eden, and when he sees the rabbit (*küngelin*) he speaks to himself and shoots it with a bow or crossbow, not with a gun (*büchsen*); and it can be arranged so, for someone to be lying in the bushes who has a rabbit, and as soon as Esau shoots the live rabbit which he is hunting in the garden this person is to thrust an arrow through the rabbit he has with him and throw it out quickly, as though it were the one Esau shot.[52]

This account suggests that the rabbit is alive when the arrow is thrust through it. Otherwise, the person 'lying in the bushes' could have prepared the dead rabbit earlier. It may appear self-evident that this description refers to conspicuous sleight of hand in order to produce illusion. The sleight of hand does not depend on 'close manipulation' ability but exists through a theatrical equivalent of the juggler's stance to licensed deception. This is theatrical sleight of hand through manipulation of staging conditions. Sometimes stage directions or stage instructions state the necessary prerequisites towards the production of desired effects, where 'skill' is often required to produce likeness to an 'original'. The original may be an object or a person. In the records concerning the *Modane Play of Antichrist* (sixteenth century) there are a number of items that require use of appropriate skill to produce verisimilitude:

Item. They shall make and paint an image looking like Antichrist which by skill they shall make move and alter its lips as a sign it is speaking.
Item. They shall by a device (*par engin*) make an earthquake when necessary with everything possible to make it convincing (*pour lui ressembler*).

. . .

Also, they will make several limbs that look like the limbs of people killed in the battle with the semblance of blood on those thus killed and wounded.

They shall paint five or six souls, and they shall find some means by skill and cunning (*par engin et industrie*) to put out the eyes of the catholic with pointed skewers (*brochettes poignantes*), and to this end they shall make the necessary eyes and false faces or some alternative as skilfully as they can.[53]

Further verisimilitude is indicated in the records concerning the indoor performance in the Household of Miguel Lucas de Iranzo at Jaen in 1461:

In front of the place where the Countess was seated, there then appeared the head of this huge dragon (*serpiente*). It was made of painted wood, and a device inside it (*su artificio*) propelled the boys out through its mouth one by one, and it breathed huge flames at the same time. And the pages, whose tunics, sleeves, and hoods were soaked in spirits (*aguardiente*), came out on fire, and it seemed that they were really being burned up in flames.[54]

The examples at Modane concerning the desire to produce verisimilitude through application of appropriate skill are different from the one from Jaen where the account is a response to the need for verisimilitude. Clearly, satisfaction of and conviction by the audience in its response to verisimilitude depends upon the concerted and collaborative sum of a number of contributory factors. The first of these concerns the context as it is affected by the narrative and nature of its presentation. Another consideration is that which focuses on the purpose of the object as it affects the context and is affected by it, e.g. scenic devises such as clouds and the space that they are permitted to occupy. Additionally, a number of other relative features bear upon this condition. Distance from the object is a critical factor. The amount of light available by which the audience is able to witness the object is also an important consideration, and verisimilitude too is affected by the way in which the object is used in relation to narrative, character, and presentational needs and functions. Communication and reception are in turn affected by audience experience and its perception.

In the present age, and notably in western societies, notions of verisimilitude are affected by public exposure to photographic and filmed objects and events. Knowledge of that which is real is affected by its filmed version. Thus, today, public reading of verisimilitude is extensively conditioned by subjection to still and moving images. Here, communicated meaning demands that an appreciation of the likeness of character, event or location be synonymous with the 'real thing'. This does not necessarily make for a more sophisticated ability, as is popularly thought, but it does modify how an audience interprets and receives verisimilitude. Despite these differences there are still similar ways in which medieval and modern audiences may react. Take, for example, Thomas Ady's description (1651) of the juggler who performs with an artificial mouse. Assuming that potential performances are of good quality there is no reason why the juggler and his simulated mouse could not create appropriate verisimilitude for both a medieval and a modern audience:

he therefore carrieth about him the skin of a Mouse stopped with feathers, or some like Artificial thing, and in the hinder part thereof sticketh a small springing Wire of about a foot long, or longer, and when he begins to act his part in a Fayr, or a Market before Vulgar people, he bringeth forth his Impe, and maketh it spring from him once or twice upon the Table, and then catcheth it up, saying, would you be gone? I will make you stay and play some Tricks for me before you go, and then he nimbly sticketh one end of the Wire upon his waste, and maketh his Impe spring up three or four times to his shoulder, and nimbly catcheth it, and pulleth it down again every time, saying, Would you be gone? in troth if you be gone I can play no Tricks, or Feats of Activity to day, and then holdeth it fast in one hand, and beateth it with the other, and slily maketh a squeeking noyse with his lips, as if his Impe cried, and then putteth his Impe in his breeches, or in his pocket, saying, I will make you stay, would you be gone? Then begin the silly people to wonder, and whisper, then he sheweth many slights of activity as if he did them by the help of his Familiar, which the silliest sort of beholders do verily beleeve.[55]

This account is yet another that refers to responses from the 'silly people'. However, the nature of verisimilitude produced by this example is mainly achieved through the performed behaviour of the juggler and is conducted with the related skill of the puppeteer and ventriloquist. Clearly, for a modern audience the juggler's patter would need to be converted to a contemporary vernacular. All the relative conditions outlined above would need to operate but it is possible that this basic situation of the relationship between the juggler and mouse might achieve verisimilitude solely through the skill of the juggler without the actual presence of an artificial mouse.

CHAPTER 8

Stage tricks

Although the word *trick* exists during the first half of the sixteenth century it is not until later in this period that it begins to be more precisely aligned to the work of jugglers. Up to this time the word was certainly used to describe crafty or fraudulent activity, deceptive appearances and mischievous or foolish acts.[1] In *Hall's Chronicle*: 'When the duke of Bedford was aduertised of these craftye trickes and sodaine inuented traines, he sent furth an army.'[2] Hall's namesake, John Hall, uses the word *trick* in a sense that draws it nearer to that of the juggler's activity with reference to the behaviour of a hobby horse as an apparent feat of dexterity:

> And some with hoby nagge
> For gayne of gold wold play trim tricks.
> With turne round kycke and wag.[3]

Definitions of *trick* frequently straddle the relationship between *deceit* and *skill*. One or both of these concerns find their way into definitions of *trick* as it applies to juggling. Towards the end of the sixteenth century the word *trick* is more firmly established in its use to describe juggler's feats. Shakespeare uses the word in connection with juggling in *Troilus and Cressida* when Cressida asks: 'What would you have me do?' Thersites replies: 'A juggling trick, to be secretly open'.[4] Henry Chettle in his *Kind-Harts Dreame* of 1592 refers to the juggler William Cuckoe and quotes or parodies his patter: 'Roome for a craftie knaue, cries William Cuckoe. Knaue, nay, it will neare hande beare an action: Bones a mee, my trickes are stale, and all my old companions turnd into Ciuill sutes.'[5] Here, it appears that Cuckoe refers to the performance of juggling tricks that are seemingly stale but in all probability are not so. Often jugglers create a deliberate contrast between the demonstrated level of skill that is witnessed by the audience and the juggler's verbal denigration of the skill itself through patter. It is as if to say: 'I am no good at performing this trick' but then being seen to perform it with consummate skill. In Act 1,

Scene i of Thomas Kyd's *Jeronimo* (1599) the word *trick* is firmly aligned to the word 'sleights': 'You ha no tricks, you ha none of all their slights.'[6] In 'An accompt of money disbursed by the Lord Haryngton for my Lady Elizabeth her grac*es* service for Apparell necessaries and other extraordinaries begonne at michelmas 1612 and ending at the Ladie Daie 1613', payment is recorded 'To A turkie Iugler, that shewed tryck*es* to her grace & the Palatine x^s'.[7] Fitzdottrel, in Jonson's *The Divell is an Asse* (1616), is taught to perform tricks, or 'counterfeiting' as he calls them, in a pretence of being possessed by the devil. Eventually, he has to own up to the pretence:

> These two Gentlemen
> Put me vpon it. (I haue faith against him)
> They taught me all my tricks. I will tell truth,
> And shame the *Feind*. See, here, Sir, are my bellowes,
> And my false belly, and my *Mouse*, and all
> That should ha' come forth![8]

'Tricks' and 'sleight of hand' are linked in *The Dramatic Records of Sir Henry Herbert*, where it is recorded that: 'A license was granted to Henry Momford, and others, "for tumbling, and vaulting, with *other tricks of slight of hand*"' (italics in original).[9] The words *trick* and *legerdemain* are linked in John Gee's *The Foot out of the Snare* in 1624, where a deceitful action is labelled as 'a trick of Leigerdemaine'.[10] Similarly, the *Coventry Chamberlains' and Wardens' Account Book III* for 1642 records payment: 'given to William Vincent who had commission for him and his company to daunce vpon the ropes & shew other trickes of legerdemeane x s'.[11] Later, in *The Foot out of the Snare*, Gee refers to the performance of a trick that was not so skilfully performed when he says: 'O but let me tell you of another trick, though not so cleanly as I could wish'.[12] At Doncaster, the *Chamberlains' Accounts* for 1631–2 record payment: 'to them that played the Artice [Antic] tricks, having the Kings privie seale v ^{s}.'[13] The Coventry *Chamberlains' and Wardens' Account Book III* for 1638 records: 'Paid given to Mr. Gyn and his Company who came with a Patent to shew Trickes. by bill v s.'[14] Just as *Hocus Pocus* was the pseudonym of William Vincent and is a term that is synonymous with juggling, so might 'Mr. Gyn' be a stage or professional name in that *gin* also means *trick, contrivance* or *device*.[15]

So, what constitutes the range of tricks performed by jugglers? The repertoire is well illustrated by Cardano in his *De svbtilitate* of 1550:

Infinita sunt huius artis inuenta, transferre, occulere, uorare, ex oculis, è fro*n*te humore*m* copiosum elicere, ab ore clauos filu*mque* educere, uitru*m* mandere,

brachia manusúe stylo penetrare, nectere cathenas ferreas circulis integris
manentibus, imò quod maius est, sursum proiectos tres annulos descendere uidi
inuicem implicitos, cu*m* integri essent & separati, antequàm & dum
proijcerentur: formas uarias in uno eodem*que* libello ostendunt, semper
prioribus abscedentibus: ensem ab acie nudo uentreus*que* ad capulu*m* premendo
flectunt, alij abdere illum & abscondere penetrantem uidentur . . . & cum
resciueris rationem qua oculos fallunt, ea autem duobus constat, instrumentis
uarijs ad hoc paratis, manuum*que* agilitate, nec si te docere uelint precario
digneris discere. Solum quæ in ore abscondunt ratione naturali constant, nam
latent post columellam in quodam amplo spacio, quod asperam arteriam at*que*
gulam & os palati in teriacet: alij uerò etiam uorant, & cum uolunt euomunt,
longa consuetudine adiuti: edunt alij uenena butiro prius copiose ingesto: alij
tractant serpentes: sed uel innoxios, uel exenteratis prius dentibus, uel fame prius
maceratos, uel frigore torpe*n*tes, uel educatos familiariter.[16]

The tricks of this art are innumerable, to transfer, to conceal, to devour, to draw
forth plentiful liquid from the eyes and forehead, to pull out nails and thread
from the mouth, to eat glass, to pierce arms or hands with a sharp object, to join
together iron chains with the links remaining intact, and indeed what is more, I
have seen three rings thrown into the air come down joined together, when they
were whole and separate before and while they were being thrown: they show
divers forms in one and the same book, always with the earlier ones disappearing:
they bend a sword, by pressing it on the naked stomach, from the point all the
way to the handle, others seem to hide and make disappear that piercing object
. . . and when you learn the method by which they deceive your eyes, it consists,
moreover, of two techniques: by various instruments prepared for this, and by
nimbleness of hands, and should they not wish to teach you the trick, you may
not be considered worthy to learn it through entreaty. They hide in their mouth
only what things agree with natural reason, for they are concealed behind the
small-column in a certain larger space, which lies between the trachea and the
gullet and the mouth of the palate: but others do even eat it, and when they want
they vomit it out, aided by long habit: others eat poisons when they have first
swallowed a great deal of butter: others handle snakes: but either harmless ones
or ones with their teeth removed beforehand, or ones previously weakened by
hunger, or ones sluggish through cold, or ones trained familiarly [i.e. 'trained to
be familiar with their owners'].

The juggler's repertoire is further extended by a description of the
tricks performed by an Irish juggler in Cardano's *De rervm varietate* of
1557:

Adolescentulus Hibernicus, octodecimu*m* agens annum, binos cultellos naribus
recta adeò inserebat, dimidij palmi longitudine, ut ad perpendiculum faciei
superstarent: nostri erant cultelli, adeò ut necesse esset transire illos per foramina,
ea quibus os naribus committitur: at*que* ita foramina illa multo ampliora esse, &
situ inferiora quàm sint naturaliter. Paleam etiam obliquam per omnes faciei

partes ad perpendiculum insistentem transferebat per frontem, supercilia, palpebras, buccas, nasi summum, mentum, solo musculorum faciei motu: unde interim miras formas effingebat. Prægrandem quoquè gladium recta super frontem abs*que* alio auxilio, & transferebat & continebat. Paleas recta hærentes uentri, gladio ut nouacula incide*n*te, maximis ictibus incidebat: nec unquam irrito ictu. Deinde similibus ictibus cum uentris cutem feriret, haud uulnerabatur. Cultellum quo*que* mordicus ex altera parte ore tenens, ei ex aduerso lignum cum ferrea cuspide superponebat, & rursus ligni cuspidi scutulum plumbeum, quem assidua celerrimè uersatione rotabat. Enses plures corpori tum pugiones cuspide admouebat, quorum capuli solo insisteba*n*t, duo*que* præterea manibus, sed acie ipsa continebantur, solis*que* manuum ac pedum extremitatibus tum gladijs ipsis innixus, mirum quanta uelocitate se inter illos uersaret. Interrogatus à me an Hibernia tales multos haberet[?] respondit, plurimos at*que* longè præstantiores, qui*que* multo mirabiliora facerent. quod uerum esse existimo, quandoquidem uiros pueris in singularis artibus præstare uideamus.[17]

A very young Irish man, in the course of his eighteenth year, inserted two small knives directly into his nostrils to such an extent (to the length of half a palm [of a hand]) that they projected perpendicular to his face. The small knives were ours, so that it was necessary for them to go through those holes by which the mouth is joined to the nostrils; and so these holes had to be much larger, and positioned further in, than they would naturally be. He even used, by movement of the muscles of his face alone, to move a bent straw around all the parts of his face – around his forehead, eyebrows, eyelids, cheeks, the bridge of his nose, and his chin – until it stood upright. And from it in the meantime he used to fashion marvellous shapes. Also he used to both move about and hold a very large sword directly on his forehead, without any other aid. He used to cut through straws clinging directly to his stomach with great blows from a razor-sharp sword, and never with an ineffectual blow. Then, when he struck the skin of his stomach with similar blows, he was not wounded. Also, holding a small knife in his mouth with his teeth from one side, from the opposite [side] he placed on top of that a piece of wood with an iron point, and again on the point of the wood a small dish of lead, and he made it spin as quickly as possible with continual turning. He applied by their point[s] several swords to his body, then daggers, whose handles were standing on their base [hilts], and with two meanwhile in his hands (but they were being held by the point itself), and then, resting by only the extremities of his hands and feet on the swords themselves, it was wonderful with how much speed he would turn himself among them. Asked by me whether Ireland might have many such men, he replied that there were many and considerably more excellent ones, and who might perform much more marvellous things. Which claim I consider to be true, seeing that we may observe that men exceed boys in remarkable arts.

Clearly, tricks involving ostensibly sharp knives, daggers and swords formed a significant part of some jugglers' repertoires. Sir Herbert

Thomas, in his *A Relation Of Some Yeares Travaile, Begvnne Anno 1626*, describes a similar range of tricks to those described by Cardano but with significant differences:

Our next nights *Manzeil* was at *Goyoam*, a Towne at least of a thousand Houses, after our reposing there, a *Persian Hocus-pocus*, affronted vs, he performed rare trickes with hands and feet, hee trod vpon two very sharpe *Persian* Semiters with his bare feet, then laid his naked backe vpon them, and suffered a heauy Anuill to be laid on his belly, on which two men beat two Horse-shooes forceably: that tricke done, he thrust Kniues and Arrowes thorow many parts of his armes and thighes, and by meere strength of his head, tooke vp a stone of sixe hundred pound waight, which was fastned to the ring with his haire, and in like sort tore asunder a Goatsheads with his fore-locke, still crying *Allough whoddow*, or great God to helpe him, we gaue him perticular requitals, and so left him and the towne.[18]

Richard Johnson, quoted in the previous chapter, in *Hakluyt's Collection of the Early Voyages* (1599), reveals his astonishment at a description of a trick performed with a sword, although he does not appear to have been totally tricked into believing that what he appears to have seen did in fact take place:

Then hee tooke a sworde of a cubite and a spanne long, (I did mete it my selfe) and put it into his bellie halfeway and sometime lesse, but no wounde was to bee seene, (they continuing in their sweete song still) Then he put the sworde into the fire till it was warme, and so thrust it into the slitte of his shirte and thrust it through his bodie, as I thought, in at his nauill and out at his fundament: the poynt beeing out of his shirt behinde, I layde my finger vpon it, then hee pulled out the sworde and sate downe.[19]

Thomas Coryat, in *Coryat's Crudities* of 1611, writes of his visit to Venice where he describes in some detail the performances and activities of mountebanks who 'oftentimes ministred infinite pleasure vnto me':

Also I haue seene a Mountebanke hackle and gash his naked arme with a knife most pittifully to beholde, so that the blood hath streamed out in great abundance, and by and by after, he hath applied a certaine oyle vnto it, wherewith he hath incontinent both stanched the blood, and so throughly healed the woundes and gashes, that when he hath afterward shewed vs his arme againe, we could not possibly perceiue the least token of a gash.[20]

The same kind of routine is alluded to in the *Chamberlains' and Wardens' Account Book II* at Coventry in 1616 where payment is: 'Gyven to an Italian that thrust himself through the side to make experiment of his oyle as appeareth by a bill vnder maister Maiors hand xx s'.[21]

A common feature of the preceding descriptions by Cardano, Thomas, Johnson and Coryat is that they take at face value that which they see – or reportedly see. They marvel that no wounds are left after cutting, slashing or stabbing with knives or swords. In the case of Johnson, he is permitted to examine the inserted sword and verify the action, for he claims that: 'I layde my finger vpon it'. Wounds appear to be miraculously healed in the description given by Coryat and it might be presumed that the Italian recorded at Coventry seemingly performed the same or similar miraculous feats by application of his 'oyle'. The possibility that actual wounds were never created in the first place does not seem to enter into the apparent truth or interpretation of the respective observations.

The ability seemingly to 'thrust Kniues and Arrowes thorow many parts of his armes and thighes' is one that is seen demonstrated in a number of plays in order to develop action. Although the purpose of the trick may be one of deceit, licensed trickery, or staged effect, it may display only subtle differences in the nature of its communicated intention, i.e. that a knife or arrow appears to penetrate a limb. The mechanism of the trick and its reception by an audience may produce effectively the same result. In Thomas Preston's *Cambises* (1561) an explicit stage direction instructs: 'Enter the King without a gowne, a swoord thrust vp into his side bleeding'.[22] A similar staged effect is contained in Barnaby Barnes' *The Divils Charter* (1607), where an explicit stage direction requires that: 'He bringeth from the same doore Gismond Viselli, his wounds gaping and after him Lucrece undrest, holding a dagger fix't in his bleeding bosome: they vanish.'[23] George Peele, in his *King Edward the First* of 1593, requires that Meredeth should stab the King: 'meredeth stabs him into the armes and shoulders'.[24] In *The Spanish Tragedy* two deaths are required by use of the same knife: 'He with the knife stabds [*sic*] the Duke and himselfe.'[25] The feigned death of Sentloe in *The Faire Maide of Bristow* is determined by an explicit stage direction: 'Heere he stabs his arme, and blodies Sentloes face, and pluckes out vallingers sword and blodies it, and laies it by him.'[26]

Stabbings are not confined to the arms and stomach. In *Edmond Ironside; or, War Hath Made All Friends* (c. 1595) two stage directions require of Canutus that: 'Hee Cutts off his Nose' and that 'Hee Cutt*es* his hand*es* and Nose.'[27] In an unusually prescriptive stage direction in Robert Yarington's *Two Lamentable Tragedies* (1601) Thomas Merry is required to murder Beech: 'Then being in the vpper Rome Merry strickes him in the head fifteene times.' Later in the play Merry is further instructed to murder Beech's boy (in order to cover up the first murder) by a similarly graphic stage direction that states: 'When the boy goeth into the shoppe Merrie striketh six blowes on his head & with the seauenth leaues the hammer sticking in his head, the boy groaning must be heard by a maide who must crye to her master. Merrie flieth.'[28] In Thomas Heywood's *The Brazen Age* (1613) an explicit stage direction instructs: 'Enter Nessus with an arrow through him.'[29] Similarly, in *The Covragiovs Tvrke; Or, Amvrath the First* (1632) by Thomas Goffe a stage direction requires: 'Enter Aladin as flying, an arrow through his arme, wounded in his forehead, his shield stucke with darts.'[30]

In the *Two Lamentable Tragedies, The Brazen Age* and *The Covragiovs Tvrke* the sought-after effects are created out of view of the audience and suddenly brought into view respectively by Beech's boy, Nessus and Aladin. Potentially, these arrivals are comic ones because of the contained surprise element. Clearly, acceptance of such effects depends on the seriousness of the communicated intention.

The relationship between these sorts of tricks as juggling ones and those created for staging purposes is encapsulated in Thomas Ingeland's *The Disobedient Child* (*c.* 1560) where it is declared:

> What iuglyng was there vpon the boordes!
> What thrustyng of knyves throughe many a nose
> What bearinge of formes! what holdinge of Swords!
> And puttynge of Botkyns throughe legge and hose!
> Yet for all that they called for dryncke.[31]

Declaration of the nature of artifice, techniques and stance towards the creation of juggling tricks and effects may be found in a number of accounts. Records for the *Bourges Effects* for the *Mystery of the Acts of the Apostles* in 1536 itemise the following: 'There must be a fake (faincte) knife for the bishop of India with which he shall strike St. Thomas in the stomach and kill him.'[32] Evidence of different kinds of fake knives exists and this varies according to whether the knife is used to 'stab' or to 'cut'. Payment for one such knife is recorded in the *Documents Relating to the Office of the Revels in the Time of Queen Elizabeth*. It reads: 'A hollowe knife of plate, heades of wier/ iiij . . . v^s'.[33] This account seems to refer to a knife that is effectively made from two thin pieces of metal plate with a space between them, and may be designed not to stab but to cut the skin and leave an artificial line of blood. An explanation of this kind of construction may be seen in two accounts in the *Volume of Secrets of a Provençal Stage Director's Book*:

los lairos qua[nt]
lor quoparon las [cam-]
bas quossas, la lor [quopa-]
ron sans lor fa [mal],
el qual fa un [quo-]
tel que sia gran e
deservi, e que lo [. . .]
s'en intre pel serv[is]
que qual que sia cr[oi]
e que sia tot ple d[edins]
de vermelo ben m[out]
e ben destrenpat, [e]
qual fa como una [. . .]
uneta an d' estopas.[34]

the thieves, when they'll wound their legs and thighs, they'll cut them without hurting them, it is necessary to have a knife that should be large and rigged [faked?], and that the . . . enters on the place that has been rigged. The knife needs to be empty and filled with vermilion, well ground and well diluted. And it is necessary to make a . . . [wounds?] with tow.

Later in the same account the construction of another hollow dagger is described where wax is used to plug the hollow knife that contains liquefied vermilion. Given the nature of the trick the author suggests that the dagger should be quickly replaced in its scabbard after use so that the audience will not be permitted to discover the trick. Knives with hollow blades and hilts were presumably used in the trick described by Richard Carew in Chapter 2 where 'vp flyes the knife, and sticks in a beame of the roofe'.[35] Here, some form of thread needs to pass through both the blades and hilts of the knives in order that the blade of the second and third knives may be guided into the hilts of the first and second knives.

Some of the most detailed revelations as to the methods of jugglers who made use of false knives are contained in Reginald Scot's *Discouerie of witchcraft*. Of the several tricks and declared techniques perhaps it will suffice to offer four tricks and their explanations since they all afford the means by which eye-witness accounts previously cited in this chapter may have been fulfilled. Similarly, these techniques also provide further explanations to the description given in Thomas Ingeland's *The Disobedient Child* and suggest that these were known stage tricks in England at least twenty-five years before Scot published *The Discouerie of witchcraft*. The first of these accounts details how: 'To thrust a bodkin through your toong, and a knife through your arme: a pittifull sight, without hurt or danger':

Make a bodkin, the blade therof being sundred in the middle, so as the one part be not neere to the other almost by three quarters of an inch, each part being kept a sunder with one small bought or crooked peece of iron, of the fashion described hereafter in place conuenient. Then thrust your toong betwixt the foresaid space; to wit, into the bought left in the bodkin blade, thrusting the said bought behind your teeth, and biting the same: and then shall it seeme to sticke so fast in and through your toong, as that one can hardlie pull it out. Also the verie like may be doone with a knife so made, and put vpon your arme: and the wound will appeare the more terrible, if a little bloud be powred therevpon.[36] (Figure 8.1).

The second of these techniques is outlined under the title: 'To cut halfe your nose asunder, and to heale it againe presentlie without anie salue':

Take a knife hauing a round hollow gap in the middle, and laie it vpon your nose, and so shall you seeme to haue cut your nose halfe asunder. Prouided alwaies, that in all these you haue an other like knife without a gap, to be shewed vpon the pulling out of the same, and words of inchantment to speake, bloud also to beeraie the wound, and nimble conueiance.

[Marginal note] This is easilie doone, howbeit being clenlie handled it will deceiue the sight of the beholders.[37] (Figure 8.2).

A more involved technique is outlined in the process of stabbing oneself in the stomach. Even so, the technique may apply equally to the stabbing of someone else. Scot describes how 'To thrust a dagger or bodkin into your guts verie strangelie, and to recouer immediatlie':

Another miracle may be shewed touching counterfet executions; namelie, that with a bodkin or a dagger you shall seeme to kill your selfe, or at the least make an unrecouerable wound in your bellie: as (in truth) not long since a iuggler caused himself to be killed at a tauerne in cheapside, from whence he presentlie went into Powles churchyard and died. Which misfortune fell vpon him through his owne follie, as being then drunken, and hauing forgotten his plate, which he should haue had for his defense. The deuise is this. You must prepare a paste boord, to be made according to the fashion of your bellie and brest: the same must by a painter be coloured cunninglie, not onelie like to your flesh, but with pappes, nauill, haire, &c: so as the same (being handsomelie trussed vnto you) may shew to be your naturall bellie. Then next to your true bellie you may put a linnen cloth, and therevpon a double plate (which the iuggler that killed himselfe forgot, or wilfullie omitted) ouer and vpon the which you may place the false bellie. Prouided alwaies, that betwixt the plate & the false bellie you place a gut or bladder of bloud, which bloud must be of a calfe or of a sheepe; but in no wise of an oxe or a cow, for that will be too thicke. Then thrust, or cause to be thrust into your brest a round bodkin, or the point of a dagger, so far as it may pearse through your gut or bladder: which being pulled out againe, the said bloud will spin or spirt out a good distance from you, especiallie if you straine your bodie to swell, and thrust therewith against the plate. You must euer remember to vse (with words, countenance, and gesture) such a grace, as may giue a grace to the action, and mooue admiration in the beholders.[38]

The false belly referred to here may well be of the kind alluded to, earlier in this chapter, by Fitzdottrel in Jonson's *The Divell is an Asse* as one of the accoutrements of the juggler. One further technique to be outlined here is how 'To thrust a bodkin into your head without hurt':

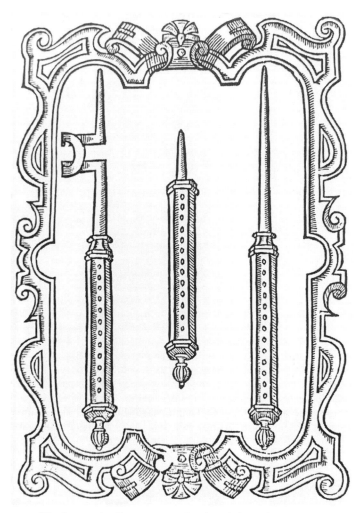

Figure 8.1.   'To thrust a bodkin into your head, and through your toong, &c.', from Scot, *Discouerie of witchcraft*, after p. 352.

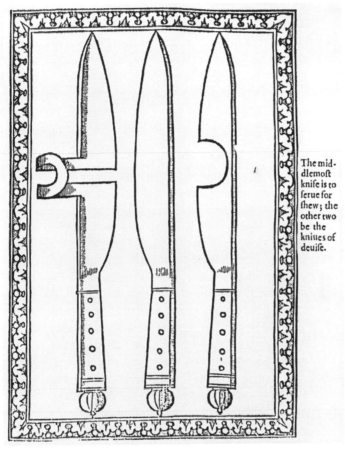

The mid-
dlemoſt
knife is to
ſerue for
ſhew; the
other two
be the
kniues of
deuiſe.

Figure 8.2. 'To thrust a knife through your arme, and to cut halfe your nose asunder, &c.', from Scot, *Discouerie of witchcraft*, after p. 352.

Take a bodkin so made, as the haft being hollowe, the blade thereof may slip thereinto as soone as you hold the point vpward: and set the same to your forehead, and seeme to thrust it into your head, and so (with a little sponge in your hand) you may wring out bloud or wine, making the beholders thinke the bloud or the wine (whereof you may saie you haue drunke verie much) runneth out of your forehead. Then, after countenance of paine and greefe, pull awaie your hand suddenlie, holding the point downeward; and it will fall so out, as it will seeme neuer to haue beene thrust into the haft: but immediatlie thrust that bodkin into your lap or pocket, and pull out an other plaine bodkin like the same, sauing in that conceipt.[39] (Figure 8.2).

The four techniques offered by Scot present some interchangeable features. For instance, use of the bodkin in which the spike retracts into the haft could easily be used to stab someone else in the stomach. Scot, however, is careful to say that the bodkin should be held either upright or downwards in order to allow the spike to be revealed or hidden. The weight of the spike allows it to move. A development of this kind of device might require a spring to enable the shaft to disappear into the haft and be released upon a supposed withdrawal. Such a technique is described with reference to a knife blade in the performance of an Irish mummers play: 'This one they had was a big long knife. You'd swear it was a bayonet. And, be jingo, you'd swear it went into him – the way the spring drives the blade back. And he'll fall, do you see, and let a big groan out of him and you'd swear he was dead.'[40]

The concomitant visual effect of stabbing may be seen through evidence of the resultant wound as illustrated in some of the earlier eye-witness accounts. In *The Croxton Play of the Sacrament* (also cited earlier in Chapter 7), a stage direction determines the appearance of the image of Christ (the imago) displaying wounds: 'Here the owyn must ryve asunder and blede owt at þe cranys, and an image appere owt with woundys bledyng.'[41] The context of this situation is that the Jews have tried a number of ways of destroying the host. They have tried to nail it, to boil it in oil and to burn it in an oven. It is after the last attempt to destroy the host that the image of Christ rises out of the oven. In *The Divils Charter* by Barnaby Barnes a stage direction, quoted earlier, declares that Gismond Viselli is brought in, 'his wounds gaping'.[42] Although the wound may be presented simply by the release of 'blood' there is some evidence of the notion of the wound as a physical representation that is applied to the body. In the *Volume of Secrets of a Provençal Stage Director's Book* a description that accompanies a sketch of one of the knives, referred to earlier, declares the technique of applying a 'wound':

> Lo quotel es aques[t];
> e qualra fa.iiii.pl[a-]
> guas e pueis bota-la[s]
> sus las cueisas en de[men-]
> [tr]as que los talo, mas qual [que]
> [las] fico que degus no vego.[43]

This is the knife; one should make four sores and then throw [stick or affix] them on the thighs while they are being cut, but it should be done in such a way that nobody can see it.

The visible wound may be seen to represent the effect of stabbing, cutting or piercing. Similarly, the sight of blood also creates communicated statements of a like kind. The *Bourges Effects* for the *Mystery of the Acts of the Apostles* require that: 'There must be a device (<u>faincte</u>) which gives blood (<u>qui rende sang</u>) for the child's wound.'[44] A stage direction for the *Mercade Vengeance* establishes: 'Then Pilate stabs himself with a knife: and he must have something on him which will spurt blood. And he must so position himself for the blow that it looks to the audience as if he had killed himself.'[45] An account concerning the *Modane Antichrist Play* makes a requirement that presumably relates to the stance taken by Scot's techniques outlined above: 'Then they shall make a dagger with which someone can be struck in the breast and die from the blow. And they will make blood issue forth in the accustomed way (<u>à la maniere accoutumée</u>).'[46] Another requirement, in the *Admont Passion Play*, states that 'Longinus rests his spear against Christ, opens up his right side, and out flows blood and water.'[47] This need could easily be satisfied by the technique outlined by Scot where he requires use of 'a gut or bladder of bloud' that is suitably camouflaged. The idea of the 'bladder of bloud' is referred to elsewhere. In *Cambises*, in order to simulate bleeding, a stage direction requires: 'A little bladder of Vinegar prickt'.[48] The *City Chamberlains' Accounts* at Canterbury for 1528–30 record payment for 'a new leder bag for ye blode vj d'.[49] This item was required for the production 'almost certainly [of] a debased survival or revival of an old St. Thomas play'.[50] Payment is also recorded in the same accounts 'for x ow, ces of vermylion x d'.[51] Presumably, this material contributed to the spilling-of-blood effect.

Use of bladders or bags containing actual or simulated blood was not the only means by which blood effects were created. At Revello during the 'Agony in the Garden' blood effects are painted on Christ:

And when he [Christ] is praying, the angel Uriel shall come and show him the Passion painted on a cloth. Then he shall stretch out on the stage (<u>zafaldo</u>) on his face, and underneath there shall be someone who shall paint his face and hands with crimson paint as if he were sweating. And when he has been like this for a time he shall rise. And one of the angels shall come and without speaking wipe away the sweat.[52]

Similarly, at Lucerne, paint is used to simulate blood:

At these words they awake and start up as if they want to pray, then the Savior goes for a third time to the mount and falls down. Then the painter inside the mount is to splash him with the blood, and when he has splashed him he is to arise with difficulty and say the following with a trembling voice . . .[53]

In Scot's trick, 'To thrust a bodkin into your head without hurt', he suggests that a sponge may be filled with blood or wine to add to the desired effect. A similar requirement is made in the *Volume of Secrets of a Provençal Stage Director's Book* during the incident of the 'Crowning of Thorns'. Here the actor playing Christ wears a metal cap under which are held sponges containing diluted vermillion. When the crown of thorns is pressed down on to Christ's head the sponges release their content.[54]

In Thomas Kyd's *The Spanish Tragedy* a stage direction requires of Hieronimo that: 'He bites out his tongue.'[55] Despite the possibility that this might be in reality a physically difficult thing to do the action does depend on the apparent successful completion of the task. The idea that this action is completed may be seen in the requirement of another stage direction that states of Hieronimo: 'He makes signes for a knife to mend his pen.'[56] It may be presumed that Hieronimo, without his tongue, is unable to speak. It seems also as if the audience must be shown the detached tongue in order to recognise the significance of his supposed behaviour. This action amounts to a simply devised trick involving sleight of hand that is also recorded in an observation in 1555: 'After this, commynge behynde hym, he conueygheth the piece of fleshe owte of his owne mouth like a iuggeler, and sheweth it to the sicke man, sayinge, behoulde what you haue eaten to muche: you shall nowe bee hole, bycause I haue taken this from you.'[57]

The basis of this trick is also alluded to in the following extract from John Gee's *The Foot out of the Snare* (1624):

A gentle-woman of England, in one of the yeers of Iubile, trauelled to Rome, where beeing arriued, shee repaired to Father Parsons, who was her Confessor: and he administring vnto her the blessed Sacrament (which, in the forme of a little Wafer, hee put in to her mouth) obserued shee was long chewing, and could not swallow the same: whereupon he asked her, whether she knew what it was shee receiued? Shee answered, Yes, a Wafer. At which answer of hers, Father Parsons beeing much offended, he thrust his finger into her mouth, and thence drew out a piece of red flesh, which after was nailed vp against a post in a Vespery or priuate Chappell within our Lady-Church: and though this were done about some twenty yeeres since or more, yet doth that piece of flesh there remaine to bee seene, very fresh and red as euer it was.[58]

Some stage tricks that are not strictly juggling tricks are those concerning strangulation and hanging. In *The Famous History of Sir Thomas Wyat* (1607), a stage direction determines that Homes enter with 'a Halter about his necke', and the Clowne speaking of Homes' state of mind suggests that 'in this moode hee would hang himselfe'. An explicit stage direction

confirms this mood by stating that 'He strangles himselfe.'[59] Homes enters
with a halter about his neck and this points to the method of hanging by
rope. The other key method of hanging was by the *furca*. This consisted of
a post at the top of which was a forked branch. The guilty party was lifted
into place so that his neck was cradled in the fork, and a piece of wood
(viniculum partibuli) was nailed behind his head and to the branches of the
fork; here he was left to strangle himself.[60] Hangings from trees could
either take place in the manner following the *furca* or by rope. In the
Cornish ordinalia the hanging of Judas appears to have been conducted
using the latter method. A stage direction states: 'paratur arbor et capistrum ad suspendendum Judam'.[61] [A tree is made ready, and a halter for
hanging Judas]. The 'capistrum' or halter, in this case, may well have
included a harness of strapwork to take the weight of the actor's body in
order to simulate hanging by noose. If it is the actor who is seen by the
audience then the noose needs to be loosely attached to the load-bearing
rope yet seem taut enough in order to create the illusion. If a dummy
substitute is used then the noose can be the natural end of the rope and
fixed tight around the neck. Such a possibility occurs in *The Life of Saint
Meriasek*, where a stage direction declares 'yᵉ galovs aredy' [the gallows
ready] in order that 'Comes' [The Earl] and the 'Doctor in Fide' [A Doctor
in Faith] may be threatened by the 'Tertius Tortor' [Third Torturer]:

> Here thou shalt be gibbeted.
> Likewise the other traitor
> By thy shoulder like a villain
> By me shall be hung.[62]

When the Earl and the Doctor are on the gallows the torturers make
further sport by cutting up the bodies with swords. The First Torturer
says: 'Let us come through them with swords / From one side to the
other'. The Second Torturer replies: 'Look at it through him put! / I will
slit him across to the head.' The Third Torturer winds up the operation:
'Look at them fallen to the ground! / Their bodies together are broken.'[63]
Given the normal caution that needs to be exercised when interpreting
action of the narrative it does seem that the bodies are cut down from the
gallows and further mutilated. This action appears to be witnessed by the
audience and further indicates use of dummies as substitutes. Recognition
of the possibility of using the actor or a dummy substitute is clearly
offered by stage directions in Sir David Lindsay's *Ane Satyre of the Thrie
Estaitis*. Here 'Commoun Thift', 'Dissait' and 'Falset' are hanged. These
characters are hanged by the rope as indicated by the First Sergeant when

he says to Thift: 'Slip in thy head into this coird.' The hanging of Thift is prepared by an explicit stage direction that states: 'Heir sal Thift be drawin vp, or his figour.' The alternative offered here indicates something of the author's awareness of the practical issues involved in this process. A similar stage direction prepares for the hanging of Dissait: 'Heir sal Dissait be drawin vp or ellis his figure.' When Falset is hanged a stage direction states: 'Heir sall thay festin the coard to his neck with ane dum countenance' and another explicit stage direction declares: 'Heir sal he be heisit [hauled] vp, and not his figure, and an Craw [crow] or ane Ke [jackdaw] salbe castin vp, as it war his saull [soul].'[64] In this case it appears that Falset is not replaced by a dummy and therefore receives different treatment. The nature of this action is unclear.

In *The Book of Sir Thomas More* (c. 1595), Lincoln is ostensibly hanged from a tree. The Sheriff says: 'Bring *Lincolne* there the first vnto the tree.' A stage direction curtly declares: 'he goes vp'. A subsequent stage direction states: 'he leapes off'. Whether the 'tree' of the text is a tree or some other physical structure within the staging is unclear, but it does seem that a harness of some kind is necessary in order to absorb the jolt of leaping off the 'tree'.[65]

A stage direction in *The Love of King David and Fair Bethsabe* (1599) by George Peele says: 'The battell, and Absolon hangs by the haire'.[66] Although this is not an example of hanging by strangulation the technical requirement is a similar one. This action also relates to hanging from a tree, for the soldier states: 'My lord I saw the young prince Absalom / Hang by the haire vpon a shadie oke, / And could by no meanes get himselfe vnlosde.'[67] The mechanism by which this hanging was achieved may be accounted for in an item recorded in *Henslowe's Diary* for 1602: 'pd for poleyes & worckmanshipp for to hange absolome ... xiiijd'.[68] 'Poleyes', in the plural, may indicate more than one pulley. This is a condition that may have been necessary to obtain the necessary 'mechanical advantage' to raise the weight of Absalom's body.[69]

The *Trinity College Junior Bursar's Accounts 1* at Cambridge for 1555 record the following payment: 'Item payd vnto Wylliam Carpenter ... & for makyn a payre of lytle gallowes for ye shew (*not* itemized)'.[70] Of the five plays recorded as having been played at Trinity College in 1555, none of them is named and it is unclear as to which play made use of the 'lytle gallowes'.[71]

The incident of the hanging of Judas was the responsibility of the Smiths at Coventry. Extant accounts offer a number of key features concerning the staging of this event. Payment is recorded in the *Smiths'*

Accounts for 1576 'ffor the gybbyt of Jeȝie xviij d'.[72] Given the subject matter of the Smiths' pageant the term 'Jeȝie' is considered to be a mistake for 'Judas'.[73] Thus, it appears that Judas was hanged on a gibbet. Other items that contribute to this action are also recorded in the *Smiths' Accounts* for 1573: 'paid for a poollye [pulley] and an yron hoke and mendyng the padgand, xvj d; paid for cowntters [the pieces of silver] and a lase [lace] and pwyntes [points] for Jwdas, iii d'.[74] Further payment is recorded to Thomas Massy in 1578: 'paid to Thomas Massy for a trwse [truss] for Judas, ij s viij d; paid for a new hoke to hange Judas, vj d'.[75] The same accounts for 1577 record payment 'ffor a lase for Judas & a corde [rope] iij d'.[76] Payment is also recorded in 1573 and 1574 to the person who operated the gibbet and effectively hanged Judas: 'paid to Fawston for hangyng Judas iiij d', and 'paid to Fawston for hangyng Jwdas and coc-croyng, viij d'.[77] Further payment is recorded in 1572 for Judas' coat: 'Paid for canvys for Jwdas coote, ij s.'[78]

From the above information it appears that Judas was hanged from a gibbet by Fawston who controlled the rope that passed over/through the pulley(s) that was attached to an iron hook that was fastened to Judas' 'trwse'. Presumably, 'Jwdas coote' was provided with a hole or slit through which the 'yron hoke' could be anchored. The word 'truss' has two potentially relevant meanings in this context. One refers to a close-fitting upper body garment and the other refers to a similarly close-fitting item that covers the buttocks and the upper thighs.[79] In this instance the former meaning seems more appropriate in that the body weight needs to be controlled from as high as possible in order to provide strength to the illusion of being hanged by the neck.

The hazards of playing Judas are recorded in relation to the *Metz Passion* of 1437:

And in this play was yet another priest called lord Jehan de Missey who was chaplain of Mairange, who took the part of Judas; and because he was left hanging too long, he also was unconscious and seemed dead, for he had fainted; therefore he was swiftly taken down and carried to a place nearby where he was rubbed with vinegar and things to restore him.[80]

The means by which Peter was able to walk on the water in the *Paris Resurrection* is divulged in the following account:

Icy va Sainct Pierre par sus la mer a Jhesus sans moiller la cheville par une grant haies mise subtillement et chevillee en l'eau et les apostres mectent leur poisson en ung aultre reth venant tousiours a la rive de la mer puis s'agenoillent tous devant Nostre Seigneur sans parlement et dit Jhesus . . .[81]

Here St Peter goes across the sea to Jesus, without wetting his ankle, on a large hurdle (<u>haies</u>) cunningly set and dug in (<u>mise . . . et chevillee</u>) in the water, and the apostles put their fish in another net, still approaching the shore of the sea. Then they all kneel before Our Lord without speaking and Jesus says . . .

The stage trick of producing springs of water from the earth is required in a number of plays. In the *Origo mundi* of the *Cornish ordinalia* a stage direction requires Moses to strike the earth:

> Et percuciet cum virga petram et exveniet aqua
> [hic percutit bis silicem et fluit aqua][82]

> And he shall strike the rock with his rod, and the
> water shall come out.

In *The Life of Saint Meriasek* the same incident is referred to by Meriasek as follows:

> Ihesu arluth me ath peys
> ihesu gront dovyr a wur speys
> ihesu dymmo der the graes
> del russys kyns the moyseys
> an men cales
> [her ye wyll sprynggyth vp water[83]

> Jesu, Lord, I beseech thee,
> Jesu, grant water in abundance,
> Jesu, to me through thy grace
> As thou didst before for Moses
> From the hard rock.
> [Here the well springeth up water.

The legend concerning the death of Paul when his head is reputed to have bounced three times is referred to in the *Bourges Effects* for the *Mystery of the Acts of the Apostles*: 'St. Paul shall be beheaded, and the head will bounce three times, and from each bounce will spring up a fountain from which will flow milk, blood, and water.'[84] This description/direction essentially repeats the legend concerning St Paul and seems to present concerns for the way in which the stipulation might have been achieved. One method that might have been used is a version of the one concerning Moses' creation of water from the earth in the *Lucerne Passion Play*:

Now the water comes with full force. They all run to drink, pressing forward in a throng. Note: the rock is to be made artificially, namely a container (<u>beheb</u>) which will take a good amount of water under a cover, arranged and made so that it looks like a rock with at three or four places glass or brazen bungs (<u>zapffen</u>) sticking out which Moses strikes out when the water is to flow.[85]

Perhaps the most demanding aspect of the trick concerning the bouncing of St Paul's head is that of contriving the three bounces. The other requirements concerning the springs of water, blood and milk could no doubt be simulated as in the Lucerne account. Additional force behind the springs might have been created by use of bellows and pipe. If it may be presumed that the audience knew of the legend concerning St Paul then the literal requirement of 'three bounces' may need to have been only of support value to the consummation of this effect by the rapid and timed ejection of the three springs. A similar technique to that used at Lucerne is contained in Thomas Ady's *A Candle in the Dark* (1651):

> then he [the juggler] saith, If this be not enough I will draw good Claret Wine out of a post, and then taketh out of his bagge [budget or gipser] a Wine-gimblet, and so he pierceth the Post quite thorow with his Gimblet; and then is one of his boys on the other side of the wall with a Bladder and a Pipe (like as when a Clister is administred by the Phisician) and conveyeth the Wine to his Master thorow the Post, which his Master (Vintner like) draweth forth into a Pot, and filleth it into a Glass, and giveth the company to drink.[86]

The action of Moses in striking the rock with his rod is effectively, in staging terms, one of timing or cueing the release of the liquid. A similar arrangement concerning cueing may be seen in a stage direction in Thomas Lodge and Robert Greene's *A Looking-Glass for London and England* (1590): 'The Magi with their rods beate the ground, and from vnder the same riseth a braue Arbour, the King returneth in an other sute while the Trumpettes sounde.'[87] Presumably, the 'braue Arbour' rises via a trap. The notion of striking the earth or rock with a rod or staff to produce liquids may be extended through the same action to produce fire. In the *Triumph of Time* (1612) by Francis Beaumont and John Fletcher a stage direction states: 'Plutus strikes the Rock and flames flie out.'[88]

The biblical narrative requirement that Moses should turn his rod into a snake is contained in Exodus 4.4 and is embraced by the *Hosiers Play* of *Moses and Pharaoh* in the *York Cycle*. Virtually the same text is contained in the *Play of Pharaoh* in the *Towneley Plays*. This is one of six plays thought to have been derived or taken from the *York Cycle*. In the *Hosiers Play* of *Moses and Pharaoh* at York, 'Moyses' is commanded by God as follows:

> [Moyses] My wande he bad by his assent,
> And þat þou shulde þe wele avise
> How it shulde turne to a serpent.
> And in his haly name

Here sal I ley it downe:
Loo ser, se her þe same.
[Rex] A! Dogg! þe deuyll þe drowne
[Moyses] He saide þat I shulde take þe tayle
So for to proue his poure playne,
And sone he saide it shuld not fayle
For to turne a wande agayne.
Loo sir, behalde.
[Rex] Hopp illa hayle!
Now tis certis þis is a sotill swayne.[89]

The York text above clearly requires that the audience witness two states: one, the rod; and two, the snake. In terms of the staging requirements of this incident two distinct methods present themselves: one is that sleight of hand is involved in producing a real snake, and the other involves an imitation snake. If the latter suggestion is involved then perhaps the most obvious method of performing the Moses trick is that of using a 'wande' made up of short hollow sections that just slot into each other, which are pulled firmly into position by a cord attached through the sections to the last one when the 'wande' is required, and slackened for the simulated behaviour of the writhing snake. This seems particularly relevant in that Moses relays God's instruction as 'He saide þat I shulde take þe tayle'. This instruction gives both practical and creative permission to hold the 'wande' in the appropriate place. Thomas Ady suggests that the trick is easy to perform:

for what is easier than for a cunning Jugler to hold up a staffe as if he would throw it down, and then to speak a lofty inchantation, to busie the intention of the Spectators, and then with slight of hand to throw down an artificial Serpent instead of his staffe, and convey away his staffe, that so they might think his staffe was turned into a Serpent[?][90]

It is not clear how much additional value might accrue if a real snake was involved but some early-seventeenth-century accounts of mountebank operations indicate ways in which docile snakes were used in their performances. In Edward Topsell's *The Historie of Serpents* (1608) some appropriate insights are offered in respect of considerations made by jugglers:

I haue heard a Gentleman of singuler learning ['Ma: Will: Morley of Glynde in Sussex'], & once my Worshipfull good friend, and daily encourager vnto all good labours, report diuers times very credibly, vppon his owne knowledge and eye sight, that beeing at *Padua* in *Italy*, hee sawe a certaine Quacksaluer, or Mountebacke [*sic*] vpon a stage, pull a Viper out of a box, and suffered the saide Viper to bite his flesh, to the great admiration of all the beholders, receiuing thereby no danger at all.

Afterward he put off his doublet and shirt, and shewed vppon his right arme a very great vnwonted blew veine, standing beyond the common course of nature; and he said, that he was of the linage of Saint *Paule*, & so were all other that had such veines, and that therefore (by speciall vertue to that Family giuen from aboue) no Viper nor Serpent could euer annoy or poyson them: but withall, the fellowe dranke a certaine compound water, or antidote, for feare of the worst, and so at one time vented both his superstitious hypocrisie, and also much of his Antidote to his great advantage. But I haue since that time also read, in Mathiolus his Commentaries vppon the sixth Booke of *Discorides*, that there were wont to be many such Iuglers in Italy, carrying in theyr bosomes liuing Serpents, of whose fraudulent Impostures hee speaketh in this sort. They take Serpents in the Winter time, when they growe dead and stiffe through cold, and yet for their better defence against their venemous byting, they defend themselues by a certaine experimentall vngeunt, knowne to bee practised in this sport, made of the Oyle pressed out of wilde Radish, the rootes of Dragonwort, the iuyce of Daffodill, the braine of a Hare, the leaues of Sabine, sprigges of Bay, & some other few things there-vnto added. As soone as they haue taken them, they instantly all to spette vpon their heads, for by reason of a secret antipathy in Nature, they grow very dull thereby, and lay aside the force and rage of venome; for the spettle of a Man, is of a cleane contrarie operation to their poyson. And when afterward they make ostentation heerof in the Market, or publique Stage, they suffer them to bite their owne flesh: but first of all, they offer them a peece of hard flesh, where-vppon they bite to clense their teeth from all spawne and spume of venome, or els sometime pull forth the little bagges of poyson, which inhaere in their chaps, and vnder their tongues, so as they are neuer more repleate or filled againe: And by this deceit they deceiue the world where euer they come, giuing foorth that they are of the linage of Saint *Paule*, who cast a Viper off from his hands, as wee reade in the holie Scripture.[91]

Thomas Coryat (1611) makes a similar observation concerning activities of mountebanks in Venice:

For I saw one of them holde a viper in his hand, and play with his sting a quarter of an houre together, and yet receiue no hurt; though another man should haue beene presently stung to death with it. He made vs all beleeue that the same viper was linealy descended from the generation of that viper that lept out of the fire vpon S. *Pauls* hand, in the Island of Melita now called Malta, and did him no hurt; and told vs moreouer that it would sting some, and not others.[92]

Observations from Topsell and Coryat accord with those of Cardano cited earlier in this chapter. Topsell communicates a clearer understanding of the processes of artifice than does Coryat, who simply describes that which he saw. Both, however, refer to the mountebank's attempts to bolster the legitimacy of the respective performances of the vipers to that of the 'linage of Saint *Paule*, who cast a Viper off from his hands, as wee reade in the holie Scripture'. This suggests considerable use of patter to create the imaginative context of the performance.

CHAPTER 9

Terminology

Appropriate terminology needs to be considered in relation to both the nature of the activity and its performers. The terms under discussion here are those listed in the Introduction as *tregetry, legerdemain, prestigiation, juggling* or *jugglery, feats, feats of activity, sleights* and *sleight of hand.* Designations of the performers of these activities are drawn from the *tregetour, prestigiator, joculator, circulator, mountebank, emperic, quacksalver* and *juggler.* The important concern here is to clarify the distinctions between performance and performers of magic with entertainment intentions and those employed or implied in the broadest sense for spiritual or witchcraft reasons. Here, it is important to consider specific purposes and contexts within which the terms arise, particularly where the terminology might overlap entertainment and spiritual concerns. Of itself, this is not a discussion about witchcraft. The focus is upon 'magic' for entertainment purposes.

Emphasis is placed upon the *MED* and the *OED* in their definitions of these relevant terms and to some extent the changing meanings over many years are apparent or implied. These sources may be basically relied upon in terms of supplied definitions, for they are clear in their expositive function and provide strong exemplification to definitions. On some occasions, however, quotations used as examples provide only neutral value to definitions and may not actively promote them. It is sometimes possible to share or move examples to another related definition. Thus, some care needs to be exercised in the use of such examples and consideration of context becomes vital.

The 'magic' referred to in this work is that which the *OED* defines as 'The art of producing (by legerdemain, optical illusion, or devices suggested by knowledge of physical science) surprising phenomena resembling the pretended results of "magic"; conjuring'. In this definition the word 'conjuring' is used in its modern sense to explain the term 'legerdemain', which in turn is defined by the *OED* as 'Sleight of hand;

the performance of tricks which by nimble action deceive the eye; jugglery; conjuring tricks'.

Explanatory notes in the *OED* concerning meanings of the word 'magic' point to the particular sense in which it is used in this work:

The 'magic' which made use of the invocation of evil or doubtful spirits was of course always regarded as sinful; but *natural magic* i.e. that which did not involve recourse to the agency of personal spirits, was in the Middle Ages usually recognised as a legitimate department of study and practice, so long as it was not employed for malificent ends . . . On the other hand, the 'natural magic' of the Middle Ages included much that from the standpoint of modern science is 'natural', but not 'magical', the processes being really, according to the now known laws of physical causation, adapted to produce the intended effects.

Many of the sources cited in this work are drawn from those dealing with *natural magic* as represented by what are generically known as *Books of secrets*.[1] Such books usually deal with the phenomena that arise out of examination and explanation of the relationship between art, science and nature, and may be seen, for example, in the works of Albertus Magnus, Heinrich Cornelius Agrippa, Giambattista Porta, Hanss Johannis Wecker, Girolamo Cardano, William Bourne, Thomas Hill, Reginald Scot, Sir Hugh Platte, John Bate, William Vincent, John Babington and Thomas Ady. One of the features that binds these authors and their works into the genre of *Books of secrets* is that they share common approaches to the explanation of various natural phenomena and their realisation. Each of the above Italian and German authors was translated into English in the sixteenth and seventeenth centuries.

The modern meaning of *conjuring*, as defined by the *OED*, and referred to earlier, did not arise until the eighteenth century (see Introduction, note 1). The earliest *OED* example of the word *conjuring*, in the modern sense, appears as the title to Garenne's *The Art of Modern Conjuring, Magic, and Illusions* of 1886.[2] There are, however, earlier nineteenth-century examples that might have been cited.[3]

The etymology of *conjure* from the Latin *conjurare* is cited by the *OED* as 'to swear together, to band, combine, or make a compact by oath, to conspire, etc, f. *con-* together + *jūrāre* to swear, make oath'. Early use of the term *conjuring* is defined by the *MED* as '(a) An urgent appeal or demand; (b) invocation (of spirits); (c) an act of magic, as by incantation or casting of spell'. The earliest examples of these three meanings are from the early fourteenth century and include ones from the *Northern Passion*, the *Cursor mundi* and *The Seven Sages of Rome*. In the *Northern Passion*, Cayphas says to Jesus: 'I coniure þe thurgh coniuryng / [If þou be Ihesus þe Iewis kyng.'[4] Here, the sense of *conjure* and *conjuring* is concerned with Cayphas making an appeal to Jesus. Joseph of Arimathea uses the term *conjuring* with the same sense in the *Cursor mundi* after it is realised that Christ has risen: 'And fand we forto bring þaim heder, / And sal we þaim wid coniuring, / Ger tell vs of þis vp-rising.'[5] *The Early South English Legendary* records that: 'þe feondes seiden: "to nime þe and þi fere; Hermogenes us made hidere wiende: þoruȝ is conIuringue'.[6] Hermogenes is an evil prince and an enchanter who has the power to create spirits able to cast spells, and the term *conIuringue* here refers to this ability. It is considered in *The Seven Sages of Rome* that Virgil could create magic through witchcraft, for he 'was whilom a clerk / þat coude of nigramancie werk. / He made a fair coniuring / Amideward Rome cheping.'[7] Equivalent definitions in the *OED* add a further meaning derived from a late-sixteenth-century example of *conspiring* as contained in William Warner's *Albions England* (1589), where he uses the word *conjuring* in this sense: 'Yet of the Yorkests neuer lackt he Princes that rebell: Nor other than confusion to their still coniuring fell.'[8] It may be seen, therefore, that these meanings and senses of *conjuring* need to be separated from a concern for *legerdemain*. However, some overlapping meaning may be seen between *conjuring*, in the sense of *conspiracy*, and *conjuring* (juggling) as *confederacy*, as used in this work. Given that the earliest appearance of the term *conjuror* as used in the modern sense is 1727, it is hardly surprising that it and its derivations of *conjurator*, *conjure*, *conjuren* and *conjurere* in the *MED* do not refer to any meaning concerning *legerdemain*.

The *OED* definition of *legerdemain*, cited above, confirms that it and *sleight of hand* are the same thing: 'Sleight of hand; the performance of tricks which by nimble action deceive the eye; jugglery; conjuring tricks'. In its definition of *legerdemain*, the *OED* offers an example of its meaning as recorded in the *Catholicon Anglicum* (*c.* 1475) as: 'To play lechardemane, *pancraciari* [juggling]'. The derivation of *legerdemain* is from the French *léger de main* with its literal translation as 'light of hand'. With reference to implicit deceit, and typical of many sixteenth-century references concerning the Catholic priesthood, William Roy is quoted in the *OED* in his *Rede me and be nott wrothe For I saye no thynge but trothe* (1528 and now ascribed to William Barlow) in saying: 'O churche men are wyly foxes / More crafty then iuggelers boxes / To play ligier du mayne teached.'[9] Similarly, implicit sleight of hand is revealed in a deception described by William Bullein in *Bulleins Bulwarke of defence against all Sicknes* (1562) when he declares: 'Although many Inkepers with their hostlers, through a cast [trick] of legerdemain: can make a pecke of draffe and Beanes, buye three bushelles of cleane Pease or Beanes.'[10]

Sleight of hand is defined by the *OED* in two relevant ways to the focus of this work: '1. Dexterity or skill in using the hand or hands for any purpose; expertness in manipulation or manual action'. The second definition is even more pertinent: '2. A dextrous trick or feat; a piece of nimble juggling or conjuring'. The earliest use of the term cited by the *OED* refers to the first of these two meanings as used in *The Gest Hystoriale of the Destruction of Troy: An Aliterative Romance* (*c.* 1400), where 'Achilles with angur come angardly fast /. . . Slough him full slawthly with sleght of his hond'.[11] Another example of this use of the phrase *sleight of hand* is contained in the *Crucifixion* of the *Towneley Plays* (*c.* 1500), where the third torturer is well satisfied with the job of tying Christ to the cross when he says: 'So, that is well, it will not brest; / Bot let now se who dos the best / With any slegthe of hand.'[12] The second and more pertinent meaning for the present discussion may be seen in the example from the *Beggars' Bush* by Beaumont and Fletcher where Prig says: 'Will ye see any feates of activity, / Some sleight of hand, leigerdemaine? Hey passe, / Presto be gone there?' (Appendix 3).

The word *sleight* or *sleights* is also to be found in this context in relation to cleverness or dextrousness. In the *Newcastle Play* of *Noah's Ark* (*c.* 1440–50), Noah's wife says: 'God give him Evil to fayre / Of Hand to have such slight, / To make Ship less or more perfect.'[13] Pilate, in the *Conspiracy and Capture* in the *Towneley Plays*, speaks of Jesus: 'Bot sleyghtys / Agans hym shall be soght.'[14] More specifically, *sleight*, is also defined in the *OED* as 'Skill in jugglery or conjuring; sleight of hand' and 'A feat of jugglery or legerdemain; a trick or action performed with great dexterity, esp. so quickly as to deceive the eye'. Such deceit, not for entertainment purposes but for criminal ones, is alluded to in 1595 through the behaviour of Judith Philips in *The Brideling, Sadling and Ryding, of a rich Churle in Hampshire etc.*, where: 'This Iudeth Philips . . . practised many cousoning sleites and deuises to deceiue the simpler sort of people in the Countrey.'[15]

The terms *tregetry* and *treget* are found in England at an earlier date than *legerdemain* and *sleight of hand*. The *OED* defines the words as 'Juggling; deception, trickery' and 'Jugglery; trickery, deceit'. Additional definitions of *treget* are offered by the *MED* as: '(a) A transverse sword stroke, thrust, lunge; (b) trickery, duplicity, deceit; also, a deception; (c) as surname'. The word *tregetrie* is also defined by the *MED* in slightly different terms from the *OED* as: '(a) Pleasurable or diverting activity, entertainment; (b) sorcery, magic; (c) deceit, trickery, chicanery'. The verb *treget* is defined by the *OED* as 'To practise juggling tricks. Hence tregetting vbl sb'. The equivalent verb *tregeten* is defined in the *MED* as '(a) To perform tricks by sleight of hand or juggling; also, practice deception, deceive; (b) to deceive (sb.), trick; also subvert (a covenant), betray'. *Tregetinge* is derived from the verb *tregeten* and is defined in the *MED* as '(a) Sleight of hand, mime, juggling, jesting, etc.; (b) duplicitous conduct, deceit'. The earliest examples of *treget* in the *OED* and the *MED* are from the *Cursor Mundi* (*c.* 1300).[16] The first use of *treget* as a surname is recorded by the *MED* as 1176.[17]

As to the etymology of *tregetry, treget* and *tregeting,* the *OED* and the *MED* refer to Old French sources in respect of *tre(s)geterie,* meaning 'enchantment, magic'. Similarly, *treget* is derived from the Old French *tresgiet* with the same meaning as *tregetry. Tregeting* originates from *tregeten* as defined above, with its sources offered by the *MED* as the Old French *tresjeter, trejeter* and *treget(t)er.* In a description of Troy in the *Destruction of Troy, tregetrie* is highlighted as one of a number of pastimes along with chess, draughts and backgammon that are played during the month of May: 'Soche soteltie þai soght to solas hom with; / The tables, the top, tregetre also.'[18] Eight tregetours are employed to watch over a garden in *The Tale of Beryn,* where they are able to use their skill:

> The which[e] been so perfite of Nygramance,
> And of þe arte of apparene, and of tregetrie,
> That they make semen (as to a mannys sight)
> Abominabill wormys, þat sore ouȝt be a-friȝte
> The hertiest man on erth, but he warnyd were
> Of the grisly siȝtis þat he shuld see there.[19]

Reference to *prestigium* in the definition of *tregetinge* in the *Promptorium parvulorum* (1440) points to the synonymity with *prestigiation,* which is defined by the *OED* as 'The practice of juggling, sorcery, or magic; deception or delusion by such practice; conjuring'. The verb *prestigiate* is similarly defined as: 'To deceive by jugglery or as by magic; to delude'. The etymology of both noun and verb arises from the Latin *præstigiare.* Charlton T. Lewis and Charles Short, in *A Latin Dictionary,* define *præstigiae* as 'deceptions, illusions, jugglers' tricks, sleights, feats of legerdemain'. It should be noted, however, that the word *prestidigitation,* which is also defined by the *OED* in respect of legerdemain, is only recorded in its earliest use in the nineteenth century. The relationship between *tregetry, juggling* and *prestigiation* is clearly seen in William Horman's *Vulgaria* of 1519:

The iugler carieth clenly vnder his gublettis
Prestigiator scite visum ludificat cum acceptabulis
A iugler with his troget castis [tricks] deceueth mens syghtis
Prestigiator suis vafrementis intuentium oculos prestringit.[20]

Jugglery, juggling and *juggle,* in their earliest citations in the *MED* as *jogelerie, jogelinge* and *jogelen,* all refer to sleight of hand, performance of conjuring tricks and deception. They also refer to other forms of entertainment such as music, jesting and pantomime, as well as further meanings concerned with enchantment and sorcery. The *MED* again cites the *Promptorium parvulorum* (1440) in its definition of *Iogulrye,* or *iogulment,* as 'Prestigium, pancracium, mimilogium'. *Jogelinge* is defined with two meanings in the *MED*: '(a) Jesting, buffoonery; (b) trickery, deception'. The *OED* also provides two meanings to the verb *juggle*: '1. intr. To act as a JUGGLER; to amuse or entertain people with jesting, buffoonery, tricks etc.' and '2. To practise the skill or art of a JUGGLER in magic or legerdemain; to play conjuring tricks; to conjure'. The two distinct strands of meaning of *juggling* and *juggle* come much closer together in the *OED* definition of *jugglery* which is: '1. The art or practice of a juggler; minstrelsy, play; pretended magic or witchcraft; conjuring, legerdemain'. and '2. The playing of tricks likened to those of a juggler; trickery, deception'. Reference to 'deception' is often made through the notion of 'falseness'. In *The Life of Saint Meriasek*, Teudar, the emperor, accuses Meriasek: 'Out on thee, thou false juggler, / To defy my flower of gods!'.[21] Reginald Scot, in his *Discouerie of witchcraft*, makes a clear distinction between *juggling* and the old meaning of *conjuring* when he says: 'our iugglers approch much neerer to resemble *Pharaos* magicians, than either witches or conjurers, & can make a more liuelie shew of working miracles than anie inchantors can doo: for these practise to shew that in action, which witches doo in words and termes.'[22] Heinrich Cornelius Agrippa (1569) explains what he means by *juggling*: 'But let vs retourne to Magicke, wherof the Juglers skil is a parte also, that is, illusions, which are onely done accordinge to the outwarde apparance: with these the Magitiens doo shewe vaine visions, and with Juglinge castes [tricks] doo plaie many miracles.'[23] Like Scot, Thomas Cooper (1617) attempted to define and distinguish between 'Witch-craft which is performed by charmes' and 'Iugling . . . When strange Feats are performed, not by reall charmes, but onely by deluding of the eye, and some extraordinarie sleight: Not that any such thing is effected in *Truth,* but onely in *Appearance,* to the deceiued judgement, being peruerted by such delusions as the eye falsely apprehends.'[24] A strong example of the nature of juggling and communication of its different realities is contained in John Frith's 'An other booke ageynst Rastell' in *The Whole workes of W. Tyndale, Iohn Frith, and Doct. Barnes* (1573), where Frith says: 'Here he iuggeleth wyth me, and would make me beleue that he tossed me mine own ball agayne, but when I beholde it, I perceaue it to be none of mine: for he hath cut out all that shoulde make for me, so that he hath geuen it cleane an other shape then euer I entended that it should haue.'[25]

A seemingly common juggling trick is referred to in an epitaph to a juggler in George Herbert's *Witts Recreations* (1640): 'Death came to see thy trickes and cut in twaine, / Thy thread, why did'st not make it whole againe[?]'.[26] In *The Vision of William concerning Piers the Plowman* (1393–8) the inability to perform a number of musical and other skilled accomplishments is acknowledged in so much as:

> Ich can nat tabre ne trompe · ne telle faire gestes,
> Farten, ne fipelen · at festes, ne harpen,
> Iapen ne Iogelen · ne gentelliche pipe,
> Noper sailen ne sautrien · ne singe with þe giterne.[27]

Confirmation of the synonymity of juggling and sleight of hand is contained in the records of the *Mayors' Court Books* at Norwich in 1624, where 'william Denny who vse slight of hand vsually called Iuglinge beinge taken vagrant in this City ys punished and sent to Ipswich with a passe where he saith he hath dwelt by the space of the most part of a yeare nowe last past & hath hired a howse'.[28] Edmund Spenser, in *The Faerie Qveene* (1596), refers to the 'villane' who did 'prate and play, / And many pleasant trickes before her show, / To turne her eyes from his intent away: / For he in slights and iugling feates did flow, / And of legierdemayne the mysteries did know'.[29] In John Bale's *King Johan* (1538), Sedwision [Sedition] regards lawyers and preachers as knowing the mysteries of legerdemain in that they 'are my most secrett fryndes / w^t falce colores procure, them to be slayne'.[30]

Feats of activity is a phrase that is not recorded in the *MED* or *OED*, yet the examples provided earlier in this work make clear the specific use of the phrase and its application to juggling, tumbling, vaulting and dancing on the rope. The word *feats* is, however, defined by the *OED*, but in a broad sense as: 'The art, knack, or trick of doing anything'. Specific use of *feats* in relation to juggling is not recorded in the *MED* or the *OED*. The earliest *OED* example of the word *feat*, in relation to juggling, is 1682.

The performers of these processes exhibit a wider range of designations beyond the nature and scope of the activities themselves. All the designated performers, with the necessary exception of tumblers, vaulters and dancers on the rope, perform sleight of hand or legerdemain. Some tumblers, vaulters and dancers on the rope also perform sleight of hand but it cannot be said that they all do this. Even so, the activities of tumbling, vaulting and dancing on the rope do not form any part of the definitions of sleight of hand or legerdemain.

The earliest references in the *OED* to illuminate the word *tregetour* come from the *Cursor mundi* (*c.* 1300) and continue with the same meaning into the nineteenth century. The *Cursor mundi* refers to the implicit deception or diversion employed by the tregetour as: 'A trigettur i hope es he be, / Or ellis god him self es he.'[31] Here the *tregetour* is defined as 'One who works magic or plays tricks by sleight of hand; a conjurer; a juggler; hence a trickster, a deceiver'. The *MED* definition of *tregetour* widens out the meaning to include '(a) An entertainer, a sleight-of-hand artist, a juggler, an illusionist, etc.; (b) one who practises black magic, a sorcerer; (c) a deceiver, charlatan; (d) as surname'. The relevant definition to this work is (a), although (c) may be appropriate too, depending on the sense and context. Definition (d) may also be relevant if supported by other information. Although the *MED* includes the term *illusionist* in its definition of *tregetour* the same is not the case with the *OED* definition. Other similar terms such as *treget*, *tregetrie* and *tregeting* are similarly not defined in the *MED* or *OED* in terms of *illusion*. The earliest example of the term *illusionist* in the *OED* is 1864, although *illusion* is recorded in the late fourteenth century by Chaucer. In *The Franklin's Tale* in *The Canterbury Tales* (1386), Chaucer explains that: 'This is to seye, to maken illusion, / By swich an apparence or jogelrye– / I ne kan no termes of astrologye.'[32] Illusion is clearly involved in what amounts to a military-inspired trick as relayed in *The Seven Sages of Rome*. Here, several English manuscripts (the earliest dating from *c.* 1320–40) contribute to a fuller acount of the creation of an image of the devil, which is exaggerated through use of a mirror in order to scare off the Saracens in their attack upon one of the gates of Rome. One of the seven wise men of Rome, Genus ('Ianus'), was responsible for making an image from clothes:

> Ase blacke ase ani arnement,
> And heng þer on squirel tail,
> A þousand and mo, wiȝ outen fail.
> A viser ȝit he made more,
> Two faces bihinde and two bifore,
> And ij nosys in eyther halfe,
> More horrybeler thenne any calfe,

And the tonge also there on rede,
As euyr was brennynge lede.[33]

The image was positioned to be reflected down from the tower walls to the Saracens below. The figure held two swords and 'made more noyse and more boste / Than wolde half a gret oste. / The sarasyns þat loked on it / Were nygh owt of their wit.'[34] The mirror appeared to make 'grete noyse', whereupon the 'gatys of Rome were vppe caste' and the emperor's men rushed out to slay the enemy. Thus, Genus was deemed to have saved the city. The practicalities of the device are limited, for the story represents one of those incidents where the narrative power is stronger than the possible reality. Realisation of the reflected image of the devil would, no doubt, demand a restricted viewing angle. The capacity to create stronger illusion might have been possible through use of additional mirrors, as demonstrated in more modern tricks of illusion.[35]

John Gower describes the tregetor's work in respect of the necessary skill and nature of its product when he says:

Mi Sone, as guile under the hat
With sleyhtes of a tregetour
Is hidd, Envie of such colour
Hath yit the ferthe deceivant,
The which is cleped Falssemblant,
Whereof the matiere and the forme
Now herkne and I thee schal enforme.[36]

In *The Pricke of Conscience* (1542) reference is made to Antichrist as follows:

He sal gader fast til hym þan
Alle þat of þe devels crafte can,
Als negremanciens and tregettours,
Wiches and false enchauntours,
þat þe devels crafte sal hym ken
Whar-thurgh he sal decayve þe men.[37]

Wynkyn de Worde records in his *Treatyse of this Galaunt* (1520) 'For trygetours ˉt tryflours / that tauernes haunte / Haue trowth and temperaunce / troden vnder foote / Talwes and talkynge / and drynkynge ataunte'.[38] Chaucer makes a number of references to 'tregetry' and the 'tregetour', some of which are extended ones while others create the impression that he only partially understood that of which he wrote. In the English translation of *The Romaunt of the Rose* (c. 1400), ascribed to Chaucer, it is declared that: 'I did hem a tregetry' and that 'They know not al my tregetrye.' In the same work it is stated that 'sith they coude not perceyve / His treget and his crueltee, They wolde him folowe', and 'Thourgh me hath many oon deth resseyved, / That my treget never aperceyved.' Later still, the accusation is made that: 'Two tregetours art thou and he.'[39] In the often-quoted reference in *The Franklin's Tale* of *The Canterbury Tales*, Chaucer refers to the nature and scope of tregetry:

> For I am siker that ther be sciences
> By whiche men make diverse apparences,
> Swiche as thise subtile tregetoures pleye.
> For ofte at feestes have I wel herd seye
> That tregetours, withinne an halle large,
> Have maad come in a water and a barge,
> And in the halle rowen up and doun.
> Somtyme hath semed come a grym leoun;
> And somtyme floures sprynge as in a mede;
> Somtyme a vyne, and grapes white and rede;
> Somtyme a castel, al of lym and stoon;
> And whan hem lyked, voyded it anon.
> Thus semed it to every mannes sighte.[40]

Although Chaucer attributes the events of this quotation to 'tregetoures pleye', the described action of 'a water and a barge' does not relate to the capacity of the tregetour to create it. A convincing case is made for the origin of this event as taking place at the Royal Palace, Paris, in 1378, and on this occasion the movement of the 'water and a barge' that was 'rowen up and doun' was created by men hidden inside the barge.[41] Thus it is possible to see why the reported action might have been attributed to the skill of the tregetour. However, such an explanation does not deny Chaucer's capacity to know what a tregetour did; it simply inflates and misaligns the skill of the tregetour when an explanation of the illusion is not forthcoming. Care needs to be taken here that understanding of the tregetour's skill is not interpreted as being different from that of the juggler. Whereas the term *illusionist* might be considered different in emphasis from that of a *conjuror* today, in terms of the scale and possible purpose of their respective activities, the examples of tregetours' work offered by Chaucer refer to both small-scale activity and larger-scale, stage-managed activity. It is inappropriate to define the 'tregetour' only by such large-scale work as might be the case with a modern illusionist.

Thomas Tyrwhitt, the eighteenth-century editor of *The Poetical Works of Geoff. Chaucer*, wrongly concluded that the tregetour performed his work with the aid of 'machinery' and cited the French word *trebuchet* in support of this assumption. There is clearly no connection between *trebuchet*, in any of its meanings, and *tregetour*. Tyrwhitt does not offer proof of this connection, instead he leaves it up to his reader to 'judge whether the *tregetour* may not possibly have been so called from his frequent use of these insidious machines in his operations'. He goes on to say that it is certain that 'a great deal of machinery was requisite to produce the apparences [*sic*] or illusions enumerated by Chaucer'. It is clear, however, that Chaucer makes no such enumerations. Tregetours may not be defined or identified in relation to the use of machinery. The notion that tregetours were different from jugglers because they worked with machines is not based on any evidence. The tregetour was not an illusionist in the modern sense although, like the juggler, he employed illusion in his sleight of hand.[42]

The following, often-quoted, passage from Chaucer's *House of Fame* (*c.* 1384) refers to a small-scale trick where the nature of illusion is alluded to as follows:

> Ther saugh I Colle tregatour
> Upon a table of sycamour
> Pleye an uncouth thyng to telle;
> Y saugh him carien a wynd-melle
> Under a walsh-note shale.[43]

The 'walsh-note shale', or walnut shell, suitably hollowed out, governs the scale of this potential trick. The windmill is a model or a sign of a windmill. The *OED* offers both possibilities and yet neither of these meanings is illustrated by this quotation from Chaucer. The fictional 'Colle tregatour' is indicative of other evidence of the word *tregetour* as a surname and/or a role.[44] Philemon Holland, in his 1609 translation of Ammianus Marcellinus' *Rerum gestarum*, records the tregetour's activity and the response of his audience:

it happened at Antioch, that when all was still and silent, at the solemne stage-playes a dauncing Tregetour sent in to make sport together with his wife, was acting and counterfeiting certaine gestures that were commonly and usually taken up, with so pleasant and delightsome a grace, that the people were astonied thereat.[45]

Ammianus Marcellinus (*c.* AD 325–95) of Antioch settled in Rome after a period in the army of Ursicinus and service under the emperor of the east, Constantius II, and later under the emperor Julian. When in Rome he wrote his history of the Roman empire, *Rerum gestarum libri* XXXI, which covered the period between AD 96 and 378. In addition to his coverage of military events he also included aspects of economic and social affairs. It is likely that the 'astonied' people in the above account reacted in such a way to the power of the tregetour. Dancing skill may be appreciated, enjoyed and admired but the astonishment is likely to come from the illusion-creating capacity of tregetour activity. Desiderius Erasmus (1534) links and defines the terms *trogeter* and *iuglere* when he records that: 'These persons do make Christe a iuglere or a trogeter and a wonderfull deceiver o men.'[46] Such an account points to the notion of the synonymity of these two terms.

The etymology of *tregetour*, as provided by the *OED*, appears to be mutually supported by Old French and Latin sources. The English word is derived from the twelfth-century French word 'tre(s)geteo(u)r', with its meaning as 'a juggler, mountebank, agent-n[oun] of *tre(s)geter* to cast across or to and fro', and the Latin 'tra(ns)jectāre', which is combined from *trans* and *jactare*, meaning 'to throw, cast'. It is this definition that has enabled the uncomfortable understanding to arise that 'to throw, cast' is the same as 'throwing up objects'. This is a misleading interpretation and it is wrong. The Italian *tragettatore* is also translated as 'juggler'. Although the word 'cast' is frequently used in its meaning as 'trick' there is another sense in which the definition concerned with 'casting' or 'throwing' actions may be defined, and that is with the implicit concern for misdirection in the production of sleight of hand. The action of seemingly casting one way and/or another is involved in sleight of hand. This sense is alluded to in the *Legends of the Saints in the Scottish Dialect of the Fourteenth Century* in respect of *tregetry*, where it is declared 'þat gere fele men*n* wene þat þai / throw tryget are goddis verray'.[47]

The earliest use of the term *conjuror*, in respect of *legerdemain*, is recorded by the *OED* for 1727 and is thus not an appropriate word to use in this context.

Although the *OED* records the earliest use of *prestigiator* as 1614 there are earlier definitions and examples of its use before this date. Sir Walter Raleigh, in his *The History of the World* (1614) describes *Praestigiators* as those who 'dazell mens eies, and make them seeme to see what they see not: as false colours, and false shapes'.[48] The *Promptorium parvulorum* (1440) in its definitions of *Ioglyn, Iogulowre* and *Iogulyre* defines the terms with reference to the *Prestigior, prestigiator* and *Prestigium*. The *OED* defines the *prestigiator* as: 'One who practises 'prestigiation'; a juggler, a conjurer; a cheat'.

Even though the word *juggler* is the most appropriate one to use in respect of the practice of legerdemain it is also recorded by the *MED* and the *OED* with other meanings. The *MED* defines *jogelour* as: '1. (a) A minstrel, harper, singer; (b) an entertainer (usually itinerant); actor, jester, clown, tumbler, dancer. 2. (a) A sleight of hand artist, prestidigitator [*sic*], an illusionist; (b) an enchanter, wizard, diviner'. The *OED* offers similar definitions, although it links the definition of 'one who plays tricks by sleight of hand; a performer of legerdemain; a conjurer' with 'One who works marvels by the aid of magic or witchcraft, a magician, wizard, sorcerer'. Consequently, specific examples need to be allowed to separate these meanings in respect of jugglers and legerdemain. For instance, the *Chamberlains' Accounts* at New Romney, Kent, for 1620–1 cite an account that ties in the function of the King's juggler with that of performing tricks: 'paid vnto the kings Iugler [presumably Brandon] in reward that he should not shew his tricks in this Towne iijs iiijd.'[49] Another definition of 'juggler' in the *OED* refers to 'One who entertains or amuses people by stories, songs, buffoonery, tricks, etc.; a jester, buffoon'. It is this definition that in etymological terms is derived from the Latin *joculator* and *joculari* – to jest. The Latin *joculator* clearly develops through different phases in its meaning. In its early use, the word is the medieval Latin one for the minstrel in its broadest sense, and E. K. Chambers acknowledges that he has 'not come across *ioculator* as a noun before the eighth century but thenceforward it is widely used for minstrels of both the *scôp* and the *mimus* type'.[50] Chambers also establishes the equivalence in meaning of the terms *ioculator, ministrallus, mimus* and *histrio*. These headings may be found too in the *Exchequer Rolls of Scotland* from 1433–50.[51] The word *juggler* also appears to have been derived or influenced by the Old French forms of *jouglere, jogeleor, jougelour* and, later, *jougleur*. In addition the *OED* indicates that some of the Middle English forms may represent the Old French synonyms *jogeler* and *jougler*. Baret, in his *Alvearie . . .* (1580), defines a juggler as 'he that deceiueth or deludeth by legier de mayn'.[52] Some development of meaning, unrecorded in the *MED* or the *OED*, occurs through the title of the *Joculator domini regis* in the early sixteenth century. This title and function was the same as the 'King's Juggler', which may be verified by the occupier of the post, Thomas Brandon, who is recorded as receiving payment for legerdemain in a number of accounts, cited earlier, in respect of both the Latin and English titles. E. K. Chambers makes much the same point when he states: 'In English documents the Latin *ioculator* itself to some extent follows suit; the *ioculator regis* of the late fifteenth or early sixteenth-century accounts is not a minstrel or musician, but the royal *juggler*.'[53] Chambers does not, however, refer to the knowledge that the 'royal *juggler*' practised legerdemain.

The French form *jougleur* has led to some confusion through its presumed association with the word *jangleur* – a 'babbler'. The seeming fusion of these two words as *jongleur* has led to an incorrect assumption that *jougleur, jougelere, jogeler* and *jugelour* are synonymous with *jongleur*. The *OED* describes the changing meaning of *jongleur*: the first meaning is: 'The Norman French term (technically used by modern writers) for an itinerant minstrel, who sang and composed ballads, told stories and otherwise entertained people'. This meaning is equated with the first of the definitions offered by the *OED* of the *juggler* (see above). The earliest use of this term is illustrated by an example of 1779. The second meaning of *jongleur* is defined by the *OED* to equate with the second definition of *juggler* in the *OED* (see above) and the earliest example of this meaning is 1851. It can be seen therefore that even if the meaning of *jongleur* has changed since the Middle Ages, such late use of the term as 1779 and 1851 (the earliest examples) is too late to make appropriate or accurate use of it. The *juggler* is not a *jongleur* in the period under investigation.

The *circulator*, the *mountebank*, the *quacksalver* and the *emperic* all made use of juggling skills even though their prime function was not that of the juggler. To some extent, these terms are interchangeable. John Gaule (1652) also refers to the synonymity of the above terms when he states that:

One *Caesarius Maltes*, a praestigious Jugler, being taken at *Paris*, escaped prison by his circulatory tricks; for which being questioned again in another place, and condemned; the Governour (by his power, and against Law) reprieved him; as much taken with his feats of Leigerdemaine.[54]

Gaule introduces the phrase 'circulatory tricks', which relates to the activity of the *circulator* or *juggler*.[55] Horman (1519) translates *Circulatores* as *Iuglers*: 'Iuglers deceyue mennys syght. / Circulatores prestigiant intuentium oculos.'[56]

The *circulator* is defined by the *OED* as: 'A mountebank who gathers a ring or crowd of spectators about him; a quack, charlatan'. The earliest reference to the *mountebank* as recorded by the *OED* is 1577, and one definition is: '1. An itinerant quack who from an elevated platform appealed to his audience by means of stories, tricks, juggling, and the like, in which he was often assisted by a professional clown or fool'. The 'quack' referred to by this definition is derived from the term *quacksalver*, which is defined by the *OED* as: '1. An ignorant person who pretends to a knowledge of medicine or of wonderful remedies'. 'Quack' is defined by the *OED* as: '1. An ignorant pretender of medical or surgical skill; one who boasts to have a knowledge of wonderful remedies; an emperic or imposter in medicine'. The earliest example of the word in the *OED* is 1659. The word *quacksalver* is considered by the *OED* to be derived from the early Dutch, sixteenth-century *kwakzalver*. The second element of the word, 'salve', refers to ointment, whereas the 'stem of *quacken* (mod. Du. *kwakken*) to quack'. The 'emperic' referred to in the definition of *quack* is another synonymous term used to describe 'An untrained practitioner in physic or surgery; a quack'. Some distinction occurs between these two terms in that the 'emperic' also refers to 'A member of the sect among ancient physicians called *Empirici*, who (in opposition to the *Dogmatici* and *Methodici*) drew their rules of practice entirely from experience, to the exclusion of philosophical theory'. Both terms, as recorded in the definition of the *circulator*, provide implicit links to the *charlatan*, and it is in this sense that the juggling skills are important in convincing an audience, often through sleight of hand, that the remedies to particular bodily complaints may be cured by the application of ointments and oils. The efficacy of these treatments is often considered to have been dubious.

Appendix 1   Edward Melton's text (1681)

[Apart from a reprint of this text in 1702 this extract does not appear to have been reproduced since its first publication in 1681. Similarly, the work has not been translated previously into English. Similarities between the observations made by Ibn Batuta and Melton are evident. The translation given here is by Elsa Strietman.]

Eduward Meltons, Engelsch Edelmans, Zeldzaame en Gedenkwaardige Zee-en Land-Reizen; Door Eygypten, West-Indien, Perzien, Turkyen, Oost-Indien, en d'aangrenzende Gewesten; behelzende een zeer naauwkeurige beschrijving der genoemde Landen/ benevens der zelver Inwoonderen Godsdienst/ Regeering/ Zeden en Gewoonten/ mitsgaders veele zeer vreemde voorvallen/ ongemeene geschiedenissen/ en wonderlijke wedervaringen.

Aangevangen in den jaare 1660. en geeindigd in den jaare 1677. Vertaald uit d'eigene Aanteekeningen en Brieven van den gedagten Heer MELTON; en met verscheidene schoone Kopere Figuuren versierd. t' AMSTERDAM, BY JAN ten HOORN, Boek-verkooper over t' Oude Heeren-Logement, Anno 1681, pp. 468–9.

Men vind onder de Chinesen ook veele Tovenaars/ Teeken-bedieders/ Waarzeggers/ en konstige Bootsemakers en Googchelaars/ die van d'eene plaats na d'andere reizen/ om in gevaar van hun leeven/ ten minsten soo't schijnt/ hun kost te verdienen. 'k Zag een diergelijk Gezelschap in de maand van December te *Batavia* dingen doen/ die te recht voor wonderlijk konden gaan/ en waar van ik den Leezer hier't verhaal zal mededeelen.

Eerstelijk kroop een van den hoop onder een mand/ die zoo eng was/ dat hy'er naauwelijks onder konde zitten. Terstond daar op stak sijn Makker met een bloote degen soo dapper door en weer door den mand/ dat den geen/ die'er onderzat/ luidskeels begon te schreeuwen/ en het bloed van alle kanten door de teenen liep; maar zoo haast hy daar onder weer van daan kroop/ kon men gantsch geen letsel aan hem bespeuren. My stonden verwonderd/ dat niet een van deeze steeken hem getroffen

had/ daar nochtans de mand zoo geweldig naauw was/ en den degen daar
t'elkens door en weer door had gescheenen te gaan/ en daar wy met onze
oogen 't bloed daar hadden zien uitloopen.

Vervolgens nam een ander met wonderlijke gebaerden een *Bamboes*, die
wel 18 of 20 voeten lang was/ en onder de dikte van omtrent anderhalve
span had/ loopende vorders na boven allengskens scherper toe. Deeze
Bamboes zettede hy met het dikste einde in den Gordel/ dien hy om sijn
middel om gewonden had; wanneer een ander van de bende/ een jongeling van omtrent 20 jaren/ met een lugtige loop den *Bamboes*-drager van
achteren op de schouderen sprong/ en in een oogenblik tot boven aan den
top palmde/ daar hy met sijn eene been op ging staan/ zonder zich ergens
aan vast te houden. Dit scheen ons geweldig wonderlijk; maar noch
wonderlijker was 't wanneer den Bamboes-drager de stok los gelaten
hebbende/ zulks dat de zelve nu niets meer als op sijn gordel steunde/
met wakkere schreeden heen en weer begon te wandelen/ zonder zijn
last te laten vallen. Dus wandelende/ stak hy den buik/ om den *Bamboes*
des te beter in 't gewigt te konnen houden/ dapper voor uit/ en zettede
de handen in de zijden/ ziende gedurig opwaarts na de beweeging van
den geen/ dien hy droeg/ en sijn lichaam daar gestadig gints en weer
na buigende; invoegen dat wy klaerlijk bespeuren konden/ dat deese
konst door geen toovery/ maar alleenlijk door een behendig en vaerdig
balanceeren toeging.

Na dat den jongeling nu weder beneden gekommen was/ en aldaar
eenige kuurtjes aangeregt had/ klom hy andermaal op de zelve manier na
boven/ en ging thans met de buik op het spits van den *Bamboes* leggen/
steekende handen en voeten van zich/ even gelijk men de vliegende
kupidootjes pleegt uit te schilderen. Met deeze vragt begon den Drager
weer als voor heen dapper met rasse schreeden heen en weer te wandelen/
zonder dat men eens bespeuren konde/ dat hy angstig voor sijn vragt was.

Voor de darde maal zettede hy de *Bamboes* vlak boven op sijn hoofd/ en
den gedachten jongeling daar kruiswijs met de beenen onder 't lichaam op
zijnde gaen sitten/ liep hy/ zonder dat de stok nu eenig steunsel had/ daar
soo geswind mee voort/ dat ik ieder oogenblik/ wanneer hy omkeerde/
niet anders dagt/ of den ander zou van boven neer gekomen hebben; maer
deese wist sich met d'armen soo wel in 't gewigt te houden/ dat hy
onbeschadigd met een vrolijk gelaat weer beneden kwam.

Maar nu zal ik een zaak gaan verhalen/ die alle geloof te boven gaat/ en
dien ik hier naauwelijks zoude durven invoegen/ indien 'er niet duizend
nevens my oog-getuigen van geweest waren. Een van deese selve bende
nam een klouwen touw/ waar van hy het eene eind in de hand hield/ en

het overige met sulk een kragt na de lugt wierp/ dat wy met ons gesigt het eind daar van niet bereiken konden. Thans klauterde hy met cen onuitspreekelijke geswindheid by dit touw op tot soo hoog/ dat wy hem niet langer sien konden. 'k Stond nu vol verwonderings/ niet weetende wat hier van worden zou; wanneer 'er een been uit de lugt kwam vallen. Een van deeze tooveragtigen hoop raapte het terstond op/ en wierp het in de mand/ daar ik hier voor af gesprooken heb. Een oogenblik daar na viel 'er een hand/ en terstond daar op het andere been. Om kort te gaan/ alle de leden des lichaams kwamen aldus uit de lugt vallen/ en wierden by malkander in de mand geworpen. 't Alderlaatste stuk/ dat wy neer sagen komen/ was het hoofd/ 't geen niet soo haast d' aarde had geraakt/ of den geen/ die de stukken opgeraapt/ en in de mand geworpen had/ stolpte deselve 't onderste boven. Thans sagen wy voor onse oogen alle deeze leeden weer aan malkander kruipen/ en in 't kort een volkomen mensch uitmaken/ die terstond weer/ gelijk voor heen/ gaan en staan konde/ zonder het minste letsel te hebben. Nooit ben ik soo verwonderd geweest/ als toen ik dit wonderlijk werk aanzag/ en ik twijfelde nu niet langer/ of deeze verblinde menschen wierden van den Duivel daar in geholpen; want het dunkt my t'eenemaal onmogelijk/ dat men door natuurlijke middelen iets diergelijks zoude konnen doen.

Translation:

Eduward Melton's, English Nobleman's, Rare and Memorable Sea and Land Voyages Through Egypt, West-Indies, Persia, Turkey, East India and the neighbouring regions; containing a very accurate description of the aforementioned countries/ as well as of the Religion of the Inhabitants thereof/ their Government/ Mores and Customs/ including many very strange incidents/ unusual histories/ and miraculous experiences.

Begun in the year 1660. And concluded in the year 1677. Translated from the personal Notes and Letters of the said Lord MELTON; And decorated with several beautiful Copper Drawings. at AMSTERDAM By JAN ten HOORN, Book-seller above the Oude Heeren-Logement, Anno 1681.

Amongst the Chinese one can find many Wizards/ Explainers of Portents/ Soothsayers/ and artful Acrobats and Magicians/ who travel from one place to the next/ and endanger their lives/ or so it would seem/ in order to earn their living. I saw such a company, in the month of December, in Batavia, do things/ which justly may be held to be miraculous/ and the account of which I will here relate to the Reader.

First of all one of them crawled under a basket/ which was so tight/ that he could barely sit underneath it. Immediately after that his companion so fiercely stabbed a dagger through the basket, high and low, that the one who was sitting underneath it began to scream loudly and the blood ran on all sides through the gaps in the basket; but as soon as he crawled out of it/ it was impossible to find any wounds on him. We stood and marvelled/ that not one of the stabs with the dagger had hit him/ since the basket was so very tight/ and the dagger had gone in and out through it so often/ and we had, with our own eyes, seen the blood run out of it.

Then another one took, with mysterious gestures, a bamboo, which was at least 18 or 20 feet long/ and was about one and a half handspan thick at the bottom and gradually became sharper towards the top. This Bamboo he placed with the thick end in the girdle/ which he had wound round his middle; whilst another of the troupe/ a youngster of about 20 years old/ jumped with a light movement from behind on to the shoulders of the Bamboo-carrier/ and in a trice palmed his way up to the top/ where he went and stood on one leg/ without holding on to anything. This seemed to us truly a marvel; but even more wondrous was it that the Bamboo-carrier, having withdrawn his hands from the stick/ so that it now rested on nothing but his girdle/ began to pace about with lively steps/ without dropping his load. Walking about thus/ he pushed out his belly as far as possible/ in order to balance the Bamboo better/ and put his hands on his hips/ looking up constantly at the movements of the one/ he carried/ and bending his body steadily one way and the other; so that we could see/ that this art was not achieved by wizardry/ but solely by clever and skilled balancing.

Now, after the youngster had come down again/ and carried out some acrobatic tricks/ he again climbed up in the same manner/ and laid himself down on his belly on the sharp point of the Bamboo/ stretching out his hands and feet/ just as one is accustomed to paint the flying little Cupidos. With this burden the Carrier began to pace about with lively steps/ without anyone being able to observe/ that he was afraid for his burden.

The third time he placed the Bamboo on the top of his head/ and the youngster having sat down with his legs crossed on its top/ the Carrier walked/ now without any other support for the stick/ so fast about/ that every moment/ that he turned around/ I could not think otherwise/ than that his companion would fall down from the top; but he was able to balance himself so well with his arms/ that he came down undamaged and with a cheerful countenance.

But now I want to relate a matter/ which defies all belief/ and which I would hardly have dared to insert here/ had there not been a thousand eyewitnesses of this as well as myself. One of this same company took a coil of rope/ of which he held one end in his hand/ and threw the rest into the air with such force/ that we could barely keep the other end in our sight. Then, with inexpressible speed he clambered so high up the rope/ that we could no longer see him. I stood, amazed/ not knowing what would transpire; when a leg came tumbling down from the sky. One of this gang of wizards instantly picked it up/ and threw it in the basket/ of which I have spoken before. A moment later a hand fell down/ and immediately thereafter the other leg. In short/ all the parts of the body came tumbling down from the sky in the same fashion/ and were thrown together in the basket. The very last bit/ which we saw coming down/ was the head/ and no sooner had it touched the earth/ than the one who had gathered together the pieces/ and thrown them into the basket/ upended this. Now we saw before our very eyes all the parts join together again/ and quite rapidly become a perfect human being again/ who, just as before/ could walk and move/ without showing any injuries. Never have I been so astonished/ as when I saw this miraculous work/ and now I did not doubt any longer/ that these benighted people were assisted in this by the Devil; for it seems to me absolutely impossible/ that one could achieve something like this by natural means.

Appendix 2   Wily Beguild *(1606)*

[This extract is taken from the prologue of *Wily Beguild* and demonstrates a synthesis of juggling language and patter.]

Anon. [Samuel Rowley?], *A Pleasant Comedie, Called Wily Begvilde* (London: H[umphrey] L[ownes] for Clement Knight, 1606), p. 2

> Enter a Iuggler
>
> IUGGLER. Why how now humorous *George*? what as me-choly as a mantletree?
> Will you see any trickes of Leigerdemaine, slight of hand,
> clenly conuayance, or *deceptio visus*? what will you see
> Gentleman to driue you out of these dumps?
> PROL. Out you soust gurnet, you Woolfist, be gon I say
> and bid the Players dispatch and come away quickly, and
> tell their fiery Poet that before I haue done with him; Ile
> make him do penance vpon a stage in a Calues skin.
> IUGGLER. O Lord sir ye are deceiued in me, I am no tale-carrier, I am a Iuggler.
> I haue the superficiall skill of all the seuen liberall sciences at my fingers end.
> Ile shew you a tricke of the twelues, and turne him ouer the thumbes with a trice.
> Ile make him fly swifter then meditation.
> Ile shew you as many toies as there be minutes in a moneth, and as many trickes as there be motes in the sunne.
> PROL. Prithee what trickes canst thou doe?
> IUGGLER. Marry sir I wil shew you a trick of cleanly con-ueiance.
> *Hei fortuna furim nunquam credo*, With a cast of cleane con-ueyance, come aloft
> *Iack* for thy masters aduantage (hees gone I warrant ye.)
> {*Spectrum* is conueied away: and *Wily*
> {*beguiled*, stands in the place of it.

PROL. Mas an tis well done, now I see thou canst doe
something, holde thee thers twelue pence for thy labour.
Goe to that barme-froth Poet and to him say,
He quite has lost the Title of his play,
His Calue skin iests from hence are cleane exil'd.
Thus once you see that Wily is beguil'd. *Exit the Iuggler.*

Appendix 3   Beggars' Bush *(1622)*

[The content of this scene is composed of tricks that if conducted in reality would rely entirely on the skills of the juggler. However, successful theatrical completion of the scene requires only limited juggling skill and provides an example of the way in which juggling skills may be fulfilled by staging arrangements.]

Francis Beaumont and John Fletcher, *The Dramatic Works in the Beaumont and Fletcher Canon*, ed. Fredson Bowers, 10 vols. (Cambridge: Cambridge University Press, 1966–96), III (1976), 279–81

> *Enter* Prig, *and* Ferret.
> PRIG. Will ye see any feates of activity,
> Some sleight of hand, leigerdemaine? hey passe,
> Presto, be gone there?
> 2. BOORE.   Sit downe Jugler.
> PRIG [aside]. Sirha, play you your art well; draw neer piper:
> Look you, my honest friends, you see my hands;
> Plaine dealing is no Divel: lend me some money;
> Twelve-pence a piece will serve.
> 1. 2. BOORES   There, there.
> PRIG. I thank ye,
> Thanke ye heartily: when shall I pay ye?
> ALL BOORES. Ha, ha, ha, by'th masse this was a fine trick.
> PRIG. A merry sleight toy: but now I'le shew your Worships A tricke indeed.
> HIGGEN. Marke him well now my Masters.
> PRIG. Here are three balls, these balls shall be three bullets,
> One, two, and three: *ascentibus malentibus.*
> *Presto*, be gone: they are vanish'd: faire play Gentlemen,
> Now these three, like three bullets, from your three noses
> Will I plucke presently: feare not, no harme boyes,
> *Titere, tu patule*——

1. BOORE.   Oh, oh, oh.

PRIG.   *Recubans sub tegmine fagi.*

2. BOORE   Ye pull too hard; ye pull too hard.

PRIG. Stand faire then:
Silvestramtrim-tram.

3. BOORE.   Hold, hold, hold.

PRIG. Come aloft bullets three, with a whim-wham:
Have ye their moneys?

HIGGEN.   Yes, yes.

1. BOORE.   Oh rare Jugler.

2. BOORE.   Oh admirable Jugler,

PRIG.   One tricke more yet;
Hey, come aloft: *sa, sa, flim, flam, taradumbis?*
East, west, north, south, now flye like *Jacke* with a *bumbis.*
Now all your money's gone: pray search your pockets.

1. BOORE.   Humh.

2. BOORE.   Ha.

3. BOORE.   The Divell a penny's here.

PRIG.   This was a rare tricke.

1. BOORE.   But 'twould be a far rarer to restore it.

PRIG. I'le doe ye that too: looke upon me earnestly,
And move not any wayes your eyes from this place,
This button here: pow, whir, whiss, shake your pockets.

1. BOORE.   By'th masse 'tis here againe boyes.

PRIG. Rest ye merry;
My first tricke has paid me.

ALL BOORES.   I, take it, take it.

2. BOORE.   And take some drinke too.

PRIG.   Not a drop now I thanke you.

HIGGEN.   Away, we are discover'd else.
    Exeunt [Prig, Ferret and Higgen].

Appendix 4   The Knave in Graine *(1640)*

[The author of the play is unknown, although 'J. D.' has been tentatively identified by some as 'John Davenport'. The scene consists of a well-structured 'scam' in which 'Julio', the knave in grain, cheats 'A country fellow' out of his 'twenty shillings peece'.]

The Knave in Graine, New Vampt. A witty Comedy, Acted at the Fortune many dayes together with great Applause. Written by J. D. Gent. (London: J.[ohn] O.[kes], 1640)

Actus quintas. Scena prima. [sigs. M^r–M2^r]
A Country fellow standing by.
COUNTRY FEL. They talke of Cheaters, here is a twenty shillings peece that I put into my mouth, let any Cheater in Christendome cousen me of this, and carry it away cleanly, and Ile not only forgive him, but hugge him and imbrace him for it, and say he is a very *Hocus Pocus* indeed.
IULIO. What said that fellow?
PUSSE. He saith he hath a peece in his mouth, that all *Europe* shall not cheate him of.
IULIO. I have markt him, 'tis mine owne: and notwithstanding all this melancholy we'le spend it at night in Wine and Musicke.
COUNT. FEL. Hee that can plucke this peece out of my jawes, spight of my teeth, and I keepe my mouth fast shut, Ile say hee is more than a Cheater, and a Doctor *Faustus*, or *Mephostophilus* at least.
PUSS. Dost heare how he brags?
JULIO. Tis mine own I warrant thee.

[Later in the same scene]

He [Julio] *draws his handkerchiefe (as to wipe his eyes) just before the Country fellow, and scatters some small mony.*

COUNTRY FELLOW. Sir, you have (I think) let fall some mony.

IULIO. Thanks honest friend. *He takes it up.*

COUNT. FEL. What do you look for? I can assure you here is all that fell.

IULIO. Nay, sure I had more mony? 'tis not in my handkerchief, nor in my pockets, I have examined them both.

SERG. Why, what do you want sir?

IULIO. A piece, a piece, and had it now, just now; sure whilst I was so high pearcht none could dive so low into my pocket, it was sure as I lighted, and dropt from mee, just as I drew my hankerchief.

PUSS. Some such thing I saw fall.

IULIO. Pray who were they that stoopt?

SERG. I saw non stoop but this Country fellow.

IULIO. Then sir, I must demand this piece of you.

COUNT. FELLOW. Of me? I professe I tooke up but two shillings and six pence, and that I gave into your hand.

IULIO. But I professe that one of them was a piece, and never came into my hand, and that I must demand of you: say did no body stoop but hee?

SERG. None I assure you.

IULIO. Thou art still my honest Sergeant.

PUSS. That fellow hath something in his mouth.

COUNT. FEL. Yes my tongue and my teeth, and what of all that.

PUSS. Nay, something else sure, for hee is not troubled with the Mumps, and yet see how one side of his cheeks bumps out.

IULIO. I am afraid, we shall finde him a Cheater.

SERG. Sirrah know I am an Officer, I charge you open your mouth, and let us see what you have in it, &c.

COUNT. FEL. Well sir, I have a twenty shillings piece, what then?

SERG. And this man misseth a twenty shilling piece out of his pocket.

IULIO. Plead well Sergeant and thou shalt have thy see.

COUNT. FEL. Well, there it is, what make you of it?

IULIO. Marry twenty shillings good and lawfull currant mony, Puss, was not this the piece that I put in my pocket this morning?

PUSS. I know it by that mark.

SERG. And she's witnesse sufficient in conscience.

IULIO. Doe you see Gentlemen, I am here brought to publike penance for a Cheater, and here's a plain fellow that (it seems) in his simplicity would out-doe me: if I be thus censured meerly for suspicion; shall he scape free that is taken in the very action?

ALL. No, no, mount him, mount him.

COUNT. FEL. Nay, by your favour Gentlemen, I have driven a Cart often for my pleasure, and would bee both loth to ride in one now for my punishment. It is penance enough for mee to part with my peece, which cannot be more currant of Coine, then his is Arrant for Knavery. *Exit.*

[A similar modern-day 'scam' was recently seen on the BBC 1 'fly-on-the-wall' film, *Hot Plastic*, where the film 'follows police squads as they trail the thieves who use cutting-edge technology to achieve their nefarious ends'. The scene is this: a woman goes up to a 'hole-in-the-wall' cash dispenser and puts her card into the machine. At this point a man comes to her side and drops a £20 note. As he does so he asks the woman if she has dropped the note. She instinctively bends to pick it up. As she does so, a second member of the gang comes behind her to extract her card from the machine. As he does this he quickly 'swipes' her card into a 'skimmer', which is a small hand-held elctronic device that will record the electronic information contained on the card. He hands the card to her but she is sufficiently flustered by now that she does not ask the important question 'How did you get hold of my card?'. The person who dropped the £20 note continues to pretend to use the cash dispenser and the one who swiped the card stops a passer-by to ask for directions. A third member of the group has been used as a look-out. At this point the woman does not know that this gang now has the necessary information to copy or 'clone' her card and use it to retrieve money from her account. *Hot Plastic*, executive producers Matt Holden and Nick Curwin, BBC 1, 9.00 pm, Wednesday 2 June, 2004.]

Notes

INTRODUCTION

1 *OED* **conjuration** 5. transf. 'Performance of magic art or sleight of hand; conjury'. The earliest use is 1734. **conjuration** 6. 'A conjuring trick'. The earliest use is 1820. **conjure** III 8. 'To affect, effect, produce, bring out, convey away, by the arts of the conjurer or juggler'. **conjurer 2**. 'One who practises legerdemain: a juggler'. The earliest use is 1727. **conjury**². The earliest use is 1855.

2 *The Oxford Companion to the Theatre*, ed. Phyllis Hartnoll, 3rd edn (London: Oxford University Press, 1951; repr. 1972), p. 526.

3 John Beckmann, *A History of Inventions and Discoveries*, trans. William Johnston, 4 vols. (London: J. Bell, 1797 (vols. I–III); J. Walker, 1814 (vol. IV), III, pp. 282–336. The term 'juggler' as used by Beckmann in 1797 was still being used to describe the activity of conjuring in its modern sense. The collection was reprinted and re-presented in 1846 in two volumes: John Beckmann, *A History of Inventions and Discoveries*, enlarged and rev. William Francis and J. W. Griffith 2 vols. (London: Henry G. Bohn, 1846), II, pp. 115–42. William Hone, however, records a description in 1826 of 'The Young American [who] will Perform after the Manner of the French Jugglers at Vauxhall Gardens, with Balls, Rings, Daggers, &c'. The description states: 'He commenced his performances by throwing up three balls, which he kept constantly in the air, as he afterwards did four, and then five, with great dexterity, using his hands, shoulders, and elbows, apparently with equal ease. He afterwards threw up three rings, each about four inches in diameter, and then four, which he kept in motion with similar success. To end his performance he produced three knives, which, by throwing up and down, he contrived to preserve in the air altogether. These feats forcibly reminded me of the Anglo-Saxon Glee-man, who "threw three balls and three knives alternately in the air, and caught them, one by one, as they fell; returning them again in regular rotation".' See William Hone, *The Every-Day Book*, 2 vols. (London: Hunt and Clarke, 1826–7), I (1826), p. 1187; Joseph Strutt, *The Sports and Pastimes of the People of England* (London: Thomas Tegg, 1834), p. 173. It seems that both meanings of the word 'juggler' ran concurrently through the nineteenth century. One possible explanation for this diversion of meaning may be accounted for in the activities of the 'French juggler' and the 'Indian

juggler'. These jugglers performed feats of juggling in both senses of the word. 'French' and 'Indian' jugglers were frequent visitors to England in the nineteenth century.

4 The activities of 'Mexicani ioculatores' are described in 1557 by Girolamo Cardano as follows: 'Mexicani ioculatores primum pedibus ea agunt, quae alij uix manibus facere solent, hastiludia exercent, iactant recipiunt*que* quae in sublime iactauerint: alij pedibus superstant humeris alienis, ita ut secundo tertius insistat. Facile est ascendere, si primum tertius secundo genibus insistat, inde eodem modo secundus primo, pòst singuli se erigant: quae autem supremus agat iactando ludendo*que* fidem quasi excedere uidentur: robore haec fiunt, quod contentione constat, tum exercitatione, at*que* agilitate, unum alteri insistere, uulgare est apud nostros gerulos, tertium secundo difficilius, non tamen ita, ut magnam admirationem pariat: quae ueró sic actitat, rara sunt, & ideo etiam admiratione digna. Dici solet robur spinae dorsi, omnibus his plurimu*m* conducere, quale hoc est.' [Mexican 'jugglers' first do things with their feet which others are scarcely accustomed to do with their hands; they practise jousts, they throw and catch what they have thrown into the air: others stand with their feet on the shoulders of others, so that the third stands on the second. It is easy to climb up, if at first the third stands on the knees of the second, then in the same way the second on the first, afterwards one at a time they raise themselves up: what things the topmost does, however, in throwing and playing, seem as if they beggar belief: these things are done by strength, which consists of effort, then of practice, and of agility; one standing on another is common among our bearers; the third on the second is harder, but not so that it attracts great admiration: those who truly behave thus are rare, and therefore even worthy of admiration. It is generally said that the strength of the spine of the back greatly conduces to all these activities such as this is.] Girolamo Cardano, *Hieronymi Cardani Mediolanensis Medici de rervm, varietate libri* xvii (Basle: H. Petri, 1557), p. 466. Translation by Philip A. Shaw.

5 Roger Bacon, *Epistola Fratris Rogerii Baconis, De Secretis Operibus Artis et Naturae, et de Nullitate Magiae. Operâ Iohannis Dee Londinensis E pluribus exemplaribus castigata olim, et ad sensum integrum restituta. Nunc verò a quodam veritatis amatore, in gratiam verae scientiae candidatorum foras emissa; cum notis quibusdam partim ipsius Johannis Dee, partim edentis* (Hamburg: Bibliopolio Frobeniano, 1618), p. 2.

6 Roger Bacon, *Frier Bacon his Discovery of the Miracles of Art, Nature, and Magick. Faithfully translated out of Dʳ Dees own Copy, by T. M. and never before in English* (London : Simon Miller, 1659), p. 2. See also Samuel Butler, *The Genuine Remains in Verse and Prose of Mr Samuel Butler*, 2 vols. (London: J. and R. Tonson, 1759), ii, p. 263.

1 JUGGLERS: THE CREATORS OF MAGIC

1 *Register of Royal and Baronial Domestic Minstrels 1272–1327*, ed. Constance Bullock-Davies (Woodbridge: Boydell, 1986), p. 77; Joseph Strutt,

Glig-Gamena Angel Deod.; or, The Sports and Pastimes of the People of England: including the Rural and Domestic Recreations, May Games, Mummeries, Pageants, Processions, and Pompous Spectacles, from the earliest Period to the present Time: Illustrated by Engravings selected from Ancient Paintings; in which are represented most of the Popular Diversions (London: T. Bensley for J. White, 1801), p. 158.

2 *Records of Early English Drama: Cambridge,* ed. Alan H. Nelson, 2 vols. (Toronto; Buffalo; London: University of Toronto Press, 1989), I, p. 78; II, p. 1099.

3 *Records of Early English Drama: Herefordshire, Worcestershire,* ed. David N. Klausner (Toronto; Buffalo; London: University of Toronto Press, 1990), p. 528.

4 *Accounts of the Lord High Treasurer of Scotland,* ed. Thomas Dickson, Sir James Balfour-Paul and Charles T. McInnes, 13 vols. (Edinburgh: H M General Register House, Her Majesty's Stationery Office, 1877–1978), X (1913), p. 167.

5 Albert Feuillerat, *Documents Relating to the Revels at Court in the Time of King Edward VI and Queen Mary: The Loseley Manuscripts* (Louvain: A. Uystpruyst, 1914), p. 90.

6 *Collections* XI, ed. David Galloway and John Wasson, Malone Society (Oxford: Oxford University Press, 1980), p. 58.

7 *Ibid.*, p. 21.

8 *Records of Early English Drama: Sussex,* ed. Cameron Louis (Toronto; Buffalo; London: Brepols Publishers and University of Toronto Press, 2000), pp. 18, 230.

9 *Anglo-Saxon Charters: An Annotated List and Bibliography,* ed. P. H. Sawyer (London: Royal Historical Society, 1968), p. 452.

10 *Collections* XI, p. 36.

11 *Records of Early English Drama: Kent,* ed. James M. Gibson, 3 vols. (Toronto; Buffalo; London: British Library and University of Toronto Press, 2002), II, p. 673.

12 *Ibid.*, I, p. 113.

13 *Collections* VII, ed. Giles E. Dawson, Malone Society (Oxford: Oxford University Press, 1965), p. 35.

14 *REED: Kent,* II, pp. 810, 834, 836.

15 *REED: Sussex,* p. 86.

16 *Ibid.*, p. 89.

17 *Collections* XI, p. 114; *Records of Early English Drama: Devon,* ed. John M. Wasson (Toronto; Buffalo; London: University of Toronto Press, 1986), p. 40. The date of 1542–3 recorded here suggests Smythe rather than Brandon as the King's juggler.

18 *Collections* XI, p. 114.

19 *Records of Early English Drama: Cumberland, Westmorland, Gloucestershire,* ed. Audrey Douglas and Peter Greenfield (Toronto; Buffalo; London: University of Toronto Press, 1986), p. 299.

20 *Records of Early English Drama: Shropshire*, ed. J. Alan B. Somerset, 2 vols. (Toronto; Buffalo; London: University of Toronto Press, 1994), I, p. 84.
21 *Ibid.*, I, 204.
22 *Records of Early English Drama: Coventry*, ed. R. W. Ingram (Toronto; Buffalo; London: University of Toronto Press and Manchester University Press, 1981), p. 429.
23 *REED: Sussex*, p. 14.
24 *REED: Shropshire*, I, p. 178; II, p. 596; *Collections* XI, p. 36.
25 *REED: Herefordshire, Worcestershire*, p. 472.
26 *REED: Shropshire*, I, 178, 193.
27 *REED: Herefordshire, Worcestershire*, p. 472.
28 *Ibid.*, pp. 478, 484, 487, 491, 494, 499, 504, 508, 514, 518, 526.
29 *Ibid.*, p. 494.
30 *Records of Early English Drama: Dorset, Cornwall*, ed. Rosalind Conklin Hays, C. E. McGee, Sally L. Joyce and Evelyn S. Newlyn (Toronto; Buffalo: Brepols and University of Toronto Press, 1999), pp. 407, 494, 585; *REED: Devon*, pp. 37, 62, 125, 132, 133, 220, 221; *Records of Early English Drama: Oxford*, ed. John R. Elliott, Jr, Alan H. Nelson, Alexandra F. Johnston and Diana Wyatt, 2 vols. (Toronto; Buffalo: British Library and University of Toronto Press, 2004), p. 77.
31 *Collections* XI, p. III.
32 *Ibid.*, pp. 110, 112, 114, 182.
33 *Ibid.*, p. 182.
34 *REED: Cambridge*, I, p. III.
35 *Ibid.*, I, p. 106.
36 *Ibid.*, I, p. 109.
37 *Collections* II:3, ed. W. W. Greg, Malone Society (Oxford: Oxford University Press, 1931), pp. 286–7.
38 Reginald Scot, *The Discouerie of witchcraft* (London: H[enry] Denham for W[illiam] Brome, 1584), pp. 308–9.
39 James I, King of England, *Daemonologie, In Forme of a Dialogue, Diuided into three Bookes* (Edinburgh: Robert Walde-graue, 1597), p. 22.
40 See Chapter 7, p. 150 and note 40. Robert Harrison's translation of Lavater's *Of ghostes and spirites walking by nyght, and of strange noyses, crackes, and sundry forewarnynges, which commonly happen before the death of men, grat slaughters, & alterations of kyngdomes* was published in 1572 (London: Henry Benneyman for Richard Watkyns) and the original was published in Zurich in 1570. The understanding outlined here predates that of Scot's *Discouerie of witchcraft*.
41 Scot, *Discouerie of witchcraft*, pp. 309, 330, 339, 343–4, 349, 352.
42 George Peele, *Merrie Conceited Iests: Of George Peele Gentleman, sometimes a Student in OXFORD. Wherein is shewed the course of his life, how he liued: a man very well knowne in the Citie of London, and elsewhere* (London: G[eorge] P[urslowe] for F[rancis] Faulkner, 1627), sig. B3^v.

43 Scot, *Discouerie of witchcraft*, p. 144.
44 *Ibid.*, p. 252.
45 Cornish Record Office, Truro, *The* MS *Works of Sir Richard Carew*, CZ/EE/ 32, pp. 85–7.
46 Scot, *Discouerie of witchcraft*, p. 336.
47 *Ibid.*, pp. 335–6.
48 S[amuel] R[id], *The Art of Iugling or Legerdemaine. Wherein is deciphered, all the conueyances of Legerdemaine and Iugling, how they are effected, & wherin they chiefly consist* (London: T[homas] B[ushell], 1612); Henry van Etten [Jean Leurechon], *Mathematicall Recreations* (London: T[homas] Cotes for R[ichard] Hawkins, 1633; Anon. [William Vincent], *Hocvs Pocvs Ivnior. The Anatomie of Legerdemain; Or, The Art of Iugling set forth in his proper colours, fully, plainely, and exactly, so that an ignorant person may thereby learne the full perfection of the same, after a little practise* (London: T[homas] H[arper] for R[alph] M[abb], 1634).
49 Cornish Record Office, MS *works of Sir Richard Carew*, pp. 87–8.
50 Scot, *Discouerie of witchcraft*, p. 327. A similar trick is outlined in 1582 under the title *Iocus alter histrionicus* [*Another Jest of Stage Players*]: 'Multis & hoc admirandum videbatur, quod tamen vbi modum quo similiter agi possit, exposuerimus, ludicrum existimabitur. Vitrum vir quidam nobis inspicientibus obtulit, in quod anulum immisit, qui sua sponte quoties id expeteremus in vitro saltitabat. Hic astus hac ratione peractus est. Subtilis cuiuspiam mulieris capillus anulo adaptatus erat, hominisque ludentis digitis. Cur ergo saltandum esset anulo, digitos histrio motitabat, quib. agitatis, simul anulus ipse mouebatur. nobis capillum nequaquam conspicientibus. Facum hic histrio subtili commento tegebat. Anulus hic (aiebat) lasciuarum puellarum more non saltat, nisi meis ipsius digitis ei tympanum pulsem. A quodam Histrione Veneto' [This also seemed strange to many, but when I shall shew you the way to do the like, you will think it a silly thing. A certain Man brought a Glass to us, we looking into it, he put in a Ring, which as oft as we desired, it would leap in the Glass. This Trick was performed thus. There was a fine hair of a Womans head made fast to the Ring, and to the fingers of the Man that made the sport: when therefore the Ring must Dance, the Stage-Player moved his fingers, and the Ring moved therewith, and we saw not the hair. The Fellow concealed this Jugling by a cunning device; saith he, this Ring will not Dance like fair Maids, unless I Pipe and Taber with my fingers to it. *A Venetian Jugler*]; Hanss Jacob Wecker, *De secretis libri* XVII (Basle [n.p.]: 1582), p. 950; Hanss Jacob Wecker, *Eighteen Books of the Secrets of Art & Nature, being the Summe and Substance of Naturall Philosophy, Methodically Digested. First designed by John Wecker D^r in Physick, and now much Augmented and Inlarged by Dr R. Read* (London: Simon Miller, 1660), p. 341. Thomas Nashe, in his *Summer's Last Will and Testament*, remarks 'Such odd trifles as mathematicians' experiments be artificial flies to hang in the air by themselves, dancing balls.' These are also presumably suspended by thread.

See Thomas Nashe, *Summer's Last Will and Testament*, in *A Select Collection of Old English Plays*, ed. Robert Dodsley, 4th edn, rev. W. Carew Hazlitt, 11 vols. (London: Reeves and Turner, 1874–6), VIII (1874), p. 18. The option of using knives in the trick as outlined by Scot is described later as: '*Three Pen-knives are put into a Silver Goblet, at the Desire of the Spectator one of the three leaps out on the Floor.* You ask three pen-knives from different persons of your company, and put them into a goblet on the table – you desire the spectators to remark that the goblet has no communication with the table, and that there is no preparation within the goblet; nevertheless at the moment required, the pen-knife, which the spectator has chosen, leaps out on the ground, and the others remain steady within. EXPLANATION. When you have placed the goblet on the table, you slip to the bottom a half-crown piece, fastened by the middle to a thread of black silk which goes up perpendicularly to the ceiling into the hands of the Confederate: he then draws the thread at the moment required, and causes the pen-knife in the middle to leap out, which is the only one that rests on the half-crown, the others rest on the bottom of the goblet'; Anon., *The Conjurer Unmasked; Or, La Magie Blanche Devoilèe: Being a Clear and Full Explanation Of all the Surprizing Performances Exhibited as well in this Kingdom as on the Continent, By the most eminent and dexterous Professors of Slight of Hand* (London: T. Denton, 1786), p. 25.

51 *Discouerie of witchcraft*, p. 327.
52 Cornish Record Office, MS *works of Sir Richard Carew*, p. 89.
53 Henrici Cornelii Agrippae ab Nettesheym, *De incertitudine & vanitate scientiarum & Artium, atque excellentia verbi Dei, declamation* (Paris: Ioannem Petrum, 1531), sig. Hiii^r.
54 Heinrich Cornelius Agrippa, *Henrie Cornelius Agrippa, of the Vanitie and vncertaintie of Artes and Sciences, Englished by Ja[mes] San[ford] Gent.* (London: Henry Wykes, 1569), fol. 62^r. Thomas Nashe refers to Agrippa by saying: 'we found intermixed that abundant scholler Cornelius Agrippa. At that time he bare the same [name?] to be the greatest coniuror in Christendome. *Scoto* that did the iugling trickes here before the Queene, neuer came neere him one quarter in magicke reputation.' Scotto, the Italian juggler, is further referred to by King James I: 'As in like maner he [the devil] will learne them manie juglarie trickes at Cardes, dice, & such like, to deceiue mennes senses thereby: and such innumerable false practicques; which are prouen by ouer-manie in this age: As they who are acquainted with that *Italian* called SCOTO yet liuing, can reporte. And yet are all these thinges but deluding of the senses, and no waies true in substance'; Thomas Nashe, *The Vnfortvnate Traveller; Or, The Life of Iacke Wilton* (London: T[homas] Scarlet for C[uthbert] Burby, 1594), sig. F3^v; James I, *Daemonologie*, p. 22. See also Edgar Heyl, 'New light on the Renaissance master', *The Sphinx*, 47:2 (April 1948), 38–42, 50; Robert Lund, 'Colorini', *The Sphinx*, 47:5 (July 1948), 128, 138.
55 Robert Burton, *The Anatomy of Melancholy. What it is, with all the kinds causes, symptoms, prognostickes, & seuerall cures of it, In three Partitions, with*

their severall Sections, members & subsections, Philiosophically, Medicinally, Historically, opened & cut vp (London: H[enry] Cripps, 1660), p. 56.

56 N. W. Bawcutt, 'William Vincent, alias Hocus Pocus: a travelling entertainer of the seventeenth century', *Theatre Notebook*, 54 (2000), 130–8 (pp. 132–3).

57 *Ibid.*, 131.

58 *English Dramatic Companies*, ed. John Tucker Murray, 2 vols. (London: Constable, 1910), II, pp. 314, 612.

59 *REED: Coventry*, p. 429.

60 *Reading Records: Diary of the Corporation*, ed. Rev. J. M. Guilding, 4 vols. (London: James Parker, 1895), II, pp. 263–5.

61 Richard Burt, *Licensed by Authority: Ben Jonson and the Discourses of Censorship* (Ithaca, NY and London: Cornell University Press, 1993), pp. 89–90; N. W. Bawcutt, 'William Vincent, alias Hocus Pocus', p. 130.

62 *The Diary of Thomas Crosfield*, ed. Frederick S. Boas (London: Oxford University Press, 1935), pp. 71, 79.

63 *The Jacobean and Caroline Stage*, ed. Gerald Eades Bentley, 7 vols. (Oxford: Clarendon Press, 1941–68), VI, p. 164n1.

64 *Records of Early English Drama: Norwich 1540–1642*, ed. David Galloway (Toronto; Buffalo; London: University of Toronto Press, 1986), p. 326.

65 *REED: Cumberland, Westmorland, Gloucestershire*, p. 326.

66 *REED: Norwich*, p. 233.

67 *REED: Coventry*, p. 442.

68 *REED: Coventry*, p. 447.

69 *Ben Jonson*, ed. C. H. Herford, Percy Simpson and Evelyn Simpson, 11 vols. (Oxford: Clarendon Press, 1925–52), VI (1938), p. 528.

70 John Kirke, *The Seven Champions of Christendome* (London: J[ohn] Okes, 1638), Act III, sig. H2^v.

71 J. D., *The Knave in Graine* (London: J[ohn] O[kes], 1640, fol.M^r. A similar 'scam' is described in *The Country Gentleman's Vade Mecum: or his companion for the town* (London: John Harris, 1699), pp. 97–100.

72 *Ben Jonson*, ed. Herford, Simpson and Simpson, VI, p. 323.

73 John Rushworth, *Historical Collections. The Second Volume of the Second Part, Containing the Principal Matters Which happened From March 26. 1639. until the Summoning of a Parliament, which met at Westminster, April 13. 1640* (London: J. D. for John Wright, 1680), pp. 803, 804 (wrongly numbered as 834).

74 *Ben Jonson*, ed. Herford, Simpson and Simpson, VII, p. 638.

75 Thomas Randolph, *The Jealous Lovers* (Cambridge: [John and Thomas Buck,] printers to the University, 1632), p. 15.

76 Randolph, *The Jealous Lovers*, 25.

77 Alazonomastix Philalethes, *Observations upon Anthroposophia Theomagica, and Anima Magica Abscondita* (Parrhesia [London]: O[ctavian] Pullen, 1650), p. 59.

78 John Cleveland, *The Character Of A London-Diurnall: With severall select POEMS. By the same author* (London?: Optima & novissima Edition, 1647), p. 41.

79 *The Harleian Miscellany: A Collection of Scarce, Curious, and Entertaining Pamphlets and Tracts, as well in Manuscript as in Print*, ed. Thomas Parke, 10 vols. (London: John White and John Murray, 1808–13), v, p. 498.

80 *Witt's Recreations refined & Augmented, with Ingenious Conceites for the wittie, and Merrie Medicines for the Melancholie as in Print*, ed. G[eorge] H[erbert] (London: M. Simmons, 1650), sig. O3ᵛ. The epitaph to *Hocus Pocus* does not appear in the 1640, 1641 or 1645 editions of this work. Since the last recorded activity of *Hocus Pocus* that is currently available is 1642 at Coventry, it is at least safe to suggest that he died sometime between this date and 1650.

81 Anon. [William Vincent], *Hocvs Pocvs Ivnior. The Anatomie of Legerdemain; Or, The Art of Iugling set forth in his proper colours, fully, plainely, and exactly, so that an ignorant person may thereby learne the full perfection of the same, after a little practise* (London: T[homas] H[arper] for R[alph] M[abb], 1634).

82 Sidney W. Clarke, *The Annals of Conjuring* (New York: Magico Magazine, 1983), p. 43. Clarke was not that careful in his acknowledgement of sources and the origin of much of his material was not known. However, a recent annotated edition of the work has been published and the editors have taken strenuous steps to rectify Clarke's omissions. See Sidney W. Clarke, *The Annals of Conjuring*, ed. Edwin A. Dawes, Todd Karr and Bob Read (Seattle: The Miracle Factory, 2001), p. 106.

83 *The Annals of Conjuring*, ed. Dawes, Karr and Read, p. 106.

84 *Ibid.*, p. 106.

85 Henry Ridgely Evans, *Some Rare Old Books on Conjuring and Magic of the Sixteenth, the Seventeenth and the Eighteenth Century* (Kenton, OH: The Linking Ring, 1943), pp. 16–18; Harry Houdini, *Miracle Mongers and Their Methods* (New York: E. P. Dutton, 1920), pp. 100–1; John Ferguson, *Bibliographical Notes on Histories of Inventions and Books of Secrets*, 2 vols. in 1 (London: Holland Press, 1959; repr. 1981), 7th Supplement, pp. 26–33.

86 Trevor H. Hall, *Old Conjuring Books: A Bibliographical and Historical Study with a Supplementary Check-List* (London: Duckworth, 1972), pp. 120–32.

87 Randle Holme, *The Academy of Armory; Or, A Storehouse Of Armory and Blazon* (Chester: Randle Holme, 1688), Book III, Chapter xii, p. 447.

88 Anon. [William Vincent], *Hocus Pocus Junior. The Anatomy of Legerdemain; or, The Art of Jugling set forth in his proper colours, fully, plainly, and exactly; so that an ignorant person may thereby learn the full perfection of the same, after a little practise* (London: G. Dawson, 1654), sigs. B2ʳ⁻ᵛ.

89 Hall, *Old Conjuring Books*, pp. 123–5.

2 FEATS OF ACTIVITY: JUGGLING, TUMBLING AND DANCING ON THE ROPE

1 *Records of Early English Drama: Norwich 1540–1642*, ed. David Galloway (Toronto; Buffalo; London: University of Toronto Press, 1984), pp. 217–8.

2 *Ibid.*, pp. 226–7.

3 *REED: Cumberland, Westmorland, Gloucestershire*, p. 299. 'Stanway' the juggler is recorded as early as 1553, and again as the Queen's juggler in 1576. See *REED: Shropshire*, 1, pp. 84, 204.

4 *Records of Early English Drama: Somerset*, ed. James Stokes and Robert Alexander, 2 vols. (Toronto; Buffalo; London: University of Toronto Press, 1996), I, pp. 220–1.

5 Robert Langham, *Robert Laneham: A Letter [1575]*, A Scolar Press Facsimile, 60 (Menston: Scolar Press, 1968), p. 24. The identity and authority of Robert Laneham remained unclear until R. J. P. Kuin identified 'Laneham' as 'Langham' in *Robert Langham: A Letter* (Leiden: E. J. Brill, 1983), pp. 10–11.

6 *Collections* VI, ed. David Cook and F. P. Wilson, Malone Society (Oxford: Oxford University Press, 1961 [1962]), p. 16.

7 *The Dramatic Works in the Beaumont and Fletcher Canon*, ed. Fredson Bowers, 10 vols. (Cambridge: Cambridge University Press, 1966–96), III, (1976), p. 279.

8 Thomas Randolph, *The Jealous Lovers*, p. 25.

9 Scot, *Discouerie of witchcraft*, p. 345.

10 *Collections* VI, ed. Cook and Wilson, p. 21.

11 *Ibid.*, p. 22.

12 *REED: Coventry*, p. 429.

13 *REED: Norwich 1540–1642*, p. 210; *Records of Early English Drama: Lancashire*, ed. by David George (Toronto Buffalo London: University of Toronto Press, 1991), p. 176.

14 *Collections* VI, ed. Cook and Wilson, p. 46.

15 *Ibid.*, p. 47.

16 *Ibid.*, p. 61; *REED: Coventry*, p. 338.

17 *REED: Coventry*, p. 447; *REED: Cumberland, Westmorland, Gloucestershire*, p. 326; *The Dramatic Records of Sir Henry Herbert*, ed. Joseph Quincy Adams (New Haven: Yale University Press, 1917), p. 47.

18 *Collections* VI, ed. Cook and Wilson, p. 23.

19 *REED: Coventry*, p. 444. See also p. 411.

20 *The Dramatic Records of Sir Henry Herbert*, ed. Adams, p. 47.

21 *The Jacobean and Caroline Stage*, ed. Bentley, II, p. 613.

22 *REED: Herefordshire, Worcestershire*, p. 394.

23 *Collections*, VI, ed. Cook and Wilson, p. 47; *REED: Herefordshire, Worcestershire*, p. 537.

24 Albert Cohn, *Shakespeare in Germany in the Sixteenth and Seventeenth Centuries: An Account of English Actors in Germany and the Netherlands and of the Plays Performed by Them During the Same Period* (London: Asher, 1865; repr. New York: Haskell House, 1971), lxxxiii.

25 *Collections*, VI, ed. Cook and Wilson, p. 144.

26 *Ibid.*, p. 61.

27 *REED: Norwich 1540–1642*, p. 147. See also pp. 156, 162.

28 *REED: Coventry*, p. 411.

29 *REED: Somerset*, I, pp. 382–3; See also *REED: Somerset*, II, p. 501; *REED: Norwich 1540–1642*, p. 147.

30 *REED: Herefordshire, Worcestershire*, pp. 539–40; *REED: Somerset*, I, pp. 382–3; II, p. 501.

31 *Collections* VI, ed. Cook and Wilson, pp. 21, 22, 23, 24; *Documents Relating to the Office of the Revels in the Time of Queen Elizabeth*, ed. Albert Feuillerat (Louvain: A. Uystpruyst, 1908), pp. 365, 390.

32 *REED: Dorset, Cornwall*, pp. 223, 350; *REED: Norwich 1540–1642*, p. 187; *REED: Herefordshire, Worcestershire*, p. 394; *The Jacobean and Caroline Stage*, ed. Bentley, 11, pp. 485–6.

33 *REED: Dorset, Cornwall*, pp. 223, 350.

34 *REED: Norwich 1540–1642*, p. 187.

35 *REED: Herefordshire, Worcestershire*, p. 394.

36 *REED: Norwich 1540–1642*, p. 227.

37 *REED: Somerset*, 1, 435; 11, 500.

38 *REED: Norwich 1540–1642*, pp. 217–8; *Records of Early English Drama: Bristol*, ed. Mark C. Pilkinton (Toronto; Buffalo; London: University of Toronto Press, 1997), p. 216.

39 *REED: Norwich 1540–1642*, p. 173.

40 *REED: Coventry*, p. 427.

41 *Collections* VI, ed. Cook and Wilson, p. 25.

42 *Ibid.*, p. 26.

43 *REED: Shropshire*, 1, p. 19; *REED: Bristol*, pp. 133, 135; *REED: Norwich 1540–1642*, p. 96; *Collections* VI, ed. Cook and Wilson, pp. 19, 25, 26, 27; Feuillerat, *Elizabeth*, pp. 349, 388; *REED: Somerset*, 1, p. 14; *REED: Dorset, Cornwall*, p. 216; *REED: Kent*, 1, p. 244.

44 *Collections* VI, ed. Cook and Wilson, p. 27.

45 Scott McMillin and Sally-Beth MacLean, *The Queen's Men and Their Plays* (Cambridge: Cambridge University Press, 1998), pp. 194–5.

46 *Records of Early English Drama: Newcastle Upon Tyne*, ed. J. J. Anderson (Toronto; Buffalo; London: University of Toronto Press and Manchester University Press, 1982), p. 73; *REED: Norwich 1540–1642*, p. 162; *REED: Kent*, 11, p. 811; *REED: CWG*, p. 359; *REED: Somerset*, 1, 14; Feuillerat, *Elizabeth*, p. 378.

47 *REED: Devon*, pp. 34, 308; *Records of Early English Drama: York*, ed. Alexandra F. Johnston and Margaret Rogerson, 2 vols. (Toronto; Buffalo; London: University of Toronto Press and Manchester University Press, 1979), 1, p. 581.

48 Some examples are: Feuillerat, *Elizabeth*, p. 380; *The Diary of Thomas Crosfield*, ed. Boas (London: Oxford University Press, 1935), p. 71; *English Dramatic Companies*, ed. Murray (London: Constable, 1910), 11, pp. 291, 304; *Records of the Borough of Leicester: Being a Series of Extracts from the Archives of the Corporation of Leicester, 1509–1603*, ed. Mary Bateson, 7 vols. (London: C. J. Clay under the authority of the Corporation of Leicester, 1899–1974), 111, p. 384; *The Jacobean and Caroline Stage*, ed. Bentley, 1, p. 150; 11, p. 456; VI, p. 159; *REED: Bristol*, p. 240; *REED: Cumberland, Westmorland, Gloucestershire*, p. 87; *REED: Shropshire*, 1, p. 203; *REED: Somerset*, 1, pp. 12, 14; *REED: Coventry*, pp. 376, 439; *REED: Devon*, pp. 33, 34, 35, 67, 154, 155, 181, 172; *REED: Kent*, 11, pp. 341, 555, 833, 918, 925; *The Dramatic Records of Sir Henry Herbert*, ed. Adams, p. 48.

49 *REED: Cumberland, Westmorland, Gloucestershire*, p. 359.

50 *REED: Norwich 1540–1642*, p. 150; *The Jacobean and Caroline Stage*, ed. Bentley, II, p. 459; Henry Farley, *St Pavles-Chvrch Her Bill For The Parliament, As it was presented to the Kings Matie on Midlent-Sunday last, and intended for the view of that most high and Honorable Court, and generally for all such as beare good will to the reflourishing estate of the said Chvrch* (London: Henry Farley, 1621), sigs. E4^{r-v}; Sir William Davenant, *The Works of Sr William Davenant K^t Consisting of those which were formerly Printed and those which he design'd for the Press: now published out of the authors originall copies* (London: T. N. for Henry Herringman, 1673), p. 291.

51 *REED: Lancashire*, p. 204.

52 *REED: Cumberland, Westmorland, Gloucestershire*, p. 83.

53 Richard Brome, *The Antipodes* (London: J[ohn] Okes, 1640), sig. D3^{v}; Ben Jonson, *Every Man Out of His Humour*, ed. F. P. Wilson, Malone Society (Oxford: Oxford University Press, 1920), sig. lii^{v}.

54 *The Dramatic Works in the Beaumont and Fletcher Canon*, ed. Bowers, III, p. 145; Davenant, *The Works of Sr William Davenant*, p. 291.

55 *REED: Kent*, II, p. 357.

56 *REED: Bristol*, p. 112.

57 *The Diary of Thomas Crosfield*, ed. Boas, pp. 54, 79.

58 William Stokes, *The Vaulting Master; or, the Art of Vaulting reduced to a method . . . Illustrated by examples* (Oxon: [n.p.], 1652), Figs. 1–13.

59 Langham, *Robert Laneham: A Letter [1575]*, pp. 24–5; *OED* **gambado**^2 2. 'A fantastic movement, as in dancing or leaping about; a caper'; *OED* **caprettie**^1 'A fantastic motion of some kind'.

60 *REED: Shropshire*, I, p. 247.

61 Feuillerat, *Edward VI and Mary*, p. 58.

62 *Ibid.*, p. 123.

63 *Ibid.*, p. 97. See also pp. 98, 100.

64 *Ibid.*, pp. 134, 145.

65 Feuillerat, *Elizabeth*, p. 365.

66 *Ibid.*, p. 349. See also p. 388.

67 *Ibid.*, p. 390.

68 W. J. Lawrence, *Old Theatre Days and Ways* (London; Bombay; Sydney: George G. Harrap, 1935), p. 64.

69 In *Old Theatre Days and Ways* Lawrence suggests that 'Gloves to an acrobat were surely more of a handicap than a help', p. 64. The term 'acrobat' is not used in England until the nineteenth century. See *OED* **acrobat**, where the earliest example of its use is recorded as 1825.

70 *Accounts of the Lord High Treasurer of Scotland*, ed. Dickson *et al.*, VII, p. 150.

71 Feuillerat, *Edward VI and Mary*, p. 79.

72 *Ibid.*, p. 123.

73 See n53.

74 Henry Chettle, *Kind-Harts Dreame. Conteining fiue Apparitions, with their Inuectiues against abuses raigning. Deliuered by seuerall Ghosts vnto him to be*

publisht, after Piers Penilesse Post had refused the carriage (London: William Wright, 1592), sig. B2ʳ.

75 Professor [Luis] Hoffmann, *Modern Magic: A Practical Treatise on the Art of Conjuring*, 12th edn (London: George Routledge, [n.d.]), p. 5. The first edition of this work was published in 1876; Professor Hoffmann, *Later Magic with New Miscellaneous Tricks and Recollections of Hartz the Wizard* (London: George Routledge, 1911; repr. 1931), pp. 102–33; [Jean Eugène] Robert-Houdin, *The Secrets of Conjuring and Magic; or, How to Become a Wizard*, ed. and trans. Professor Hoffmann (London: George Routledge, 1878), p. 65.

76 Girolamo Cardano, *Hieronymi Cardani Medici Mediolanensis de svbtilitate libri* xxi (Nuremberg: Ioh. Petreium, 1550), p. 343. Translation by Philip A. Shaw.

77 Io[a]nnis Wieri, *De praestigiis daemonum, & incantationibus ac ueneficiis libri sex, postrema editioni sexta aucti & recogniti* (Basle: ex officina Oporiniana, 1583), Book 1, Chapter 18, sig. g3ᵛ. The translation of this account is taken from Johann Weyer *Witches, Devils, and Doctors in the Renaissance: Johannn Weyer, 'De praestigiis daemonum'*, ed. George Mora *et al.*, Medieval and Renaissance Texts and Studies (Tempe, AZ: Center for Medieval and Early Renaissance Studies, State University of New York at Binghamton, 1991; repr. 1998), p. 59.

78 Raphael Holinshed, *Holinshed's Chronicle of England, Scotland and Ireland*, 6 vols. (London: Richard Taylor for J. Johnson; F. C. and J. Rivington; T. Payne; Wilkie and Robinson; Longman, Hurst, Rees, and Orme; Cadell and Davies; and J. Mawman, 1807–8), iii, p. 866.

79 John Leland, *Joannis Lelandi antiquarii de rebvs Britannicis collectanea. Cvm Thomae Hearnii praefatione notis et indice ad editionem primam*, 6 vols. (London: apud Benj[amin] White, 1774), iv, pp. 320–1.

80 Cardano, *de svbtilitate*, p. 344; Wecker, *De secretis libri* xvii. *Ex varijs authoribus collecti, methodiceque digesti*, p. 933; Wecker, *Eighteen Books of the Secrets of Art & Nature*, pp. 335–6.

81 Strutt, *The Sports and Pastimes of the People of England*, pp. 168–9; John Evelyn records the following description of dancing on the rope: 'Going to London with some company, we stept in to see a famous Rope-dauncer call'd *The Turk*. I saw even to astonishment yᵉ agilitie with which he perform'd; he walk'd barefooted taking hold by his toes only of a rope almost perpendicular, and without so much as touching it with his hands; he daunc'd blindfold on yᵉ high rope and with a boy of 12 yeares old tied to one of his feete about 20 foote beneath him, dangling as he daunc'd, yet he mov'd as nimbly as if it had ben but a feather. Lastly he stood on his head on yᵉ top of a very high mast, daunc'd on a small rope that was very slack, and finally flew downe yᵉ perpendiculer, on his breast, his head foremost, his legs and arms extended, with divers other activities.' *Memoirs, Illustrative of the Life and Writings of John Evelyn, Esq. F. R. S.*, ed. William Bray, 2 vols. (London: Henry Colburn, 1819), i, 306–7.

82 Strutt, *The Sports and Pastimes of the People of England*, p. 169.

83 Robert Birrel, *The Diarey of Robert Birrel, containing Divers Passages of Staite, and Uthers Memorable Accidents. Frome the 1532 zeir of our redemptione, till ye beginning of the zeir 1605*, in *Fragments of Scottish History* (Edinburgh: Archibald Constable, 1798), p. 47; Anna Jean Mill, *Mediaeval Plays in Scotland* (New York, London: Benjamin Blom, 1969), pp. 297–8.

84 Holinshed, *Holinshed's Chronicles*, IV, p. 63; Robert Chamberlain records the death 'Of one dancing upon the Ropes' in his *A New Booke of Mistakes; or, Bulls with Tales, and Buls without Tales. but no lyes by any meanes* (London: N[icholas] O[kes], 1637), pp. 121–2.

85 Cardano, *De svbtilitate*, p. 344; Translation by Philip A. Shaw. See also Wecker, *De secretis*, p. 934; Wecker, *Eighteen Books of the Secrets of Art & Nature*, pp. 335–6.

86 *Records of Early English Drama: Chester*, ed. Lawrence Clopper (Toronto; Buffalo; London: Manchester University Press and University of Toronto Press, 1979), p. 218; William Cavendish, *The Country Captain*, ed. Anthony Johnson and H. R. Woudhuysen, Malone Society (Oxford: Oxford University Press, 1999), p. 17. A. H. Bullen printed this text under the title *Captain Underwit: A Comedy* in his *A Collection of Old English Plays in Four Volumes* (London: Wyman, 1883).

87 *REED: Cambridge*, I, p. 573; payment is recorded for a specialised form of footwear as: 'a pair of daunsing pumpes ijs vjd' in the Howard Household Books 3 for 1620–1, *REED: Cumberland, Westmorland, Gloucestershire*, p. 138.

88 *REED: Shropshire*, I, p. 247.

89 *English Dramatic Companies*, ed. Murray, II, p. 291.

90 James Melvill, *The Autobiography and Diary of Mr James Melvill, with a Continuation of the Diary. Edited from Manuscripts in the Libraries of the Faculty of Advocates and University of Edinburgh*, ed. Robert Pitcairn (Edinburgh: Printed for the Wodrow Society, 1842), p. 487 and n1; *Mediaeval Plays in Scotland*, ed. Mill, p. 298.

91 *REED: Newcastle*, p. 136.

92 *REED: Norwich 1540–1642*, p. 133.

93 *Ibid.*, p. 96; Tho[mas] Nashe, *Strange Newes, Of the intercepting certaine Letters and a Conuoy of Verses, as they were going Priuilie to victuall the Low Countries* (London: [J. Danter], 1592), B2ᵛ; *Collections* X, ed. F. P. Wilson and R. F. Hill, Malone Society (Oxford: Oxford University Press, 1975 [1977]), p. 13.

94 *English Dramatic Companies*, ed. Murray, II, p. 293.

95 *REED: Bristol*, p. 135.

96 *The Dramatic Records of Sir Henry Herbert*, ed. Adams, p. 47.

97 *REED: Kent*, II, p. 470; *Collections VII*, p. 45; *English Dramatic Companies*, ed. Murray, II, p. 261.

98 Langham, *Robert Laneham: A Letter*, pp. 24–5.

99 *The Dramatic Records of Sir Henry Herbert*, ed. Adams, p. 47; *The Jacobean and Caroline Stage*, ed. Bentley, II, p. 517.

3 CONVEYANCE AND CONFEDERACY

1 Edwin Sachs, *Sleight of Hand: A Practical Manual of Legerdemain for Amateurs and Others*, 2nd edn (London: L. Upcott Gill, 1885), p. 40; David Devant, *Secrets of My Magic* (London: Hutchinson, 1936), pp. 23–4; Peter Lamont and Richard Wiseman, *Magic in Theory: An Introduction to the Theoretical and Psychological Elements of Conjuring* (Hatfield: University of Hertfordshire Press, 1999), pp. 28–81.

2 Scot, *The Discouerie of witchcraft*, p. 307.

3 Giovanni Boccaccio, *A Treatise excellent and compendious, shewing and declaring, in maner of Tragedye, the falles of sondry most notable Princes and Princesses with other Nobles, through ye mutabilitie and change of vnstedfast fortune together with their most detestable & wicked vices*, trans. John Lydgate (London: Richard Tottelli, 1554), fol. ccxxiiii; *The Dance of Death: Edited from MSS Ellesmere 26/A.13 and B. M. Lansdowne 699, Collated with the Other Extant MSS*, ed. Beatrice White, Early English Text Society (London: Humphrey Milford for Oxford University Press, 1931), p. 64.

4 Scot, *Discouerie of witchcraft*, p. 352.

5 Robert Tailor, *The Hogge Hath Lost His Pearl*, ed. D. F. McKenzie, Arthur Brown and G. R. Proudfoot, Malone Society (Oxford: Oxford University Press, 1967 [1972]), sig. G1^v.

6 Sir Roger L'estrange, *The Loyal Observator; Or, Historical Memoirs of the Life and Actions of Roger the Fidler; Alias, The Observator* (London: W. Hammond, 1683), p. 6.

7 Scot, *Discouerie of witchcraft*, p. 323; see also Thomas Cooper, *Thesavrvs lingvae romanae & britannicae etc.* (London: Henry Denham, 1573), fol. Ddddd.i: 'A iuggler that playeth his conueighances with little rounde balles'.

8 Scot, *Discouerie of witchcraft*, p. 326.

9 John Baret, *An Alvearie or Triple Dictionarie, in Englishe, Latin, and French* (London: Henry Denham, 1580), sig. Piv^v.

10 John Stephens, *Satyrical Essayes Characters and Others; Or, Accurate and quick Descriptions, fitted to the life of their Subjects* (London: Nicholas Okes, 1615), p. 277.

11 Thomas Elyot, *The boke named the Gouernour* (London: Tho[mas] Bertheleti, 1531) [The firste boke], fol. 95^r.

12 Edward Hall, *Hall's Chronicle; containing The History of England, during The Reign of Henry the Fourth, and the Succeeding Monarchs, to the end of the Reign of Henry the Eighth, in which are particularly described the Manners and Customs of those Periods*, ed. Sir Henry Ellis (London: J. Johnson; F. C. and J. Rivington; T. Payne; Wilkie and Robinson; Longman, Hurst, Rees and Orme; Cadell and Davies; and J. Mawman, 1809), p. 428. See also p. 403.

13 *Ballads from Manuscripts: Ballads Relating Chiefly to the Reign of Queen Elizabeth*, ed. W. R. Morfill, Ballad Society, 2 vols. (Hertford: Stephen Austin, 1873), II, Part II, 355.

14 John Skelton, *Magnyfycence: A Moral Play*, ed. Robert Lee Ramsay, Early English Text Society (London: Oxford University Press, 1908; repr. 1958), p. 42.

15 *Ibid.*, p. 42.

16 *Ibid.*, p. 42.

17 William Pemble, *Vindicae fidei; or, A Treatise of Ivstification by Faith, wherein that point is fully cleared, and vindicated from the cauils of its aduersaries* (Oxford: John Lichfield and William Turner for Edward Forrest, 1625), p. 33.

18 R. W[illis], *Mount Tabor; or, Private Exercises of a Penitent Sinner. Serving for a daily Practice of the Life of Faith, Reduced to speciall heads comprehending the chiefe comforts and refreshings of true Christians: Also Certain occasionall Observations and Meditations profitably applyed* (London: R. B[adger] for P[hilemon] Stephens and C[hristopher] Meredith, 1639), p. 111; *REED: Cumberland, Westmorland, Gloucestershire*, p. 363.

19 John Day, *Law-trickes; or, Who Wovld have Thovght it* (London: [Edward Allde] for Richard More, 1608), sig. D4^r.

20 *Ibid.*, sig. G3^v.

21 Thomas Lupton, *All for Money*, ed. John S. Farmer, Tudor Facsimile Texts (Amersham: John S. Farmer, 1910), sigs. Aiiii^r, Bi^r, Bi^v, Bii^r.

22 John Palsgrave, *L'éclaircissement de la Langue Francaise par Jean Palsgrave suivi de la grammaire de Giles du Guez, publiés pour la premiere fois en France par F. Génin* (Paris: Imprimerie Nationale, 1852), p. 592.

23 Stephens, *Satyrical Essayes*, p. 229.

24 Anon., *Wily Beguild*, ed. John S. Farmer, Tudor Facsimile Texts (Amersham: John S. Farmer, 1912), p. 2 (see Appendix 2).

25 William Shakespear and William Rowley, *The Birth of Merlin; Or, The Childe hath found his Father* (London: Tho[mas] Johnson for Francis Kirkman, and Henry Marsh, 1662), sig. FI^r. Harbage dates this text to 1608 and suggests that it is based upon the anonymously penned *Uther Pendragon* of 1597. Alfred Harbage, *Annals of English Drama 975–1700: An Analytical Record of all Plays, Extant or Lost, Chronologically Arranged and Indexed by Authors, Titles, Dramatic Companies, &c*, rev. S. Schoenbaum (London: Methuen, 1964), p. 94.

26 Scot, *Discouerie of witchcraft*, p. 348.

27 *Ibid.*, p. 351.

28 *Ibid.*, p. 322.

29 *Ibid.*, pp. 337, 346.

30 Skelton, *Magnyfycence*, p. 43.

31 Sir John Harington, *A New Discovrse of a Stale Svbiect, called the Metamorphosis of Ajax. Written by Misacmos to his friend and cosin Philostilpnos* (London: R[ichard] Field, 1596), sig. E4^v.

32 [Thomas Nash ?], *The Returne of the renowned Caualiero Pasquill of England, from the other side of the Seas, and his meeting with Marforius at London vpon the Royall Exchange* (London: If my breath be so hote that I burne my

mouth, suppose I was Printed by Pepper Allie, J[ohn] Charlewood?], 1589), sig. Div^v; James Harrison, *An exhortacion to the Scottes, to conforme them selfes to the honorable expedient, and godly vnion, betwene the twoo realmes of Englande and Scotlande* (London: Richard Grafton, 1547), sig. b.i^v.

33 Eddie Joseph, *How to Pick Pockets: A Treatise on the Fundamental Principle, Theory and Practice of Picking Pockets, for Entertainment Purposes Only* (London: Vampire Press, [1946]; Eddie Joseph, *How to Pick Pockets for Fun and Profit* (Colorado Springs: Piccadilly Books, 1992); Eddie Joseph, *Body Loading and Productions* (Colon, MI: Abbott, 1950).

34 Robert Greene, *A notable discouery of coosnage*, 1591; *The second part of Conny-catching*, 1592 (London: John Lane, Bodley Head, [1923]), [The second part], p. 34.

35 Skelton, *Magnyfycence*, p. 38.

36 *OED* **confederacy** 1. and 2. **confederate** B sb. 1. and 2.; *MED* **confederacie** n. 1.(b); n. 2; **confederat** ppl 1. (a) and (b); 2 (a).

37 Scot, *Discouerie of witchcraft*, pp. 308–9.

38 John Northbrooke, *Spiritus est vicarius Christi in [terra]. A Treatise wherein Dicing, Dauncing, Vaine playes or Enterluds with other idle pastimes &c. commonly vsed on the Sabboth day, are reproued by the Authoritie of the word of God and auntient writers* (London: H[enry] Bynnenian for George Byshop, 1577 [?BL copy has '1579' pencilled in]), pp. 110–11; Girolamo Cardano, *Hieronymi Cardani Mediolanensis medici de Subtilitate libri* xxi (Basle: ex officina Petrina, 1560), [Liber xviii], pp. 1121–4. See *OED* **bumb**. 'A pimple'. A 'Bumbe carde' may be a pricked card resulting in a pimple that may be felt. A 'Bumbe carde finely vnder ouer' may simply be one that is pricked and turned to face the other way in the deck.

39 Scot, *Discouerie of witchcraft*, p. 332.

40 *Ibid.*, p. 332.

41 *Ibid.*, p. 332.

42 *The Dramatic Works in the Beaumont and Fletcher Canon*, ed. Bowers, x, pp. 622–4.

43 Scot, *Discouerie of witchcraft*, p. 339.

44 Margaret Flower, *The Wonderful Discoverie of the Witchcrafts of Margaret and Phillip Flower, daughters of Ioan Flower neere Beuer Castle: Executed at Lincolne, March 11. 1618* (London: G[eorge] Eld for I[ohn] Barnes, 1619), sig. B 2v.

45 Scot, *Discouerie of witchcraft*, p. 339.

46 *Ibid.*, p. 309.

47 *Ibid.*, p. 330.

48 *Ibid.*, p. 338.

49 Sir Thomas Roe, *Sir Thomas Roe's journal of his voyage to the East Indies, and observations there during his residence at the Mogul's court, as Embassador from King James the first of England, taken from his own manuscripts*, in *A Collection of Voyages and Travels, some now printed from Original Manuscripts, others now first published in English*, 6 vols. (London: Churchill,

1732), I, p. 732; *The Embassy of Sir Thomas Roe to the Court of the Great Mogul, 1615–1619, as Narrated in His Journal and Correspondence*, ed. William Foster, Hakluyt Society, 2 vols. (London: Hakluyt Society, 1899), II, p. 318.

50 Edward Terry, *A Voyage to East-India. Wherein some things are taken notice of in our passage thither, but many more in our abode there, within that rich and most spacious Empire of the Great Mogol* (London: T. W. for J. Martin, and J. Allestrye, 1655), pp. 403–4.

51 Anon., *A Trve Relation Withovt All Exception, of Strange and Admirable Accidents, which lately happened in the Kingdome of the great Magor, or Magvll, who is the greatest Monarch of the East Indies* (London: I[ohn] D[awson] for Thomas Archer, 1622), pp. 5–7; Michael Drayton, *The Battaile of Agincovrt. Fovght by Henry the fift of that name, King of England, against the whole power of the French: vnder the Raigne of their Charles the sixt, Anno Dom. 1415* (London: William Lee, 1627), p. 173; *The Dramatic Works in the Beaumont and Fletcher Canon*, ed. Bowers, X, p. 592; Farley, *St Pavles-Church Her Bill For The Parliament*, sigs. E4$^{r–v}$; John Taylor, *All The Workes of Iohn Taylor The Water-Poet. Beeing Sixty and three in Number. Collected into one Volume by the Avthor: With sundry new Additions, corrected, reuised, and newly Imprinted* (London: J. B. for Iames Boler, 1630), II, p. 159; Jonson, *Every Man Out of His Humour*, sig. M iv^{r}.

52 Roe, *Roe's journal*, p. 732; Terry, *A Voyage to East-India*, p. 403.

53 Terry, *A Voyage to East-India*, p. 405.

54 *Ibid.*, p. 405.

55 Roe, *Roe's journal*, p. 732.

56 *REED: Norwich 1540–1642*, p. 150.

57 Scot, *Discouerie of witchcraft*, p. 252.

58 Francis Douce, *Illustrations of Shakspeare, and of Ancient Manners: with Dissertations on the Clown and Fools of Shakspeare; on the Collection of Popular Tales entitled Gesta Romanorum; and on the English Morris Dance*, 2 vols. (London: Longman, Hurst, Rees and Orme, 1807), I, pp. 212–14; *The Works of William Shakespeare, the Text Formed from a New Collation of the Early Editions: to Which are Added All the Original Novels and Tales on Which the Plays Are Founded; Copious Archaeological Annotations on Each Play; an Essay on the Formation of the Text; and a Life of the Poet*, ed. James O. Halliwell, 16 vols. (London: C. & J. Adlard, 1853–65), IV, pp. 227, 243–54; *Collectanea anglo-poetica; or, a Bibliographical and descriptive catalogue of a portion of a collection of early English poetry, with occasional extracts and remarks biographical and critical*, ed. Thomas Corser, Remains Historical and Literary Connected with the Palatine Counties of Lancaster and Chester, 52 (Manchester: Chetham Society, 1860), pp. 152–6; J. O. Halliwell-Phillipps, *Memoranda on Love's Labour's Lost, King John, Othello and on Romeo and Juliet* (London: James Evan Adlard, 1879), pp. 70–3; Constance Russell, 'Thinking horses', *Notes and Queries*, 10th Series, II (July–December 1904), 282.

59 Lucius Apuleius, *Les metamorphoses, ov l'asne d'or*, trans. J. de Montlyard (Paris: S. Thiboust, 1623), p. 250. Since Banks did not return from Paris until 1608, the memory of his performances in Paris was presumably vivid enough for Montlyard to include them in his augmented translation.

60 *Dictionary of National Biography*, ed. Leslie Stephen, 63 vols. (London: Smith, Elder, 1885), III, pp. 125–6.

61 John Dando and Harrie Runt, *Maroccus extaticus. Or, Bankes Bay Horse in a Trance: A Discourse set downe in a merry Dialogue, between Bankes and his beast: Anatomizing some abuses and bad trickes of this age* (London: [Thomas Scarlet] for C[uthbert] Burby, 1595), title page.

62 Patrick Anderson, *The historie of Scotland, since the death of King James the first, where Boetius left off, untill the death of King James the sixt of happie memorie*, Adv. MS 35.5.3, 3 vols. (Edinburgh: Advocates Library, National Library of Scotland, c. 1600?), fol. 285^r; C[hristopher] M[arlowe], *All Ovids Elegies: 3. Bookes. By C. M. Epigrams* ed. J[ohn] D[avies] (Middlebovrgh: [n.p.], 1630?), sig. G4v; Iohn Webster, *The White Divel; Or, The Tragedy of Paulo Giordano Vrsini,Duke of Brachiano, With The Life and Death of Vittoria Corombona the famous Venetian Curtizan* (London: N[icholas] O[kes] for Thomas Archer, 1612), sig. D4^r.

63 *REED: Shropshire*, I, p. 276.

64 John Marston, *Iacke Drums Entertainment; or, The Comedie Of Pasquill and Katherine*, ed. John S. Farmer, Tudor Facsimile Texts (Amersham: John S. Farmer, 1912), sig. B3^v.

65 *DNB*, III, **BANKS**, p. 125.

66 Anderson, *The historie of Scotland*, fol. 285^r; *REED: Shropshire*, I, p. 276; Apuleius, *Les metamorphoses*, p. 250; *DNB*, III, **BANKS**, p. 125.

67 Sir Walter Raleigh, *The History of the World* (London: Walter Bvrre, 1614), Chapter XI, Section VI, p. 209.

68 *Ben Jonson*, ed. Herford, Simpson and Simpson, VIII, p. 88.

69 Thomas Heywood, *Hogs Character of a Projector, Being a Relation of his Life and Death, with his Funerall* (London: [n.], 1642), sig. A2^r.

70 Thomas Killigrew, *Comedies, and Tragedies* (London: Henry Herringman, 1664), p. 140; Tho[mas] Dekker, *The Seuen deadly Sinnes of London: Drawne in seuen seuerall Coaches, Through the seuen seuerall Gates of the Citie Bringing the Plague with them* (London: E[dward] A[llde], 1606), sig. F2^r.

71 Gervase Markham, *Cavalarice; Or, The English Horseman: Contayning all the Art of Horse-manship, asmuch as is necessary for any man to vnderstand, whether hee be Horse-breeder, horse-ryder, horse-hunter, horse-runner, horse-ambler, horse-farrier, horse-keeper, Coachman, Smith or Sadler. Together, with the discouery of the subtil trade or mystery of hors-coursers, and an explanation of the excellency of a horses vnderstanding: or how to teach them to do trickes like Bankes his Curtall etc.* (London: Edward White, 1607), p. 27.

72 *REED: Shropshire*, I, p. 276.

73 Thomas Bastard, *Chrestoleros. Seuen bookes of Epigrames written by T. B.* (London: Richard Bradocke for I[ohn] B[rome], 1598), p. 62.

74 Richard Brathwait, *A Strappado for the Diuell. Epigrams and Satyres alluding to the time, with diuers measures of no lesse Delight* (London: I[ohn] B[eale] for Richard Redmer, 1615), p. 159; Thomas Nash, *Haue with you to Safronwalden. Or, Gabriell Harueys Hunt is vp. Containing a full Answere to the eldest sonne of the Halter-maker. Or, nashe his Confutation of the sinfull Doctor. etc.* (London: Iohn Danter, 1596), sigs. D2^r, K3^r.

75 Thomas Morton, *A Direct Answer vnto The Scandalovs Exceptions, which Theophilus Higgons hath lately obiected against D. Morton etc* (London: Edmvnd Weaver, 1609), p. 11.

76 *Ibid.*, p. 11.

77 The transcription offered here from *The Booke of Bulls* is that presented by J. O. Halliwell-Phillipps in his *Memoranda on Love's Labour's Lost, King John, Othello and on Romeo and Juliet*, p. 72. According to Pollard and Redgrave's *Short Title Catalogue* two copies of the original work are said to exist: one at Harvard University, the other at Wadham College, Oxford; see A. W. Pollard and G. R. Redgrave, *A Short-Title Catalogue of Books Printed in England, Scotland, and Ireland and of English Books Printed Abroad 1475–1640*, 2nd edn, 3 vols. (London: Bibliographical Society, 1976–91), I, p. 222. Staff at Wadham College have no record of *The Booke of Bulls* ever having been part of their collection.

78 Richard Tarlton, *Tarltons Jests. Drawne into these three parts. 1 His Court-witty Iests. 2 His sound City Iests. 3 His Country-pretty Iests. Full of delight, Wit, and honest Mirth* (London: I[ohn] H[aviland] for Andrew Crook, 1638), sig. C2^v.

79 George Sandys, *Sandys Travailes: Containing A History of the Original and present state of the Turkish Empire: Their Laws, Government, Policy, Military Force, Courts of Justice and Commerce etc*, 6th edn (London: R. and W. Leybourn, 1658), p. 98. It seems that Thomas Fuller thought that Banks taught his horse to 'reason': '*Bancks of London*, (who taught his horse reason to perform feats above belief,)'; see Thomas Fuller, *The History of the Worthies of England* (London: J. G. W. L. and W. G. for Thomas Williams, 1662), p. 217. See also Scot, *Discouerie of witchcraft*, p. 252, where Scot makes the following statement: 'For the snake hath neither such reason; nor the words such effect: otherwise the snake must know our thoughts.'

80 Markham, *Cavalarice*, p. 25.

81 Apuleius, *Les metamorphoses*, pp. 253–4.

82 Sir Kenelm Digby, *Two Treatises. In the one of which, the natvre of bodies; in the other, the natvre of mans sovle; is looked into: in way of discovery, of the immortality of reasonable sovles* (Paris: Gilles Blaizot, 1644), p. 321.

83 Apuleius, *Les metamorphoses*, p. 250.

84 *REED: Shropshire*, I, p. 276.

85 Edmund Gayton, *Pleasant Notes upon Don Quixot* (London: William Hunt, 1654), p. 289.

86 Bastard, *Chrestoleros*, p. 62.

87 Joseph Hall, *Virgidemiarvm, Sixe Bookes. First three Bookes, Of Tooth-lesse Satyrs. 1. Poeticall. 2. Academicall. 3. Morall* (London: Thomas Creede, for Robert Dexter, 1597); *The three last Bookes. Of byting Satyres* (London: Richard Bradocke for Robert Dexter, 1598), p. 18.

88 Anderson, *The historie of Scotland*, fol. 285^r.

89 Digby, *Two Treatises*, p. 321.

90 Apuleius, *Les metamorphoses*, pp. 251–2.

91 *Ibid.*, p. 252.

92 Anderson, *The historie of Scotland*, fol. 285^{r-v}.

93 Apuleius, *Les metamorphoses*, pp. 252–3.

94 Bastard, *Chrestoleros*, p. 62; Thomas Dekker, *The Wonderfull Yeare. 1603. Wherein is shewed the picture of London, lying sicke of the Plague etc.* (London: Thomas Creede, [1603?]), sig. A4^v.

95 Digby, *Two Treatises*, p. 321; See also Nashe, *The Vnfortvnate Traveller*, sig. D2^v.

96 Anderson, *The historie of Scotland*, fol. 285v.

97 Apuleius, *Les metamorphoses*, p. 254; Aristophanes, *Ploutophthalmia ploutogamia: A Pleasant Comedie, Entituled Hey For Honesty, Down with Knavery*, trans. Tho[mas] Randolph (London: F. J., 1651), p. 24; Gabriel Harvey [Richard Lichfield], *The Trimming of Thomas Nashe Gentleman, by the high-tituled patron Don Richardo de Medicio* [Richard Lichfield], *Barber Chirgion to Trinitie Colledge in Cambridge* (London: Edward Allde for Philip Scarlet, 1597), sig. F1^v. Other dancing horses are recorded at Leicester (1547–8), Norwich (1624), Coventry (1628) and Oxford (1631). See *Records of the Borough of Leicester*, ed. Bateson, III, p. 57; *REED: Norwich*, p. 187; *REED: Coventry*, p. 425; *The Diary of Thomas Crosfield*, ed. Boas, p. 54.

98 Mary Sullivan, *Court Masques of James I: Their Influence on Shakespeare and the Public Theatres* (New York and London: G. P. Putnam, 1913), p. 192; Moll Cutpurse, *The Life and Death of M$^{rs.}$ Mary Frith. Commonly Called Mal Cutpurse. Exactly Collected and now Published for the Delight and Recreation of all Merry disposed Persons* (London: W. Gilbertson, 1662), sig. E2^r; Basilivs Mvsophilus [Samuel Holland], *Don Zara Del Fogo: A Mock-Romance. Written Originally in the British Tongue, and made English by a person of much Honor* (London: T. W. for Tho[mas] Vere, 1656), p. 114; Henry Parrot, *The Mastive; Or, Young-Whelpe of the Olde-Dogge. Epigrams and Satyrs* (London: Tho[mas] Creede for Richard Meighen and Thomas Jones, 1615), sig. G3^v; Henry Hammond, *Of A Late, Or, A Death-Bed Repentance* (Oxford: Henry Hall Printer to the Universitie, 1645), p. 25; Anon., *Old Meg Of Hereford-shire, for a Mayd-Marian: And Hereford Towne for a Morris-daunce. Or Twelve Morris-Dancers in Hereford-shire, or twelue hundred yeares old* (London: Iohn Budge, 1609), sig. A4^r.

99 Rid, *The Art of Iugling or Legerdemaine*, sig. G^{r-v}.

100 Thomas Dekker, *Satiro-mastix; Or, The vntrussing of the Humorous Poet* (London: Edward White, 1602), sig. C2^r; Thomas Dekker?, *The Meeting of Gallants at an Ordinarie; Or, The Walkes in Powles* (London: T[homas] C[reede], 1604), sig. C3^v.

101 T[homas] Deckar, *The Gvls Horne-booke: Stultorum plena sunt omnia. Al Sauio meza parola, Basta.* (London: [Nicholas Okes] for R[ichard] S[ergier], 1609), p. 21; T[homas] M[iddleton], *The Blacke Booke* (London: T[homas] C[reede] for Ieffrey Chorlton, 1604), sigs. D4^v–E^r.

102 Sir William Dugdale, *The History of St Paul's Cathedral in London, from its foundation. Extracted out of Original Charters, Records, Leiger-Books, and other Manuscripts*, 2nd edn (London: Edward Maynard, George James for Jonah Bowyer, 1716), pp. 135–6.

103 John Stow, *The Annales of England, Faithfully collected out of the most authenticall Authors, Records, and other Monuments of Antiquitie, lately corrected, encreased, and continued, from the first inhabitation vntill this present yeere 1601* (London: [Peter Short and Felix Kingston] for Ralfe Newbery, 1601), pp. 1095–6; T[homas] Dekker, *The Dead Tearme. Or Westminsters Complaint for long Vacations and short Termes. Written in manner of a Dialogue betweene the two Cityes of London and Westminster* (London: [n.p.], 1608), sigs. D3^r–D4^r.

104 T[homas] D[ekker] and George Wilkins, *Iests to make you Merie: With The Coniuring vp of Cock Watt (the walking Spirit of Newgate) To tell Tales: Vnto which is Added, the miserie of a Prison, and a Prisoner. And a Paradox in praise of Serieants* (London: N[icholas] O[kes] for N[athaniell] Butter, 1607), p. 12.

105 William Rowley, *A Search for Money; or, The Lamentable complaint for the losse of the wandring Knight Mounsieur l'Argent; or, Come along with me, I know thou louest Money* (London: Ioseph Hunt, 1609), sig. A4^r; Lo[rding] Barry, *Ram-Alley or Merry Tricks*, ed. John S. Farmer, Tudor Facsimile Texts (Amersham: John S. Farmer, 1913), sig. G2^r; Davenant, *The Works of Sr William Davenant*, p. 291.

106 Gayton, *Pleasant Notes upon Don Quixot*, p. 289.

107 Thomas Dekker and John Webster, *North-Ward Hoe*, ed. John S. Farmer, Tudor Facsimile Texts (Amersham: John S. Farmer, 1914), sig. E3^v.

108 Cavendish, *The Country Captain*, p. 74.

109 *DNB*, III, **BANKS**, p. 125.

4 APPEARANCES AND DISAPPEARANCES

1 Philip Butterworth, 'Comings and goings: English medieval staging conventions', *The Early Drama, Art, and Music Review*, 18:1 (1995), 25–34.

2 *The Towneley Plays*, ed. Martin Stevens and A. C. Cawley, Early English Text Society, 2 vols. (Oxford: Oxford University Press, 1994), I, p. 227.

3 *Ibid.*, I, 270, 287.

4 R. J. E. Tiddy, *The Mummers' Play* (Oxford: Clarendon Press, 1923), pp. 141, 157, 159, 161, 163, 170, 174, 185, 189, 192, 195, 200, 217, 219, 222, 226, 232, 237, 246; E. K. Chambers, *The English Folk Play* (Oxford: Clarendon Press, 1933), p. 46; Alex Helm, *Eight Mummers' Plays* (Aylesbury: Ginn, 1971), pp. 21, 26, 35, 45, 53. All the above references represent examples from different plays.

The related phrase of 'Here comes I . . .' is also to be found in many of the above plays.

5 Philip Butterworth, 'Timing theatrical action in the English medieval theatre', *Early Theatre: A Journal Associated with the Records of Early English Drama*, 4 (2001), 87–100.

6 *The Chester Mystery Cycle*, ed. R. M. Lumiansky and David Mills, Early English Text Society, 2 vols. (London: Oxford University Press, 1974, 1986), 1, p. 361.

7 *The N-Town Play Cotton* MS *Vespasian D. 8*, ed. Stephen Spector, Early English Text Society, 2 vols. (Oxford: Oxford University Press, 1991), 1, p. 376.

8 *The Towneley Plays*, ed. Stevens, 1, p. 364.

9 *The Chester Mystery Cycle*, ed. Lumiansky and Mills, 1, p. 242.

10 *Ibid.*, 1, p. 366.

11 *Ibid.*, 1, p. 367.

12 *The Late Medieval Religious Plays of Bodleian MSS Digby 133 and E Museo 160*, ed. Donald C. Baker, John L. Murphy and Louis B. Hall Jr, Early English Text Society (Oxford: Oxford University Press, 1982), p. 18.

13 *OED* **vanish** v.1 and 1.a.

14 *The Late Medieval Religious Plays*, ed. Baker *et al.*, pp. xxvi–xxviii; Mary Del Villar, 'The staging of the conversion of Saint Paul', *Theatre Notebook*, 25:2 (Winter 1970–1), 64–72; Richard Hoseley, 'Three kinds of outdoor theatre before Shakespeare', *Theatre Survey*, 12:1 (1971), 1–33; Glynne Wickham, 'The staging of saint plays in England' in *The Medieval Drama*, ed. Sandro Sticca (Albany: State University of New York Press, 1972), pp. 99–119 (pp. 106–11); Raymond J. Pentzell, 'The medieval theatre in the streets', *Theatre Survey*, 14:1 (1973), 1–21; Mary Del Villar, 'The medieval theatre in the streets: a rejoinder', *Theatre Survey*, 14:2 (1973), 76–81; Raymond J. Pentzell, 'A reply to Mary Del Villar', *Theatre Survey*, 14:2 (1973), 82–90.

15 *The Staging of Religious Drama in Europe in the Later Middle Ages: Texts and Documents in English Translation*, ed. Peter Meredith and John E. Tailby, trans. Raffaella Ferrari, Peter Meredith, Lynette R. Muir, Margaret Sleeman and John E. Tailby, Early Drama, Art, and Music Monograph Series, Medieval Institute Publications, 4 (Kalamazoo: Western Michigan University, 1983), p. 101.

16 *Ibid.*, pp. 102, 103.

17 John Fletcher and William Shakespeare, *The Two Noble Kinsmen*, ed. John S. Farmer, Tudor Facsimile Texts (Amersham: John S. Farmer, 1910), p. 74.

18 *Ibid.*, p. 75.

19 John Marston, *Histrio-Mastix*, ed. John S. Farmer, Tudor Facsimile Texts (Amersham: John S. Farmer, 1912), sig. D^r.

20 *OED* **mist** 2. b. 'Hence used in phrases with reference to the obscuring of vision (physical or mental), esp. *to cast* or *throw a mist before* (a person's) *eyes*; also simply, *to cast a mist* or *mists*: to produce mystification.' Henry Chettle writes: 'Let me see, if I can see, beleeue mee theres nothing but iugling in

euery corner; for euery man hath learnd the mysterie of casting mysts': Chettle, *Kind-Harts Dreame*, sig. F3ᵛ. Similarly, James Harrison talks of 'casting before your eyes, mystes, shadowes, & colors (suche as Juglers vse to doo)', in *An exhortacion to the Scottes, to conforme them selfes to the honorable, expedient, and godly vnion, betwene the twoo realmes of Englande and Scotlande* (London: Richard Grafton, 1547), sig. hvʳ; Stephen Gosson says 'The Juggler casteth a myst to worke the closer', in *The Schoole of Abuse* (London: Thomas Woodcocke, 1579), sig. A.2ᵛ. In Dekker's *The Whore of Babylon* the King declares: 'They say you can throw mists before our eyes, To make vs thinke you faire': *The Dramatic Works of Thomas Dekker*, ed. Fredson Bowers, 4 vols. (Cambridge: Cambridge University Press, 1953–61), II, p. 563.

21 Scot, *Discouerie of witchcraft*, pp. 340, 341; *Il quaderno di segreti d'un regista provenzale del Medioevo: note per la messa in scena d'una passione*, ed. Alessandro Vitale-Brovarone (Alessandria: Edizioni Dell'Orso, 1984), p. 49; Véronique Plesch, 'Notes for the staging of a late medieval passion play', in *Material Culture and Medieval Drama*, ed. Clifford Davidson, Early Drama, Art, and Music Monograph Series, 25 (Kalamazoo: Medieval Institute Publications, 1999), pp. 75–102 (p. 80). In George Peele's *The Old Wives Tale* (1595) Fantastic says of Huanebango, a braggart armed with a two-handed sword, 'Me thinkes the Coniurer [Sacrapant] should put the foole into a Iugling boxe.' Such an action may not only put Huanebango in his place but there is a further implication that by putting him in a juggling box he may be seen to disappear. It is not clearly established what a 'Iugling boxe' might be. It does appear, however, that such a box is big enough to contain a person and that use of the word 'Iugling' indicates use of sleight of hand. To what might this allude if not to an apparent disappearance? See George Peele, *The Old Wives Tale*, ed. W. W. Greg, Malone Society (Oxford: Oxford University Press, 1908), sig. D2ᵛ; William Roy [William Barlow], *Rede me and be nott wrothe For I saye no thynge but trothe. I will ascende makynge my state so hye/ That my pompous honoure shall never dye* (Strasburg: [n.p.], 1528; facs. repr. C. Whittingham for W. Pickering, 1845), sig. J8ʳ. Here Jef*raye* says: 'O churche men are wyly foxes More crafty then iuggelers boxes To play ligier du mayne teached.' Pollard and Redgrave's *Short Title Catalogue* has now re-classified this work under the authorship of William Barlow (I, p. 65 (STC 1462.7)); see also *The Knave in Graine*, where *Tom* asks: 'Is that your Father *Phoebus* his Chariot, and will he allow you never a Boxe to sit in?' *Iulio* replies: 'No juglers Boxe Ile assure thee friend: for here's neither passe, nor repasse', sig. Mʳ. (Appendix 4).

22 *Il quaderno di segreti d'un regista provenzale del Medioevo*, ed. Vitale-Brovarone, p. 49; Plesch, 'Notes for the staging of a late medieval passion play', p. 80; *The Staging of Religious Drama*, ed. Meredith and Tailby, p. 114.

23 *The Buke of John Maundeuill Being the Travels of Sir John Mandeville Knight 1322–1356*, ed. George F. Warner (London: Roxburghe Club, 1889), pp. 116–117.

24 *Mandeville's Travels*, ed. P. Hamelius, Early English Text Society, 2 vols. (London: Kegan Paul, Trench, Trübner; Humphrey Milford, Oxford University Press, 1919–23), 1, p. 156.

25 *The Staging of Religious Drama*, ed. Meredith and Tailby, p. 114.

26 Sir Hugh Platte, *The Jewell House of Art and Natvre* (London: Peter Short, 1594), pp. 31, 32; *The Renaissance Stage: Documents of Serlio, Sabbattini and Furttenbach*, ed. Barnard Hewitt (Coral Gables, FL: University of Miami Press, 1958; repr. 1969), p. 226; Sebastiano Serlio, *The Five Books of Architecture: An Unabridged Reprint of the English Edition of 1611* (New York: Dover, 1982), fol. 26^v.

27 Casimir Simienowicz, *The Great Art of Artillery of Casimir Simienowicz, Formerly Lieutenant-General of the Ordanance to the King of Poland*, trans. George Shelvocke (London: J. Tonson, 1729), pp. 121, 168. The principle is alluded to with reference to the work of Cornelius Drebbel: 'He could make a glass that, placed in the dark near to him or another, drew the light of a candle, standing at the other end of a long room, with such force, that the glass near him reflected so much light as to make him see to read perfectly.' The strength of this illumination presupposes that the glass is filled with water. If the candle is brought closer to the glass then the illumination will be stronger. See *England as Seen by Foreigners in the Days of Elizabeth and James the First*, ed. William Brenchley Rye (London: John Russell, 1865), p. 234; Philip Butterworth, *Theatre of Fire: Special Effects in Early English and Scottish Theatre* (London: Society for Theatre Research, 1998), pp. 70–8.

28 *Mandeville's Travels*, ed. Hamelius, 1, pp. 153–4.

29 John Nichols, *The Progresses, Processions, and Magnificent Festivities of King James the Sixth*, 4 vols. (London: J. B. Nichols, 1828), 11, p. 537.

30 Agrippa, *De incertitudine & vanitate scientarum & artium*, fol. lviiii; Agrippa, *Henry Cornelius Agrippa, of the Vanitie and vncertaintie of Artes and Sciences*, p. 62^r.

31 William Shakespeare, *The Tempest*, ed. Peter Alexander (London and Glasgow: Collins, 1951; repr. 1965), p. 18.

32 Anon., *The Wasp or Subject's Precedent*, ed. J. W. Lever and G. R. Proudfoot, Malone Society (Oxford: Oxford University Press, 1974 [1976]), pp. 93, 95.

33 *The Staging of Religious Drama*, ed. Meredith and Tailby, p. 102.

34 Albert A. Hopkins, *Magic: Stage Illusions and Scientific Diversions Including Trick Photography* (New York: Munn, 1897), pp. 529–32; Will Goldston, *Tricks and Illusions* (London: Routledge & Kegan Paul, 1908; repr. 1955), pp. 186–9.

35 *The Works of Geoffrey Chaucer*, ed. F. N. Robinson, 2nd edn (Boston: Houghton Mifflin, 1961), p. 130. Further skill is demonstrated by a juggler at a banquet in 1541 where some imaginative provision of light is created: 'Item payd the same day to a joggeller that shoyd hes connyng in makyng off a lyght for the banckyt, xxd'. For an instrument to be described as 'connyng' suggests an instrument(s) that makes use of mirrors; *The Manuscripts of His Grace the Duke of Rutland, K. G. preserved at Belvoir Castle*, ed. Sir H. Maxwell Lyte,

4 vols. (London: His Majesty's Stationery Office, 1905), IV, p. 322; Butterworth, *Theatre of Fire*, pp. 65–8.

36 Rid, *The Art Of Iugling or Legerdemaine*, sigs. B3v–B4r.

37 Scot, *Discouerie of witchcraft*, pp. 323, 329, 339, 350.

38 *Ibid.*, pp. 323, 325, 326, 327, 329.

39 *Ibid.*, p. 324.

40 *Ibid.*, p. 327.

41 *Ibid.*, p. 327.

42 *Ibid.*, p. 309; *Ben Jonson*, ed. Herford and Simpson, VII, 571.

43 Chettle, *Kind-Harts Dreame*, sig. F3ᵛ. Chettle's use of patter plays upon the French term for sleight of hand, 'passe-passe' as demonstrated by John Palsgrave's translation: 'I playe a caste of legyer demayne, Je joue ung tour de passe passe. Wyll you playe a caste of legyer demayne with me nowe: voulez vous jouer ung tour de passe passe auecques moy?': *L'éclaircissement de la langue Française*, p. 658.

44 Anon., *Wily Beguild*, sig. A2ᵛ.

45 Scot, *Discouerie of witchcraft*, p. 323.

46 *The Dramatic Works in the Beaumont and Fletcher canon*, III, pp. 279–80. Some similar patter occurs in Thomas Randolph's *The Jealous Lovers* (1632) where Asotus, the prodigal son to Simo, declares: 'I think Cupid be turn'd jugler. Heres nothing but Hocas pocas. Praesto be gon, Come again Jack; and such feats of activitie.' These phrases of patter appear to be the ones used by Hocus Pocus [William Vincent] as do the following ones recorded in the same play by Paegnium [a Page]: 'If I do not think women were got with ridling, whippe me: Hocas, pocas, here you shall have me, and there you shall have me': Thomas Randolph, *The Jealous Lovers*, pp. 25, 15. Further patter that may be ascribed to Hocus Pocus indicates something of his accompanying actions: 'Here Philalethes like the Angell of the bottomlesse Pit, comes jingling with the Keyes of Magick in his hands. But hee opens as Hokus Pokus do's his fists, where we see here is nothing and there is nothing.' Philalethes, *Observations upon Anthroposophia Theomagica, and Anima Magica Abscondita*, p. 59.

47 *OED* **presto** A. adv. (interj.) 'Quickly, immediately, at once; used by conjurers and jugglers in various phrases of command, esp. *Presto, be gone, Hey presto, pass,* etc; hence = immediately, forthwith, instanter'; C. adj. or attrib. 'At hand, in readiness; active, ready, rapid, quick, instantaneous; of the nature of a magical transformation; juggling.' Among the meanings ascribed to 'praesto' by Thomas Eliot is one that states: 'to exhibite, to represent or shewe'. As an adverb Eliot also defines 'presto' as 'redy, at hande'. The sense, therefore, of 'Presto, be gone' is 'hear it is and now it is gone'. See Thomas Eliot, *The Dictionary of syr Thomas Eliot knyght* (London: Thomas Bertheleti, 1538).

48 The origin of this patter is from the beginning of Virgil's *Eclogues*: 'Tityre tu patulae recubans sub tegmine fagi silvestrem tenui musam meditaris avena' [You, Tityrus, lie under the canopy of a spreading beech, wooing the

woodland Muse on slender reed]: *Virgil Eclogues. Georgics. Aeneid* 1–vi, trans. H. Rushton Fairclough, and rev. G. P. Goold (Cambridge, MA; London: Harvard University Press, 1999), pp. 24–5.

49 [Vincent], *Hocvs Pocvs Ivnior,* sig. B^r.

50 *Ibid.,* sig. B^v-B2^r; Francisco Mario Grapaldi, *Francisci Marij Grapaldi poete laureati . . . vita: de partibus Aedium,* etc. (Venice: A. de Bindonis, 1517), p. 178.

51 [Vincent], *Hocvs Pocvs Ivnior,* sig. c^v.

52 *Ibid.,* sig. c2^r.

53 *Ibid.,* sig. c2^v.

54 *OED* **budget** 1. A 'A pouch, bag, wallet, usually of leather'. The *OED* refers **gipciere** to **gipser.** 'A purse, pouch, or wallet, suspended from a belt or girdle'. See *OED* **budget** 1. C for 'hangman's budget' and Robert Yarrington's *Two Lamentable Tragedies* where a sack containing a dead body is referred to as a hangman's budget: Robert Yarrington, *Two Lamentable Tragedies,* ed. John S. Farmer (Amersham: John S. Farmer, 1913), sig. G^r. Stephen Gosson in his *The Schoole of Abuse* (1579) refers to the analogous role of the 'quacksalver' and his 'budget' by saying: 'And so wading too farre in other mens manners, whilst they fill their Bookes with other mens faultes, they make their volumes no better then an Apothecaries Shop, of pestilent Drugges; a quackesaluers Budget of filthy receites; and a huge Chaos of foule disorder', sig. c.4^v. Also, lawyers seem to have made use of budgets. In John Day's *Law-Trickes,* Emilia says: 'Prittie yfaith, haue ye any more of these tricks? / I may be out-fac'd of my selfe with a Carde of ten, but / yfaith Vncle, the best knaue 'ith bunch, nor all the law / in your Budget cannot doo't, & as for you Sisley bum-trinkets, ile haue about with you at the single Stackado are you a woman?'; Day, *Law Tricks,* sig. H4^v. The devil is also targeted as a possessor of a budget in Thomas Gainsford's *Rich Cabinet,* where it is claimed that 'Knauery is an instrument out of the diuells budget, and serueth for as many purposes, as his workman will apply it vnto': Thomas Gainsford, *The Rich Cabinet Furnished with varietie of Excellent discriptions, exquisite Characters, witty discourses, and delightfull Histories, Deuine and Morrall* (London: I[ohn] B[eale] for R[oger] Iackson, 1616), p. 80. Many decorative and seemingly elaborate budgets were made for a masque performed at Court in 1625. George Binnion was paid for 'Two hundred twenty and nine ounces more of gold and silver lace to trimme twelve suits hatts budgetts shooes and other such like necessaryes for the said Masque iiij^{xx} iij^{li} xix^s iiij^d and 'for tassells for seaventeene budgetts xxxiiij^s'. At the same event Edmond Harrison and Charles Gentill were paid for 'seaven budgetts of Carnacion satten with silver vij^{li} xiiij^s'. George Wilson was paid 'lvj^s iiij^d for 'making vp seventeene budgetts of satten and for silke imploid therein'. Hugh Pope was paid 'lj^s . . . for foure and thirty yards of broad ribben for the Budgetts'. The budgets seem to have been lined since 'Io[hn] Morrall' was paid for 'three ellnes of fine holland to line the budgetts xxix^{li} xvj^s': *Collections* 11:3, pp. 329–31. A more functional use of the budget is recorded by Joseph Moxon: 'Some use a *Budget* or *Pocket* to hang by their sides, to put their *Nails* in when they *Lath,*

and others Tuck and tye up their *Aprons*, and put the Nails therein': Joseph Moxon, *Mechanick Exercises; or, the Doctrine of Handy-Works. Applied to the Arts of Smithing, Joinery Carpentry Turning Bricklayery* (London: Dan[iel] Midwinter and Tho[mas] Leigh, 1703), p. 250. See also: Henry Ridgely Evans, *The Old and the New Magic* (Chicago and London: Open Court and Kegan Paul, Trench, Trübner, 1906), pp. 17–18; Edwin A. Dawes, *The Great Illusionists* (Newton Abbot: David and Charles, 1979), p. 19.

55 [Vincent], *Hocvs Pocvs Ivnior*, sig. B ᵛ. In *The Country Captain* (*c.* 1640) by William Cavendish, Thomas, Captain Vnderwit's 'man', speaking of the devil says: 'his arme flew out, wᵗh open mouth, and his very fingers cryed, giue me the gold, wᶜh presumeing to be wieght [sic], he put into his hocas pocas, a litle dormer vnder his right skirt'. The *OED* offers the above example from '[SHIRLEY] *Capt:.* II. ii in Bullen *O[ld] P[lays]* II. 342' as one of the meanings of 'hocus pocus': *OED* **hocus pocus** 4, 'A bag or "poke" used by jugglers'. Bullen wrongly ascribes the play *Captain Vnderwit* to James Shirley; *Captain Vnderwit* and *The Country Captain* are the same play written by Cavendish. See Cavendish, *The Country Captain*, ed. Johnson and Woudhuysen, p. 18.

56 Joh[n] Amos Comenius, *Orbis sensualium pictus: hoc est omnium principalium in mundo rerum, & vita actionum, pictura & nomenclatura*, trans. Charles Hoole (London: S. Leacroft, 1777), p. 170.

57 [Vincent], *Hocvs Pocvs Ivnior*, sig. B ᵛ.

58 *Ibid.*, sig. B ᵛ.

59 Merlinus Cocaius [Teofilo Folengo], *Histoire Maccaronique de Merlin Coccaie, prototype de Rablais. ou est traicté les Ruses de Cingar, les tours de Boccal, les adventures de Leonard, les forces de Fracasse, les enchantemens de Gelfore & Pandrague, & les recontres heureufes de Balde, &c.*, 2 vols. (Paris: [n.p.], 1606), I, pp. 366–8. Translation by Cécile Brabban. See also Clarke, *The Annals of Conjuring*, ed. Dawes *et al.*, p. 563.

60 Skelton, *Magnyfycence*, p. 69.

61 *Cathay and the Way Thither; Being a Collection of Medieval Notices of China*, ed. and trans. Colonel Henry Yule, 2 vols. (London: Hakluyt Society, 1866), II, pp. 500–1; *The Travels of Ibn Battuta AD 1325–1354*, ed. and trans. C. Defrémery, B. R. Sanguinetti, H. A. R. Gibb and C. F. Beckingham, 5 vols. (Cambridge: Hakluyt Society, 1958–94), IV, pp. 903–4.

62 *The Book of Ser Marco Polo, The Venetian, Concerning the Kingdoms and Marvels of the East*, ed. and trans. Colonel Henry Yule, 2 vols. (London: John Murray, 1875), I, pp. 306–11.

63 *Cathay and the Way Thither*, ed. Yule, II, pp. 500–1. The earliest English account of the entertainments said to be witnessed by Marco Polo and played before the Great Khan is offered by John Frampton in 1579 although his version does not include Ibn Batuta's description. Frampton says: 'When the great Cane will drinke, all the Musitians that bee in Hall doe play, and euery one that serueth, kneeleth downe tyll hee haue drunke. In the Hall be alwayes Jesters, Juglers, and fooles, attending vpon the Tables, to make pastime all dynner

tyme, and after Dinner is done, and the Tables taken vppe, euerie man goeth aboute his businesse.' John Frampton, *The most noble and famous trauels of Marcus Paulus, one of the nobilitie of the state of Venice, into the East partes of the world, as Armenia, Persia, Arabia, Tartary, with many other kingdoms and Prouinces* (London: Ralph Newbery, 1579), p. 59.

64 *Drama and the Performing Arts in Pre-Cromwellian Ireland: A Repertory of Sources and Documents from the Earliest Times until c. 1642*, ed. Alan J. Fletcher (Cambridge: D. S. Brewer, 2001), pp. 598, 480. Fletcher's use of alternative designations in his translation to the juggler is quite understandable but the acts are ones performed by jugglers. *Catalogue of Irish Manuscripts in the British Museum*, ed. S. H. O'Grady and R. Flower, 3 vols. (London: printed for the Trustees, 1926–53), II, p. 350.

65 Ioannis Wieri, *De praestigiis daemonvm, et incantationibus ac ueneficijs, libri* v (Basle: Ioannem Opoinum, 1566), Chapter 11, p. 158; Weyer, *Witches, Devils, and Doctors in the Renaissance,* p. 122.

66 *Memoirs of The Emperor Jahangueir written by Himself; and Translated From a Persian Manuscript,* trans. Major David Price (London: Oriental Translation Committee, 1829), p. 102.

67 *The Book of Ser Marco Polo,* ed. Yule, p. 309; Eduward Melton, *Zee-en Land-Reizen; door Egypten, West-Indien, Perzien, Turkyen, Ost-Indien, en d'aangrenzende Gewesten . . . Aangevangen in den jaare 1660. en geeindigd in den jaare 1677* (Amsterdam: Jan ten Hoorn, 1681), between pp. 468 and 469.

68 Robert Henry Elliot, *The Myth of the Mystic East* (Edinburgh and London: Blackwood, 1934), pp. 83–4, 85–106; Richard Wiseman and Peter Lamont, 'Unravelling the Indian rope-trick', *Nature,* 383 (19 December 1996), 212–13; Lee Siegel, *Net of Magic: Wonders and Deceptions in India* (Chicago and London: University of Chicago Press, 1991), pp. 193–221.

69 Peter Lamont, *The Rise of the Indian Rope Trick: The Biography of a Legend* (London: Little, Brown, 2004), p. 208.

70 J. N. Maskelyne, *The Fraud of Modern 'Theosophy' Exposed* (London: George Routledge, [1912]), p. 22.

71 Maskelyne, *The Fraud of Modern 'Theosophy' Exposed,* pp. 23–4.

5   MAGIC THROUGH SOUND: ILLUSION, DECEPTION
AND AGREED PRETENCE

1 *The Ancient Cornish Drama,* ed. and trans. Edwin Norris, 2 vols. (Oxford: Oxford University Press, 1859), I, pp. 28–9.

2 *Ibid.,* II, pp. 156–7, 158–9.

3 The immediate comparison is that with the treatment meted out to Mac in the Towneley *Second Shepherds' Play.* See *The Towneley Plays,* ed. Stevens and Cawley I, p. 152. In *A Pleasant Conceyted Comedy of George a Greene, the Pinner of Wakefield* (1599) by Robert Greene, a stage direction requires of Ienkin that: 'He throwes the ground in, and she comes out.' This refers to a

staged trick performed by Ienkin to produce George a Greene's 'sweete heart', Bettris. George is unsure of what he sees. He says: 'Is this my love, or is it but her shadow?' Ienkin replies: 'I this is the shadow, but heere is the substance.' Perhaps the simplest way of envisaging this requirement is for a cloth to cover the hole produced by an open trap and for Bettris to rise up under the cloth and for it to be removed to reveal the 'substance' from the 'shadow'. Robert Greene, *A Pleasant Conceyted Comedy of George a Greene, the Pinner of Wakefield*, ed. F. W. Clarke and W. W. Greg, Malone Society (Oxford: Oxford University Press, 1911), sig. D. 4^r.

4 *Ancient Cornish Drama*, ed. Norris, 1, pp. 458–9.
5 *Il quaderno di segreti d'un regista provenzale del Medioevo*, ed. Vitale-Brovarone, pp. 44; Plesch, 'Notes for the staging of a late medieval passion play', p. 78.
6 Plesch, 'Notes for the staging of a late medieval passion play', p. 78.
7 Holinshed, *Holinshed's Chronicles of England, Scotland and Ireland*, ed. Ellis, 6 vols., IV, p. 6; see also John Stow [Edmund Howes], *The Annales Or Generall Chronicle of England* (London: Thomas Adams, 1615), p. 616; Robert Withington, *English Pageantry: An Historical Outline*, 2 vols. (Cambridge, MA: Harvard University Press, 1918; repr. New York/London: Benjamin Blom, 1963), 1, p. 188.
8 Langham, *Robert Laneham: A Letter* [*1575*], pp. 9–10; R. J. P. Kuin, *Robert Langham: A Letter* (Leiden: E. J. Brill, 1983), p. 40.
9 George Gascoigne, *The Whole woorkes of George Gascoigne Esquyre: Newlye compyled into one Volume, that is to say: His Flowers, Hearbes, Weedes, the Fruites of warre . . . the Complaint of Phylomene, the Storie of Ferdinando Ieronimi, and the pleasure at Kenelworth Castle* (London: Abel Ieffres, 1587), sig. A.1^r.
10 John Nichols, *The Progresses and Public Processions of Queen Elizabeth. Among which are interspersed other solemnities, public expenditures, and remarkable events. During the reign of that illustrious princess. Collected from Original Manuscripts, Scarce Pamphlets, Corporation Records, Parochial Registers, etc, etc.* 3 vols. (London: John Nichols, 1823), I, p. 488.
11 *The Staging of Religious Drama*, ed. Meredith and Tailby, p. 112; J. Voskuil 'The speaking machine through the ages', Transactions of *the Newcomen Society*, 26 (1953 for 1947–9) 259–67. Arthur Prince, writing on ventriloquy, refers to the deception of positioning people inside dummy figures: 'I was nearly forgetting the trick ventriloquist. His figures *did* speak with different voices, and the voices *did* come from the figures themselves. But the effects were not obtained by ventriloquism. The figures were all of a large size, and boys and girls, sometimes even men and women, were concealed within them. They did the talking; the performer only pretended to be a ventriloquist'; Arthur Prince, *The Whole Art of Ventriloquism* (London: Will Goldston, [1921]), p. 9.
12 *The Staging of Religious Drama*, ed. Meredith and Tailby, p. 101.
13 Peele, *The Old Wives Tale*, sigs. D.3^v–E.1^r.

14 Robert Greene, *The Honorable Historie of Frier Bacon, and Frier Bongay*, ed. John S. Farmer, Tudor Facsimile Texts (Amersham: John S. Farmer, 1914), sig. G. 2^r.

15 *Ibid.*, sigs. G . 1^v, G . 2^r.

16 For discussion of the range and significance of 'posts' in texts and stage directions see: George Fullmer Reynolds, *The Staging of Elizabethan Plays at the Red Bull Theater 1605–1625* (New York; London: Modern Language Association of America and Oxford University Press, 1940), pp. 92–3; *A Dictionary of Stage Directions in English Drama, 1580–1642*, ed. Alan C. Dessen and Leslie Thomson (Cambridge: Cambridge University Press, 1999), pp. 168–9.

17 Robert Greene, *Alphonsus King of Aragon*, ed. W. W. Greg, Malone Society (Oxford: Oxford University Press, 1926), sigs. F. 1^r–F. 2^v. See also pp. viii–ix.

18 Dekker, *The Dramatic Works of Thomas Dekker*, ed. Bowers, III, pp. 161, 168–9.

19 William Bourne, *Inuentions or Deuises* (London: Thomas Woodcock, 1578), pp. 98–9. Similar automaton technology is recorded during the Progress of Henry VII at Bristol in 1486, where a number of pageants were performed that included one of 'The Resurrection of oure Lorde in the highest Tower of the same, with certeyne Imagerye smytyng Bellis, and al went by Veights, merveolously wele done'; Leland, *De rebus Britannicus collectanea*, IV, pp. 201–2. The transcription of this quotation differs in significant detail from that in *REED: Bristol*. The latter reads: 'The Resurreccion of our lorde in the highest Tower of the same with certeyne Imagerye smyting bellis And al went by vices marveolously weldone . . .' The difference between 'Veights' and 'vices' may change the meaning of the account: *REED: Bristol*, p. 13. Early claims to the construction of speaking heads were made by Albertus Magnus, Roger Bacon, Gerbert, Robert Grosseteste and Johannes Müller (alias Regiomontanus). See Voskuil, 'The speaking machine through the ages', pp. 260–1; Derek J. De Solla Price, 'Automata and the origins of mechanism and mechanistic philosophy', *Technology and Culture*, 5:1 (1964), 9–23; Silvio A. Bedini, 'The role of automata in the history of technology', *Technology and Culture*, 5:1 (1964), 24–42.

20 Records concerning the Modane play of *Antichrist* state that: 'They shall make and paint an image looking like Antichrist which by skill they shall make and move and alter its lips as a sign it is speaking'; *The Staging of Religious Drama*, ed. Meredith and Tailby, p. 105.

21 Bourne, *Inuentions or Deuises*, p. 99.

22 'Acme Whistle Company', T. Hudson and Co. (Whistles), 244 Barr Street, Birmingham B19 3AH, UK: instruction leaflet *c.* 1975.

23 Io[hn] Bapt[ista] Portae, *Magiae natvralis libri XX. Ab ipso authore expurgati, & superaucti, in quibus scientiarum Naturalium diuitiae, & delitae demonstrantur cvm privilegio.* (Naples: apud Horatium Saluianum, 1589), XVIIII, I, p. 288. This description is not contained in the earlier editions of 1558, 1561 or 1564: John Baptista Porta, *Natural Magick*, ed. Derek J. Price

(London: Thomas Young and Samuel Speed, 1658; repr. New York: Basic Books, 1957), p. 353. See also pp. 385–6.

24 Etten, *Mathematicall Recreations*, p. 87. In Henri Decremps, *The Conjurer Unmasked; or, La Magie Blanche Dèvoilèe: Being a Clear and Full Explanation of all the Surprizing Performances Exhibited as well in this Kingdom as on the Continent, By the most eminent and dexterous Professors of Slight of Hand* (London: T. Denton, 1785), p. 79 the following account describes the use of speaking and hearing trumpets: 'We were then shewn by Mr. Van Estin the figure of an infant suspended by a ribbon, and apparently quite detached from any other object, this figure gave rational answers to questions put to it, either in French, English, German, or Italian Languages. He thus explained it to us. – "This (said he) does not merit much of your attention, altho' the multitude have gaped, and paid, and the learned have puzzled themselves by their own conjectures on this simple trick. This figure has in its mouth a tin speaking trumpet, through which the questions are put, and the answers received; this trumpet has communication with a similar one concealed in the head of the figure, the widest part being uppermost, each serving alternately as a speaking and a hearing trumpet. Two other trumpets of the same construction are in the ceiling, immediately over the head of the figure, and the confederate being in the room above, answers to the questions, thro' these two trumpet."' The disposition of the 'tin speaking trumpet' in the head of the figure and the ones placed in the ceiling do not appear to be effective of themselves. The clue to the appropriate operation of this trick seems to be related to the description that 'an infant [was] suspended by a ribbon, and apparently quite detached from any other object'. It may be conjectured that the ribbon concealed a pipe that connected the trumpets.

25 Nicolo Sabbatini, *Pratica di fabricar scene e machine ne' teatri* (Ravenna: Pietro de' Paoli and Gio[vanni] Battista Giouannelli, 1638; facs. repr. Rome: Carlo Bestetti, Edizioni D'Arte, 1955), p. 131; *The Renaissance Stage*, ed. Hewitt, p. 176.

26 Ludwig Lavater, *Of ghostes and spirites walking by nyght*, trans. H[arrison], p. 34.

27 Nash, *The Vnfortvnate Traveller*, sig. κ. 1ᵛ. James Sandford, in his translation of Heinrich Cornelius Agrippa's *De incertitudine & vanitate scientiarum & artium*, alludes to the same devices when he declares that: 'Thou art determined to knowe difficulte matters, and so shewe miracles: with the passinge skill of thy Arte mettales do belowe, *Diomedes* bloweth alowde in Brasse, the Brasen Serpente hisseth, birdes be counterfaited, and they that haue no proper voice be hard to vtter sweetnesse of songe'; Agrippa, *Vanitie and vncertaintie of Artes and Sciences*, sig. 55ʳ.

28 Wecker, *De Secretis Libri*, pp. 949–50; Wecker, *Eighteen Books Of the Secrets of Art & Nature*, pp. 340–1. The method of producing this illusion is contained in a nineteenth-century account by Sir David Brewster. See *Letters on Natural Magick: Addressed to Sir Walter Scott, Bart. By Sir David Brewster K. H.* (London: John Murray, 1834), pp. 161–4. Sir Samuel Morland, in his

Tuba Stentoro-Phonica, states that: 'The first Instrument of this kind (though the Invention had been long before digested in my thoughts!) was by my directions made in Glass, in the Year 1670 . . . being about 2 Foot 8 Inches in length, the Diameter of the great end 11 Inches, and the Diameter of the little end 2½. In this Instrument I was heard speaking at a considerable distance, by several Persons, and they likewise were heard by me, and found that it did very considerably magifie (or rather multiply) the Voice. Whereupon I caused another to be made in Brass, about 4 Foot 1/2 in length, the Diameter of the greater end 12 Inches, and of the less, 2 Inches . . . And for the better conveniency of opening and shutting the mouth without losing any part of the breath (the loss of a small part whereof sensibly abates the lowdness of the voice) I caused the Mouth-piece to be made somewhat after the manner of Bellows, that so by opening and shutting, it might answer the motion of the mouth exactly, and yet be held so close, that it might not lose any part of the breath in speaking. Of this second Instrument, there were two tryals made very successfully in St. *James'* Park; where, at one time, the Lord *Angier* standing by the Park-wall near *Goring-House*, heard me speaking (and that very distinctly) from the end of the Mall near *Old Spring*-Garden: And at another time, His Majesty, His Royal Highness, Prince *Rupert*, and divers of the Nobility and Gentry, standing at the end of the Mall near *Old Spring-Garden*, heard me speaking (word for word) from the other end of the Mall, (though the wind were contrary;) which is 850 Yards, or near 1/2 of a measured *English* Mile': Samuel Morland, *An Instrument of Excellent Use, As well at Sea, as at Land; Invented, and variously Experimented in the Year 1670* (London: W. Godbid, 1671), sig. A. 2ᵛ; Evelyn, *Memoirs*, 1, p. 278; John Wilkins, *Mathematical Magick: Or, the Wonders That may be Performed by Mechanical Geometry* (London: Ric[hard] Baldwin, 1691), p. 176; Charles F. Partington, *The Century of inventions of the Marquis of Worcester from the Original* MS *with Historical and Explanatory Notes and a Biographical Memoir* (London: John Murray, 1825), pp. 85–8. The account contained in this work is that employed by Robert Charles in his presentation of *The Invisible Lady* in London in 1803; see Clarke, *The Annals of Conjuring*, ed. Dawes *et al.*, pp. 188–9; Sir David Brewster, *Letters on Natural Magick, addressed to Sir Walter Scott*, pp. 158–64.

29 Nevil Maskelyne and David Devant, *Our Magic: The Art in Magic; The Theory of Magic; The Practice of Magic* (London: George Routledge & Sons, [1911]), p. 231.

30 Some of the earliest references to ventriloquy are those included in Scot, *Discouerie of witchcraft*, pp. 126–32; George McIntyre, *George McIntyre's Bibliography on Ventriloquism* (Seattle: Gregory & Walter Berlin, 1970).

31 Lack of trust or, indeed, lack of understanding of the need for such trust, forms a critical part of the adventures of Valentine Vox where the stories are based upon a misconception of the ventriloquist's ability to 'throw his voice'. Here, Cockton gives Vox the opportunity to fool various gathered assemblies that his voice actually emanates from another part of the room and not as a

disguised voice of the ventriloquist. See Henry Cockton, *The Life and Adventures of Valentine Vox, the Ventriloquist* (London: Robert Tyas, 1840); Frederic Maccabe, *The Art of Ventriloquism. Including Full Directions to Learners How to Acquire a Pleasing Vocalization; with Amusing Dialogues* (London: Frederick Warne, [1875]), p. 5.

32 Bacon, *Epistola Fratris Rogerii Baconis*, p. 2; Bacon, *Frier Bacon his Discovery of the Miracles of Art, Nature, and Magick*, p. 2. Similarly poor understanding is recorded by Francis Bacon in his *Sylva sylvarvm*; he states: 'There haue beene some, that could counterfeit the *Distance* of *Voices* (which is a *Secondary Object* of *Hearing*) in such sort; As when they stand fast by you, you would thinke the *Speech* came from a farre off, in a fearefull manner. How this is done, may be further enquired. But I see no great vse of it, but for Imposture, in counterfeiting Ghosts or Spirits'; Francis Bacon, *Sylva sylvarvm; or, A Naturall History In ten Centuries* (London: W. Rawley, 1628), p. 65. Further reference to this poorly understood technique is made by Sir Kenelm Digby when he states: 'In the like manner they that are called ventriloqui, do persuade ignorant people that the Diuell speaketh from within them deepe in their belly) by their sucking their breath inwardes in a certaine manner whiles they speake: whence it followeth that their voice seemeth to come, not from them, but from somewhat else hidden within them; if (att the least) you perceiue it cometh out of them: but if you do not, then it seemeth to come from a good way off. To this art belongeth the making of sarabatanes [sarbacanes], or trunkes, to helpe the hearing; and of Eccho glasses, that multiply soundes, as burning glasses, do light': Digby *Two Treatises*, p. 251. In *The Art of Ventriloquism*, pp. 4–6, Maccabe corrects some of the above false assumptions in a re-published letter to the editor of *Land and Water*.

33 Maccabe, *The Art of Ventriloquism* pp. 47–8; Fred Russell, *Ventriloquism and Kindred Arts: An Historical and Practical Treatise, Giving Explicit and Reliable Directions Whereby the Whole Art of Distant Voice Illusion, Figure Working and Vocal Mimicry May Be Acquired* (London: Keith, Prowse, 1898), p. 53; Robert Ganthony, *Practical Ventriloquism and Its Sister Arts* (London: L. Upcott Gill, 1903), pp. 28–31; Harold G. King and John E. T. Clark, *Ventriloquism and Juggling* (London: C. Arthur Pearson, 1921), pp. 58–63; Douglas Craggs, *Ventriloquism from A to Z: A Complete Treatise on the Art of Voice-Throwing and Doll Manipulation* (London: Faber, 1969), pp. 31–6, 48–57; Valentine Vox, *I Can See Your Lips Moving: The History and Art of Ventriloquism* (London: Kaye & Ward, 1981), pp. 154–5.

34 Russell, *Ventriloquism and Kindred Arts*, pp. 39, 41–2; Craggs, *Ventriloquism from A to Z*, p. 25; Robert-Houdin, *The Secrets of Stage Conjuring*, ed. and trans. Professor [Luis] Hoffmann (London: George Routledge, 1881, pp. 143–53.

35 Ganthony, *Practical Ventriloquism*, pp. 43, 53, 80, 81; Russell, *Ventriloquism and Kindred Arts*, p. 54.

36 Russell, *Ventriloquism and Kindred Arts*, p. 53.

37 Maccabe, *The Art of Ventriloquism*, pp. 50–1; Russell, *Ventriloquism and Kindred Arts*, pp. 27, 46; Ganthony, *Practical Ventriloquism*, pp. 92–115.

38 *REED: Coventry*, pp. 265, 269, 289.

39 *The Staging of Religious Drama*, ed. Meredith and Tailby, p. 157.

40 John Bate, *The Mysteries Of Nature and Art. In foure seuerall parts. The first of Water works. The second of Fire works. The third of Drawing, Washing, Limming, Painting, and Engraving. The fourth of sundry Experiments. The Second Edition; with many additions unto every part* (London: Ralph Mabb, 1635), pp. 82–8. In *The Araygnement of Paris* (1584) a stage direction requires: 'An artificiall charme of birdes being harde within, Pan speakes.' George Peele, *The Araygnement of Paris A Pastorall* (London: Henrie Marsh, 1584), sig. A 4^v. Sounds of the cuckoo, nightingale and quail are required by stage directions in the following seventeenth-century plays: Thomas Dekker, *The Sun's Darling* in *The Dramatic Works of Thomas Dekker*, ed. Bowers, IV, pp. 4, 27; James Shirley, *Hide Park. A Comedie* (London: Andrew Crooke and William Cooke, 1637), sigs. F. 3^r, F. 4^v–G. 1^r. Thomas Randolph, *Amyntas*, in *Poems with the Mvses Looking-glasse: and Amyntas* (Oxford: Leonard Lichfield, 1638), p. 97; Richard Brome, *A Joviall Crew; or, The Merry Beggars* (London: J. Y. for E. D. and N. E., 1652), sig. B. 4^r. Verisimilar sound is sought by stage directions for the wren, lark, cuckoo, owl, lamb, cow, fawn, swallow, thrush and pig in the masque of Sir Thomas Kynaston, *Corona Minervæ* (London: William Sheares, 1635), sigs. A. 4^r, B. 2^r, B. 3^v.

41 Bate, *The Mysteries Of Nature and Art*, p. 86.

42 Frank Bellew, *The Art of Amusing* (London: S. Low, 1866), pp. 220–1.

43 *The Staging of Religious Drama*, ed. Meredith and Tailby, p. 102; Ganthony, *Practical Ventriloquism*, p. 80.

6 MECHANICAL IMAGES, AUTOMATA, PUPPETS AND MOTIONS

1 George Puttenham, *The Arte of English Poesie. Contriued into three Bookes: The first of Poets and Poesie, the second of Proportion, the third of Ornament* (London: Richard Field, 1589), Book 3, p. 128. Something of the skill and imagination used in the construction of these 'vglie Gyants' may be compared with that recorded in the *Bridge house Rentals* that refer to preparations for the coronation of Elizabeth Woodville in 1464: 'And for rods of hazel bought for making images 4d . . . And for eight pairs of gloves bought for the hands of eight images 9d. And for one pound of flock wool bought for stuffing the said gloves 1½d. And for six kerchiefs of "pleasaunce" bought for the apparel of six images of women 8s. 8d . . . And for a thousand pins bought and used in fixing the clothes on the images 14d . . . And to William Parys and Richard Westmyll, tailors, preparing and making clothes for diverse images . . . for 3½ days, 6s.'; Glynne Wickham, *Early English Stages 1300 to 1660*, 3 vols. (London: Routledge & Kegan Paul, 1966–81), I, p. 102, Appendix B.

2 Withington, *English Pageantry*, I, 138n1.

3 Cornelius Grapheus Scribonius, *Spectaculorum in susceptione Philippi Hispani Principis Caroli V.* (Antwerp: Petro Alosten, 1550), sig. L4ᵛ.

4 Nichols, *The Progresses and Public Processions of Queen Elizabeth*, 11, pp. 372–73.

5 Johannes Bochius, *The Ceremonial Entry of Ernst Archduke of Austria into Antwerp, June 14, 1594* (New York: Benjamin Blom, 1970), p. 108.

6 *OED* **vice** sb² 2b. 'A mechanical contrivance or device by which some piece of apparatus, etc., is worked'. Something of the range of use of the term may be seen from two different examples. At Christmas, 1511, an allegorical pageant was presented to Henry VIII at Richmond. On 'Epiphanie at nighte, before the banket in the Hall at Richemond, was a pageaunt deuised like a mountayne, glisteringe by night, as though it had bene all of golde and set with stones, on the top of the which mountayne was a tree of golde, the braunches and bowes frysed with gold, spredynge on euery side ouer the mountayne, with Roses and Pomegarnettes, the which mountayne was with vices brought vp towardes the kyng, & out of thesame came a ladye, appareiled in cloth of golde, and the chyldren of honor called the Henchemen, whiche were freshly disguised, and daunced a Morice before the kyng. And that done, reentred the moutaine and then it was drawen backe, and then was the wassaill or banket brought in, and so brake vp Christmas.' Another use of the term 'vice' may be seen to refer more specifically to a winch mechanism at Canterbury, Kent between 1514 and 1534. The event was performed annually on a wagon and it is thought to be 'a debased survival or revival of an old St. Thomas play'. Payment is recorded here throughout this period 'to hym that turned the vyce' that presumably lifted 'yᵉ Angell'. In the accounting year for 1520–1 payment is recorded 'for wyre for the vyce of yᵉ Angell jᵈ'. Hall, *Hall's Chronicle*, pp. 516–17; *Collections* VII, pp. 188, 192–7.

7 Bourne, *Inuentions or Deuises*, p. 98.

8 *OED* **picture** sb 2d. 'By extension, an artistic representation in the solid, esp. a statue or a monumental effigy; an image'; Charles Wriothesley, *A Chronicle of England during the Reigns of the Tudors, from A.D. 1485 to 1559*, ed. William Douglas Hamilton, 2 vols. (London: Camden Society, 1875), 11, p. 1. See also Mark C. Pilkinton, 'The Easter Sepulchre at St Mary Redcliffe, Bristol, 1470', *The EDAM Newsletter* 5:1 (Fall 1982), 10–12 for another device of the same subject.

9 Withington, *English Pageantry*, 1, p. 178.

10 *Ibid.*, 1, p. 177.

11 *Ibid.*, 1, p. 186.

12 Thomas Middleton, *A Game at Chess*, ed. T. H. Howard-Hill, Malone Society (Oxford: Oxford University Press, 1990), p. 80.

13 Thomas Middleton, *The Works of Thomas Middleton*, ed. A. H. Bullen, 8 vols. (London: John C. Nimmo, 1885–6), VII (1886), pp. 112–13.

14 *Ibid.*, VII, pp. 112–13.

15 John Babington, *Pyrotechnia; Or, A Discovrse of Artificial Fire- works* (London: Thomas Harper for Ralph Mab, 1635; facs. repr. Amsterdam/New York: Da

Capo Press Theatrvm Orbis Terrarvm Ltd, 1971), pp. 36–7. George Chapman, in his *The Revenge of Bussy D'Ambois* of 1613 makes disparaging comments about the present state of theatre: 'Nay, we must now haue nothing brought on Stages, / But puppetry, and pide ridiculous Antickes': George Chapman, *The Revenge of Bussy D'Ambois* (Menston: Scolar Press, 1968), sig. C1^v. Payments in the *Ironmongers' Court Books* and *Rough Book* for 1609 concerning the Lord Mayors' Show record details of 'the maine Pageant wth a golden feild, and an Ocean about it wth Mermaid*es* and Tritons artificiallie moovinge'. This may well be a similar device that enables the mermaids and tritons to circle the 'golden feild'; *Collections* III, ed. Jean Robertson and D. J. Gordon, Malone Society (Oxford: Oxford University Press, 1954), p. 74.

16 Thomas Hill, *A briefe and pleasaunt treatise, entituled, Naturall and Artificiall conclusions* (London: Iohn Kyngston for Abraham Kitson, 1581), pages not numbered.

17 See for example: Cyprian Lucar, *Three Bookes of Colloqvies concerning the Arte of Shooting in great and small pieces of Artillerie . . . written in Italian, and dedicated by Nicholas Tartaglia . . . And now translated into English by* CYPRIAN LVCAR *. . .* (London: Thomas Dawson for Iohn Harrison, 1588), Appendix, p. 82; Robert Norton, *The Gvnner Shewing The Whole Practise Of Artillerie: With all the Appurtenances therevnto belonging. Together with the making of Extraordinary Artificiall Fireworkes, as well for Pleasure and Triumphes, as for Warre and Seruice* (London: A. M. for Hvmphrey Robinson, 1628), p. 147; Francois de Malthe, *A Treatise of Artificial Fire-works both for Warres and Recreation: with divers pleasant Geometricall obseruations, Fortifications and Arithmeticall Examples. In fauour of Mathematicall Students. Newly written in FRENCH, and Englished by the Authour THO:MALTHVS* (London: Richard Hawkins, 1629), p. 91; Bate *The Mysteryes of Natvre and Art* (London: Thomas Harper for Ralph Mab, 1634), II, p. 65; Butterworth, *Theatre of Fire*, p. 217.

18 Leland, *Johannis Lelandi antiquarii de rebvs Britannicis collectanea*, IV, pp. 201–2. See this book, Chapter 5, note 19.

19 Michael Glenny, 'Ingenious and efficient: the Wells Cathedral clock', *Country Life*, 180 (1986), 852–4 (p. 853). An account in *Coryat's Crudities* of 1611 relates an apocryphal description of the maintenance of one of these clocks. However, the story may well be an early account of what is today referred to as an 'urban legend'. It reads: 'in which gate are two pretty conceits to be obserued, the one at the very top, which is a clocke with the images of two wilde men by it made in brasse, a witty deuice and very exactly done. At which clocke there fell out a very tragicall and rufull accident on the twenty fifth day of Iuly being munday about nine of the clocke in the morning, which was this. A certaine fellow that had charge to looke to the clocke, was very busie about the bell, according to his vsuall custome euery day, to the end to amend something in it that was amisse. But in the meane time one of those wilde men that at the quarters of the howers doe vse to strike the bell, strooke the man in the head with his brasen hammer, giving

him such a violent blow, that therewith he fel down dead presently in the place, and neuer spake more. Surely I will not iustifie this for an vndoubted truth, because I saw it not. For I was at that time in the Dukes Palace obseruing of matters: but as soone as I came forth some of my country-men that tolde me they saw the matter with their owne eies, reported it vnto me, and aduised me to mention it in my iornall for a most lamentable chance.' Thomas Coryat, *Coryat's Crudities Hastily gobled vp in five Moneths trauells in France, Sauoy, Italy, Rhetia comonly called the Grisons country, Heluetia aliàs Switzerland, some parts of high Germany, and the Netherlands; Newly digested in the hungry aire of Odcombe in the County of Somerset, & now dispersed to the nourishment of the trauelling Members of this Kingdome* (London: William Stansby for the author, 1611), p. 187.

20 *The Travels of Leo Rozmital through Germany, Flanders, England, France, Spain, Portugal and Italy 1465–1467*, ed. and trans. Malcolm Letts, Hakluyt Society (Cambridge: Cambridge University Press, 1957), p. 57. Coryat also refers to the same subject matter in what appears to be a similar mechanism: 'The other conceit that is to be obserued in this gate is the picture of the Virgin *Mary* made in a certaine dore aboue a faire Dyal, neare to whom on both sides of her are painted two Angels on two little dores more. These dores vpon any principall holiday doe open of themselues, and immediately there come forth two Kings to present themselues to our Lady, vnto whom after they haue done their obeysance by vncouering of their heads, they returne againe into their places: in the front of this sumptuous gate are presented the twelue celestiall signes, with the Sunne, Moone, and Starres, most excellently handled.' Coryat, *Coryat's Crudities*, p. 187.

21 *The Travels of Leo Rozmital*, ed. Letts, p. 61.

22 Christopher Wordsworth, *Notes on Mediæval Services in England* (London: Thomas Baker, 1898), p. 132.

23 *The Staging of Religious Drama*, ed. Meredith and Tailby, p. 119. See also p. 115 for an account of 'mechanical figures moved by springs' at Dieppe in 1443.

24 Bourne, *Inuentions or Deuises*, p. 98; *The Chester Plays*, ed. Hermann Deimling, Early English Text Society, 2 vols. (Oxford: Oxford University Press, 1892; repr. 1968), I, p. 59; *The Chester Mystery Cycle: A New Edition with Modernised Spelling*, ed. David Mills, Medieval Texts and Studies, 9 (East Lansing: Colleagues Press, 1992), p. 60.

25 Bourne, *Inuentions or Deuices*, p. 99.

26 William Lambarde, *Dictionarium Angliæ topographicum & historicum. An Alphabetical Description of the Chief Places in England and Wales; With an Account of the most Memorable Events which have distinguish'd them* (London: Fletcher Gyles, 1730), p. 459.

27 Butterworth, *Theatre of Fire*, pp. 23–5.

28 Hopkins, *Magic: Stage Illusions and Scientific Diversions*, pp. 413–14.

29 *Letters and Papers, Foreign and Domestic, of the Reign of Henry VIII: Preserved in the Public Record Office, the British Museum, and Elsewhere in England*, ed. J. S. Brewer, 21 vols. (London: Longman, 1862–1910), IV, Part 1 (1870), p. 127.

30 See for example the account in William Lambarde, *A Perambulation of Kent: Conteining the description, Hystorie, and Customes of that Shyre (for the most part) in the yeare. 1570* (London: Ralphe Newberie, 1576), pp. 182–5. Here, Lambarde states: 'he compacted of wood wyer, paste, and paper, a Roode of suche exquisite arte, and workmanship, that it not onely matched in comelynesse, and due proportion of the partes, the beste of the common sorte: but in straunge motion, varietie of gesture, and nimblenesse of ioynts, passed all other that before had beene seene: the same being able to bowe downe, and lift vp it selfe, to shake and stirre the handes and feete, to nod the heade, to roll the eyes, to wagge the chappes, to bende the browes, and finally, to represent to the eye bothe the proper motion of eche member of the bodye, and also a liuely, expresse, and significant shewe of a well contented, or displeased mynde, byting the lippe, and gathering a frowning, frowarde, and disdainefull face, when it woulde pretende offence'. See also Scot, *Discouerie of witchcraft*, pp. 110–11.

31 *Letters and Papers, Foreign and Domestic, of the Reign of Henry VIII: preserved in the Public Record Office, the British Museum, and elsewhere in England,* arranged and catalogued by J. S. Brewer, J. Gairdner and R. H. Brodie (London: Longman, 1862–1910), XIII (1892), part 1, p. 79.

32 *Ibid.*, XIII, Part 1, pp. 116–17.

33 *Ibid.*, XIII, Part 1, p. 120. Reference to these effects created by the 'juggler' are no doubt what the author of *The second Tome of Homilees* had in mind when the work states: 'And yf it were to be admitted, that some miraculous actes were by illusion of the deuill done where images be: (For it is evident that the moste part were fayned iyes, and craftie iuglynges of men) yet foloweth it not therefore, that suche images are eyther to be honoured, or suffered to remayne.' Anon., *The second Tome of Homilees, of such matters as were promised, and intituled in the former part of Homilees. Set out by the aucthoritie of the Queenes Maiestie: And to be read in euerie parishe Church agreeably* (London: R. Jugge and J. Cawood, 1571), p. 111.

34 *Letters and Papers*, ed. Brewer, Gairdner and Brodie, XIII, Part 1, pp. 283–4.

35 Wriothesley, *A Chronicle of England*, I, p. 74. Ability to 'move the eyes' is referred to in a description of a 'picture' in *Coryat's Crudities*: 'The other was the picture of a Gentlewoman, whose eies were contriued with that singularitie of cunning, that they moued vp and down of themselues, not after a seeming manner, but truly and indeed. For I did very exactly view it. But I beleeue it was done by a vice.' Coryat, *Coryat's Crudities*, p. 254; see note 8 to this chapter.

36 Wriothesley, *A Chronicle of England*, I, pp. 74–5; J. Brownbill, 'Boxley Abbey and the Rood of Grace', *The Antiquary*, 7 (1883), 162–5, 210–13.

37 *Three Chapters of Letters Relating to the Suppression of Monasteries*, ed. Thomas Wright (London: Camden Society, 1843), p. 172.

38 *Original Letters Relative to the English Reformation Written during the Reigns of King Henry VIII., King Edward VI., and Queen Mary: Chiefly from the Archives of Zurich*, ed. Hastings Robinson, Parker Society, 2

vols. (Cambridge: Cambridge University Press, 1846), II, p. 604. See also pp. 606–10.

39 *The Antiquarian Repertory: A Miscellaneous Assemblage of Topography, History, Biography, Customs, and Manners*, ed. Francis Grose and Thomas Astle, 4 vols. (London: Edward Jeffery, 1807–9), III [1808], pp. 349–50.

40 *OED* **puppetry** 1.

41 William Tyndale, *The obedience of a Christen man and howe Christen rulers ought to gouernel where in also (yf thou marke diligently) thou shalt fynde eyes to perceave the crafty conveyaunce of all iugglers.* (Marlborow, Hans Luft [Antwerp, Johannes Hoochstraten], 1528; facs. repr. Menston: Scolar Press, 1970), fol. 53^v.

42 John Bale, *King Johan*, Malone Society (Oxford: Oxford University Press, 1931), p. 10.

43 George Speaight, *The History of the English Puppet Theatre*, 2nd edn (London: Robert Hale, 1990), p. 54.

44 *Ibid.*, p. 53.

45 Of the assembled evidence, *The Romance of Alexander* is perhaps the strongest in its visual confirmation of the existence of glove puppets, although the drawing by Bruegel (engraving by van der Heyden) of the glove puppet and its puppeteer together (1565) constitutes the strongest visual evidence of puppeteers with glove puppets in the sixteenth century. Reference to the Chaucer examples is not strong, for other interpretations of 'popet' are possible. See *OED* **puppet** sb 2. 'A figure (usually small) representing a human being; a child's doll; = POPPET sb 2.' *The second Tome of Homilees* employs the sense when it declares 'that as litle girles playe with litle puppettes, so be these decked images great puppettes for olde fooles to play with'. Anon., *The second Tome of Homilees*, p. 151.

46 Speaight, *The History of the English Puppet Theatre*, p. 52.

47 Ian Lancashire, ' "Ioly Walte and Malkyng": a Grimsby puppet play in 1431', *Records of Early English Drama Newsletter*, 2 (1979), 6–8.

48 *REED: York*, 1, pp. 70, 72. The translations used here are slightly different from those used in *REED: York*. The second translation makes it possible that the reference could refer to a dialogue between two actors.

49 Lancashire, ' "Ioly Walte and Malkyng" ', p. 6.

50 *Ibid.* p. 7n5. The suggested connection of this material to the *Interludium de clerico et puella* is not conclusive, although it is an attractive proposition. See *Early Middle English Verse and Prose*, ed. J. A. W. Bennett and G. V. Smithers, 2nd edn (Oxford: Clarendon Press, 1968; repr. 1974), pp. 196–200. See also *OED* **malkin** sb. 4. 'A scarecrow; a ragged puppet or grotesque effigy; a guy'.

51 Sir Philip Sidney, *Syr P. S. His Astrophel and Stella. Wherein the excellence of sweete Poesie is concluded To the end of which are added, sundry other rare Sonnets of diuers Noble men and Gentlemen* (London: Thomas Newman, 1591; facs. repr. Menston: Scolar Press, 1970), fol. A3^r.

52 Bentley, *The Jacobean and Caroline Stage*, III, p. 45.

53 John Hall, *The Courte of Vertu: Contayning many holy or Spretuall Songes, Sonnettes, psalmes, & Shorte Sentences, as well of holy Scripture as others* (London: Thomas Marshe, 1565), p. 140^r.

54 *Ibid.*, p. 141^v.

55 Thomas Nashe, *Lenten Stuffe, Containing, the Description and first Procreation and Increase of the towne of Great Yarmouth in Norfolke: With a new Play neuer played before, of the praise of the Red Herring. Fitte of all Clearkes of Noblemens Kitchins to be read: and not vnnecessary by all Seruing men that haue short boord-wages, to be remembred.* (London: N. L. and C. B., 1599), p. 64.

56 Thomas Nashe, *The Terrors of the night; Or, A Discourse of Apparitions* (London: Iohn Danter for William Iones, 1594), sig. c.iv^r.

57 *Ben Jonson*, v, 305.

58 *Collections* v: *The Academic Drama in Oxford: Extracts from the Records of Four Colleges*, ed. R. E. Alton, Malone Society (Oxford: Oxford University Press, 1961 [1962]) p. 21.

59 *REED: Hereforshire, Worcestershire*, p. 383.

60 Edmund Spenser, *Prosopoia; Or, Mother Hubberds Tale. By Ed. Sp. Dedicated to the right Honorable the Ladie Compton and Mountegle* (London: William Ponsonbie, 1591), sig. pi^v.

61 Lambarde, *Dictionarium Angliæ topographicum*, p. 459.

62 William Horman, *Vulgaria* (London: R. Pynson, 1519), p. 409. 'Hiding' of the puppeteer is referred to by William Davenant in his *Works*: 'and Man in Chimney hid to dress, / Puppit that acts our old Queen Bess, / And Man that whilst the Puppits play, / Through Nose expoundeth what they say'. Davenant, *The Works of Sr William Davenant K^t*, p. 291.

63 Gervase Babington, *An Exposition of the Catholike Faith; Or, the* xii. *Articles of the Apostles Creede. Learnedly Expovnded (According to the Scriptures) Wherein all heretiques as well Auncient as Moderne against the Deity of Christ and the Holy Ghost, are plainely discouered, pithely disproued, and the trueth faithfully confirmed* (London: G[eorge] Elde for Henry Featherstone, 1615), p. 270. Evidence concerning the nature and making of puppets in England is scant. Payment is recorded in the *Drapers' Repertory* for 1521 concerning the Midsummer Shows in London: 'makyng of iiij^{or} popys'; *Collections* iii, p. 9.

64 Cardano, *De svbtilitate*, p. 342. Translation by Philip A. Shaw.

65 Wecker, *De secretis libre*, p. 953. Translation by Philip A. Shaw. See also Wecker, *Eighteen Books of the Secrets of Art & Nature*, p. 342.

66 Ferguson, *Bibliographical Notes on the Histories of Inventions and Books of Secrets*, ii, p. 22.

67 W. R. Streitberger, *Court Revels 1485–1559* (Toronto; Buffalo; London: University of Toronto Press, 1994), p. 245.

68 *Collections* iii, p. 25.

69 *Ibid.*, p.26.

70 William Turner, *The first and seconde partes of a Herbal of William Turner . . . lately ouersene corrected and enlarged with the Thirde parte lately gathered and nowe set oute with the names of the herbes in Greke Latin English Duche Frenche*

and in the Apothecaries and Herbaries Latin with the properties degrees and naturall places of the same (London: Arnold Birckman, 1568), pp. 45^v–46^r.

71 Bourne, *Inuentions or Deuises*, p. 99.

72 Adams, *The Dramatic Records of Sir Henry Herbert*, p. 47.

73 Boas, *The Diary of Thomas Crosfield*, pp. 26–9.

74 *Ibid.*, p. 29.

75 *Ibid.*, p. 54.

76 Ben Jonson, *Everyman Out of his Humour*, sig. F ij^v.

77 N. W. Bawcutt, 'Craven Ord transcripts of Sir Henry Herbert's office-book in the Folger Shakespeare Library', *English Literary Renaissance*, 14 (1984), 83–94 (p. 91); N. W. Bawcutt, 'Sir Henry Herbert and William Sands the puppeteer: some corrections', *Records of Early English Newsletter*, 20:1 (1995), 17–19.

78 *REED: Lancashire*, p. 87.

79 *REED: Dorset, Cornwall*, pp. 121–2.

80 Harold C. Gardner, *Mysteries' End: An Investigation of the Last Days of the Medieval Religious Stage* (Yale: Yale University Press, 1946; repr. Archon, 1967), p. 78.

81 N. W. Bawcutt, 'New revels documents of Sir George Buc and Sir Henry Herbert, 1619–1662', *Review of English Studies* 35 n.s. (1984), 316–31 (p. 327).

82 *REED: CWG*, pp. 319–20.

83 Adams, *The Dramatic Records of Sir Henry Herbert*, p. 47.

84 *REED: Coventry*, p. 442.

85 *Ibid.*, p. 443.

86 *Acts of the Privy Council of England*, ed. John Roche Dasent, New Series, 8 (London: Public Record Office, 1894), p. 131. See also p. 132; E. K. Chambers, *The Elizabethan Stage*, 4 vols. (Oxford: Clarendon Press, 1923; repr. 1974), IV, p. 271.

87 Chambers, *The Elizabethan Stage*, IV, p. 271.

88 *Collections II:3*, p. 316.

89 *REED: Cambridge*, I, p. 487.

90 *REED: Coventry*, p. 419.

91 Adams, *The Dramatic Records of Sir Henry Herbert*, p. 47.

92 *The Court and Times of James the First; Containing a Series of Historical and Confidential Letters, in which will be found a detail of the Public Transactions and Events in Great Britain during that Period, with a variety of Particulars not mentioned by our Historians*, ed. Thomas Birch, 2 vols. (London: Henry Colburn, 1849), I, p. 72.

93 *REED: Coventry*, p. 442. The 'Robert Browne' recorded here appears to be the same person recorded at Carlisle in 1641–2 and Norwich in 1641–2. See *REED: Cumberland, Westmorland, Gloucestershire*, p. 125; *REED: Norwich*, p. 236.

94 Murray, *English Dramatic Companies*, II, p. 313.

95 *REED: Norwich*, p. 232.

96 *Ibid.*, p. 222.

97 *REED: Coventry*, p. 433. See also p. 434.

98 *Ibid.*, p. 434.
99 *Ibid.*, p. 444.

7   SUBSTITUTION

1 *Non-Cycle Plays and Fragments*, ed. Norman Davis, Early English Text
   Society (London: Oxford University Press, 1970), p. 73.
2 *Ibid.*, p. 74.
3 *Ibid.*, p. 82.
4 Jacobus de Voragine, *Legenda aurea*, in *Lombardica historia* (Cologne:
   Ludwig von Renchen, 1485), fols. x^{vii}–y; Jacobus de Voragine, *Legenda aurea:
   vulgo historia lombardica dicta; ad optimorum liborum fidem/ Recensuit Dr. Th.
   Graesse*, ed. Theodor Graesse, 3rd edn (Breslau: Gulielmum Koebner, 1890),
   p. 508; Jacobus de Voragine, *The Golden Legend: Readings on the Saints*, trans.
   William Granger Ryan, 2 vols. (Princeton: Princeton University Press, 1993),
   ii, p. 81. See also: *The Blickling Homilies*, ed. Richard Morris, Early English
   Text Society (London: Oxford University Press, 1967), pp. 151–3; *Cursor
   Mundi (The Cursor o the world): A Northumbrian Poem of the* xivth *Century*,
   ed. Richard Morris, Early English Text Society, 3 vols. (London: Kegan Paul,
   Trench, Trübner, 1874–93), iii, pp. 1186–7; *The South English Legendary*, ed.
   Charlotte D'Evelyn and Anna J. Mill, Early English Text Society, 3 vols.
   (London: Oxford University Press, 1956–9), ii, p. 371; *Mirk's Festial: A
   Collection of Homilies*, ed. Theodore Erbe, Early English Text Society
   (London: Kegan Paul, Trench, Trübner, 1905), pp. 222–3.
5 *The N-Town Play: Cotton* ms *Vespasian* d. 8, ed. Spector, i, 404.
6 *The Staging of Religious Drama*, ed. Meredith and Tailby, pp. 101–2.
7 *REED: York*, i, pp. 47–8; ii, p. 732.
8 *REED: York*, i, p. 23; ii, p. 709.
9 *REED: York*, i, p. 110; *The York Plays*, ed. Richard Beadle, York Medieval
   Texts, second series (London: Edward Arnold, 1982), p. 460.
10 William Hutchinson Shoemaker, *The Multiple Stage in Spain during the
   Fifteenth and Sixteenth Centuries* (Westport, CT: Greenwood Press, 1973),
   p. 82.
11 *Ibid.*, pp. 20–4; N. D. Shergold, *A History of the Spanish Stage from Medieval
   Times until the End of the Seventeenth Century* (Oxford: Clarendon Press,
   1967), p. 66.
12 Vitale-Brovarone, *Il quaderno di segreti*, pp. 35–6; Plesch, 'Notes for the
   staging of a late medieval passion play', pp. 75–102 (p. 81).
13 Anon., *Edmond Ironside; or, War Hath Made All Friends*, ed. Eleanore Boswell
   and W. W. Greg, Malone Society (Oxford: Oxford University Press, 1927),
   pp. 32–5.
14 Anon., *The Tragedy of Claudius Tiberius Nero*, ed. John S. Farmer, Tudor
   Facsimile Texts (Amersham: John S. Farmer, 1913), sig. m3^{v}.
15 Dekker, *The Dramatic Works of Thomas Dekker*, iii, p. 203.
16 *The Staging of Religious Drama*, ed. Meredith and Tailby, pp. 236, 238.

17 Alfons Llorens, Rafael Navarro Mallebrera and Joan Castaño Garcí, *La festa d'Elx*, trans. Pamela M. King and Asunción Salvador-Rabaza Ramos (Elche: Patronato Nacional del Misterio de Elche, 1990), p. 24.
18 *The Staging of Religious Drama*, ed. Meredith and Tailby, p. III.
19 *Ibid.*, p. 102.
20 *Ibid.*, p. 103.
21 *Ibid.*, p. 113.
22 *Ibid.*, pp. 110–11.
23 *Ibid.*, p. 113.
24 Vitale-Brovarone, *Il quaderno di segreti*, p. 20; Plesch, 'Notes for the staging of a late medieval passion play', pp. 79–80.
25 *The Staging of Religious Drama*, ed. Meredith and Tailby, p. 113.
26 *Ibid.*, p. 102.
27 *Ibid.*, p. 105.
28 *Teatre Hagiogràfic*, ed. Josep Romeu, 3 vols. (Barcelona: Editorial Barcino, 1957), III, p. 200; *The Staging of Religious Drama*, ed. Meredith and Tailby, p. 110; Shergold, *A History of the Spanish Stage*, pp. 62–4.
29 *The Staging of Religious Drama*, ed. Meredith and Tailby, p. 110.
30 *Ibid.*, p. 110.
31 *Ibid.*, pp. 111–12.
32 *Ibid.*, p. 112.
33 Dekker, *The Dramatic Works of Thomas Dekker*, III, p. 448.
34 John Marston, *The Works of John Marston*, ed. A. H. Bullen, 3 vols. (London: John C. Nimmo, 1887), III, p. 232.
35 R. B. [Richard Bower?], *A new Tragicall Comedie of Apius and Virginia*, ed. Ronald B. McKerrow and W. W. Greg, Malone Society (London: C. Whittingham, Chiswick Press, 1911), sigs. D3^v–D4^r.
36 Yarrington, *Two Lamentable Tragedies*, sigs. F4^v–G1^r. See Thomas Heywood's *The Golden Age*, where a stage direction determines that 'A banquet [is] brought in, with the limbes of a Man in the service'. Thomas Heywood, *The Dramatic Works of Thomas Heywood: Now First Collected with Illustrative Notes and a Memoir of the Author*, 6 vols. (London: J. Pearson, 1874; repr. New York: Russell and Russell, 1964), III, p. 21.
37 John Fletcher and Philip Massinger, *Sir John van Olden Barnavelt*, ed. T. H. Howard-Hill, Malone Society (London: Oxford University Press, 1979 [1980]), p. 94.
38 *Mankind*, in *The Macro Plays*, ed. Mark Eccles, Early English Text Society, (London: Oxford University Press, 1969), p. 168.
39 Cardano, *De svbtilitate libri XXI* (1550), p. 342.
40 Ludwig Lavater, *Of ghostes and spirites walking by nyght*, p. 18.
41 Scot, *The Discouerie of witchcraft*, pp. 349–50; Francesco Maria Guazzo, *Compendivm maleficarvm in tres libros distinctum ex plvribvs avthoribus per fratrem franciscvm Mariam Gvaccivm* (Milan: [n.p.], 1608), p.4. Brother Guazzo refers to the work of Ioannes Trithemius in his ability to perform the decapitation trick: 'Ioannes Trithemius refert ex antiquioribus, quod anno

876. tempore Ludouici Imperatoris, Sedechias quidam Religione Iudeus, professione Medicus, stupenda quaedam coram principibus uiris fecit; videbatur enim hominibus ipsum deuorare currum onustum foeno, cum equis, & Auriga: insuper amputare capita, manus, & pedes, quae pelui coram imposita sanguine stillantia, cunctis spectanda praebebat, & ea statim hominibus illesis suo quoque loco restituebat.' [John Trithemius tells that much earlier, in the year 876 during the time of the Emperor Louis, a certain Zedechias, a Jew by religion and a physician by profession, worked wonders in the presence of Princes. For he appeared to devour a cart loaded with straw, together with the horses and the driver; he used to cut off men's heads and hands and feet, and exhibit them in a bowl dripping with blood, and then suddenly he would restore the men unharmed each to his own place.'] Francesco Maria Guazzo, *Compendium maleficarum*, trans. E. A. Ashwin (New York: Dover, 1988), p. 5.

42 Vincent (attrib.), *Hocvs Pocvs Ivnior*, sig. E2^v.
43 *Ibid.*, sig. E3^r.
44 David Calderwood, *The History of the Kirk of Scotland*, 8 vols. (Edinburgh: Wodrow Society, 1842–9), I, p. 142.
45 Richard Johnson, *The thirde voyage into Persia, begun in . . . 1565*, in *The Principal Navigations, Voyages, Traffiqves, and Discoveries of the English Nation, made by sea or Ouer-Land to the Remote and Farthest Distant Quarters of the Earth . . . Richard Haklvyt Preacher* (London: George Bishop, Ralph Newberie and Robert Barker, 1599), pp. 317–18.
46 Lambard, *A Perambulation of Kent*, p. 182.
47 John Gee, *The Foot out of the Snare* (London: H[umphrey] L[ownes] for Robert Milbourne, 1624), p. 51.
48 Bourne, *Inuentions or Deuises*, p. 99.
49 *Ibid.*, p. 99.
50 Agrippa, *Heinrich Cornelius Agrippa*, fol. 62^r.
51 *Life in the Middle Ages*, ed. G. G. Coulton, 4 vols. (Cambridge: Cambridge University Press, 1929), II, p. 138.
52 *The Staging of Religious Drama*, ed. Meredith and Tailby, p. 118.
53 *Ibid.*, p. 105.
54 Wickham, *Early English Stages 1300 to 1660*, I, p. 326. See also an account concerning the St George play, Turin, for 1429, where it is recorded 'for flax to make hair of the angels and of the souls: 6lbs., 6 gross'; *The Staging of Religious Drama*, ed. Meredith and Tailby, p. 121.
55 Thomas Ady, *A Candle in the Dark* (London: Robert Ibbitson, 1655), pp. 36–7.

8 STAGE TRICKS

1 *OED* **trick** sb. 1. 'A crafty or fraudulent device of a mean or base kind; an artifice to deceive or cheat; a stratagem, ruse, wile'; sb. 2. 'A freakish or

mischievous act; a roguish prank; a frolic; a piece of roguery or foolery; a hoax, practical joke'.

2 Hall, *Hall's Chronicle*, p. 120.

3 Hall, *The Courte of Vertu*, p. 141ᵛ.

4 William Shakespeare, *Troilus and Cressida*, ed. Peter Alexander (London and Glasgow: Collins, 1951; rpr. 1965), p. 820.

5 Chettle, *Kind-Harts Dreame*, sig. F3ᵛ.

6 *The Works of Thomas Kyd*, ed. Frederick S. Boas (Oxford: Clarendon Press, 1901), p. 300. See also *REED: Chester*, pp. 218, 303.

7 *Collections* VI, p. 150.

8 *Ben Jonson*, VI, pp. 268–9. See also pp. 254–5, 258. The implication here is that the 'bellowes', the 'false belly' and the 'Mouse' are stock items of the juggler's equipment. See this book, Chapter 7, note 55 and text.

9 Adams, *The Dramatic Records of Sir Henry Herbert*, p. 47.

10 Gee, *The Foot out of the Snare*, p. 28.

11 *REED: Coventry*, p. 447.

12 Gee, *The Foot out of the Snare*, p. 49.

13 Murray, *English Dramatic Companies 1558–1642*, II, p. 257.

14 *REED: Coventry*, p. 442.

15 *OED* **gin** sb. 1. 'Skill, ingenuity. Also in a bad sense: Cunning, craft, artifice. *Quaint of gin*: clever in contriving or planning; also of things, curiously contrived'; sb. 2. 'An instance or product of ingenuity; contrivance, scheme, device. Also a cunning stratagem, artifice, trick'.

16 Cardano, *De svbtilitate*, pp. 342–3. Translation by Philip A. Shaw. For descriptions of how 'To make solid metal rings link one into another, and to form therewith chains of various kinds', see Robert-Houdin, *The Secrets of Conjuring and Magic; or, How to Become a Wizard*, pp. 291–300; Herbert L. Becker, *All the Secrets of Magic Revealed* (Hollywood: Lifetime Books, 1994; repr. 1997), pp. 83–5. A version of stabbing someone through the stomach may be seen in a 'Sword trick – a stab through the abdomen', in Hopkins, *Magic: Stage Illusions and Scientific Diversions* (New York: Munn, 1897), pp. 152–3. Further insight is offered by Cardano in this work into those tricks concerned with eating and blowing fire. He says: 'Etenim quid iuuat, aut igne*m* uorare, aut efflare? Namqui uorant illum, prius collecta sub lingua saliua extinguunt: qui efflant, cotto & stup*ae* inuoluunt.' [And indeed, what helps either to eat fire, or to blow it forth? For those who eat it extinguish it with saliva that they have earlier collected beneath their tongue: those who blow it forth cover [themselves] with tow and with a coat.] Protection that is offered by the 'cotto & stup*ae*' is that which is necessary for the trick involving Maximilla in the *Origo mundi* of the *Cornish Ordinalia*. See *The Ancient Cornish Drama* ed. Norris, I, pp. 200–1. Norris wrongly translates 'stuppa' as a 'stove' whereas it refers to use of 'oakum' or 'hardis'. See also Butterworth, *Theatre of Fire*, p. 31.

17 Cardano, *De rervm varietate*, pp. 466–7; see also *Drama and the Performing Arts in Pre-Cromwellian Ireland*, pp. 482, 599.

18 Sir Thomas Herbert, *A Relation Of Some Yeares Travaile, Begvnne Anno 1626. Into Afrique and the greater Asia, especially the Territories of the Persian Monarchie: and some parts of the Orientall Indies, and Iles adiacent. Of their Religion, Language, Habit, Discent, Ceremonies, and other matters concerning them* (London: William Stansby and Jacob Bloome, 1634), p. 55.

19 Richard Hakluyt, *The Principal Navigations, Voyages, Traffiqves and Discoveries of the English Nation, made by Sea or ouerland, to the remote and farthest distant quarters of the Earth, at any time within the compasse of these 1600 yeres* (London: George Bishop, Ralph Newberie and Robert Barker, 1599), p. 284.

20 Coryat, *Coryat's Crudities*, p. 274.

21 *REED: Coventry*, p. 397.

22 Thomas Preston, *A lamentable Tragedie, mixed full of plesant mirth, containing the life of Cambises king of Percia*, ed. John S. Farmer, Tudor Facsimile Texts (Amersham: John S. Farmer, 1910), sig. F3^v.

23 Barnaby Barnes, *The Divils Charter: A Tragedie Conteining the Life and Death of Pope Alexander the sixt*, ed. John S. Farmer, Tudor Facsimile Texts (Amersham: John S. Farmer, 1913), sig. G2^r; Dekker, *The Dramatic Works of Thomas Dekker*, III, pp. 530–1.

24 George Peele, *King Edward the First*, ed. W. W. Greg, Malone Society (Oxford: Oxford University Press, 1911), sig. D3^v.

25 Thomas Kyd, *The Spanish Tragedie: Containing the lamentable end of Don Horatio, and Bel-imperia: with the pittifull death of olde Hieronimo*, ed. by W. W. Greg, Malone Society (Oxford: Oxford University Press, 1925), sig. M^v.

26 Anon., *The Faire Maide of Bristow*, ed. John S. Farmer, Tudor Facsimile Texts (Amersham: John S. Farmer, 1912), sig. D2^v.

27 Anon., *Edmond Ironside; or, War Hath Made All Friends*, pp. 34–5.

28 Yarington, *Two Lamentable Tragedies*, sigs. B4^r, C4^r. In *The Honorable Historie of Frier Bacon , and Frier Bongay* by Robert Greene, a stage direction determines: 'Heere the Head speakes and a lightning flasheth forth, and a hand appeares that breaketh down the Head with a hammer'; Greene, *The Honorable Historie of Frier Bacon, and Frier Bongay*, sig. G2^v.

29 Heywood, *The Dramatic Works of Thomas Heywood*, III, p. 181.

30 Thomas Goffe, *The Covragiovs Tvrke: Or, Amvrath the First*, ed. David Carnegie and Peter Davison, Malone Society (Oxford: Oxford University Press, 1968 [1974], sig. G^v.

31 Thomas Ingeland, *A pretie and Mery new Enterlude: called the Disobedient Child*, ed. John S. Farmer, Tudor Facsimile Texts (Amersham: John S. Farmer, 1908), sig. E3^r. Simple staging tricks that are made to appear as 'Art Magicke' are contained in *A New Tricke to Cheat the Divell* by Robert Davenport. The earliest printed text of the play is from 1639 and Fryer Iohn juggles the components of a meal that includes bread from Spain, wine from France and chicken from Germany. The bread is discovered on stage in 'that Corner'; the wine is revealed 'Upon that place' and the 'Pullet' is found in 'that same Cupboord' that is seemingly locked. However, 'A hot fat Pullet, newly dress'd and save'd' is

retrieved from the cupboard. The feats of Fryer Iohn are regarded by one of the assembled gathering as 'above wonder' but not so by Fryer Iohn, who says 'You see what Art can doe': R[obert] D[avenport], *A Pleasant and Witty Comedy: Called, A New Tricke to Cheat the Divell* (London: Iohn Okes, for Humphrey Blunden, 1639), sigs. E3ᵛ–E4ʳ. Similar staged tricks are contained in Thomas Heywood's *The Late Lancashire Witches*, in which a milk pail is seen to traverse the stage with no apparent aid. An important eye-witness account of this play in performance describes the moving pail as 'walking of pailes of milke by themselues'. Immediately prior to this description, the eye witness, Nathaniel Tomkyns, offers something of a staging stance to these tricks when he talks of the witches being served with 'all sorts of meat and drinke conveyed vnto them by their familiars vpon the pulling of a cord'. The moving pail may similarly have moved by being pulled along a cord. Depending on the tautness of the presumed cord and the weight of the pail the latter may have been seen to bounce along the line when pulled. Heywood, *The Late Lancashire Witches*, in *The Dramatic Works of Thomas Heywood*, IV, pp. 201–2, 204–5; Herbert Berry, 'The Globe bewitched and El Hombre Fiel', *Medieval and Renaissance Drama in England*, I (1984), 211–30; *REED: Somerset*, I, p. 416; Alan C. Dessen, *Recovering Shakespeare's Theatrical Vocabulary* (Cambridge: Cambridge University Press, 1995), pp. 262–3.

32 *The Staging of Religious Drama*, ed. Meredith and Tailby, p. 103.

33 *Documents Relating to the Office of the Revels in the Time of Queen Elizabeth*, ed. Feuillerat, p. 327.

34 Vitale-Brovarone, *Il quaderno di segreti*, pp. 7, 8, 43; Plesch, 'Notes for the staging of a late medieval passion play', p. 82. Similar artifice regarding the use of blood is referred to in the *Volume of Secrets of a Provençal Stage Director's Book*, ed. Vitale-Brovarone, for the Crucifixion. Here, wooden nails are made hollow so that they may contain diluted vermilion. Small holes in the nails allow the 'blood' to seep out.

35 Cornish Record Office, MS *Works of Sir Richard Carew*, pp. 85–7.

36 Scot, *Discouerie of witchcraft*, pp. 347–8.

37 *Ibid.*, p. 348.

38 *Ibid.*, p. 350. Payment is recorded for false stomachs or bellies employed during 'Show day' in the *Churchwardens' Accounts* at Chelmsford in 1563: 'Item paide to Robᵗ Mathews for a paier of wombs. xvi d.' See Karl Pearson, *The Chances of Death and Other Studies in Evolution*, 2 vols. (London: Edward Arnold, 1897), II, p. 415. See also *OED* **womb** sb.1; *Non-Cycle Plays and Fragments*, ed. Davis, pp. 77, 163.

39 Scot, *Discouerie of witchcraft*, p. 347.

40 Henry Glassie, *All Silver and No Brass: An Irish Christmas Mumming* (Philadelphia: University of Pennsylvania Press, 1975), p. 31.

41 *Non-Cycle Plays and Fragments*, ed. Davis, p. 80. An example of one method of presenting wounds to an audience occurs in the records of the *Modane Antichrist Play* where 'They will paint the body of Jesus on pigskins with his wounds and the marks of his having been flogged . . . They will also paint the

pigskins of the bodies of Elijah and Enoch and the patriarch to put on over the flesh (vestir sur la chair)'; *The Staging of Religious Drama*, ed. Meredith and Tailby, p. 106.

42 Barnes, *The Divils Charter*, sig. G2ʳ.

43 Vitale-Brovarone, *Il quaderno di segreti*, p. 6; Plesch, 'Notes for the staging of a late medieval passion play', p. 81. Véronique Plesch, whose translation is used here, faces the same problem that I encountered in translating the word 'bota' for use in Butterworth, *Theatre of Fire* (p. 27). A literal translation suggests that the 'sores' are 'thrown' but the sense requires them to be stuck in place.

44 *The Staging of Religious Drama*, ed. Meredith and Tailby, p. 103.

45 *Ibid.*, p. 113.

46 *Ibid.*, p. 105.

47 *Ibid.*, p. 109.

48 Preston, *A lamentable Tragedie*, sig. D4ʳ. The technique used here may well satisfy the requirements made through an explicit stage direction in *The Creation of the World* where Cain is struck by an arrow: 'when cayme is stryken lett bloud appeare & let hem tomble'. *Gwreans An Bys, The Creation of the World: A Cornish Mystery*, ed. and trans. Whitley Stokes (London: Williams and Norgate, 1864), p. 122.

49 *REED: Kent*, I, p. 137.

50 *Collections* VII, pp. 188, 195.

51 *REED: Kent*, p. 137; *Collections* VII, p. 195.

52 *The Staging of Religious Drama*, ed. Meredith and Tailby, p. 108.

53 *Ibid.*, p. 108.

54 Vitale-Brovarone, *Il* quaderno di segreti, pp. 34–5; Plesch, 'Notes for the staging of a late medieval passion play', p. 82.

55 Kyd, *The Spanish Tragedie*, sig. Mʳ.

56 *Ibid.*, sig. Mᵛ.

57 Petrus Martyr Anglerius, *The Decades of the newe worlde or west India, Conteynyng the nauigations and conquestes of the Spanyardes, with the particular description of the moste ryche and large landes and Ilandes lately founde in the west Ocean perteynyng to the inheritaunce of the kinges of Spayne*, trans. Rycharde Eden (London: Guilhelmi Powell, 1555), p. 46ᵛ.

58 Gee, *The Foot out of the Snare*, p. 28.

59 Thomas Dickers [Dekker] and Iohn Webster, *The Famovs History of Sir Thomas Wyat*, ed. John S. Farmer (Amersham: John S. Farmer, 1914), sig. C3ʳ·ᵛ. See also note 31 to this chapter.

60 Lynn White, 'The legacy of the Middle Ages in the American wild west', in *Medieval Religion and Technology: Collected Essays*, ed. Lynn White., Jr. (London: University of California Press, 1978), pp. 105–20 (p. 117).

61 *The Ancient Cornish Drama*, ed. Norris, I, pp. 342–3. A degree of realism is implied during the hanging of Judas in *The Volume of Secrets of a Provençal Stage Director's Book:* see note 24 to this chapter. Plesch, 'Notes for the staging of a late medieval passion play', pp. 79–80.

62 *The Life of Saint Meriasek, Bishop and Confessor: A Cornish Drama*, ed. and trans. Whitley Stokes (London: Trübner, 1872), pp. 70–1.
63 *Ibid.*, p. 73.
64 Sir David Lindsay, *Ane Satyre of the Thrie Estaits*, (Edinbvrgh: Robert Charteris, 1602; facs. repr. Amsterdam and New York: Theatrum Orbis Terrarum and Da Capo Press, 1969), pp. 134, 138, 141, 142.
65 Anthony Munday, *The Book of Sir Thomas More*, ed. W. W. Greg, Malone Society (Oxford: Oxford University Press, 1911), pp. 22–3. The same sort of action is implied in *A Warning for Faire Women* (1599), where a stage direction requires of Browne, who goes to his death, that 'He leapes off'. See Anon., *A Warning for Faire Women*, ed. John S. Farmer, Tudor Facsimile Texts (Amersham: John S. Farmer, 1912), sig. 14^r.
66 George Peele, *The Love of King David and Fair Bethsabe*, ed. W. W. Greg, Malone Society (Oxford: Oxford University Press, 1912), sig. G3^r.
67 *Ibid.*, sig. G3^r.
68 *Henslowe's Diary*, ed. R. A. Foakes and R. T. Rickert (Cambridge: Cambridge University Press, 1968), p. 217.
69 'Mechanical advantage' refers to the principle of raising heavy objects through reduced effort by use of more than one pulley. This is well illustrated through use of the 'block and tackle'.
70 *REED: Cambridge*, I, p. 192.
71 *Ibid.*, II, p. 967.
72 *REED: Coventry*, p. 281.
73 *Ibid.*, p. 624. See 'jeʒie' in glossary.
74 *Ibid.*, p. 260.
75 *Ibid.*, p. 289.
76 *Ibid.*, p. 285.
77 *Ibid.*, pp. 265, 269.
78 *Ibid.*, p. 260.
79 *OED* **truss** sb. 3.a. and 3.b.
80 *The Staging of Religious Drama*, ed. Meredith and Tailby, p. 116.
81 *Ibid.*, pp. 279, 114–5.
82 *The Ancient Cornish Drama*, ed. Norris, I, pp. 140–1.
83 *The Life of Saint Meriasek*, ed. and trans. Stokes pp. 38–9.
84 *The Staging of Religious Drama*, ed. Meredith and Tailby, p. 103.
85 *Ibid.*, p. 115.
86 Ady, *A Candle in the Dark*, p. 38.
87 Thomas Lodge and Robert Greene, *A Looking-Glass for London and England*, ed. W. W. Greg, Malone Society (Oxford: Oxford University Press, 1932), sig. C2^v.
88 Francis Beaumont and John Fletcher, *Four Plays or Moral Representations in One, The Triumph of Time*, ed. by A. R. Waller, 10 vols. (Cambridge: Cambridge University Press, 1905–12), X (1912), p. 362.
89 *The York Plays*, ed. Beadle, p. 106; Richard Beadle, 'The York Hosiers' play and Pharaoh: a Middle English dramatist at work', *Poetica*, 19 (1984), 3–26; *The Staging of Religious Drama*, ed. Meredith and Tailby, p. 136.

90 Ady, *A Candle in the Dark*, p. 31.
91 Edward Topsell, *The Historie of Serpents; Or, The second Booke of liuing Creatures: Wherein is contained their Diuine, Naturall, and Morall descriptions, with their liuely Figures, Names, Conditions, Kindes and Natures of all venemous Beasts: with their seuerall Poysons and Antidotes; their deepe hatred of Mankind, and the wonderfull worke of God in their Creation, and Destruction* (London: William Jaggard, 1608), p.4.
92 Coryat, *Coryats Crudities*, p. 274.

9   TERMINOLOGY

1 John Ferguson, Regius Professor of Chemistry at the University of Glasgow, first identified the genre of 'Books of secrets' in the late nineteenth century. Not only did he examine these works but he built up a large collection of them which is now held at the University of Glasgow. Bibliographical details of his lectures and publications exist in his *Bibliographical Notes on Histories of Inventions and Books of Secrets*. See also: W. R. Cunningham, *Catalogue of the Ferguson Collection of Books Mainly Relating to Alchemy, Chemistry, Witchcraft and Gipsies in the Library of the University of Glasgow*, 2 vols. (Glasgow: Robert Maclehose, 1943; facs. repr. Connecticut: Mansfield Centre, n. d.); Elizabeth H. Alexander, *A Bibliography of John Ferguson* (Glasgow: Glasgow Bibliographical Society, 1920); Elizabeth H. Alexander, *A Further Bibliography of the Late John Ferguson* (Glasgow: Glasgow Bibliographical Society, 1934); William Eamon, *Science and the Secrets of Nature: Books of Secrets in Medieval and Early Modern Culture* (Princeton, NJ: Princeton University Press, 1994).
2 Henri Garenne [Dr Frank Lind], *The Art of Modern Conjuring, Magic, and Illusions* (London: n.p., *c.* 1886).
3 Hoffmann, *Modern Magic: A Practical Treatise on the Art of Conjuring*; Robert-Houdin, *The Secrets of Conjuring and Magic*.
4 *The Northern Passion: Four Parallel Texts and the French Original, with Specimens of Additional Manuscripts*, ed. Frances A. Foster, Early English Text Society, 3 vols. (London: Kegan Paul, Trench, Trübner, 1913), 1, p. 67.
5 *Cursor mundi*, ed. Morris, 11, p. 1021.
6 *The Early South-English Legendary; or, Lives of Saints*, ed. Carl Horstmann, Early English Text Society (London: Trübner, 1887), p. 35.
7 *The Seven Sages of Rome (Southern Version)*, ed. Karl Brunner, Early English Text Society (London: Oxford University Press, 1933), p. 87.
8 William Warner, *The First and Second Parts of Albions England* (London: Thomas Orwin for Thomas Cadman, 1589), Book 6, Chapter 29, p. 128.
9 Roy, *Rede me and be nott wrothe*, p. 128.
10 William Bulleyn, *Bullein's Bulwarke of defence againste all Sicknes, Sornes, and woundes, that dooe daily assaulte mankinde, whiche Bulwarke is kepte with Hillarius the Gardiner, Health the Phisician, with their Chyrurgian, to helpe the wounded soldiers. Gathered and practised from the moste worthie learned, bothe*

old and newe: to the greate comforte of mankinde (London: Iohn Kyngston, 1562), fol. xxxᵛ.

11 *The Gest Hystoriale of the Destruction of Troy: An Alliterative Romance*, ed. Geo[rge] A. Panton and David Donaldson, Early English Text Society (London: Trübner, 1869), p. 336.

12 *The Towneley Play*, I, p. 292.

13 *Non-Cycle Plays and Fragments*, ed. Davis, p. 24.

14 *The Towneley Plays*, ed. Spector, I, p. 229.

15 Anon., *The Brideling, Sadling and Ryding, of a rich Churle in Hampshire, by the subtill practise of one Iudeth Philips, a professed cunning woman or Fortune teller* (London: T[homas] C[reede], 1595), sig. A3ᵛ.

16 *Cursor mundi*, ed. Morris, II, p. 500.

17 *The Great Roll of the Pipe for the Twenty-Second Year of the Reign of King Henry the Second, AD 1175–1176*, ed. J. H. Round, Pipe Roll Society (London: Spottiswoode, 1904), p. 44: here 'Willelmus de Treget' is recorded. *The Great Roll of Pipe for the Second Year of the Reign of King Richard the First Michaelmas 1190*, ed. Doris M. Stenton, Pipe Roll Society (London: Pipe Roll Society, 1925), pp. 46, 48: here 'Robertus Treget' is recorded; *Rotuli hundredorum temp. Hen. III & Edw. I. In turr' Lond. et in curia receptoe scaccarij Westm. asservati*, 2 vols. (London: George Eyre and Andrew Strahan, 1812 and 1818), II, p. 497: here 'Symon le Tregetor' is recorded; *REED: Kent*, II, p. 905: here payment of 12d is recorded to 'Iohanni trigettour de Rofa' (John Trigettour of Rochester) in the *Boxley Bursars' Accounts for 1354–5*. 'Rob. Trechetour' is recorded twice in the *Borough Court Roll* in the *Bridgewater Corporation Documents* for 1378 and 1380: *Bridgewater Borough Archives 1377–1399*, ed. Thomas Bruce Dilks (Somerset: Somerset Record Society, 1938), LIII, pp. 21, 71. See also *Middle English Occupational Terms*, ed. Bertil Thuresson (Lund: Håkan Ohlssons, 1950), p. 190; *A Dictionary of British Surnames*, ed. P. H. Reaney (London: Routledge and Kegan Paul, 1958), p. 326.

18 *Destruction of Troy*, ed. Panton and Donaldson, p. 54.

19 *The Tale of Beryn, with A Prologue of the merry Adventure of the Pardoner with a Tapster at Canterbury*, ed. F. J. Furnivall and W. G. Stone, Early English Text Society (London: Kegan Paul, Trench, Trübner, 1909), p. 84.

20 Horman, *Vulgaria*, p. 278ʳ⁻ᵛ (wrongly numbered; it should be p. 280ʳ⁻ᵛ). The term 'gublettis' and its potential variant spellings are not to be found in the *OED*. However, the sense appears to be that objects may be hidden under the 'gublettis'. This points to a skirt-like feature of the juggler's dress. The possibility exists that use of 'gublettis' is a mistake for 'dublettis' as a form of 'doublet'; Some doublets did have a skirt-like appearance. William Caxton, in his *The Book of Fayttes of Armes and of Chyualrye*, states: 'they hadd couertly vndre theyre lytel doublettes rasers wher wyth all they dyde cutte the synewes of the legges of the Rommayns whyle they faught'; *The Book of Fayttes of Armes and of Chyualrye*, trans. William Caxton, ed. A. T. P. Byles, Early English Text Society (London: Oxford University Press, 1932; rev. and repr. 1937), p. 134.

21 *The Life of Saint Meriasek*, ed. and trans. Stokes, p. 53.

22 Scot, *Discouerie of witchcraft*, p. 320.

23 Agrippa, *The Vanitie and vncertaintie of Artes and Sciences*, p. 62^r.

24 Thomas Cooper, *The Mystery of Witchcraft. Discouering, The Truth, Nature, Occasions, Growth and Power thereof. Together With the Detection and Punishment of the same. As Also, The seuerall Stratagems of Sathan, ensnaring the poore Soule by this desperate practize of annoying the bodie: with seuerall Vses thereof to the Church of Christ. Very necessary for the redeeming of those Atheisticall and secure times* (London: Nicholas Okes, 1617), p. 171.

25 John Frith, *An other booke agaynst Rastell*, in *The Whole workes of W. Tyndall, Iohn Frith, and Doct. Barnes, three worthy Martyrs, and principall teachers of this Churche of England, collected and compiled in one Tome togither, beyng before scattered, & now in Print here exhibited to the Church* (London: Iohn Daye, 1573), p. 63. Pollard and Redgrave's *Short-Title Catalogue of English Books 1475–1640* suggests an initial publication date of Frith's work as 1537.

26 George Herbert, *Witts Recreations, Selected from the finest Fancies of Moderne Muses. With a Thousand out Landish Proverbs* (London: Humph[ry] Blunden, 1640), sig. Bb3.

27 William Langland, *The Vision of William concerning Piers the Plowman*, ed. Walter W. Skeat, Early English Text Society (London: Trübner, 1873), p. 272.

28 *REED: Norwich*, p. 180.

29 Ed[mund] Spenser, *The Faerie Qveene. Disposed into twelve books, Fashioning XII. Morall vertues* (London: William Ponsonbie, 1590). *The Second Part of the Faerie Qveene. Containing The Fovrth, Fifth, and Sixth Bookes* (London: William Ponsonby, 1596), v, p. 299.

30 Bale, *King Johan*, p. 7.

31 *Cursor mundi*, ed. Morris, ii, p. 703.

32 Geoffrey Chaucer, *The Works of Geoffrey Chaucer*, ed. Walter W. Skeat, 7 vols. (Oxford: Clarendon Press, 1894–7) p. 141.

33 *The Seven Sages of Rome*, ed. Brunner, pp. 132–3.

34 *Ibid.*, p. 134.

35 Hopkins, *Magic: Stage Illusions and Scientific Diversions including Trick Photography*, pp. 55–88.

36 John Gower, *The Complete Works of John Gower*, ed. G. C. Macaulay, 4 vols. (Oxford: Clarendon Press, 1899–1902), ii (1901), p. 180.

37 Richard Rolle, *The Pricke of Conscience (Stimulus conscientiae): A Northumbrian Poem by Richard Rolle de Hampole*, ed. Richard Morris, Philological Society (Berlin: A. Asher, 1863), p. 115.

38 *Ballads from Manuscripts*, ed. Frederick J. Furnivall, 2 vols., Ballad Society (London: Taylor, 1868–72), i (1868), p. 449.

39 Chaucer, *The Complete Works*, i (1894), pp. 236–8.

40 Geoffrey Chaucer, *The Works of Geoffrey Chaucer*, ed. F. N. Robinson, 2nd edn (Boston: Houghton Mifflin, 1961) p. 139.

41 Laura Hibbard Loomis, 'Secular dramatics in the royal palace, Paris, 1378, 1389, and Chaucer's "Tregetoures"', in *Medieval English Drama: Essays Critical and Contextual*, ed. Jerome Taylor and Alan H. Nelson (Chicago and London: University of Chicago Press, 1972), pp. 98–115.

42 Chaucer, Geoffrey, *The Poetical Works of Geoff. Chaucer*, ed. Thomas Tyrwhitt, 14 vols. (Edinburgh: Apollo Press, by the Martins, 1782–83), IV, pp. 24–6.

43 Chaucer, *The Complete Works*, III, p. 38.

44 Ambiguity exists surrounding identification of jugglers who appear to possess the surname, 'juggler'. Does the name 'juggler' reflect the surname, role or both? In the event of insufficient evidence to determine possible answers to this question, the safer assumption may rest with designation of the surname. Even so, some of the following examples may suggest that the name exists as the role as well. 'Radulpho le Jugler' is recorded in *Collections for a History of Staffordshire*, ed. William Salt Archaeological Society, XVI (London: Harrison, 1895), p. 277. 'William le Jugelour of Barton' and 'Walter le Jugelour of Barton' were both involved in an inquisition in 1300. 'Andrew le Jugelur of Barton' is recorded as one of a number involved in an extent and valuation made at Horecross, Mercinton and Rolviston 'before the Sheriff of Stafford and Robert the Coroner of the said County' in 1255. The involvement of 'William le Jugelour' is recorded in an inquisition as one of a number of witnesses in 1323: *Collections for a History of Staffordshire*, Third Series, 38 vols., 1911 volume (unnumbered), ed. William Salt Archaeological Society (London: Harrison, 1911), pp. 125, 268, 355. In Sussex, 'Robertus Jugler' is recorded in a list of Members of Parliament between 1407 and 1414: *Sussex Archaeological Collections. Relating to the History and Antiquities of the County* (Lewes: H. H. Wolff for the Sussex Archaeological Society, 1881), XXXI, pp. 114, 116, 117, 118. Payment is recorded in the *Exchequer Lay Subsidies* to 'Richardo Juggolir vjd' in 1327: *Kirby's Quest for Somerset*, ed. F. H. Dickenson, 3 vols. (London: Somerset Record Society, 1889), III, p. 273. Further ambiguity occurs over surnames in *An Abstract of Feet of Fines Relating to the County of Sussex From 1 Edward II. To 24 Henry VII*, ed. L. F. Salzmann (Lewes: Sussex Record Society, 1916), pp. 207, 286: here, 'Robert Ingler (or Jugler)' and 'John Jugler (or Ingler)' are respectively recorded in 1397 and 1488. See note 17 above.

45 Ammianus Marcellinus, *The Roman Historie, Containing such Acts and occurrents as passed under Constantius, Iulianus, Iovianus, Valentinianus, and Valens, Emperours*, trans. Philemon Holland (London: Adam Islip, 1609), p. 223.

46 Desiderius Erasmus, *A playne and godly Exposityon or Declaration of the Commune Crede (which Latin tonge is called Symbolum apostolorum) And of the .X. Commaundementes of goddes law. Newly made and put forth by the famouse clarke Mayster Erasmus of Rotterdame. At the Requeste of the moste honorable lorde, Thomas Erle of Wyltshyre: father to the moste gratious and vertuous Quene Anne wyf to our most gracyous soueraygne lorde kynge Henry*

the .VIII. (London: [n.p.], 1720?), p. 65ʳ. The preface is dated: 'Yeuen at Friburge. the yere of our Lord 1533.'

47 *Legends of the Saints in the Scottish Dialect of the Fourteenth Century*, ed. W. M. Metcalfe, Scottish Text Society, 3 vols. (Edinburgh and London: William Blackwood, 1896), 1, p. 193.

48 Raleigh, *The History of the World*, second book, first part, p. 321.

49 *Collections VII*, p. 142; *REED: Kent*, 11, p. 810.

50 E. K. Chambers, *The Mediaeval Stage*, 2 vols. (London: Oxford University Press, 1903; repr. 1967), 11, pp. 230–1.

51 Mill, *Mediaeval Plays in Scotland*, pp. 42, 311.

52 Iohn Baret, *An Alvearie or Triple Dictionarie*, sig. Ll.iiiᵛ.

53 Chambers, *The Mediaeval Stage*, 11, p. 231.

54 John Gaule, *The Mag-Astro-Mancer; or, the Magicall-Astrologicall Diviner Posed, and Puzzeled* (London: Joshua Kirton, 1652), p. 348.

55 *Ibid.*, pp. 196, 275, 348.

56 Horman, *Vulgaria*, p. 282ʳ.

Bibliography

Note. Works are arranged alphabetically by author or editor, with the exception of the Malone Society *Collections,* and *Records of Early English Drama.* For ease of reference, publications from each of these series are grouped together under their title, and are listed in numerical/alphabetical order. Where publications give variant spellings of authors' names these are listed according to the spelling on the title page, but are arranged alphabetically according to the accepted modern spelling for ease of reference.

Adams, Joseph Quincy, ed., *The Dramatic Records of Sir Henry Herbert, Master of the Revels, 1623–1673* (New Haven: Yale University Press, 1917)

Ady, Thomas, *A Candle in the Dark* (London: Robert Ibbitson, 1655)

Agrippa ab Nettesheym, Henricus Cornelius, *De incertitudine & vanitate scientiarum & artium, atque excellentia verbi Dei, declamatio* (Paris: Ioannem Petrum, 1531)

Agrippa, Heinrich Cornelius, *Henry Cornelius Agrippa, of the Vanitie and vncertaintie of Artes and Sciences, Englished by Ja*[mes] *San*[ford] Gent. (London: Henry Wykes, 1569)

Alexander, Elizabeth H., *A Bibliography of John Ferguson* (Glasgow: Glasgow Bibliographical Society, 1920)

A Further Bibliography of the Late John Ferguson (Glasgow: Glasgow Bibliographical Society, 1934)

Anderson, Patrick, *The historie of Scotland, since the death of King James the first, where Boetius left off, untill the death of King James the sixt of happie memorie,* Adv. MS 35.5.3, 3 vols. (Edinburgh: Advocates Library, National Library of Scotland, *c.* 1600?)

Anon., *The Booke of prittie conceites, taken out of Latin, Italian, French, Dutch and Englishe. Good for them that loue alwaies newe conceites* (London: Edward White, 1586?)

The Brideling, Sadling and Ryding, of a rich Churle in Hampshire, by the subtill practise of one Iudeth Philips, a professed cunning woman or Fortune teller (London: T[homas] C[reede], 1595)

The Country Gentleman's Vade Mecum; or, his companion for the town (London: John Harris, 1699)

Edmond Ironside; or, War Hath Made All Friends, ed. Eleanore Boswell and W. W. Greg, Malone Society (Oxford: Oxford University Press, 1927)

The Faire Maide of Bristow, ed. John S. Farmer, Tudor Facsimile Texts (Amersham: John S. Farmer, 1912)

Old Meg Of Hereford-shire, for a Mayd-Marian: And Hereford Towne for a Morris-daunce. Or Twelve Morris-Dancers in Hereford-shire, or twelue hundred yeares old (London: Iohn Budge, 1609)

The second Tome of Homilees, of such matters as were promised, and intituled in the former part of Homilees. Set out by the aucthoritie of the Queenes Maiestie: And to be read in euerie parishe Church agreeably (London: R. Jugge and J. Cawood, 1571)

The Tragedy of Claudius Tiberius Nero, ed. John S. Farmer, Tudor Facsimile Texts (Amersham: John S. Farmer, 1913)

A Trve Relation Without All Exception, of Strange and Admirable Accidents, which lately happened in the Kingdome of the great Magor, or Magvll, who is the greatest Monarch of the East Indies (London: I[ohn] D[awson] for Thomas Archer, 1622)

A Warning for Faire Women, ed. John S. Farmer, Tudor Facsimile Texts (Amersham: John S. Farmer, 1912)

The Wasp or Subject's Precedent, ed. J. W. Lever and G. R. Proudfoot, Malone Society (Oxford: Oxford University Press, 1974 [1976])

Wily Beguild, ed. John S. Farmer, Tudor Facsimile Texts (Amersham: John S. Farmer, 1912)

Apuleius, Lucius, *Les metamorphoses, ov l'asne d'or*, trans. J. de Montlyard (Paris: S. Thiboust, 1623)

Aristophanes, *Ploutophthalmia ploutogamia: A Pleasant Comedie, Entituled Hey For Honesty, Down with Knavery*, trans. Tho[mas] Randolph (London: F. J., 1651)

Babington, Gervase, *An Exposition of the Catholike Faith; Or, the* xii. *Articles of the Apostles Creede. Learnedly Expovnded (According to the Scriptures) Wherin all heretiques as well Auncient as Moderne against the Deity of Christ and the Holy Ghost, are plainely discouered, pithely disproued, and the trueth faithfully confirmed* (London: G[eorge] Elde for Henry Featherstone, 1615)

Babington, John, *Pyrotechnia; Or, A Discovrse of Artificial Fire-works* (London: Thomas Harper for Ralph Mab, 1635; facs. repr. Amsterdam/New York: Da Capo Press Theatrum Orbis Terrarum, 1971)

Bacon, Francis, *Sylva sylvarvm; or, A Naturall History In ten Centuries* (London: W. Rawley, 1628)

Bacon, Roger, *Epistola Fratris Rogerii Baconis, De Secretis Operibus Artis et Naturae, et de Nullitate Magiae. Operâ Iohannis Dee Londinensis E pluribus exemplaribus castigata olim, et ad sensum integrum restituta. Nunc verò a quodam veritatis amatore, in gratiam verae scientiae candidatorum foras emissa; cum notis quibusdam partim ipsius Johannis Dee, partim edentis* (Hamburg: Bibliopolio Frobeniano, 1618)

Frier Bacon his Discovery of the Miracles of Art, Nature, and Magick. Faithfully translated out of D' Dees own Copy, by T. M. and never before in English (London: Simon Miller, 1659)

Baker, Donald C., John L. Murphy and Louis B. Hall Jr, eds., *The Late Medieval Religious Plays of Bodleian MSS Digby 133 and E Museo 160*, Early English Text Society (Oxford: Oxford University Press, 1982)

Bale, John, *King Johan*, Malone Society (Oxford: Oxford University Press, 1931)

Baret, John, *An Alvearie or Triple Dictionarie, in Englishe, Latin, and French* (London: Henry Denham, 1580)

Barnello, E., *The Red Demons or Mysteries of Fire* (Chicago?: E. Barnello?, 1893?)

Barnes, Barnaby, *The Divils Charter: A Tragedie Conteining the Life and Death of Pope Alexander the sixt*, ed. John S. Farmer, Tudor Facsimile Texts (Amersham: John S. Farmer, 1913)

Barry, Lo[rding], *Ram-Alley or Merry Tricks*, ed. John S. Farmer, Tudor Facsimile Texts (Amersham: John S. Farmer, 1913)

Bastard, Thomas, *Chrestoleros. Seuen bookes of Epigrames written by T. B.* (London: Richard Bradocke for I[ohn] B[rome], 1598)

Bate, John, *The Mysteryes of Natvre and Art: Conteined in foure. severall Tretises, The first of water workes The second of Fyer workes, The third of Drawing, Colouring, Painting, and Engrauing. The fourth of divers Experiments, as wel serviceable as delightful: partly Collected, and partly of the Authors Peculiar Practice, and Invention* (London: Ralph Mab, 1634)
  The Mysteries Of Nature and Art. In foure seuerall parts. The first of Water works. The second of Fire works. The third of Drawing, Washing, Limming, Painting, and Engraving. The fourth of sundry Experiments. The second Edition; with many additions unto every part (London: Ralph Mabb, 1635)

Bateson, Mary, ed., *Records of the Borough of Leicester: Being a Series of Extracts from the Archives of the Corporation of Leicester 1509–1603*, 7 vols. (London: C. J. Clay under the authority of the Corporation of Leicester, 1899– 1974)

Bawcutt, N. W., 'Craven Ord transcripts of Sir Henry Herbert's office-book in the Folger Shakespeare Library', *English Literary Renaissance*, 14 (1984), 83–94
  'Sir Henry Herbert and William Sands the puppeteer: some corrections', *Records of Early English Newsletter*, 20:1 (1995), 17–19.
  'New revels documents of Sir George Buc and Sir Henry Herbert, 1619–1662', *Review of English Studies*, 35 n.s. (1984), 316–31
  'William Vincent, alias Hocus Pocus: a travelling entertainer of the seventeenth century', *Theatre Notebook*, 54 (2000), 130–8

Beadle, Richard, 'Dramatic records of Mettingham College, Suffolk, 1403–1527', *Theatre Notebook*, 33:3 (1979), 125–31
  ed., *The York Plays, York Medieval Texts, second series* (London: Edward Arnold, 1982)
  'The York Hosiers' play and Pharaoh: a Middle English dramatist at work', *Poetica*, 19 (1984), 3–26

Beaumont, Francis and John Fletcher, *The Dramatic Works in the Beaumont and Fletcher Canon*, ed. Fredson Bowers, 10 vols. (Cambridge: Cambridge University Press, 1966–96)

Becker, Herbert L., *All the Secrets of Magic Revealed* (Hollywood: Lifetime Books, 1994; repr. 1997)

Beckmann, John, *A History of Inventions and Discoveries*, trans. William Johnston, 4 vols. (London: J. Bell, 1797 (vols. I–III); J. Walker, 1814 (vol. IV))

    A History of Inventions and Discoveries, enlarged and rev. William Francis and J. W. Griffith, 2 vols. (London: Henry G. Bohn, 1846)

    A Concise History of Ancient Institutions, Inventions, and Discoveries in Science and Mechanic Art, 2 vols. (London: G. and W. B. Whittaker, 1823)

Bedini, Silvio A., 'The role of automata in the history of technology', *Technology and Culture*, 5:1 (1964), 24–42

Bell, John, *Travels from St Petersburg in Russia, to Diverse Parts of Asia*, 2 vols. (Glasgow: printed for the author by Robert and Andrew Foulis, 1763)

Bellew, Frank, *The Art of Amusing* (London: S. Low, 1866)

Bennett, J. A. W. and G. V. Smithers, eds., *Early Middle English Verse and Prose*, 2nd edn (Oxford: Cleverdon Press, 1968; repr. 1974)

Bentley, Gerald Eades, *The Jacobean and Caroline Stage*, 7 vols. (Oxford: Clarendon Press, 1941–68)

Berry, Herbert, 'The Globe bewitched and El Hombre Fiel', *Medieval and Renaissance Drama in England*, 1 (1984), 211–30

Birch, Thomas, ed., *The Court and Times of James the First; Containing a Series of Historical and Confidential Letters, in which will be found a detail of the Public Transactions and Events in Great Britain during that Period, with a variety of Particulars not mentioned by our Historians*, 2 vols. (London: Henry Colburn, 1849)

Birrel, Robert, *The Diarey of Robert Birrel, containing Divers Passages of Staite, and Uthers Memorable Accidents. Frome the 1532 zeir of our redemptione, till ye beginning of the zeir 1605*, in *Fragments of Scottish History* (Edinburgh: Archibald Constable, 1798)

Boas, Frederick S., ed., *The Works of Thomas Kyd* (Oxford: Clarendon Press, 1901)

    ed., *The Diary of Thomas Crosfield* (London: Oxford University Press, 1935)

Boccaccio, Giovanni, *A Treatise excellent and compe[n]dious, shewing and declaring, in maner of Tragedye, the falles of sondry most notable Princes and Princesses with other Nobles, through ye mutabilitie and change of vnstedfast fortune together with their most detestable & wicked vices*, trans. John Lydgate (London: Richard Tottelli, 1554)

Bochius, Johannes, *The Ceremonial Entry of Ernst Archduke of Austria into Antwerp, June 14, 1594* (New York: Benjamin Blom, 1970)

Bourne, William, *Inuentions or Deuises* (London: Thomas Woodcock, 1578)

B., R. [Richard Bower?], *A new Tragicall Comedie of Apius and Virginia*, ed. Ronald B. McKerrow and W. W. Greg, Malone Society (London: C. Whittingham, Chiswick Press, 1911)

Brathwait, Richard, *A Strappado for the Diuell. Epigrams and Satyres alluding to the time, with diuers measures of no lesse Delight* (London: I[ohn] B[eale] for Richard Redmer, 1615)

Brewer, J. S., ed., *Letters and Papers, Foreign and Domestic, of the Reign of Henry VIII: Preserved in the Public Record Office, the British Museum, and Elsewhere in England*, 21 vols. (London: Longman, 1862–1910)

Brewster, Sir David, *Letters on Natural Magick: Addressed to Sir Walter Scott, Bart. By Sir David Brewster K. H.* (London: John Murray, 1834)

Brome, Richard, *The Antipodes* (London: J[ohn] Okes, 1640)

A Joviall Crew; or, The Merry Beggars (London: J. Y. for E. D. and N. E., 1652)

Brownbill, J., 'Boxley Abbey and the Rood of Grace', *The Antiquary*, 7 (1883), 162–5, 210–13

Brunner, Karl, *The Seven Sages of Rome (Southern Version)*, Early English Text Society (London: Oxford University Press, 1933)

Bullen, A. H., ed., *A Collection of Old English Plays in Four Volumes* (London: Wyman, 1883)

Bulleyn, William, *Bullein's Bulwarke of defence againste all Sicknes, Sornes, and woundes, that dooe daily assaulte mankinde, whiche Bulwarke is kepte with Hillarius the Gardiner, Health the Phisician, with their Chyrurgian, to helpe the wounded soldiors. Gathered and practised from the moste worthie learned, bothe old and newe: to the greate comforte of mankinde* (London: Iohn Kyngston, 1562)

Bullock-Davies, Constance, ed., *Register of Royal and Baronial Domestic Minstrels 1272–1327* (Woodbridge: Boydell, 1986)

Burt, Richard, *Licensed by Authority: Ben Jonson and the Discourses of Censorship* (Ithaca, NY, and London: Cornell University Press, 1993)

Burton, Robert, *The Anatomy of Melancholy. What it is, with all the kinds causes, symptoms, prognostickes, & sewerall cures of it, In three Partitions, with their severall Sections, members & subsections, Philosophically, Medicinally, Historically, opened & cut vp* (London: H[enry] Cripps, 1660)

Butler, Samuel, *The Genuine Remains in Verse and Prose of Mr Samuel Butler*, 2 vols. (London: J. and R. Tonson, 1759)

Butterworth, Philip, 'Comings and goings: English medieval staging conventions', *The Early Drama, Art, and Music Review*, 18:1 (1995), 25–34

Theatre of Fire: Special Effects in Early English and Scottish Theatre (London: Society for Theatre Research, 1998)

'Magic through sound: illusion, deception, and agreed pretence', *Medieval English Theatre*, 21 (1999), 52–65

'Timing theatrical action in the English medieval theatre', *Early Theatre: A Journal Associated with the Records of Early English Drama*, 4 (2001), 87–100

'Brandon, Feats and Hocus Pocus: jugglers three', *Theatre Notebook*, 57:2 (2003), 89–106

Byles, A. T. P., ed., *The Book of Fayttes of Armes and of Chyualrye*, trans. William Caxton, Early English Text Society (London: Oxford University Press, 1932; rev. and repr. 1937)

Calderwood, David, *The History of the Kirk of Scotland*, 8 vols. (Edinburgh: Wodrow Society, 1842–9)

Cardano, Girolamo, *Hieronymi Cardani Medici Mediolanensis de svbtilitate libri* XXI (Nuremburg: Ioh. Petrium, 1550)

Hieronymi Carda ni Mediolanensis Medici de rervm, varietate Libri XVII (Basle: H. Petri, 1557)

Hieronymi Cardani Mediolanensis medici de Subtilitate libri XXI (Basle: ex officina Petrina, 1560)

Cavendish, William, *The Country Captain*, ed. Anthony Johnson and H. R. Woudhuysen, Malone Society (Oxford: Oxford University Press, 1999)

Chamberlain, Robert, *A New Booke of Mistakes; or, Bulls with Tales, and Buls without Tales. but no lyes by any meanes* (London: N[icholas] O[kes], 1637)

Chambers, E. K., *The English Folk Play* (Oxford: Clarendon Press, 1933)

The Mediaeval Stage, 2 vols. (London: Oxford University Press, 1903; repr. 1967)

The Elizabethan Stage, 4 vols. (Oxford: Clarendon Press, 1923; repr. 1974)

Chapman, George, *The Revenge of Bussy D'Ambois* (Menston: Scolar Press, 1968)

Charney, David H., *Magic: The Great Illusions Revealed and Explained* (London: Robert Hale, 1975)

Chaucer, Geoffrey, ed., *The Poeticall Works of Geoff. Chaucer*, ed. Thomas Tyrwhitt, 14 vols. (Edinburgh: Apollo Press, by the Martins, 1782–3)

The Complete Works of Geoffrey Chaucer, ed. Walter W. Skeat, 7 vols. (Oxford: Clarendon Press, 1894–7)

The Works of Geoffrey Chaucer ed. F. N. Robinson, 2nd edn (Boston: Houghton Mifflin, 1961)

Chettle, Henry, *Kind-Harts Dreame. Conteining fiue Apparitions, with their Inuectiues against abuses raigning. Deliuered by seuerall Ghosts vnto him to be publisht, after Piers Penilesse Post had refused the carriage* (London: William Wright, 1592)

Clarke, Sidney W., *The Annals of Conjuring* (New York: Magico Magazine, 1983)

The Annals of Conjuring, ed. Edwin E. Dawes, Todd Karr and Bob Read (Seattle: The Miracle Factory, 2001)

Clarke, Sidney W. and Adolphe Blind, eds., *The Bibliography of Conjuring and Kindred Deceptions* (London: George Johnson, 1920)

Cleveland, John, *The Character Of A London-Diurnall: With severall select POEMS. By the same author* (London?: Optima & novissima Edition, 1647)

Cocaius, Merlinus [Teofilo Folengo], *Histoire Maccaronique de Merlin Coccaie, prototype de Rablais. ou est traicté les Ruses de Cingar, les tours de Boccal, les adventures de Leonard, les forces de Fracasse, les enchantemens de Gelfore & Pandrague, & les recontres heureuses de Balde, &c.*, 2 vols. (Paris: [n.p.], 1606)

Cockton, Henry, *The Life and Adventures of Valentine Vox, the Ventriloquist* (London: Robert Tyas, 1840)

Cohn, Albert, *Shakespeare in Germany in the Sixteenth and Seventeenth Centuries: An Account of English Actors in Germany and the Netherlands and of the Plays Performed by Them During the Same Period* (London: Asher, 1865; repr. New York: Haskell House, 1971)

Collections 11:3, ed. W. W. Greg, Malone Society (Oxford: Oxford University Press, 1931)

Collections 111, ed. Jean Robertson and D. J. Gordon, Malone Society (Oxford: Oxford University Press, 1954)

Collections v: *The Academic Drama in Oxford: Extracts from the Records of Four Colleges*, ed. R. E. Alton, Malone Society (Oxford: Oxford University Press, 1959 [1960])

Collections vi, ed. David Cook and F. P. Wilson, Malone Society (Oxford: Oxford University Press, 1961 [1962])

Collections vii, ed. Giles E. Dawson, Malone Society (Oxford: Oxford University Press, 1965)

Collections x, ed. F. P. Wilson and R. F. Hill, Malone Society (Oxford: Oxford University Press, 1975 [1977])

Collections xi, ed. David Galloway and John Wasson, Malone Society (Oxford: Oxford University Press, 1980)

Comenius, Joh[n] Amos, *Orbis sensualium pictus: hoc est omnium principalium in mundo rerum, & vita actionum, pictura & nomenclatura*, trans. Charles Hoole (London: S. Leacroft, 1777)

Connor, Steven, *Dumbstruck: A Cultural History of Ventriloquism* (Oxford: Oxford University Press, 2000)

Cooper, Charles Henry, *Annals of Cambridge*, 5 vols. (Cambridge: Warwick (vols. 1–111), Metcalfe and Palmer (vol. iv), Cambridge University Press (vol. v), 1842–1908)

Cooper, Thomas, *Thesavrvs lingvae romanae & britannicae etc.* (London: Henry Denham, 1573)

The Mystery of Witchcraft. Discouering, The Truth, Nature, Occasions, Growth and Power thereof. Together With the Detection and Punishment of the same. As Also, The seuerall Stratagems of Sathan, ensnaring the poore Soule by this desperate practize of annoying the bodie: with seuerall Vses thereof to the Church of Christ. Very necessary for the redeeming of those Atheisticall and secure times (London: Nicholas Okes, 1617)

Cornish Record Office, Truro, *The MS Works of Sir Richard Carew*, CZ/EE/32

Corser, Thomas, ed., *Collectanea anglo-poetica; or, a Bibliographical and descriptive catalogue of a portion of a collection of early English poetry, with occasional extracts and remarks biographical and critical*, Remains Historical and Literary Connected with the Palatine Counties of Lancaster and Chester, 52 (Manchester: Chetham Society, 1860)

Coulton, G. G., *Life in the Middle Ages*, 4 vols. (Cambridge: Cambridge University Press, 1929)

Coryat, Thomas, *Coryat's Crudities Hastily gobled vp in five Moneths trauells in France, Sauoy, Italy, Rhetia comonly called the Grisons country, Heluetia aliàs Switzerland, some parts of high Germany, and the Netherlands; Newly digested in the hungry aire of Odcombe in the County of Somerset, & now dispersed to the nourishment of the trauelling Members of this Kingdome* (London: William Stansby for the author, 1611)

Craggs, Douglas, *Ventriloquism from A to Z: A Complete Treatise on the Art of Voice-Throwing and Doll Manipulation* (London: Faber, 1969)

Cunningham, W. R. *Catalogue of the Ferguson Collection of Books Mainly Relating to Alchemy, Chemistry, Witchcraft and Gipsies in the Library of the University of Glasgow*, 2 vols. (Glasgow: Robert Maclehose, 1943; facs. repr. Connecticut: Mansfield Centre, 2002)

Cutpurse, Moll, *The Life and Death of M$^{rs.}$ Mary Frith. Commonly Called Mal Cutpurse. Exactly Collected and now Published for the Delight and Recreation of all Merry disposed Persons* (London: W. Gilbertson, 1662)

Dando, John and Harrie Runt, *Maroccus extaticus; Or, Bankes Bay Horse in a Trance: A Discourse set downe in a merry Dialogue, between Bankes and his beast: Anatomizing some abuses and bad trickes of this age* (London: [Thomas Scarlet] for C[uthbert] Burby, 1595)

Dasent, John Roche, ed., *Acts of the Privy Council of England*, New Series, 8 (London: Public Record Office, 1894)

Davenant, Sir William, *The Works of Sr William Davenant K^t Consisting of those which were formerly Printed and those which he design'd for the Press: now published out of the authors originall copies* (London: T. N. for Henry Herringman, 1673)

D[avenport], R[obert], *A Pleasant and Witty Comedy: Called, A New Tricke to Cheat the Divell* (London: Iohn Okes, for Humphrey Blunden, 1639)

Davies, Owen, *Cunning-Folk: Popular Magic in English History* (London: Hambledon, 2003)

Davis, Norman, ed., *Non-Cycle Plays and Fragments*, Early English Text Society (London: Oxford University Press, 1970)

Dawes, Edwin A., *The Great Illusionists* (Newton Abbot: David and Charles, 1979)

Day, John, *Law-Trickes; or, Who Would have Thovght it* (London: [Edward Allde] for Richard More, 1608)

D., J., *The Knave in Graine* (London: J[ohn] O[kes], 1640)

Decremps, Henri, *The Conjurer Unmasked; Or, La Magie Blanche Dèvoilèe: Being a Clear and Full Explanation of all the Surprizing Performances Exhibited as well in this Kingdom as on the Continent, By the most eminent and dexterous Professors of Slight of Hand* (London: T. Denton, 1785)

Defrémery, C., B. R. Sanguinetti, H. A. R. Gibb and C. F. Beckingham, eds., *The Travels of Ibn Battuta* A D *1325–1354*, 5 vols. (Cambridge: Hakluyt Society, 1958–94)

Dekker, Thomas, *Satiro-mastix; Or, The vntrussing of the Humorous Poet* (London: Edward White, 1602)

The Wonderfull Yeare. 1603. Wherein is shewed the picture of London, lying sicke of the Plague etc. (London: Thomas Creede, [1603?])

. . .?, *The Meeting of Gallants at an Ordinarie; or, The Walkes in Powles* (London: T[homas] C[reede], 1604)

The Seuen deadly Sinnes of London: Drawne in seuen seuerall Coaches, Through the seuen seuerall Gates of the Citie Bringing the Plague with them (London: E[dward] A[llde], 1606)

The Dead Tearme. Or Westminsters Complaint for long Vacations and short Termes. Written in manner of a Dialogue betweene the two Cityes of London and Westminster (London: [n.p.], 1608)

Deckar, T[homas], *The Gvls Horne-booke: Stultorum plena sunt omnia. Al Sauio meza parola, Basta.* (London: [Nicholas Okes] for R[ichard] S[ergier], 1609)

The Owles Almanacke. Prognosticating many strange accidents which shall happen to this Kingdome of Great Britaine this yeare, 1618 (London: E[dward] G[riffin] for Laurence Lisle, 1618)

Dekker, Thomas and George Wilkins, *Jests to make you Merie: With The Conjuring vp of Cock Watt (the walking Spirit of Newgate) To tell Tales: Vuto which is Added, the miserie of a Prison, and a Prisoner. And a Paradox in praise of Serieants* (London: N[icholas] O[kes] for N[athaniel] Butter, 1607)

Decker, Thomas and Iohn Webster, *North-Ward Hoe*, ed. John S. Farmer, Tudor Facsimile Texts (Amersham: John S. Farmer, 1914)

Dekker, Thomas, *The Dramatic Works of Thomas Dekker*, ed. Fredson Bowers, 4 vols. (Cambridge: Cambridge University Press, 1953–61)

Dickers [Dekker], Thomas and Iohn Webster, *The Famovs History of Sir Thomas Wyat*, ed. John S. Farmer (Amersham: John S. Farmer, 1914)

Del Villar, Mary, 'The staging of the conversion of Saint Paul', *Theatre Notebook*, 25:2 (Winter 1970–1), 64–72

'The medieval theatre in the streets: a rejoinder', *Theatre Survey*, 14:2 (1973), 76–81

Deimling, Hermann, ed., *The Chester Plays*, Early English Text Society, 2 vols. (Oxford: Oxford University Press, 1892; repr. 1968)

Demoriane, Hermine, *The Tightrope Walker* (London: Secker & Warburg, 1989)

Dessen, Alan C., *Recovering Shakespeare's Theatrical Vocabulary* (Cambridge: Cambridge University Press, 1995)

Dessen, Alan C. and Leslie Thomson, *A Dictionary of Stage Directions in English Drama, 1580–1642* (Cambridge: Cambridge University Press, 1999)

De Solla Price, Derek J., 'Automata and the origins of mechanism and mechanistic philosophy', *Technology and Culture*, 5:1 (1964), 9–23

Devant, David, *Secrets of My Magic* (London: Hutchinson, 1936)

D'Evelyn, Charlotte and Anna J. Mill, eds., *The South English Legendary*, Early English Text Society, 3 vols. (London: Oxford University Press, 1956–9)

Dickenson, F. H., ed., *Kirby's Quest for Somerset*, 3 vols. (London: Somerset Record Society, 1889)

Dickson, Thomas, Sir James Balfour-Paul and Charles T. McInnes, eds., *Accounts of the Lord High Treasurer of Scotland*, 13 vols. (Edinburgh: HM General Register House, Her Majesty's Stationery Office, 1877–1978)

Digby, Sir Kenelm, *Two Treatises. In the one of which, the natvre of bodies; in the other, the natvre of mans sovle; is looked into: in way of discovery, of the immortality of reasonable sovles* (Paris: Gilles Blaizot, 1644)

Dilks, Thomas Bruce, ed., *Bridgewater Borough Archives 1377–1399* (Somerset: Somerset Record Society, 1938)

Douce, Francis, *Illustrations of Shakspeare, and of Ancient Manners: with Dissertations on the Clown and Fools of Shakespeare; on the Collection of Popular Tales entitled Gesta romanorum; and on the English Morris Dance*, 2 vols. (London: Longman, Hurst, Rees and Orme, 1807)

Drayton, Michael, *The Battaile of Agincovrt. Fovght by Henry the fift of that name, King of England, against the whole power of the French: vnder the Raigne of their Charles the sixt, Anno Dom. 1415* (London: William Lee, 1627)

Dugdale, Sir William, *The History of St Pauls Cathedral in London, from its Foundation untill these Times: Extracted out of Originall Charters. Records. Leiger Books, and other Manuscripts. Beautified with sundry Prospects of the Church, Figures of Tombes, and Monuments* (London: Tho[mas] Warren, 1658)

The History of St Paul's Cathedral in London, from its foundation. Extracted out of Original Charters, Records, Leiger-Books, and other Manuscripts, 2nd edn (London: Edward Maynard, George James for Jonah Bowyer, 1716)

Dymond, David, ed., *The Register of Thetford Priory: Part 1 1482–1517; Part 2 1518–1540*, 2 vols. (Oxford: Norfolk Record Society/British Academy/Oxford University Press, 1995)

Eamon, William, *Science and the Secrets of Nature: Books of Secrets in Medieval and Early Modern Culture* (Princeton, NJ: Princeton University Press, 1994)

Eccles, Mark, ed., *The Macro Plays*, Early English Text Society (London: Oxford University Press, 1969)

Elyot, Thomas, *The boke named the Gouernour* (London: Tho[mas] Bertheleti, 1531)

Eliot, Thomas, *The Dictionary of syr Thomas Eliot knyght* (London: Thomas Bertheleti, 1538)

Elliot, Robert Henry, *The Myth of the Mystic East* (Edinburgh and London: Blackwood, 1934)

Erasmus, Desiderius, *A playne and godly Exposytion or Declaration of the Commune Crede (which Latin tonge is called Symbolum apostolorum) And of the .X. Commaundementes of goddes law. Newly made and put forth by the famouse clarke Mayster Erasmus of Rotterdame. At the Requeste of the moste honorable lorde, Thomas Erle of Wyltshyre: father to the moste gratious and vertuous Quene Anne wyf to our most gracyous soueraygne lorde kynge Henry the .VIII.* (London: [n.p.], 1720?)

Erbe, Theodore, ed., *Mirk's Festial: A Collection of Homilies*, Early English Text Society (London: Kegan Paul, Trench, Trübner, 1905)

Etten, Henry van [Jean Leurechon], *Mathematicall Recreations* (London: T[homas] Cotes for R[ichard] Hawkins, 1633)

Evans, Henry Ridgely, *Magic and Its Professors* (Philadelphia: David McKay, 1902)

The Old and the New Magic (Chicago and London: Open Court and Kegan Paul, Trench, Trübner Ltd, 1906)

Some Rare Old Books on Conjuring and Magic of the Sixteenth, the Seventeenth and the Eighteenth century (Kenton, OH: The Linking Ring, 1943)

Evelyn, John, *Memoirs, Illustrative of the Life and Writings of John Evelyn, Esq. F. R. S.*, ed. William Bray, 2 vols. (London: Henry Colburn, 1819)

Farley, Henry, *St Pavles-Chvrch Her Bill For The Parliament, As it was presented to the Kings Matie on Midlent-Sunday last, and intended for the view of that most high and Honorable Court, and generally for all such as beare good will to the reflourishing estate of the said Chvrch* (London: Henry Farley, 1621)

Ferguson, John, *Bibliographical Notes on Histories of Inventions and Books of Secrets*, 2 vols. in 1 (London: Holland Press, 1959; repr. 1981)

Feuillerat, Albert, ed., *Documents Relating to the Office of the Revels in the Time of Queen Elizabeth* (Louvain: A. Uystpruyst, 1908)
    Documents Relating to the Revels at Court in the Time of King Edward VI and Queen Mary: The Loseley Manuscripts (Louvain: A. Uystpruyst, 1914)

Fletcher, Alan J., ed., *Drama and the Performing Arts in Pre-Cromwellian Ireland: A Repertory of Sources and Documents from the Earliest Times until c. 1642* (Cambridge: D. S. Brewer, 2001)

Fletcher, John and Philip Massinger, *Sir John van Olden Barnavelt*, ed. T. H. Howard-Hill, Malone Society (London: Oxford University Press, 1979 [1980])

Fletcher, John and William Shakespeare, *The Two Noble Kinsmen*, ed. John S. Farmer, Tudor Facsimile Texts (Amersham: John S. Farmer, 1910)

Florus, Publius Annius, *The Roman Histories of Lucius Iulius Florus from the foundation of Rome, till Caesar Augustus, for above DCC. yeares, etc from thence to Traian*, trans. E. M. B[olton] (London: Will[iam] Stansby, [1618])
    Ivli flori epitomae de Tito Livio bellorvm omnivm DCC libri dvo. Reconovit Carolvs Halm. (Leipsig: Edvardvs Woelfflin, 1854)

Flower, Margaret, *The Wonderfvl Discoverie of the Witchcrafts of Margaret and Phillip Flower, daughters of Ioan Flower neere Beuer Castle: Executed at Lincolne, March 11. 1618* (London: G[eorge] Eld for I[ohn] Barnes, 1619)

Foakes, R. A. and R. T. Rickert, eds., *Henslow's Diary* (Cambridge: University Press, 1968)

Foster, Frances A., ed., *The Northern Passion: Four Parallel Texts and the French Original, with Specimens of Additional Manuscripts*, Early English Text Society, 3 vols., (London: Kegan Paul, Trench, Trübner, 1913)

Foster, William, ed., *The Embassy of Sir Thomas Roe to the Court of the Great Mogul, 1615–1619, as Narrated in His Journal and Correspondence*, Hakluyt Society, 2 vols. (London: Hakluyt Society, 1899)

Frampton, John, *The most noble and famous trauels of Marcus Paulus, one of the nobilitie of the state of Venice, into the East partes of the world, as Armenia, Persia, Arabia, Tartary, with many other kingdoms and Prouinces* (London: Ralph Newbery, 1579)

Frith, John, *An other booke agaynst Rastell*, in *The Whole workes of W. Tyndale, Iohn Frith, and Doct. Barnes, three worthy Martyrs, and principall teachers of this Churche of England, collected and compiled in one Tome togither, beyng before scattered, & now in Print here exhibited to the Church* (London: Iohn Daye, 1573)

Frost, Thomas, *The Old Showmen, and the Old London Fairs* (London: Tinsley Brothers, 1874)
  Circus Life and Circus Celebrities (London: Tinsley Brothers, 1876)
  The Lives of the Conjurors (London: Tinsley Brothers, 1876)
Fuller, Thomas, *The History of the Worthies of England* (London: J. G. W. L. and W. G. for Thomas Williams, 1662)
Furnivall, Frederick J., *Ballads from Manuscripts*, 2 vols., Ballad Society (London: Taylor, 1868–72)
Furnivall, F. J. and W. G. Stone, eds. *The Tale of Beryn, with A Prologue of the merry Adventure of the Pardoner with a Tapster at Canterbury*, Early English Text Society (London: Kegan Paul, Trench, Trübner, 1909)
Gainsford, Thomas, *The Rich Cabinet Furnished with varietie of Excellent discriptions, exquisite Characters, witty discourses, and delightfull Histories, Deuine and Morall* (London: I[ohn] B[eale] and R[oger] Iackson, 1616)
Ganthony, Robert, *Practical Ventriloquism and Its Sister Arts* (London: L. Upcott Gill, 1903)
Gardner, Harold C., *Mysteries' End: An Investigation of the Last Days, of the Medieval Religious Stage* (Yale: Yale University Press, 1946; repr. 1967)
Garenne, Henri, [Dr Frank Lind], *The Art of Modern Conjuring, Magic, and Illusions* (London: [n.p.], *c.* 1886)
Gascoigne, George, *The Whole woorkes of George Gascoigne Esquyre: Newlye compyled into one Volume, that is to say: His Flowers, Hearbes, Weedes, the Fruites of warre . . . the Complaint of Phylomene, the Storie of Ferdinando Ieronimi, and the pleasure at Kenelworth Castle* (London: Abel Ieffres, 1587)
Gaule, John, *The Mago-Astro-Mancer; or, the Magicall-Astrologicall Diviner Posed, and Puzzeled* (London: Joshua Kirton, 1652)
Gayton, Edmund, *Pleasant Notes upon Don Quixot* (London: William Hunt, 1654)
G., D., *The Harangues or Speeches of Several Famous Mountebanks in Town and Country* (London: T. Warner, [1700]?)
Gee, John, *The Foot out of the Snare* (London: H[umphrey] L[ownes] for Robert Milbourne, 1624)
Gill, Robert, *Magic as a Performing Art: A Bibliography of Conjuring*, College of Librarianship Wales Bibliographies (London and New York: Bowker, 1976)
Glassie, Henry, *All Silver and No Brass: An Irish Christmas Mumming* (Philadelphia: University of Pennsylvania Press, 1975)
Glenny, Michael, 'Ingenious and efficient: the Wells Cathedral clock', *Country Life*, 180 (1986), 852–4
Goffe, Thomas, *The Covragiovs Tvrke; Or, Amvrath the First*, ed. David Carnegie and Peter Davison, Malone Society (Oxford: Oxford University Press, 1968 [1974])
Goldston, Will, *Tricks and Illusions* (London: Routledge & Kegan Paul, 1908; repr. 1955)

Gosson, Stephen, *The Schoole of Abuse* (London: Thomas Woodcocke, 1579)

Gower, John, *The Complete Works of John Gower*, ed. G. C. Macaulay, 4 vols. (Oxford: Clarendon Press, 1899–1902)

Grapaldi, Francisco Mario, *Francisci Marij Grapaldi poete laureati . . . vita: de partibus Aediu*m, etc. (Venice: A. de Bindonis, 1517)

Greene, Robert, *A Pleasant Conceyted Comedy of George a Greene, the Pinner of Wakefield*, ed. F. W. Clarke and W. W. Greg, Malone Society (Oxford: Oxford University Press, 1911)

  The Honorable Historie of Frier Bacon, and Frier Bongay, ed. John S. Farmer, Tudor Facsimile Texts (Amersham: John S. Farmer, 1914)

  A notable discouery of coosnage, 1591; *The second part of Conny-catching*, 1592 (London: John Lane, Bodley Head, [1923])

  Alphonsus King of Aragon, ed. W. W. Greg, Malone Society (Oxford: Oxford University Press, 1926)

Grose, Francis and Thomas Astle, eds., *The Antiquarian Repertory: A Miscellaneous Assemblage of Topography, History, Biography, Customs, and Manners*, 4 vols. (London: Edward Jeffery, 1807–9)

Guazzo, Francesco Maria, *Compendivm maleficarvm in tres libros distinctum ex plvribvs avthoribus per fratrem franciscvm Mariam Gvaccivm* (Milan: [n.p.] 1608)

  Compendium maleficarum, trans. E. A. Ashwin (New York: Dover, 1988)

Guilding, Rev. J. M., ed., *Reading Records: Diary of the Corporation*, 4 vols. (London: James Parker, 1895)

Hakluyt, Richard, *The Principal Navigations, Voyages, Traffiqves and Discoveries of the English Nation, made by Sea or ouerland, to the remote and farthest distant quarters of the Earth, at any time within the compasse of these 1600 yeres* (London: George Bishop, Ralph Newberie and Robert Barker, 1599)

Hall, Edward, *Hall's Chronicle; containing The History of England, during The Reign of Henry the Fourth, and the succeeding Monarchs, to the end of the Reign of Henry the Eighth, in which are particularly described the Manners and Customs of those Periods*, ed. by Sir Henry Ellis (London: J. Johnson; F. C. and J. Rivington; T. Payne; Wilkie and Robinson; Longman, Hurst, Rees and Orme; Cadell and Davies; and J. Mawman, 1809)

Hall, John, *The Courte of Vertu: Contayning many holy or Spretuall Songes, Sonnettes, psalmes, & Shorte Sentences, as well of holy Scripture as others* (London: Thomas Marshe, 1565)

Hall, Joseph, *Virgidemiarvm, Sixe Bookes. First three Bookes, Of Tooth-lesse Satyrs. 1. Poeticall. 2. Academicall. 3. Morall* (London: Thomas Creede, for Robert Dexter, 1597); *The three last Bookes. Of byting Satyres* (London: Richard Bradocke for Robert Dexter, 1598)

Hall, Trevor H., *A Bibliography of Books on Conjuring in English from 1580 to 1850* (Lepton: Palmyra Press, 1957)

  Old Conjuring Books: A Bibliographical and Historical Study with a Supplementary Check-List (London: Duckworth, 1972)

Halliwell, James O., ed., *The Works of William Shakespeare, the Text Formed from a New Collation of the Early Editions: to Which Are Added All the Original Novels and Tales on Which the Plays Are Founded; Copious Archaeological Annotations on Each Play; an Essay on the Formation of the Text; and a Life of the Poet*, 16 vols. (London: C. & J. Adlard, 1853–65)

Halliwell-Phillipps, J. O., *Memoranda on Love's Labour's Lost, King John, Othello and on Romeo and Juliet* (London: James Evan Adlard, 1879)

Hamelius, P., ed., *Mandeville's Travels*, Early English Text Society, 2 vols. (London: Kegan Paul, Trench, Trübner; Humphrey Milford, Oxford University Press, 1919–23)

Hammond, Henry, *Of A Late, Or A Death-Bed Repentance* (Oxford: Henry Hall Printer to the Universitie, 1645)

Harbage, Alfred, *Annals of English Drama 975–1700: An Analytical Record of all Plays, Extant or Lost, Chronologically Arranged and Indexed by Authors, Titles, Dramatic Companies, &c*, rev. S. Schoenbaum (London: Methuen, 1964)

Harington, Sir John, *A New Discovrse of a Stale Svbiect, called the Metamorphosis of Ajax. Written by Misacmos to his friend and cosin Philostilpnos* (London: R[ichard] Field, 1596)

Harrison, James, *An exhortacion to the Scottes, to conforme them selfes to the honorable expedient, and godly vnion, betwene the twoo realmes of Englande and Scotlande* (London: Richard Grafton, 1547)

Hartnoll, Phyllis, ed. *The Oxford Companion to the Theatre*, 3rd edn (London: Oxford University Press, 1951; repr. 1972)

Harvey, Gabriel [Richard Lichfield], *The Trimming of Thomas Nashe Gentleman, by the high-tituled patron Don Richardo de Medicio* [Richard Lichfield], *Barber Chirgion to Trinitie Colledge in Cambridge* (London: Edward Allde for Philip Scarlet, 1597)

Helm, Alex, *Eight Mummers' Plays* (Aylesbury: Ginn, 1971)

Herbert, George, *Witts Recreations, Selected from the finest Fancies of Moderne Muses. With a Thousand out Landish Proverbs* (London: Humph[ry] Blunden, 1640)

H[erbert], G[eorge], *Witt's Recreations refined & Augmented, with Ingenious Conceites for the wittie, and Merrie Medicines for the Melancholie as in Print* (London: M. Simmons, 1650)

Herbert, Sir Thomas, *A Relation Of Some Yeares Travaile, Begvnne Anno 1626. Into Afrique and the greater Asia, especially the Territories of the Persian Monarchie: and some parts of the Orientall Indies, and Iles adiacent. Of their Religion, Language, Habit, Discent, Ceremonies, and other matters concerning them* (London: William Stansby and Jacob Bloome, 1634)

Herford, C. H., Percy Simpson and Evelyn Simpson, eds., *Ben Jonson*, 11 vols. (Oxford: Clarendon Press, 1925–52)

Herrtage, Sidney J. H., ed., *Catholicon anglicum, an English–Latin Wordbook, Dated 1483. Edited from the MS No. 168 in the Library of Lord Monson, Collated with the Additional MS 15, 562, British Museum*, Early English Text Society (London: N. Trübner, 1881)

Hewitt, Barnard, ed., *The Renaissance Stage: Documents of Serlio, Sabbattini and Furttenbach* (Coral Gables, FL: University of Miami Press, 1958; repr. 1969)

Heyl, Edgar, 'New light on the Renaissance master', *The Sphinx*, 47:2 (April 1948), 38–42, 50

 A Contribution to Conjuring Bibliography: English Language 1580 to 1850 (Baltimore: Edgar Heyl, 1963; repr. Mansfield Centre, CT: Maurizo Martino, [n.d.])

Heywood, Thomas, *Hogs Character of a Projector, Being a Relation of his Life and Death, with his Funerall* (London: [n.b.], 1642)

 The Dramatic Works of Thomas Heywood: Now First collected with Illustrative Notes and a Memoir of the Author, 6 vols. (London: J. Pearson, 1874; repr. New York: Russell and Russell, 1964)

Hill, Thomas, *A briefe and pleasaunt treatise, entituled, Naturall and Artificiall conclusions* (London: Iohn Kyngston for Abraham Kitson, 1581)

Hoffmann, Professor [Louis] *Modern Magic: A Practical Treatise on the Art of Conjuring*, 12th edn (London: George Routledge, [n.d.])

Hoffmann, Professor, *Later Magic with New Miscellaneous Tricks and Recollections of Hartz the Wizard* (London: George Routledge, 1911; repr. 1931)

Holinshed, Raphael, *Holinshed's Chronicles of England, Scotland and Ireland*, ed. Sir Henry Ellis, 6 vols. (London: Richard Taylor for J. Johnson; F. C. and J. Rivington; T. Payne; Wilkie and Robinson; Longman, Hurst, Rees, and Orme; Cadell and Davies; and J. Mawman, 1807–8)

Holland, Charlie, *Strange Feats & Clever Turns* (London: Holland & Palmer, 1998)

Holme, Randle, *The Academy of Armory; Or, A Storehouse Of Armory and Blazon* (Chester: Randle Holme, 1688)

Hone, William, *The Every-Day Book*, 2 vols. (London: Hunt and Clarke, 1826–7)

Hopkins, Albert A., *Magic: Stage Illusions and Scientific Diversions Including Trick Photography* (New York: Munn, 1897)

Horatio, Napolitano, *Libretto de secreti nobilissimi, et alcuni giochi con destrezza di mano, cose vere, & experimentate a instanza de Horatio Napolitano, gioctor di mano* (Milan: [n.p.], 1585)

Horman, William, *Vulgaria* (London: R. Pynson, 1519)

Horstmann, Carl, ed., *The Early South-English Legendary; or, Lives of Saints*, Early English Text Society (London: Trübner, 1887)

Hoseley, Richard, 'Three kinds of outdoor theatre before Shakespeare', *Theatre Survey*, 12:1 (1971), 1–33

Houdini, Harry, *Miracle Mongers and Their Methods* (New York: E. P. Dutton, 1920)

Huloet, Richard, *Abcedarivm* (London: Gulielmi Riddel, 1552)

Ingeland, Thomas, *A pretie and Mery new Enterlude: called the Disobedient Child*, ed. John S. Farmer, Tudor Facsimile Texts (Amersham: John S. Farmer, 1908)

James I, King of England, *Daemonologie, In Forme of a Dialogue, Diuided into three Bookes* (Edinburgh: Robert Walde-graue, 1597)

Johnson, Richard, *The thirde voyage into Persia, begun in . . . 1565*, in *The Principal Navigations, Voyages, Traffiqves, and Discoveries of the English Nation, made by sea or Ouer-Land to the Remote and Farthest Distant Quarters of the Earth . . . Richard Haklvyt Preacher* (London: George Bishop, Ralph Newberie and Robert Barker, 1599)

Jonson, Ben, *Every Man Out of His Humour*, ed. F. P. Wilson, Malone Society (Oxford: Oxford University Press, 1920)

Joseph, Eddie, *How to Pick Pockets: A Treatise on the Fundamental Principle, Theory and Practice of Picking Pockets, for Entertainment Purposes Only* (London: Vampire Press, [1946])

Body Loading and Productions (Colon, MI: Abbott, 1950)

How to Pick Pockets for Fun and Profit (Colorado Springs: Piccadilly Books, 1992)

Killigrew, Thomas, *Comedies, and Tragedies* (London: Henry Herringman, 1664)

King, Harold G. and John E. T. Clark, *Ventriloquism and Juggling* (London: C. Arthur Pearson, 1921)

Kirke, John, *The Seven Champions of Christendome* (London: J[ohn] Okes, 1638)

Klein, Arthur H., ed., *Graphic Worlds of Peter Bruegel the Elder* (New York: Dover, 1963)

Kuin, R. J. P., *Robert Langham: A Letter* (Leiden: E. J. Brill, 1983)

Kyd, Thomas, *The Spanish Tragedie: Containing the lamentable end of Don Horatio, and Bel-imperia: with the pittifull death of olde Hieronimo*, ed. W. W. Greg, Malone Society (Oxford: Oxford University Press, 1925)

Kynaston, Sir Thomas, *Corona Minervae* (London: William Sheares, 1635)

Lambarde, William, *A Perambulation of Kent: Conteining the description, Hystorie, and Customes of that Shyre (for the most part) in the yeare. 1570* (London: Ralphe Newberie, 1576)

Dictionarium Angliæ topographicum & historicum. An Alphabetical Description of the Chief Places in England and Wales; With an Account of the most Memorable Events which have distinguish'd them (London: Fletcher Gyles, 1730)

Lamont, Peter, *The Rise of the Indian Rope Trick: The Biography of a Legend* (London: Little, Brown, 2004)

Lamont, Peter and Richard Wiseman, *Magic in Theory: An Introduction to the Theoretical and Psychological Elements of Conjuring* (Hatfield: University of Hertfordshire Press, 1999)

Lancashire, Ian, '"Ioly Walte and Malkyng": a Grimsby puppet play in 1431', *Records of Early English Drama Newsletter*, 2 (1979), 6–8.

Laneham, Robert, *Robert Laneham: A Letter [1575]*, A Scolar Press facsimile, 60 (Menston: Scolar Press, 1968)

Langland, William, *The Vision of William concerning Piers the Plowman*, ed. Walter W. Skeat, Early English Text Society (London: Trübner, 1873)

Lavater, Ludwig, *Of ghostes and spirites walking by nyght, and of strange noyses, crackes, and sundry forewarnynges, whiche commonly happen before the death of menne, grat slaughters, & alterations of kyngdomes*, trans. R[obert] H[arrison] (London: Henry Benneyman for Richard Watkyns, 1572)

Lawrence, W. J., *Old Theatre Days and Ways* (London; Bombay; Sydney: George G. Harrap, 1935)

Leland, John, *Joannis Lelandi antiquarii de rebvs Britannicis collectanea. Cvm Thomae Hearnii praefatione notis et indice ad editionem primam,* 6 vols. (London: apud Benj[amin] White, 1774)

Le Roux, Hugues & Jules Garnier, *Acrobats and Mountebanks,* trans. A. P. Morton (London: Chapman and Hall, 1890)

L'estrange, Sir Roger, *The Loyal Observator; Or, Historical Memoirs of the Life and Actions of Roger the Fidler; Alias, The Observator* (London: W. Hammond, 1683)

Letters and Papers, Foreign and Domestic, of the Reign of Henry VIII: preserved in the Public Record Office, the British Museum, and elsewhere in England, arranged and catalogued by J. S. Brewer, J. Gairdner and R. H. Brodie, 21 vols. (London: Longman, 1862–1910)

Letts, Malcolm, ed. and trans., *The Travels of Leo Rozmital through Germany, Flanders, England, France, Spain, Portugal and Italy 1465–1467,* Hakluyt Society (Cambridge: Cambridge University Press, 1957)

Lindsay, Sir David, *Ane Satyre of the Thrie Estaits* (Edinbvrgh: Robert Charteris, 1602; facs. repr. Amsterdam and New York: Theatrum Orbis Terrarum and Da Capo Press, 1969)

Llorens, Alfons, Rafael Navarro Mallebrera and Joan Castaño Garcí, *La festa d'Elx,* trans. Pamela M. King and Asunción Salvadov-Rabaza Ramos (Elche: Patronato Nacional del Misterio de Elche, 1990)

Lodge, Thomas and Robert Greene, *A Looking-Glass for London and England,* ed. W. W. Greg, Malone Society (Oxford: Oxford University Press, 1932)

Loomis, Laura Hibbard, 'Secular dramatics in the royal palace, Paris, 1378, 1389, and Chaucer's "Tregetoures"', in *Medieval English Drama: Essays Critical and Contextual,* ed. Jerome Taylor and Alan H. Nelson (Chicago and London: University of Chicago Press, 1972), pp. 98–115.

Lucar, Cyprian, *Three Bookes of Colloqvies concerning the Arte of Shooting in great and small pieces of Artillerie . . . written in Italian, and dedicated by Nicholas Tartaglia . . . And now translated into English by* CYPRIAN LVCAR . . . (London: Thomas Dawson for Iohn Harrison, 1588)

Lumiansky, R. M. and David Mills, eds., *The Chester Mystery Cycle,* Early English Text Society, 2 vols. (London: Oxford University Press, 1974, 1986)

Lund, Robert, 'Colorini', *The Sphinx,* 47:5 (July 1948), 128, 138

Lupton, Thomas, *All for Money,* ed. John S. Farmer, Tudor Facsimile Texts (Amersham: John S. Farmer, 1910)

Lyte, Sir H. Maxwell, ed., *The Manuscripts of His Grace the Duke of Rutland, K. G. preserved at Belvoir Castle,* 4 vols. (London: His Majesty's Stationery Office, 1905)

Maccabe, Frederic, *The Art of Ventriloquism. Including Full Directions to Learners How to Acquire a Pleasing Vocalization; with Amusing Dialogues* (London: Frederick Warne, [1875])

Malthe, Francois de, *A Treatise of Artificial Fire-works both for Warres and Recreation: with divers pleasant Geometricall obseruations, Fortifications and Arithmeticall Examples. In fauour of Mathematicall Students. Newly written in FRENCH, and Englished by the Authour THO:MALTHVS* (London: Richard Hawkins, 1629)

Marcellinus, Ammianus, *The Roman Historie, Containing such Acts and occurrents as passed under Constantius, Iulianus, Iouianus, Valentinianus, and Valens, Emperours*, trans. Philemon Holland (London: Adam Islip, 1609)

Markham, Gervase, *Cavalarice; Or, The English Horseman: Contayning all the Art of Horse-manship, asmuch as is necessary for any man to vnderstand, whether hee be Horse-breeder, horse-ryder, horse-hunter, horse-runner, horse-ambler, horse-farrier, horse-keeper, Coachman, Smith or Sadler. Together, with the discouery of the subtil trade or mystery of hors-coursers, and an explanation of the excellency of a horses vnderstanding: or how to teach them to do trickes like Bankes his Curtall etc.* (London: Edward White, 1607)

M[arlowe], C[hristopher], *All Ovids Elegies: 3 Bookes. By C. M. Epigrams* ed. J[ohn] D[avies] (Middlebovrgh: [n.p.] 1630?)

Marston, John, *The Works of John Marston*, ed. A. H. Bullen, 3 vols. (London: John C. Nimmo, 1887)

  Iack Drvms Entertainment; or, The Comedie Of Pasquill and Katherine, ed. John S. Farmer, Tudor Facsimile Texts (Amersham: John S. Farmer, 1912)

  Histrio-Mastix, ed. John S. Farmer, Tudor Facsimile Texts (Amersham: John S. Farmer, 1912)

Maskelyne, J. N., *The Fraud of Modern 'Theosophy' Exposed* (London: George Routledge, [1912])

Maskelyne, Nevil and David Devant, *Our Magic: The Art in Magic; The Theory of Magic; The Practice of Magic* (London: George Routledge & Sons Ltd, [1911])

McIntyre, George, *George McIntyre's Bibliography on Ventriloquism* (Seattle: Gregory & Walter Berlin, 1970)

McMillin, Scott and Sally-Beth MacLean, *The Queen's Men and Their Plays* (Cambridge: Cambridge University Press, 1998)

Melton, Eduward, *Zee-en Land-Reizen; door Egypten, West-Indien, Perzien, Turkyen, Ost-Indien en d'aangrenzende Gewesten . . . Aangevangen in den jaare 1660. en geeindigd in den jaare 1677* (Amsterdam: Jan ten Hoorn, 1681)

Melvill, James, *The Autobiography and Diary of Mr James Melvill, with a Continuation of the Diary. Edited from Manuscripts in the Libraries of the Faculty of Advocates and University of Edinburgh*, ed. Robert Pitcairn (Edinburgh: Wodrow Society, 1842)

Meredith, Peter and John E. Tailby, eds., *The Staging of Religious Drama in Europe in the Later Middle Ages: Texts and Documents in English Translation*, trans. Raffaella Ferrari, Peter Meredith, Lynette R. Muir, Margaret Sceeman and John E. Tailby, Early Drama, Art, and Music Monograph Series, Medieval Institute Publications, 4 (Kalamazoo: Western Michigan University, 1983)

Metcalf, W. M., ed., *Legends of the Saints in the Scottish Dialect of the Fourteenth Century*, Scottish Text Society, 3 vols. (Edinburgh and London: William Blackwood, 1896)

M[iddleton], T[homas], *The Blacke Booke* (London: T[homas] C[reede] for Ieffrey Chorlton, 1604)

    ed., *The Works of Thomas Middleton*, ed. A. H. Bullen, 8 vols. (London: John C. Nimmo, 1885–6)

    A Game at Chess, ed. T. H. Howard-Hill, Malone Society (Oxford: Oxford University Press, 1990)

Mill, Anna Jean, *Mediaeval Plays in Scotland* (Edinburgh, London: Blackwood, 1927; repr. New York, London: Benjamin Blom, 1969)

Mills, David, ed., *The Chester Mystery Cycle: A New Edition with Modernised Spelling*, Medieval Texts and Studies, 9 (East Lansing: Colleagues Press, 1992)

Morfill, W. R. ed., *Ballads from Manuscripts: Ballads Relating Chiefly to the Reign of Queen Elizabeth*, Ballad Society, 2 vols. (Hertford: Ballad Society, Stephen Austin, 1873)

Morland, Samuel, *An Instrument of Excellent Use, As well at Sea, as at Land; Invented, and variously Experimented in the Year 1670* (London: W. Godbid, 1671)

Morley, Henry, *Memoirs of Bartholomew Fair* (London: Chapman and Hall, 1859)

Morris, Richard, ed., *Cursor mundi (The Cursor o the World): A Northumbrian Poem of the* xiv *th Century*, Early English Text Society, 3 vols. (London: Kegan Paul, Trench, Trübner, 1874–93)

    ed., *The Blickling Homilies*, Early English Text Society (London: Oxford University Press, 1967)

Morton, Thomas, *A Direct Answer vnto The Scandalovs Exceptions, which Theophilus Higgons hath lately obiected against D. Morton etc* (London: Edmvnd Weaver, 1609)

Moxon, Joseph, *Mechanick Exercises; or, the Doctrine of Handy-Works. Applied to the Arts of Smithing Joinery Carpentry Turning Bricklayery* (London: Dan[iel] Midwinter and Tho[mas] Leigh, 1703)

Munday, Anthony, *The Book of Sir Thomas More*, ed. W. W. Greg, Malone Society (Oxford: Oxford University Press, 1911)

Murray, John Tucker, ed., *English Dramatic Companies*, 2 vols. (London: Constable, 1910)

Mvsophilus, Basilivs [Samuel Holland], *Don Zara Del Fogo: A Mock-Romance. Written Originally in the Brittish Tongue, and made English by a person of much Honor* (London: T. W. for Tho[mas] Vere, 1656)

[Nashe, Thomas?], *The Returne of the renowned Caualiero Pasquill of England, from the other side of the Seas, and his meeting with Marforius at London vpon the Royall Exchange* (London: If my breath be so hote that I burne my mouth, suppose I was Printed by Pepper Allie, J[ohn] Charlewood?], 1589)

Strange Newes, Of the intercepting certaine Letters and a Conuoy of Verses, as they were going Priuilie to victuall the Low Countries (London: [J. Danter], 1592)

The Terrors of the night; Or, A Discourse of Apparitions (London: Iohn Danter for William Iones, 1594)

The Vnfortvnate Traveller; Or, The Life of Iacke Wilton (London: T[homas] Scarlet for C[uthbert] Burby, 1594)

Nash, Thomas, *Haue with you to Safron-walden. Or, Gabriell Harueys Hunt is vp. Containing a full Answere to the eldest sonne of the Halter-maker. Or, Nashe his Confutation of the sinfull Doctor. etc.* (London: Iohn Danter, 1596)

Nashe, Thomas, *Lenten Stuffe, Containing, the Description and first Procreation and Increase of the towne of Great Yarmouth in Norfolke: With a new Play neuer played before, of the praise of the Red Herring. Fitte of all Clearkes of Noblemens Kitchins to be read: and not vnnecessary by all Seruing men that haue short boord-wages, to be remembred.* (London: N. L. and C. B., 1599)

Summer's Last Will and Testament, in *A Select Collection of Old English Plays*, ed. Robert Dodsley, 4th edn, rev. W. Carew Hazlitt, 11 vols. (London: Reeves and Turner, 1874–6), VIII (1874)

Nelms, Henning, *Magic and Showmanship: A Handbook for Conjurers* (New York: Dover, 1969)

Neve, Richard, *The Merry Companion; or, Delights for the Ingenious* (London: Eben[ezer] Tracey, [1716])

Nichols, John, *The Progresses and Public Processions of Queen Elizabeth. Among which are interspersed other solemnities, public expenditures, and remarkable events. During the reign of that illustrious princess. Collected from Original Manuscripts, Scarce Pamphlets, Corporation Records, Parochial Registers, etc, etc.* 3 vols. (London: John Nichols, 1823)

The Progresses, Processions, and Magnificent Festivities of King James the Sixth, 4 vols. (London: J. B. Nichols, 1828)

Norris, Edwin, ed. and trans, *The Ancient Cornish Drama*, 2 vols. (Oxford: University Press, 1859)

Northbrooke, John, *Spiritus est vicarius Christi in [terra]. A Treatise wherein Dicing, Dauncing, Vaine playes or Enterluds with other idle pastimes &c. commonly vsed on the Sabboth day, are reproued by the Authoritie of the word of God and auntient writers* (London: H[enry] Bynnenian for George Byshop, 1577?)

Norton, Robert, *The Gvnner Shewing The Whole Practise Of Artillerie: With all the Appurtenances therevnto belonging. Together with the making of Extraordinary Artificiall Fireworkes, as well for Pleasure and Triumphes, as for Warre and Seruice.* (London: A. M. for Hvmphrey Robinson, 1628)

O'Grady, S. H. and Robin Flower, ed., *Catalogue of Irish Manuscripts in the British Museum*, 3 vols. (London: printed for the Trustees, 1926–53)

Palsgrave, Jean, *L'éclaircissement de la Langue Française par Jean Palsgrave, suivi de la grammaire de Giles du Guez, publiés pour la première fois en France par F. Génin* (Paris: Imprimerie Nationale, 1852)

Panton, Geo[rge] A. and David Donaldson, *The Gest Hystoriale of the Destruction of Troy: An Alliterative Romance*, Early English Text Society (London: Trübner, 1869)

Parke, Thomas, ed., *The Harleian Miscellany: A Collection of Scarce, Curious, and Entertaining Pamphlets and Tracts, as well in Manuscript as in Print*, 10 vols. (London: John White and John Murray, 1808–13)

Parrot, Henry, *The Mastive; Or, Young-Whelpe of the Olde-Dogge. Epigrams and Satyrs* (London: Tho[mas] Creede for Richard Meighen and Thomas Jones, 1615)

Partington, Charles F., *The Century of Inventions of the Marquis of Worcester from the Original MS with Historical and Explanatory Notes and a Biographical Memoir* (London: John Murray, 1825)

Pearson, Karl, *The Chances of Death and Other Studies in Evolution*, 2 vols. (London: Edward Arnold, 1897)

Peele, George, *The Araygnement of Paris A Pastorall* (London: Henrie Marsh, 1584)

    Merrie Conceited Iests: Of George Peele Gentleman, sometimes a Student in OXFORD. Wherein is shewed the course of his life, how he liued: a man very well knowne in the Citie of London, and elsewhere (London: G[eorge] P[urslowe] for F[rancis] Faulkner, 1627)

    The Old Wives Tale, ed. W. W. Greg, Malone Society (Oxford: Oxford University Press, 1908)

    King Edward the First, ed. W. W. Greg, Malone Society (Oxford: Oxford University Press, 1911)

    The Love of King David and Fair Bethsabe, ed. W. W. Greg, Malone Society (Oxford: Oxford University Press, 1912)

Pemble, William, *Vindicae fidei; or, A Treatise of Iustification by Faith, wherein that point is fully cleared, and vindicated from the cauils of its aduersaries* (Oxford: John Lichfield and William Turner for Edward Forrest, 1625)

Pentzell, Raymond J., 'The medieval theatre in the streets', *Theatre Survey*, 14:1 (1973), 1–21

    'A reply to Mary Del Villar', *Theatre Survey*, 14:2 (1973), 82–90

Petit, Philippe, *To Reach the Clouds: My High Wire Walk between the Twin Towers* (London: Faber, 2002)

Petrus Martyr Anglerius, *The Decades of the newe worlde or west India, Conteynyng the nauigations and conquestes of the Spanyardes, with the particular description of the moste ryche and large landes and Ilandes lately founde in the west Ocean perteynyng to the inheritaunce of the kinges of Spayne*, trans. Rycharde Eden (London: Guilhelmi Powell, 1555)

Philalethes, Alazonomastix, *Observations upon Anthroposophia Theomagica, and Anima Magica Abscondita* (Parrhesia [London]: O[ctavian] Pullen, 1650)

Pilkinton, Mark C., 'The Easter Sepulchre at St Mary Redcliffe, Bristol, 1470', *The EDAM Newsletter* 5:1 (Fall 1982), 10–12

Platte, Sir Hugh, *The Jewell House of Art and Natvre* (London: Peter Short, 1594)

Plesch, Véronique, 'Notes for the staging of a late medieval passion play', in *Material Culture and Medieval Drama*, ed. Clifford Davidson, Early Drama, Art, and Music Monograph Series, 25 (Kalamazoo: Medieval Institute Publications, 1999), 75–102

Pollard, A. W. and G. R. Redgrave, *A Short-Title Catalogue of Books Printed in England, Scotland, and Ireland and of English Books Printed Abroad 1475–1640*, 2nd edn, 3 vols. (London: Bibliographical Society, 1976–91)

Portae, Io[hn] Bapt[ista], *Magiae natvralis libri XX. Ab ipso authore expurgati, & superaucti, in quibus scientiarum naturalium diuitiae, & delitae demonstrantur cvm privilegio.* (Naples: apud Horatium Saluianum, 1589)

Porta, John Baptista, *Natural Magick*, ed. Derek J. Price (London: Thomas Young and Samuel Speed, 1658; repr. New York: Basic Books, 1957)

Preston, Thomas, *A lamentable Tragedie, mixed full of plesant mirth, containing the life of Cambises king of Percia*, ed. John S. Farmer, Tudor Facsimile Texts (Amersham: John S. Farmer, 1910)

Price, Major David, trans., *Memoirs of The Emperor Jahangueir written by Himself; and Translated From a Persian Manuscript* (London: Oriental Translation Committee, 1829)

Prince, Arthur, *The Whole Art of Ventriloquism* (London: Will Goldston, [1921])

Puttenham, George, *The Arte of English Poesie. Contriued into three Bookes: The first of Poets and Poesie, the second of Proportion, the third of Ornament* (London: Richard Field, 1589)

Raleigh, Sir Walter, *The History of the World* (London: Walter Bvrre, 1614)

Randolph, Thomas, *The Jealous Lovers* (Cambridge: [John and Thomas Buck,] printers to the University, 1632)
    Poems with Mvses Looking-glasse: and Amyntas (Oxford: Leonard Lichfield, 1638)

Reaney, P. H., ed., *A Dictionary of British Surnames* (London: Routledge and Kegan Paul, 1958)

Records of Early English Drama [REED]: Bristol, ed. Mark C. Pilkinton (Toronto; Buffalo; London: University of Toronto Press, 1997)

Records of Early English Drama [REED]: Cambridge, ed. Alan H. Nelson, 2 vols. (Toronto; Buffalo; London: University of Toronto Press, 1989)

Records of Early English Drama [REED]: Chester, ed. Lawrence Clopper (Toronto; Buffalo; London: Manchester University Press and University of Toronto Press, 1979)

Records of Early English Drama [REED]: Coventry, ed. R. W. Ingram (Toronto; Buffalo; London: University of Toronto Press and Manchester University Press, 1981)

Records of Early English Drama [REED]: Cumberland, Westmorland, Gloucestershire, ed. Audrey Douglas and Peter Greenfield (Toronto; Buffalo; London: University of Toronto Press, 1986)

Records of Early English Drama [REED]: Devon, ed. John M. Wasson (Toronto; Buffalo; London: University of Toronto Press, 1986)

Records of Early English Drama [REED]: Dorset, Cornwall, ed. Rosalind Conklin Hays, C. E. McGee, Sally L. Joyce and Evelyn S. Newlyn (Toronto; Buffalo: Brepols and University of Toronto Press, 1999)

Records of Early English Drama [REED]: Herefordshire, Worcestershire, ed. David N. Klausner (Toronto; Buffalo; London: University of Toronto Press, 1990)

Records of Early English Drama [REED]: Kent, ed. James M. Gibson, 3 vols. (Toronto; Buffalo; London: British Library and University of Toronto Press, 2002)

Records of Early English Drama: Lancashire [REED], ed. David George (Toronto: Buffalo; London: University of Toronto Press, 1991

Records of Early English Drama [REED]: Newcastle Upon Tyne, ed. J. J. Anderson (Toronto; Buffalo; London: University of Toronto Press and Manchester University Press, 1982)

Records of Early English Drama [REED]: Norwich 1540–1642, ed. David Galloway (Toronto; Buffalo; London: University of Toronto Press, 1984)

Records of Early English Drama [REED]: Oxford, ed. John R. Elliott, Jr, Alan H. Nelson, Alexandra F. Johnston and Diana Wyatt, 2 vols. (Toronto; Buffalo: British Library and University of Toronto Press, 2004)

Records of Early English Drama [REED]: Shropshire, ed. J. Alan B. Somerset, 2 vols. (Toronto; Buffalo; London: University of Toronto Press, 1994)

Records of Early English Drama [REED]: Somerset, ed. James Stokes and Robert J. Alexander, 2 vols. (Toronto; Buffalo; London: University of Toronto Press, 1996)

Records of Early English Drama [REED]: Sussex, ed. Cameron Louis (Toronto; Buffalo; London: Brepols Publishers and University of Toronto Press, 2000)

Records of Early English Drama [REED]: York, ed. by Alexandra F. Johnston and Margaret Rogerson, 2 vols. (Toronto; Buffalo; London: University of Toronto Press and Manchester University Press, 1979)

Reynolds, George Fullmer, *The Staging of Elizabethan Plays at the Red Bull Theater 1605–1625* (New York; London: Modern Language Association of America and Oxford University Press, 1940)

R[id], S[amuel], *The Art of Iugling or Legerdemaine. Wherein is deciphered, all the conueyances of Legerdemaine and Iugling, how they are effected, & wherin they chiefly consist* (London: T[homas] B[ushell], 1612)

Robert-Houdin, [Jean Eugène], *The Secrets of Conjuring and Magic; or, How to Become a Wizard*, ed. and trans. Professor Hoffmann (London: George Routledge, 1878)

The Secrets of Stage Conjuring, ed. and trans. Professor [Luis] Hoffmann (London: George Routledge, 1881)

Robinson, Hastings, ed., *Original Letters Relative to the English Reformation Written during the Reigns of King Henry VIII., King Edward VI., and Queen Mary: Chiefly from the Archives of Zurich*, Parker Society, 2 vols. (Cambridge: Cambridge University Press, 1846)

Roe, Sir Thomas, *Sir Thomas Roe's journal of his voyage to the East Indies, and observations there during his residence at the Mogul's court, as Embassador from King James the first of England, taken from his own manuscripts*, in *A Collection of Voyages and Travels, some now printed from Original Manuscripts, others now first published in English*, 6 vols. (London: Churchill, 1732)

Rolle, Richard, *The Pricke of Conscience (Stimulus conscientiae): A Northumbrian Poem by Richard Rolle de Hampole*, ed. Richard Morris, Philological Society (Berlin: A. Asher, 1863)

Romance of Alexander, The, collotype facsimile of MS Bodley 264 (Oxford: Clarendon Press, 1933)

Romeu, Josep, ed., *Teatre Hagiogràfic*, 3 vols. (Barcelona: Editorial Barcino, 1957)

Rose, Martial and Julia Hedgecoe, *Stories in Stone: The Medieval Roof Carvings of Norwich Cathedral* (London: Herbert Press, 1997; repr. 2000)

Rotuli hundredorum temp. Hen. III & Edw. 1. In turr' Lond. et in curia receptoe scaccarij Westm. asservati, 2 vols. (London: George Eyre and Andrew Strahan, 1812 and 1818)

Round, J. H., ed., *The Great Roll of the Pipe for the Twenty-Second Year of the Reign of King Henry the Second, AD 1175–1176*, Pipe Roll Society (London: Spottiswoode, 1904)

Rowley, William, *A Search for Money; or, The Lamentable complaint for the losse of the wandring Knight Mounsieur l'Argent; or, Come along with me, I know thou louest Money* (London: Ioseph Hunt, 1609)

Roy, William [William Barlow], *Rede me and be nott wrothe/ For I saye no thynge but trothe. I will ascende makynge my state so hye/ That my pompous honoure shall never dye/ O Caytyfe when thou thynkest least of all/ With confusion thou shalt have a fall* (Strasburg: [n.p.], 1528; facs. repr. C. Whittingham for W. Pickering, 1845)

Rushworth, John, *Historical Collections. The Second Volume of the Second Part, Containing the Principal Matters Which happened From March 26. 1639. until the Summoning of a Parliament, which met at Westminster, April 13. 1640* (London: J. D. for John Wright, 1680)

Russell, Constance, 'Thinking horses', *Notes and Queries*, 10th series, 11 (July–December 1904)

Russell, Fred, *Ventriloquism and Kindred Arts: An Historical and Practical Treatise, Giving Explicit and Reliable Directions Whereby the Whole Art of Distant Voice Illusion, Figure Working and Vocal Mimicry May Be Acquired* (London: Keith, Prowse, 1898)

Rye, William Brenchley, ed., *England as Seen by Foreigners in the Days of Elizabeth and James the First*, (London: John Russell, 1865)

Sabbatini, Nicolo, *Pratica di fabricar scene e machine ne' teatri* (Ravenna: Pietro de' Paoli and Gio[vanni] Battista Giouannelli, 1638; facs. repr. Rome: Carlo Bestetti, Edizioni D'Arte, 1955)

Sachs, Edwin, *Sleight of Hand: A Practical Manual of Legerdemain for Amateurs and Others*, 2nd edn (London: L. Upcott Gill, 1885)

Salzmann, L. F., ed., *An Abstract of Feet of Fines Relating to the County of Sussex From 1 Edward II. To 24 Henry VII*, (Lewes: Sussex Record Society, 1916)

Sandys, George, *Sandys Travailes: Containing A History of the Original and Present state of the Turkish Empire: Their Laws, Government, Policy, Military Force, Courts of Justice and Commerce etc*, 6th edn (London: R. and W. Leybourn, 1658)

Sawyer, P. H., ed., *Anglo-Saxon Charters: An Annotated List and Bibliography* (London: Royal Historical Society, 1968)

Schneideman, Robert Ivan, 'Elizabethan legerdemain, and its employment in the drama, 1576–1642' (unpublished doctoral thesis, Northwestern University, 1956)

Scot, Reginald, *The Discouerie of witchcraft* (London: H[enry] Denham for W[illiam] Brome, 1584)

Scribonius, Cornelius Graphens, *Spectaculorum in Susceptione Philippi Hispani Principis Caroli V.* (Antwerp: Petro Alosten, 1550)

Serlio, Sebastiano, *The Five Books of Architecture: An Unabridged Reprint of the English Edition of 1611* (New York: Dover, 1982)

Shakespear, William and William Rowley, *The Birth of Merlin; Or, The Childe hath found his Father* (London: Tho[mas] Johnson for Francis Kirkman, and Henry Marsh, 1662)

Shakespeare, William, *The Tempest*, ed. Peter Alexander (London and Glasgow: Collins, 1951; repr. 1965)

  Troilus and cressida, ed. Peter Alexander (London and Glasgow: Collins, 1951; repr. 1965)

Shergold, N. D., *A History of the Spanish Stage from Medieval Times until the End of the Seventeenth Century* (Oxford: Clarendon Press, 1967)

Shirley, James, *Hide Park. A Comedie* (London: Andrew Crooke and William Cooke, 1637)

Shoemaker, William Hutchinson, *The Multiple Stage in Spain during the Fifteenth and Sixteenth Centuries* (Westport, CT: Greenwood Press, 1973)

Sidney, Sir Philip, *Syr P. S. his Astrophel and Stella. Wherein the excellence of sweete Poesie is concluded To the end of which are added, sundry other rare Sonnets of diuers Noble men and Gentlemen* (London: Thomas Newman, 1591; facs. repr. Menston: Scolar Press, 1970)

Siegel, Lee, *Net of Magic: Wonders and Deceptions in India* (Chicago and London: University of Chicago Press, 1991)

Simienowicz, Casimir, *The Great Art of Artillery of Casimir Simienowicz, Formerly Lieutenant-General of the Ordanance to the King of Poland*, trans. George Shelvocke (London: J. Tonson, 1729)

Skelton, John, *Magnyfycence: A Moral Play*, ed. Robert Lee Ramsay, Early English Text Society (London: Oxford University Press, 1908; repr. 1958)

Speaight, George, *The History of the English Puppet Theatre*, 2nd edn (London: Robert Hale, 1990)

Spector, Stephen, ed., *The N-Town Play Cotton MS Vespasian D. 8*, Early English Text Society, 2 vols. (Oxford: Oxford University Press, 1991)

Spenser, Edmund, *Prosopoia; Or, Mother Hubberds Tale. By Ed. Sp. Dedicated to the right Honorable the Ladie Compton and Mountegle* (London: William Ponsonbie, 1591)

The Faerie Qveene. Disposed into twelve books, Fashioning XII. Morall vertues (London: William Ponsonbie, 1590). *The Second Part of the Faerie Qveene. Containing The Fovrth, Fifth, and Sixth Bookes* (London: William Ponsonby, 1596)

Standage, Tom, *The Mechanical Turk: The True Story of the Chess-Playing Machine that Fooled the World* (London: Penguin, 2002)

Stenton, Doris M., ed., *The Great Roll of Pipe for the Second Year of the Reign of King Richard the First Michaelmas 1190*, Pipe Roll Society (London: Pipe Roll Society, 1925)

Stephen, Leslie, ed., *Dictionary of National Biography [DNB]*, 63 vols. (London: Smith, Elder, 1885)

Stephens, John, *Satyrical Essayes Characters and Others; Or, Accurate and quick Descriptions, fitted to the life of their Subjects* (London: Nicholas Okes, 1615)

Stevens, Martin and A. C. Cawley, eds., *The Towneley Plays*, Early English Text Society, 2 vols. (Oxford: Oxford University Press, 1994)

Stokes, Whitley, ed. and trans., *Gwreans An Bys, The Creation of the World: A Cornish Mystery* (London: Williams and Norgate, 1864)

ed. and trans., *The Life of Saint Meriasek, Bishop and Confessor: A Cornish Drama* (London: Trübner, 1872)

Stokes, William, *The Vaulting Master; or, the Art of Vaulting reduced to a method . . . Illustrated by examples* (Oxon: [n.p.], 1652)

Stow, John, *The Annales of England, Faithfully collected out of the most authenticall Authors, Records, and other Monuments of Antiquitie, lately corrected, encreased, and continued, from the first inhabitation vntill this present yeere 1601* (London: [Peter Short and Felix Kingston] for Ralfe Newbery, 1601)

Stow, John [Edmund Howes], *The Annales Or Generall Chronicle of England* (London: Thomas Adams, 1615)

Streitberger, W. R., *Court Revels 1485–1559* (Toronto; Buffalo; London: University of Toronto Press, 1994)

Strutt, Joseph, *Glig-Gamena Angel Deod.; or, The Sports and Pastimes of the People of England: including the Rural and Domestic Recreations, May Games, Mummeries, Pageants, Processions, and Pompous Spectacles, from the earliest Period to the present Time: Illustrated by Engravings selected from Ancient Paintings; in which are represented most of the Popular Diversions* (London: T. Bensley for J. White, 1801)

The Sports and Pastimes of the People of England (London: Thomas Tegg, 1834)

Sullivan, Mary, *Court Masques of James I: Their Influence on Shakespeare and the Public Theatres* (New York and London: G. P. Putnam, 1913)

Sussex Archaeological Society, ed., *Sussex Archaeological Collections. Relating to the History and Antiquities of the County*, XXXI (Lewes: H. H. Wolff for the Sussex Archaeological Society, 1881)

Tailor, Robert, *The Hogge Hath Lost His Pearl*, ed. D. F. McKenzie, Arthur Brown and G. R. Proudfoot, Malone Society (Oxford: Oxford University Press, 1967 [1972])

Tarlton, Richard, *Tarltons Jests. Drawne into these three parts. 1 His Court-witty Iests. 2 His sound City Iests. 3 His Country-pretty Iests. Full of delight, Wit, and honest Mirth* (London: I[ohn] H[aviland] for Andrew Crook, 1638)

Taylor, John, *All The Workes of John Taylor The Water-Poet. Beeing Sixty and three in Number. Collected into one Volume by the Avthor: With sundry new Additions, corrected, reuised, and newly Imprinted* (London: J. B. for Iames Boler, 1630)

Terry, Edward, *A Voyage to East-India. Wherein some things are taken notice of in our passage thither, but many more in our abode there, within that rich and most spacious Empire of the Great Mogol* (London: T. W. for J. Martin, and J. Allestrye, 1655)

Thuresson, Bertil, ed., *Middle English Occupational Terms* (Lund: Håkan Ohlssons, 1950)

Tiddy, R. J. E., *The Mummers' Play* (Oxford: Clarendon Press, 1923)

Tillotson, John, *The Works Of the Most Reverend Dr. John Tillotson, Late Lord Archbishop of Canterbury: Containing Fifty four Sermons and Discourses, On Several Occasions. Together with The Rule of Faith* (London: B. Aylmer and W. Rogers, 1696)

Toole Stott, Raymond, *Circus and Allied Arts: A World Bibliography*, 5 vols. (Derby: Harpur, 1958–80)

A Bibliography of English Conjuring 1581–1876, 2 vols. (Derby: Harpur, 1976–8)

Topsell, Edward, *The Historie of Serpents; Or, The second Booke of liuing Creatures: Wherein is contained their Diuine, Naturall, and Morall descriptions, with their liuely Figures, Names, Conditions, Kindes and Natures of all venemous Beasts: with their seuerall Poysons and Antidotes; their deepe hatred of Mankind, and the wonderfull worke of God in their Creation, and Destruction* (London: William Jaggard, 1608)

Turner, William, *The first and seconde partes of a Herbal of William Turner . . . lately ouersene corrected and enlarged with the Thirde parte lately gathered and nowe set oute with the names of the herbes in Greke Latin English Duche Frenche and in the Apothecaries and Herbaries Latin with the properties degrees and naturall places of the same* (London: Arnold Birckman, 1568)

Tyndale, William, *The obedience of a Christen man and howe Christen rulers ought to gouernel where in also (yf thou marke diligently) thou shalt fynde eyes to perceaue the crafty conveyaunce of all iugglers.* (Marlborow, Hans Luft [Antwerp, Johannes Hoochstraten], 1528; facs. repr. Menston: Scolar Press, 1970)

Vincent, William (attrib.), *Hocvs Pocvs Ivnior. The Anatomie of Legerdemain; Or, The Art of Iugling set forth in his proper colours, fully, plainely, and exactly, so that an ignorant person may thereby learne the full perfection of the same, after a little practise* (London: T[homas] H[arper] for R[alph] M[abb], 1634) (attrib.) *Hocus Pocus Junior. The Anatomy of Legerdemain; or, The Art of Jugling set forth in his proper colours, fully, plainly, and exactly; so that an ignorant person may thereby learn the full perfection of the same, after a little practise* (London: G. Dawson, 1654)

Virgil, *Virgil Eclogues. Georgics. Aeneid* I–VI, trans. H. Rushton Fairclough, rev. G. P. Goold (Cambridge, MA; London: Harvard University Press, 1999)

Vitale-Brovarone, Alessandro, ed., *Il quaderno di segreti d'un regista provenzale del Medioevo: note per la messa in scena d'una passione* (Alessandria: Edizioni Dell'Orso, 1984)

Voragine, Jacobus de, *Legenda aurea*, in *Lombardica historia* (Cologne: Ludwig von Renchen, 1485)

    Legenda aurea: vulgo historia lombardica dicta; ad optimorum liborum fidem/ recensuit Dr. Th. Graesse, ed. Theodor Graesse, 3rd edn (Breslau: Gulielmum Koebner, 1890)

    The Golden Legend: Readings on the Saints, trans. William Granger Ryan, 2 vols. (Princeton: Princeton University Press, 1993)

Voskuil, J., 'The speaking machine through the ages', *Transactions of the Newcomen Society*, 26 (1953 for 1947–9), 259–67

Vox, Valentine, *I Can See Your Lips Moving: The History and Art of Ventriloquism* (London: Kaye & Ward, 1981)

Waller, A. R., ed., *The Works of Francis Beaumont and John Fletcher*, 10 vols. (Cambridge: Cambridge University Press, 1905–12)

Warner, George F., ed., *The Buke of John Maundeuill Being the Travels of Sir John Mandeville Knight 1322–1356* (London: Roxburghe Club, 1889)

Warner, William, *The First and Second Parts of Albions England* (London: Thomas Orwin for Thomas Cadman, 1589)

Way, Albert, ed., *Promptorium parvulorum sive clericorum, lexicon Anglo-Latinum princeps, auctore fratre Galfrido grammatico dicto e predicatoribus lenne episcopi, northfolciensi, A.D. circa M.CCCC.XL*, 3 vols. (London: Camden Society, 1843–65)

Webster, Iohn, *The White Divel; Or, The Tragedy of Paulo Giordano Vrsini, Duke of Brachiano, With The Life and Death of Vittoria Corombona the famous Venetian Curtizan* (London: N[icholas] O[kes] for Thomas Archer, 1612)

Wecker, Hanss Jacob, *De secretis libri* XVII. *Ex varijs authoribus collecti, methodiceque digesti* (Basle: [n.p.], 1582)

    Eighteen Books Of the Secrets of Art & Nature, being the Summe and Substance of Naturall Philosophy, Methodically Digested. First designed by John Wecker Dr in Physick, and now much Augmented and Inlarged by Dr R. Read (London: Simon Miller, 1660)

Wieri, Ioannis, *De praestigiis daemonvm, et incantationibus ac ueneficijs, libri* V (Basle: Ioannem Oporinum, 1566)

    De praestigiis daemonum, & incantationibus ac ueneficiis libri sex, postrema editioni sexta aucti & recogniti (Basle: ex officina Oporiniana, 1583)

Weyer, Johann, *Witches, Devils, and Doctors in the Renaissance: Johann Weyer, 'De praestigiis daemonum'*, ed. George Mora *et al.*, Medieval and Renaissance Texts and Studies (Tempe, AZ: Center for Medieval and Early Renaissance Studies, State University of New York at Binghamton, 1991; repr. 1998)

White, Beatrice, ed., *The Dance of Death: Edited from MSS Ellesmere 26/A.13 and B. M. Lansdowne 699, Collated with the Other Extant MSS*, Early English Text Society (London: Humphrey Milford for Oxford University Press, 1931)

White, Lynn, 'The legacy of the Middle Ages in the American Wild West', in *Medieval Religion and Technology: Collected Essays*, ed. Lynn White, Jr. (London: University of California Press, 1978)

Wickham, Glynne, *Early English Stages 1300 to 1660*, 3 vols. (London: Routledge & Kegan Paul, 1966–81)

  'The staging of saint plays in England', in *The Medieval Drama*, ed. Sandro Sticca (Albany: State University of New York Press, 1972)

William Salt Archaeological Society, ed., *Collections for a History of Staffordshire* First Series, 18 vols., XVI (London: Harrison, 1895)

  ed., *Collections for a History of Staffordshire*, Third Series, 38 vols., 1911 volume (unnumbered) (London: Harrison, 1911)

W[illis], R., *Mount Tabor; or, Private Exercises of a Penitent Sinner. Serving for a daily Practice of the Life of Faith, Reduced to speciall heads comprehending the chiefe comforts and refreshings of true Christians: Also Certain occasionall Observations and Meditations profitably applyed* (London: R. B[adger] for P[hilemon] Stephens and C[hristopher] Meredith, 1639)

Wilkins, John, *Mathematical Magick; Or, the Wonders That may be Performed by Mechanical Geometry* (London: Ric[hard] Baldwin, 1691)

Wing, Donald, *Short-Title Catalogue of Books Printed in England, Scotland, Ireland, Wales, and British America and of English Books Printed in Other Countries 1641–1700*, 3 vols. (New York: Index Society, 1945; repr. Mansfield Centre, CT: Martino Publishing, 2003)

Wiseman, Richard and Peter Lamont, 'Unravelling the Indian rope-trick', *Nature*, 383 (19 December 1996), 212–13

Withington, Robert, *English Pageantry: An Historical Outline*, 2 vols. (Cambridge, MA: Harvard University Press, 1918; repr. New York/London: Benjamin Blom, 1963)

Wood, Gaby, *Living Dolls: A Magical History of the Quest for Mechanical Life* (London: Faber, 2002)

Wordsworth, Christopher, *Notes on Mediæval Services in England* (London: Thomas Baker, 1898)

Wright, Louis B., 'Juggling tricks and conjury on the English stage before 1642', *Modern Philology*, 24 (1926–7), 269–84

Wright, Thomas, ed., *Three Chapters of Letters Relating to the Suppression of Monasteries* (London: Camden Society, 1843)

Wriothesley, Charles, *A Chronicle of England during the Reigns of the Tudors, from A.D. 1485 to 1559*, ed. William Douglas Hamilton, 2 vols. (London: Camden Society, 1875)

Yarington, Robert, *Two Lamentable Tragedies*, ed. John S. Farmer (Amersham: John S. Farmer, 1913)

Yule, Colonel Henry, ed. and trans., *Cathay and the Way Thither; Being a Collection of Medieval Notices of China*, 2 vols. (London: Hakluyt Society, 1866)

ed. and trans., *The Book of Ser Marco Polo, The Venetian, Concerning the Kingdoms and Marvels of the East*, 2 vols. (London: John Murray, 1875)

Index